"What hope do I have for dealing with the sin in my life?" is the agonized cry of the believer in Jesus Christ. Robert Saucy gives a biblically based, spiritually powerful, experientially liveable answer. . . . He combines the deep wisdom of the sage and godly heart of the man of God to show us the way of growing to a truly satisfying Christlikeness."

—GERRY BRESHEARS, Phd, Professor of Theology, Western Seminary

"Dr. Robert Saucy's *Minding the Heart* should be on your list of must-read books. Certain to become a classic, Bob's insights in this volume are transformative. Well researched and deeply grounded in God's Word, with solid interpretive methodology, he has produced a work both profound and practical. I am happy to commend it in the highest terms to any who seek spiritual transformation."

—W. BINGHAM HUNTER, Executive Vice President and Provost, Phoenix Seminary

"Dr. Saucy's work on the 'theological heart' provides a much needed addition to our understanding of biblical anthropology and psychology. Sanctification has been defined as 'the work of God that we participate in.' Dr. Saucy's book shows how the Christian participates in his or her spiritual growth and maturity. Every Bible teacher or student needs to read and digest this important study."

—DR. EDWIN BLUM, general editor/translator of Holman Christian Standard Bible

"What do the Scriptures mean with all of the references to the heart? For most, such passages evoke warm fuzzies but very little light. *Minding the Heart*, by veteran scholar and gracious man of God Robert Saucy, causes these references to leap from the pages of the Bible and grip your heart with ethos, logos, and pathos. I love it when a top-level scholar writes something as cogent and helpful to the masses as this great read."

—PAIGE PATTERSON, President, Southwestern Baptist Theological Seminary

"*Minding the Heart* is a product of the lifelong research, teaching, and personal transformation of Robert Saucy. It is now arguably the most important and comprehensive biblical and theological study of the spiritual heart, and culminates over fifty years of teaching on this subject. But it also draws upon Dr. Saucy's personal transformation, as his spiritual heart has weathered and grown through personal tragedies and suffering. He is a wise, learned, profound, loving, and insightful man of God."

—MICHAEL J. WILKINS, Distinguished Professor of New Testament and Dean of Faculty, Talbot School of Theology, Biola University

"So much of what is published under the banner of spiritual formation these days is little more than personality theory splashed with holy water. *Minding the Heart* goes straight to the source of spirituality, theology, and transformation—the Scriptures—and displays, in a highly accessible style, a solid command of the linguistic, historical, and theological issues involved in authentic transformation of the heart."

—Dr. Leslie T. Hardin, Professor of New Testament, Florida Christian College and author of *The Spirituality of Jesus*

Minding the Heart

The Way of Spiritual Transformation

ROBERT L. SAUCY

Kregel
Publications

For Nancy,
my blessed, loving companion on the
journey to true life

Contents

Preface

This book is about the personal transformation of life that the Bible teaches is for everyone who believes in the gospel of Jesus Christ. According to the Scripture, the person who believes in Christ and trusts him and his saving work for salvation receives a new life and becomes a new creation in his or her deepest inner person—a newness that is designed to grow in power and scope in the experience of daily life. Jesus said, "I came that they may have life, and have it abundantly" (John 10:10). The goal of this work is to help those who have received Christ as Savior to know that this abundant life can begin in the here and now and not just in eternity, and to know how they can grow in the daily experience of it.

This book has been simmering for a long time—admittedly on the back burner at times, but always there. As both a believer and a teacher of theology in a seminary the concept of growth was always present. But my interest in the direction of this work was particularly stimulated through co-teaching a course on the theology of human nature with a number of psychology professors. I was intrigued by the psychology readings that dealt with the depth of the person and how the unconscious affected life, and how those corresponded to things the Scriptures said about the heart. This developed into a lecture series that I presented at Western Seminary and subsequently used as reading material in our course on human nature and various other presentations.

On a personal level, I began to pay more attention to my attitudes and actions in relation to their source—which Scripture says is the heart—especially regarding my emotions, which up to that point I, like many men, had essentially ignored. I recognized that my emotions revealed the thoughts and beliefs in the depth of my heart, thoughts which shaped my attitudes and actions in life. All of this fueled my desire for further study.

As I gained more information, I began to realize that discussions related to the biblical heart were not prominent in church teachings or theology books. I had taught theology courses including the doctrine of sanctification, or spiritual growth. But aside from relatively brief explanations of the means of growth—the

Scriptures, prayer, church sacraments, fellowship, and so on—little was said as to how these means actually worked to bring about growth. Churches faithfully proclaimed what Christ had done for our salvation, and how to be saved; the Christian walk was rightly set forth, telling us what we should and shouldn't do; but not much was said concerning how to actually do some of these important things so that I actually knew what it was to experience them. For example, I knew that reading the Bible and studying it was important, but I don't remember hearing much about *meditating* on it, or how to actually practice meditation—something that according to Scripture is crucial for experiencing God in our life. The Christian life seemed more of a holy walk keeping away from sin rather than an abundant life of love, joy, and peace.

My life was blessed in these churches. Lives were changed. But I suspect that in many people there was a quiet longing for more. Daily life didn't seem to square with the abundant life Jesus talked about. The power of God was not very effective for overcoming life's problems. So many sought help elsewhere.

Once, after I had delivered a message about the power of God's love and challenged the people to a similar love, a young woman approached me. "We often hear messages like this which tell us what to do," she said, "but no one tells us how we can do it."

I came to see that the motivation and power for a holy walk and the experience of new life ultimately come not from knowing the Bible and theology, or even from trying to keep the commandments, but only from knowing God through a heart-to-heart relationship with him, through Jesus, by the Spirit. This led me to the focus of this work, which may be broadly described as seeking to understand the dynamics of Proverbs 4:23: "Watch over your heart with all diligence, for from it flow the springs of life." What are the dynamics of the heart that make it the source of all that we do in life, and how can we watch over or guard our heart so that our life is different?

Without denying the value of what can be learned about living the spiritual life from the traditions of the church and its practices, this work is basically a study of scriptural teaching on the nature of spiritual growth or spiritual formation, and how any believer can experience a transformation of the heart and all of the daily activities and attitudes that come from it. Aspects of psychology, philosophy of psychology, and even neuroscience are utilized at times for their insight into the dynamic of human nature. These can be very useful in understanding how we tick and in diagnosing our condition, and therefore the underlying process of spiritual change revealed in Scripture. But since only God has the power to overcome sin and affect genuine spiritual transformation, in a very real sense this work seeks to help the reader understand how we can come to have God actively working in our lives and actually experience more of his abundant life.

Many people have contributed to this work to whom I gladly give thanks. For arranging publication though Kregel Publications and continually encouraging me along the way with much patience, and reading over the work with editorial suggestions, I thank Jim Weaver. Thanks also to those who read parts or all of the manuscript and contributed helpful thoughts and wording: Mary Barnett, Ed Blum, Barbara Hillaker, Cameron Jung, John Mosqueda, and especially Ting Guevarra-Small who provided many helpful illustrations. Thanks also to Sandra Orr, my gracious and efficient secretary, who helped in obtaining books and essays and checking details in the manuscript. Thanks to Isaac Blois for help with the transliteration of Hebrew and Greek.

My gratitude also to the people at Kregel Publications who have been so gracious and helpful to work with: Dennis Hillman, Steve Barclift, Dawn Anderson, and Paul Brinkerhoff, whose careful editing was so helpful, along with the others who had a hand in producing this work.

I am grateful also to the administration, faculty colleagues, and staff at the Talbot School of Theology, Biola University, for their constant encouragement during the rather lengthy writing of this book. Their provision of an environment in which the transformation of the heart was highly valued along with academics was a great blessing.

For her help in ways that she doesn't even realize, I give my heartfelt gratitude to my dear life companion, Nancy. Her encouragement when progress seemed slow, prodding when I needed it, graciousness in letting me spend hours in the study, and most of all her love and provision of a good home undergird this work.

Above all, I am grateful to our Lord for drawing me to this study on the spiritual transformation of the heart. I count it a great blessing to have had the privilege of spending much time giving thought to this topic vital to all followers of Christ—how we grow in the experiential knowledge of our great God and Savior in our daily walk. Thank you, Father, for enriching my life!

Introduction

Change my heart oh God
Make it ever true
Change my heart oh God
May I be like you

EDDIE ESPINOSA[1]

These simple yet profound lyrics echo the cry of David: "Create in me a clean heart, O God, and renew a steadfast spirit within me" (Ps. 51:10).*

But questions about having this kind of heart arise. How exactly does God communicate his life-transforming power? What does God do in this process? And what do *I* have to do? In other words, *how does growth take place?*

The answer is the heart—the most important biblical term for the human person's nature and actions. Indeed, the heart is the control center of life. It is the very place where God works to change us—and the place where *we* must work if growth is to take place.

The heart is one's core. According to Scripture, it is who you and I are at our deepest and most private level. So profound is the hidden person of the heart that only God himself is able to plumb its unfathomable depths. The psalmist declared, "O LORD, You have searched me and known me" (Ps. 139:1). For the believer, that is good news, because God is the ultimate heart-changer.

"Spiritual formation for the Christian," writes Dallas Willard in *Renovation of the Heart*, "basically refers to the Spirit-driven process of forming the inner world of the human self in such a way that it becomes like the inner being of

---

* Unless otherwise indicated, all Scripture quotations are from the New American Standard Bible (NASB). The NASB uses more literal translations of the Hebrew and Greek words for "heart" than most other modern translations, and it frequently provides a marginal note indicating the literal sense when the original language word for "heart" is translated as some other word. This aids in understanding the biblical meaning of the heart as the seat of all personal functions (see chapter 4).

Christ himself."[2] Willard adds: "Christlikeness of the inner being is not a human attainment. It is, finally, a gift of grace."[3]

But it is also a process in which we participate. In fact, we are responsible before God for embarking on a spiritual journey that produces ever-increasing change and renewal within our hearts. God works to effect this change—and so do we. "Work out your salvation," wrote Paul, "for it is God who works in you" (Phil. 2:12–13 NIV).

The transformation of which I speak is nothing less than the liberating, joyful experience of increasing freedom from the power of sin's bondage. It is exchanging the dysfunctional and dark works of our self-centered, sinful nature in favor of the wholesomeness and delight of the fruit of God's Spirit.

The focus of this book will be on the command center: your heart. We'll compare the biblical description of our natural heart (the heart in its fallen and sinful condition, with which we were born) with the heart that God desires for his spiritually born children. In doing so, we'll come to see that, in reality, life's problems are none other than *heart problems*. Or, as has been said, "The heart of every problem is a problem of the heart."

Thus, we'll discover that *spiritual growth, at its root, is the transformation of the heart.* "Watch over your heart with all diligence, for from it flow the springs of life" (Prov. 4:23).

This pithy statement reminds us that the heart is the center of our thoughts, emotions, and actions. But how do they function together? How can they be harnessed so that deep spiritual transformation happens? By using the Bible, along with selected scientific studies, we will explore how to make lasting heart change and show how we can achieve the joys of Christlikeness in an intentional manner, not in a hit-or-miss kind of way. We'll also consider the social dimension of human nature and how relationships with other believers contribute to spiritual growth.

Finally, we will seek to tie our study together by looking at some fundamentals of biblical spiritual formation. What is the essential nature of our growth—what really changes in our life as we grow more like Christ? And how does this finally take place?

In the end, of course, all glory goes to God whenever we are changed. The renewing of the heart is an inescapable human need, but the solution lies only within the realm of the divine. A growing relationship with God through Jesus Christ is the only means by which our hearts can be transformed. He alone has power over sin; he alone can break its hold on us.

Abbreviations

AB	Anchor Bible
BCOT	Biblical Commentary on the Old Testament
BDAG	Bauer, W., W. F. Arndt, F. W. Gingrich, and F. W. Danker, *A Greek-English Lexicon of the New Testament and Other Early Christian Literature*, 3rd ed. Chicago, 2000
EBC	*Expositor's Bible Commentary*
ESV	English Standard Version
GNT	Good News Translation
HCSB	Holman Christian Standard Bible
IDB	*The Interpreter's Dictionary of the Bible*. Edited by G. A. Buttrick. 4 vols. Nashville, 1962
lit.	literally
MSG	*The Message*, Eugene H. Peterson
NASB	New American Standard Bible
NEB	New English Bible
NET	NET Bible
NICNT	New International Commentary on the New Testament
NICOT	New International Commentary on the Old Testament
NIDNTT	*New International Dictionary of New Testament Theology*. Edited by C. Brown. 4 vols. Grand Rapids, 1975–85
NIGTC	New International Greek Testament Commentary
NIV	New International Version
NKJV	New King James Version
NLT	New Living Translation
NRSV	New Revised Standard Version
OTL	Old Testament Library
PNTC	Pillar New Testament Commentary
TDNT	*Theological Dictionary of the New Testament*. Edited by G. Kittel and G. Friedrich. Translated by G. W. Bromiley. 10 vols. Grand Rapids, 1964–76

TDOT	*Theological Dictionary of the Old Testament.* Edited by G. J. Botterweck and H. Ringreen. Translated by J. T. Willis, G. W. Bromiley, and D. E. Green. 8 vols. Grand Rapids, 1974–2006
TLOT	*Theological Lexicon of the Old Testament.* Edited by E. Jenni and C. Westermann. Translated by M. E. Biddle. 3 vols. Peabody, MA, 1997
TOTC	Tyndale Old Testament Commentaries
TWOT	*Theological Wordbook of the Old Testament.* Edited by R. L. Harris, and G. L. Archer Jr. 2 vols. Chicago, 1980
WBC	Word Biblical Commentary

▪▪ 1 ▪▪

Born to Grow

Moving beyond Forgiveness to an Abundant Life

I came that they may have life and have it abundantly.

JESUS OF NAZARETH

It is only when we live with Christ that life becomes really worthy living, and that we begin to live at all in the real sense of the word.

WILLIAM BARCLAY

No one is going to catch me and make me a man." So said Peter Pan, a fictional character who never grew up from childhood. Though he had exciting adventures in Neverland with fairies, pirates, and mermaids, soon enough other children in the story grew up to be adults, even Wendy, Peter's dear companion. At the tearful ending of the book, she said to him, "I grew up long ago." Peter protested, "You promised not to!" To which she retorted, "I couldn't help it."

Written by J. M. Barrie more than a hundred years ago and still a popular children's story, *Peter Pan* is often associated with escapism, or even developmental disorder. Growing up is a fundamental fact of human existence.

Change simply happens. Life is a constant progression (or regression), both in the body and the inner person. We see and feel change in our bodies, but in the inner person, change is often subtle, giving an illusion that we're somehow standing still. But we are changing even when we are not aware of it.

When it comes to the life of the person who believes in Jesus Christ, that change should ever be *upward*. In the same way that we are born physically to grow to maturity, we are born again spiritually to grow to maturity. We are not born again just so we can be in heaven someday, but we are born from above by the Spirit of God to actually live a brand-new life in Christ now. A life that grows. *Excelsior!*

The message of Scripture is that our life in Christ is more than the forgiveness of sins, more than the escape from God's condemnation, but a new way to live, a new source of zest that thirsts and hungers for more.

All too often, sincere believers find themselves trying the usual Christian practices—reading the Bible, attending church, praying—with little, if any, success. Disappointed and defeated, they wonder: "Why is nothing really *different?* The same fears and anxieties are with me. My attitudes and actions toward things don't seem to be any different. What do I have to do to experience more of this new life? How does it all work?"

Believers want more than knowledge of biblical and theological doctrines. *They want to experience God.* They want to know how this new life operates. They want to know how they can grow in this new life. Like all important areas of our life—physical, intellectual, and ethical—spiritual growth involves time and effort. It is a process, and Scripture gives light to the *means* of growth and the *dynamic operations* of these means.

Born to Grow

The gospel is not only the "Good News," but the "best news" anyone could ever receive. Through simple faith in Jesus Christ, God's Son, a person can be born again into a new life, an *eternal* life.

Unfortunately, the meaning of "eternal life" is lost to many Christians. Instead of conceiving eternal life in terms of its *quality*, their thought is more on its *quantity*—the fact that it lasts forever. This is certainly understandable. Our sins are forgiven and we are given Christ's righteousness. Consequently, we are freed from God's wrath and sin's punishment of eternal death—thus we live forever.

Our new relationship with God, as children freed from his wrath, is correctly seen by believers as the foundation of the Christian life. But for too many Christians the matter ends there. Radical transformation of our life takes place only when we meet Christ. Yet in the meantime we live as heaven-bound, forgiven sinners with very little expectation of any real change in the quality of our life and our behavior, except perhaps for some reduction in the most blatant outward forms of sin.

Scripture paints a totally different picture. Our "new birth" is the starting point of a continuous process of growth in a new kind of life. As "newborn babies," we are told to "crave pure spiritual milk, so that by it you may grow up in your salvation" (1 Peter 2:2 NIV). In the words of a song by the popular rock band Switchfoot, "There's a new way to be human." This new kind of life is the quality of life lived first by Jesus Christ and subsequently by those who've known him well and followed him closely.

The apostle Paul exemplified this in his own life. Meeting Christ on the road to Damascus was only the beginning of his new life. His passion was to "gain Christ" and to "know Him" (Phil. 3:8, 10). The Christian life for Paul was not simply waiting and hoping for his final perfection. Rather, as he expressed it, "I press on to take hold of that for which Christ Jesus took hold of me. . . . Forgetting what is behind and straining toward what is ahead, I press on toward the goal to win the prize for which God has called me heavenward in Christ Jesus" (Phil. 3:12–14 NIV).

In saying that he "pressed on" Paul uses strong language, a Greek word that refers to *zealous pursuit*. From the time that Christ laid hold of him, his life took off in a completely new direction. He would not allow either his past failures or achievements to divert him from his pursuit of Christlikeness. We "are *being transformed* into . . . [Christ's] image with ever-increasing glory" (2 Cor. 3:18 NIV).*

Our growth as believers is *a continuous process*. This is underscored by the frequent use of Greek present-tense verbs that denote continuous action. In the verse above, 2 Corinthians 3:18, and in Romans 12:2, "Be transformed by the renewing of your mind," the word translated as "transformed," literally means, "be continually being transformed." Likewise, we are to be "renewed [continually] in the spirit of our mind" (Eph. 4:23; see also Col. 3:10).

Moreover, our present outward life, which C. K. Barrett has described as "subject to a thousand troubles and under sentence of death,"[1] may be trending downward, but our inner person is designed to continually grow. "Though outwardly we are wasting away, yet inwardly we are *being renewed* day by day" (2 Cor. 4:16 NIV).

God's design for our continuous spiritual growth can be both encouraging and challenging. On the one hand, it is encouraging to know that though our physical bodies are going through wear and tear, our spiritual life can still go from strength to strength. On the other hand, this is a challenge, because it does not allow any excuse for complacency or neglect or being "too old" to make any spiritual progress.

The growth of believers as a continuous process is also underscored by Scripture's use of the imagery of "journey." A journey is more than developing a good road map or having knowledge to navigate the way, that is, it's more than

---

* Throughout, italics in Scripture quotations were added for emphasis.

Living Step by Step

Because nomadic life in ancient times was defined by a continual walking from place to place, the Bible emphasizes the importance of a person's steps and feet. As one Old Testament scholar explained, "Although the Hebrew is keenly aware of the role the hand plays in human actions, [it] still places more emphasis on the significance of the foot than modern languages. Human action consists of spatial forward movement to a goal."[2] Old Testament wisdom and poetry frequently use the metaphors of "steps" ('ashur) for "living." This is picked up by New Testament authors, who use the term for "walking around" (peripateō) as a metaphor for "living" or one's "lifestyle."

"My steps have held fast to Your paths. My feet have not slipped." (Ps. 17:5)

"The steps of a man are established by the LORD, and He delights in his way." (Ps. 37:23; cf. 31)

"Our heart has not turned back, and our steps have not deviated from Your way." (Ps. 44:18)

"He set my feet upon a rock making my footsteps firm." (Ps. 40:2)

"Therefore we have been buried with Him through baptism into death, so that as Christ was raised from the dead through the glory of the Father, so we too might walk in newness of life." (Rom. 6:4; cf. 2 Cor. 12:18)

constructing a philosophy or theology of life. It is the actual travel on the road, the living of this new life. A journey is more than its destination. As Derek Kidner put it, the "path of life" (Ps. 16:11) is so called, "not only because of its goal but because to walk that way is to live, in the true sense of the word, already."[3]

In the ancient world, especially among nomadic people, life was lived on foot. They walked step by step along a "path" or "way" in search of food and water for their flocks and herds. As a result, walking became a metaphor for the journey of life. We are called "to live [our lives] before God in such a way that every single step is made with reference to [him] and every day experiences him close at hand."[4] To each of us, God says as He did to Abraham centuries ago, "Walk before me" (Gen. 17:1).

Walking, however, is never simply walking per se. It is always walking along a particular way. We can walk along "the way of the LORD" (Gen. 18:19)—"the way of the righteous" (Ps. 1:6; cf. Prov. 8:20; 2 Peter 2:21), "the path of life" (Ps. 16:11; Prov. 10:17), "the good way" (Jer. 6:16), and "the way of the truth" (2 Peter 2:2). Or we can tread the alternative route—"the way of the wicked" (Pss. 1:6; 146:9), the "dark and slippery" way (Ps. 35:6), and "the false way" (Ps. 119:104, 128).

The point is that each one of us is on our own spiritual journey, always walking, always stepping, always moving along *a path*. One path is like the "light of dawn, that shines brighter and brighter until the full day" (Prov. 4:18), while the other is a path of pain and grief and ultimately final destruction (Ps. 1:6). Thus we need to pray with the psalmist: "Search me, O God, and know my heart; try me and know my anxious thoughts; and see if there be any *hurtful way* in me, and lead me in the *everlasting way*" (Ps. 139:23–24).

The picture of continually walking may be unpleasant and tiring to us. To constantly pay attention to our next step—always thinking about whether it's along the path of life or along the way of destruction—takes a lot of thought and effort. Wouldn't it be nice just to be able to get off the road and relax for a while? Or, as someone put it, "Lord, please give me the vacation of a second!"

We may never have thought of the Christian life in this way. But in reality, we may be practicing it by relegating our spiritual walk to well-defined religious activities such as church attendance, group Bible studies, and personal times of "devotion." The rest of our life—whatever else consumes our time—is not part of the journey. It's a vacation. It doesn't count.

This is contrary to Scripture. In God's eyes, our journey includes *all* of our life. We are always on our journey, making decisions and taking steps in one direction or another. Even when we avoid deciding about something, we are deciding, taking a step in some direction—no decision is a decision. Thus our spiritual growth or heart transformation includes all of the activities of our life—work, family life, social life, recreation, physical exercise (if we do it), and so on. Later we will see that changing our heart involves changing our thoughts, emotion, and will and thus our actions to conform to the thoughts, emotions, and will of God. Since these functions are continually active in our life, there is no aspect of our life that is not involved in our transformation.

The Scriptures say, "Whether, then, you eat or drink or whatever you do, do all to the glory of God" (1 Cor. 10:31). As the goal of our life is to live to the glory of God, this is also the goal of our spiritual transformation. As such, therefore, no matter where we are or what we are doing, we are either nourishing and strengthening our new life or weakening and stunting it.

In many ways, the new life of the Christian is like all of life. According to Erwin Schrödinger, the Nobel Prize–winning physicist, something is considered to be alive "when it goes on 'doing something,' moving, exchanging material with its environment, and so forth." A living organism avoids decay and death, only "by eating, drinking, breathing and (in the case of plants) assimilating" life-nourishing elements from outside itself. This continuous process is called *metabolism*, which comes from the Greek word *metaballein*, meaning change or exchange.[5]

Plants absorb light and other elements from the atmosphere. They extend their roots into the soil in search of nutrients and moisture in order to sustain life and to grow. Animals also look for similar life-giving provisions. In the same manner, human life is a continual metabolism, drawing in life from outside of ourselves. One of the key Hebrew words related to human nature, *nefesh*, is often translated "soul." The term depicts the human person as a being of desires, drives, and appetites that must be fulfilled in order to be alive.[6] In short, *it is our very nature to live by hungering and thirsting for nourishment from sources beyond ourselves.*

However, we do not always take in what is good for us or what is truly life-enhancing. For example, a glazed donut and a rich, bold cup of coffee gives a surge of life, but the subsequent letdown lets us know that some "life sources" can be specious. Nevertheless, as long as we're alive, this fundamental process of drawing life from outside of ourselves never ceases. We're continually taking in either healthy nourishment that promotes life and growth or imbibing harmful toxic material that leads to sickness and death.

This reality in our physical life is equally valid in our spiritual life. Understanding this truth is vital for understanding our spiritual growth. We are continually assimilating from our environment either true life from our Creator/Redeemer, or counterfeit "life" from the Deceiver, which is no life at all. As we will see later, it is the very nature of our heart—our inner person—to be open to outside influences that shape and form who we really are. It is no wonder that Scripture urges us to "watch over your heart with all diligence, for from it flow the springs of life" (Prov. 4:23).

Growth in the Life of God

But what does this spiritual growth in our new life look like? How do we know if we are really growing? Are we growing in our spiritual life when we gain more Bible and theological knowledge? Does growth mean increased faithfulness in Christian practices—Bible reading, church attendance, witnessing, good behavior, loving actions and so forth? Or does spiritual transformation mean more religious feelings, more zeal and passion in worship, or more "spiritual" experiences?

All of these things may be evidences of growth. But they also could be of our own doing rather than actually flowing from our new life. Genuine spiritual growth is an increase in the experience of the new life of which Jesus spoke when he said, "I came that they may have life, and have it abundantly" (NASB) or "life in all its fullness" (John 10:10 GNT). Or as Paul described it, "life indeed" (1 Tim. 6:19 NASB) or "that which is truly life" (ESV).

This new life is the indestructible life of the living God himself. It is Christ's life lived in us *as our own life*—this is what the apostle had in mind when he wrote "Christ, who is our life" (Col. 3:4) and said of himself "it is no longer I who live, but Christ lives in me" (Gal. 2:20). In short, it is Christ's life produced in us by the "Spirit of life" (Rom. 8:2; cf. 8:6; Gal. 6:8).

Our natural human life manifests itself in thoughts, feelings, and actions. The more we think, feel, and act, the more we are alive. *These same capacities are also the means through which our new life is expressed.* Our new life in God is also evident in thoughts, feelings, and actions that are according to the pattern of God's life. Instead of confused thoughts, feelings, and desires that are corrupted by the patterns of this world and complicated by the burden of guilt and depression, in our new life in God, we think Christ's thoughts, feel his emotions, and live our life as it was designed by our Creator.

According to the Scripture, Christ has made it possible for us to "become partakers of the divine nature" (2 Peter 1:4). We are becoming like God in "life and godliness," taking on a divine quality of life that exhibits a godly moral walk, as opposed to the "corruption" or destructive decay of the world (2 Peter 1:3–4)—a life that increasingly reflects "the image of God" we were created to embody as human beings.

We are also said to be "partakers of Christ" (Heb. 3:14; see also 1 Cor. 1:9) and participate (or fellowship) in the Spirit (Phil. 1:2; 2 Cor. 13:14). All of this does not mean that growing spiritually is becoming a divine being. No, God will always be God and we will always be human. But what it means is that God through his Spirit is continually working to form us into Christlikeness. Like an embryo develops into the form of a human, so our new life is gradually taking the shape of Christ's life (Gal. 4:19).

What this new life looks like is therefore exemplified in the human earthly life of Christ. It is also seen in the many instructions and commands for our life and the biblical examples of the lives of many godly men and women. Perhaps there is no better description of this life than the qualities described as the "fruit of the Spirit" who is himself "the Spirit of life"—"love, joy, peace, patience, kindness, goodness, faithfulness, gentleness, self-control" (Gal. 5:22–23). These are rightly termed "fruit," for they are the produce or product of the "Life-Giver," rather than human manufacture.

The understanding of this Spirit-produced life is enhanced when we consider its opposite described as "the deeds of the flesh," or the dysfunctional outcome of living apart from the life of God—"immorality, impurity, sensuality, idolatry, sorcery, enmities, strife, jealousy, outbursts of anger, disputes, dissensions, factions, envying, drunkenness, carousing, and things like these" (Gal. 5:19–21). As Christians, we are not totally free from these old "deeds of the flesh." But at the core of our being, our heart, the life of God through the Spirit is implanted and designed to grow the fruit of the Spirit.

Love

The first three elements of the Spirit's fruit—love, joy, and peace—are especially prominent throughout the Bible as the qualities of the life that God designed for us. The prime position of love at the head of the list suggests that the other virtues somehow flow from love.

It is only natural that our new life in God is characterized by love since God himself is love. As John wrote, "Everyone who loves is born of God and knows God. . . . if we love one another, God abides in us, . . . *God is love,* and the one who abides in love abides in God, and God abides in him" (1 John 4:7, 12, 16). Moreover, "We know that we have passed out of death into life, because we love the brethren. He who does not love abides in death" (1 John 3:14).

This love is not the love of the world's songs and poetry—a natural love that cares for those who are dear to us and who usually treat us as we would like to be treated. It is the radical, unlimited, unconditional love of Christ, who willingly gave up his glory, power, honor, and finally his very life, not just for his friends, but also for his enemies. It is the perfect love that has existed between the Father, Son, and Spirit in eternity that has been "poured out within our hearts through the Holy Spirit who was given to us" (Rom. 5:5).

Joy

Joy is another prominent trait of our new life in God. As William Barclay rightly stated, "Joy is *the distinguishing atmosphere of the Christian life.* We may put it this way—whatever be the ingredients of the Christian life, and in whatever proportions they are mixed together, joy is one of them."[7]

Like love, this joy is of God. The joy of our new life is joy "in the Lord" (Phil. 4:4). It is Christ's joy of which he said to his disciples, "These things I have spoken to you so that My joy may be in you, and that your joy may be made full" (John 15:11; see also 17:13). It is the joy with which he welcomes his servants into his presence for eternity—"Enter into the joy of your master" (Matt. 25:21, 23).

Again, this is not the joy that depends on something in this world—the present world system that is passing away and can never be permanent (1 John 2:17).

What Is Joy and Happiness?

Joy is "that spiritual gladness which acceptance with God and change of heart produce. . . . It is opposed to dullness, despondency, indifference, and all the distractions and remorses which are wrought by the works of the flesh. This joy is the spring of energy, and praise wells out of the joyful heart. Where the heart is gladness, the instinctive dialect is song."[8]

It is sometimes said, "God wants us to be holy, not happy," suggesting that God is not really interested in our happiness. While happiness may come at times as a side benefit, his real goal for us is obedience to his commands. To be sure God desires that we walk in obedience with him, but does that exclude joy also as his goal? The objective of wise parents is not to make their children happy every moment by giving them everything they desire or protecting them from every hurt. But any hurtful maturing experience that parents allow their child to experience or active discipline they administer has the goal of a richer future life of peace and joy for their child.

It is no doubt correct to say that God wants more for us than "happiness" if our happiness is determined merely by *happenings*. But if happiness is conceived in a broader biblical sense, we cannot exclude it from God's desire for us. For included in the Spirit's fruit life is not only love and peace, but joy. In fact, "Joy is more conspicuous in Christianity than in any other religion and in the Bible more than any other literature."[9]

In reality there is no disjunction between holiness and an abundant, joyful life. Holiness means that we're set apart for the living God, who is the source of all life. And, as Fenton John Anthony Hort rightly says, "There is no life, worthy to be called life, entirely separate from joy and gladness."[10]

It is not based on our circumstances, as in the example of Paul repeatedly mentioning "joy" (seven times) and exhorting to "rejoice" (nine times) in his letter to Philippi while he was in prison.

The troubles and sorrows of this world cannot extinguish this joy. Paul Tournier, the well-known Christian Swiss psychiatrist, knew something of this joy. Telling of his deep sense of loss in the passing away of his dear wife, he said, "I can truly say that I have a great grief and that I am a happy man." The joy of Tournier is well expressed in Fenton John Anthony Hort's explanation: "He whose heart has learned to make answer to the Lord comes to find that the power of life and joy lives on with him while outward things are taking their course of obstruction or decay. He has a life exempt from being dried up, for it flows not from within himself or from any part of the perishable creation but from an ever living fountain in the heavens."[11]

Peace

Perhaps the most comprehensive description of our experience of God's kind of life is the third term of the life-giving Spirit's fruit—peace. The association of peace with life is apparent in Paul's words, "For the mind set on the flesh [i.e., the self-centered mind] is death, but the mind set on the Spirit is *life and peace*" (Rom. 8:6; cf. Prov. 3:16–18). Peace is also often found as the equivalent of salvation. The Savior is the "Prince of Peace" (Isa. 9:6; cf. Acts 10:36), and the gospel of his saving work is the "the gospel of peace" (Eph. 6:15; cf. 2:17).

The peace of the Bible is more than the absence of turmoil or hostilities. The fundamental meaning of the Hebrew word for "peace" (*shalom*) denotes "completeness, wholeness, harmony." It has the idea of "unimpaired relationship with others and fulfillment in one's undertakings."[12] Thus the peace produced by the Spirit may be summed up as "everything that makes for a person's highest good and that promotes the best relationships."[13] Praying for the blessing of peace as in the climax and culmination of the well-known Old Testament priestly blessing—"the LORD lift up His countenance on you, and give you peace" (Num. 6:24–26)—is therefore asking for "the sum total of all God's good gifts to his people."[14]

We all know something of this peace and we long for it. It is, to put it simply, the way things ought to be—that sense that everything is right. As a sick person knows the feeling of health and longs for its return, so every human being in the depth of his heart longs for this peace—the health of "*universal flourishing, wholeness,* and *delight*."[15] It is the peace of life for which we were created—though now disordered—that still remains in us, even as the memory of health remains in the sick person.

Abundant Life

The new life in Christ through the Spirit characterized by love, joy, and peace expresses itself in various ways depending on our personality type. But whether we are affable, melancholic, cranky, pragmatic, or any combination thereof, this life is an abundant life (John 10:10)—it will always have a certain enthusiasm. The Bible describes it as "living water" that satisfies and brings renewed vitality—a picture that had powerful meaning in arid biblical lands (Ps. 63:1; Jer. 2:13).

The psalmist described God as the "fountain of life" who gives his people "drink [from] . . . the river of [his] delights" (Ps. 36:8–9). Jesus offered "living water" to the Samaritan woman, telling her that it becomes "a well of water *springing up* to eternal life" in everyone who drinks of it (John 4:14). Eugene Peterson captured the exuberance of the Greek expression "springing up"* in

---

* A related form of the Greek word is used to describe the man who had been crippled from birth and was now "leaping" joyfully in the temple after being healed through Peter and John (Acts 3:8).

his paraphrase: "The water I give will be an artesian spring within, gushing fountains of endless life" (MSG). An artesian spring has ground water that flows upward by natural pressure, without any need for pumping. The new life is life that bubbles up—it just flows.

Jesus later describes this life bubbling up *in* the believer's heart as *flowing out* as rivers of living water in love and service to others (John 7:38). Leon Morris aptly summed up the zest of this life: "The life that Jesus gives is no tame and stagnant thing. It is much more than merely the entrance into a new state, that of being saved instead of lost. It is the abundant life ([John] 10:10), and the living Spirit within people is evidence of this. . . . When the believer comes to Christ and drinks, that believer not only slakes his thirst but receives such an abundant supply that veritable rivers flow from him."[16] Our salvation is not only *from* sin, but also *to* newness of life.

In short, our new life in Christ—and the transformed lifestyle it produces—should be felt in our daily experience in increasing measure during our journey on earth. According to the Bible, that's exactly what God intended.

Fountain of Life

The great nineteenth-century Irish-born Cambridge biblical scholar Fenton John Anthony Hort, referring to the psalmist's words "with You is the fountain of life" (Ps. 36:9), gives us a good description of our new abundant life in Christ:

> The perennial spring of water that leaps and flashes as though it were a living thing, breaking ceaselessly forth from a hidden source, is the best image of that higher life bestowed on him to whom God has unveiled His face. . . . He whose heart has learned to make answer to the Lord comes to find that the power of life and joy lives on with him while outward things are taking their course of obstruction or decay. He has a life exempt from being dried up, for it flows not from within himself or from any part of the perishable creation but from an ever living fountain in the heavens. . . .
>
> In Christ life was given in its fullness . . . . This is the one character of the Gospel which takes precedence of all others: its many partial messages are unfoldings of its primary message of life. Salvation according to the Scripture is nothing less than the preservation, restoration, or exaltation of life.[17]

Understanding the Way of Growth

The presence of the new life in a person inevitably creates a hunger and thirst for more. The more we experience the abundant nature of this life, the greater our desire for it. Once we realize that God designed us to grow in our new life, and graciously makes available to us everything that we need to grow, we're left with practical questions such as: How does growth take place? What does God do in this process, and what must I do? How does God's power transform my daily walk? How can I have a lasting change in my thoughts, attitudes, and actions?

The answers to these questions lie in the heart, the most important biblical term in relation to man's nature and actions. The heart is the control center of life. It is the place where God works to change us and the place we also must work if growth is to take place. Hence the Bible counsels, "Watch over your heart with all diligence, for from it flow the springs of life" (Prov. 4:23).

We will begin with the biblical teaching on the importance of the heart as the center of our being. Because God works his renewal in and through our heart, it will be helpful to understand something of its nature and how it functions. *The heart is who we are.* It is the seat of our thoughts, emotions, and actions. Understanding the heart will help us grasp the process of our transformation.

We will also study what God does and what we can do in the process of transformation. The Bible makes it clear that God is the ultimate heart-changer. Ultimately, only a growing relationship with our Savior Jesus Christ can transform our heart since he is the One who has power over sin and has broken its hold on us. After all, our growth is nothing less than an increasing freedom from the power of sin's bondage and enduring experience of God's bubbling zest in our daily lives.

But our growth also entails our activity. The apostle Paul's words, "Work out your salvation . . . for it is God who is at work in you" (Phil. 2:12–13), are central to our spiritual transformation. This process, as the Bible indicates, involves two elements: the part that God plays, and the role that the believer plays. A greater understanding of both of these can help us grow in our new life in Christ.

Unlike Peter Pan, we can indeed, and in fact must, grow up. And Scripture tells how.

Questions for Thought

1. Since you became a Christian, what has been your attitude toward growth in your new life? If you were concerned to grow, what was your concept of spiritual growth and how one grows in one's spiritual life?
2. Looking back on your life since you became a Christian, what changes if any do you see in your spiritual life along the way—times of positive

growth or times of slipping back? Describe them and explain why you think they occurred.

3. From the description of our new life in Christ, what characteristics of that life are most prominent in your life? What are least prominent?

▪▪ 2 ▪▪

The Real Person

The Meaning of "Heart"

As water reflects the face, so the heart reflects the person.

Proverbs 27:19 HCSB

The deepest sense of "heart" is the genuine, the authentic man. . . .
Man is made up of many layers. He who penetrates into the deepest
layer (the heart) comes to know himself thoroughly.

F. H. von Meyenfeldt

The trademarked I♥NY logo was created by American graphic designer
Milton Glaser in 1975 for a campaign commissioned by the New York State
Commerce Department in an effort to reverse the decay of New York City and to
spur on tourism. The idea came to Glaser while on board a taxi after the state had
approved another logo he had submitted. Working pro bono, he managed to convince them to use this logo, which now has had an unwitting impact on culture.

The I♥NY logo is known not only to New Yorkers, who could not walk ten
feet without seeing it on shirts, caps, pins, and cars, but to all Americans, and to
the rest of the world. It is now a universal shorthand, with replications such as
"I♥Chocolate" or "I♥Dogs." More recently, the logo's pioneering use of the heart
icon has been adopted into social networking websites, text messaging lingo, and
other forms of colloquialism.

In a recent interview with *Haddash Magazine*, Glaser explained the essence
of his most recognizable design, "The image of 'I♥NY' is basically a little puzzle. There is a complete word, 'I.' There is a symbol for an emotion, which is the
heart, and there are initials for a place. These require three little mental adjustments to understand the message. But they are so easy to achieve that there is
very little possibility that somebody won't be able to figure it out."[1]

But is the meaning of the "heart" really that easy to figure out? The heart is used in common expressions more than any other part of the body. People say things like this:

"We had a heart-to-heart talk."
"His heart is on the right place."
"I meant it from the bottom of my heart."
"My heart is set on it."
"In your heart you know it's true."

The heart is commonly associated with emotions, feelings, or some type of fondness or affinity. But looking closely at the above expressions and slogans, we see that the heart is so much more.

In truth, the heart represents the whole person—who we really are. Scripture tells us that life flows from the heart, hence it urges, "Watch over your *heart* with all diligence, for from it flow the springs of life" (Prov. 4:23). The faith of a person is never expressed with any faculty other than the heart, "Believe in your *heart* that God has raised Him from the dead . . . for with the *heart* a person believes" (Rom. 10:9–10).* Christ dwells in the *heart* and it is in the *heart* that we acknowledge him as Lord (Col. 3:14; 1 Peter 3:15).

The heart stands for the whole person. Ultimately, "heart" and "person" are virtually synonymous. To understand ourselves and how we grow, therefore, requires an understanding of the real nature of the heart.

The Most Important Word for "Person"

If anything clearly emerges from a careful study of what Scripture says about humanity, it is that *the word* heart *is the most significant term for understanding the person.* In his classic study *Anthropology of the Old Testament*, Hans Walter Wolff declared, "The most important word in the vocabulary of Old Testament anthropology is generally translated 'heart.'"[2] The Hebrew words for "heart" (*lev* and *levav*) occurs a total of 858 times in the Old Testament,[3] 814 of which are related solely to the human heart with an additional 4 references to the heart of animals as metaphorical illustrations of human hearts (e.g., "the heart of a lion," i.e., courageous (2 Sam. 17:10).

A few of the 814 occurrences to the human heart refer to the physical heart or to its general location in the center of the chest (e.g., mourning includes

---

* As human persons our belief is never expressed with any faculty other than the heart.

The Heart of God and the Human Heart

In addition to the 818 Old Testament uses of "heart" related to the human heart, there are 26 references to the "heart" of God that are used in an anthropomorphic sense for the deep center of the person. It is interesting that the very first reference to "heart" in Scripture is the "evil" heart of humans at the time of the flood (Gen. 6:5). And the second, which follows immediately, tells us that God as a result this human condition "was grieved in his heart" (v. 6). This "heart-to-heart" pattern of the human relationship with God continues throughout Scripture as is evident when later, God promised to his still imperfect but redeemed people, "My eyes and My heart will be there [in the temple] perpetually" (1 Kings 9:3) to commune with those who love him with all their heart.

In addition there are 13 figurative uses of "heart" for the deep center or interior of something—the "heart" of the sea" (11), "heart" of heaven (1), "heart" of a tree (1), and one reference to the literal "heart" of an animal, the awesome Leviathan in Job 41:24 that is said to have a "heart . . . as hard as stone" which probably refers to his hard rocklike chest area (cf. NIV).

beating one's "heart," i.e., chest or breast [Nah. 2:7; cf. Exod. 28:29; 2 Sam. 18:14; 2 Kings 9:24]) But most are metaphorical, referring to the inner life of the person. The number of references to the human heart in the Old Testament outnumbers other terms associated with the inner life of the person. For example, the Hebrew word *nefesh*, often translated "soul," occurs only 755 times, many of which are unrelated to the human person.* The Hebrew term for the human "spirit," *ruakh*, has even fewer mentions. The same numerical frequency of "heart" is found in the New Testament.

For our understanding of the "heart," it will be helpful to briefly consider how this term relates to some other significant terms used to denote the human makeup. The basic components of our essential constitution as human beings are provided in the account of the creation of man: "The LORD God formed man of dust from the ground, and breathed into his nostrils the breath of life; and man became a living being [lit. soul]" (Gen. 2:7). As human beings we are a union of material substance, "dust from the ground," and immaterial substance, "the breath of life," or spirit.†

This union of material (body) and immaterial (spirit) results in "a living soul."

---

* The Hebrew word for "soul," *nefesh*, is also used for animals as living "creatures" (e.g., Gen. 1:20, 21, 24; 9:10; Lev. 11:10; Job 12:10; Prov. 12:10). It also has a number of other meanings and uses including "life," "person," "self," "desire" or "appetite," and "emotion."
† The equivalency of "breath of life" in Gen. 2:7 with "spirit" is evident in Gen. 7:22, "the breath [*neshamah*] of the spirit [*ruakh*] of life." See also the "breath [*ruakh*, spirit] of life" in 6:17; 7:15. Eichrodt notes here that "as God's own breath it shares with *ruakh* the significance of God's life-giving power in creation." Walther Eichrodt, *Theology of the Old Testament*, trans. John A. Baker, OTL (London: SCM Press, 1967), 2:142.

Soul is thus the term for man's total human nature—the total person, what he is, not just what he has. Soul represents the human as alive with life that consists of emotions, passions, drives, and appetites.[4] As depicted in the three-part diagram, the body (the plain figure) and the spirit (the figure filled with wind representing its animating quality), together making up the soul or the whole person, and at its core is the heart.

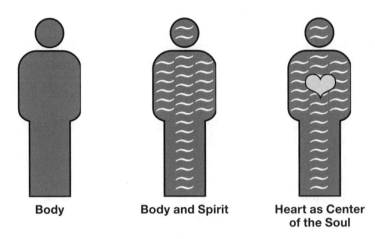

Body   **Body and Spirit**   **Heart as Center of the Soul**

Because soul is the whole person, it can also be used for the "person" who survives death, though temporarily separated from the body, as spirit (Matt. 10:28; Rev. 6:9). Such a person, however, is an incomplete soul, for the soul, or human person, by creation is body and spirit, and it will be completed again following the resurrection of the body.

Spirit is the principle of life that animates the body (Ps. 104:29; James 2:26). It is the vitalizing power by which the person or soul lives.[*] Created in the likeness of God, the human spirit images God's own personal life. Thus the characteristics of personality—self-conscious reason, emotion, and volition—are viewed in Scripture as the faculties of our spirit that function holistically with our material body. For example, the mind (spirit) and brain (material) operate as a functional unity. Since these holistic activities of spirit and body are finally the actions of the total person they can also be described as activities of the soul.

---

* *Spirit* is life as effective power; *soul* is the subject or bearer of that life, or life actively realized in the creature. *Soul* emphasizes the living individual, *spirit* the vitalizing power by which the individual or *soul* lives. John Laidlaw, *The Bible Doctrine of Man; or The Anthropology and Psychology of Scripture*, rev. ed., Cunningham Lectures, Seventh Series (1879; Edinburgh: T&T Clark, 1895), 88–91. See also Walther Eichrodt, *Theology of the Old Testament*, trans. John A. Baker, OTL (London: SCM Press, 1967), 2:136.

For example, we find instances where functions involving thought are attributed to the spirit (e.g., "For who among men knows the thoughts of a man except the spirit of the man which is in him?" (1 Cor. 2:11), and also to the soul (e.g., "Bless the Lord, O my soul, and forget none of His benefits" (Ps. 103:2). The idea in such instances is that the whole person or "soul" thinks by virtue of having a spirit that has the capacity to think—much like saying "I see" because "my eyes see." In short, the functions of the body and spirit are at the same time expressed as the functions of the person or soul.

The human being, as far as his constitutional makeup, is therefore biblically depicted as a "soul" composed of a material body and immaterial spirit. Many other terms referring to parts of the body (e.g., head, eye, ear, mouth, hand, arm, feet, kidneys, bowels, and so on) are used simply for the anatomical part, or as a way of speaking of the human function associated with the bodily part. It is important to recognize that although Scripture pictures the human as having a dualistic composition of a material body and an immaterial spirit, these dimensions function together and also holistically. The ear, for example, is used to depict the function of hearing. But technically other parts of the body such as the brain are also involved in hearing and thereby the whole "person" hears.

The biblical heart as we have seen is used like the other body parts, both for the physical organ, but most often and certainly most importantly as the figure of the center of the human person. As the deep center of the person, the heart is the center of the soul or the person. It is the place "in which the soul is at home with itself, and is conscious of all its doing and suffering as its own."[5] As the center of the soul the heart is the deep seat of the personal capacities of the spirit associated with personhood that function through the soul. "More than the soul and spirit, 'the heart' is the all-embracing term for the human psychological phenomena."[6]

When we add to the 800-plus Old Testament references some 156 uses of the Greek term for "heart," *kardia*, in the New Testament, it's evident that if we desire to understand our nature as human persons, we must understand the biblical heart.

The importance of the "heart" is highlighted by its presence in many significant biblical teachings in addition to the ones mentioned earlier:

+ "You shall love the Lord your God with all your heart" (Mark 12:30).
+ "Blessed are the pure in heart" (Matt. 5:8).
+ "Trust in the Lord with all your heart" (Prov. 3:5).
+ "Forgive [your] brother from your heart" (Matt. 18:35).

+ "God has sent forth the Spirit of His Son into our hearts, crying, 'Abba! Father!'" (Gal. 4:6).
+ "The LORD has sought out for Himself a man [David] after His own heart" (1 Sam. 13:14).
+ "The goal of our instruction is love from a pure heart" (1 Tim. 1:5).

Many more Scriptures could be mentioned, but these are enough to tell us that human life focuses on the heart. Most telling, *your heart is the point of your personal contact with God*. As Martyn Lloyd-Jones noted, "The gospel of Jesus Christ is concerned about the heart: all its emphasis is upon the heart. Read the accounts which we have in the gospels of the teaching of our blessed Lord, and you will find that all along He is talking about the heart."[7]

The Heart: Our True Identity

Who Am I, Really?

Most of us at one time or another have pondered the question, "Who am I, really?" Or perhaps even more importantly, "Who am I *becoming*?"

Knowing ourselves is vital for our spiritual life, and to do so, Scripture tells us we must look deep into our heart. The writer of Proverbs said, "As in water face reflects face, so the heart of man reflects man" (27:19). The cryptic nature of the original wording of this text, "As water face to face / so a man's heart to a man," has led to some debate over the precise meaning. But the general sense seems clear: as we see our reflection in calm water, so we see our real person when we gaze into our heart. No more and no less.

It is not how we look or what status or position we have or what we have accomplished or even what others think of us that determines who we really are. Nor do any of these criteria give us understanding of our self. True self-knowledge comes from looking inwardly at the "thoughts and attitudes" that reside deep in our heart (Heb. 4:12 NIV). As William McKane said, "[A man's] self is mirrored in his *lev* [heart] . . . . It is through introspection, through self-examination in depth, that a man acquires self-knowledge."[8]

Since the real identity of a person is his heart, the heart often equals the person. For example, the writer of Proverbs asked, "Who can say, 'I have cleansed my heart, I am pure from my sin?'" (20:9). A cleansed heart is a clean person. So also Delilah finally got to Samson with her question: "How can you say, 'I love you,' when your heart is not with me?" (Judg. 16:15). A person ("I") loves when his or her "heart" loves.

Jesus made the same equation of heart and person when he told his disciples, "You now have sorrow, but . . . your heart will rejoice" (John 16:22 NKJV). The heart speaks for the person even as the psalmist said, "My heart said to You, 'Your face, O Lord, I shall seek" (Ps. 27:8). In Scripture, therefore, the "heart" is often a precise synonym for "'self' in its most profound meaning."[9]

The heart is also the center of the natural life of the person. Food and drink refresh and sustain the heart, that is, the person (e.g., Gen. 18:5; Judg. 19:5; Pss. 102:4; 104:15; Acts 14:17). To tell someone, "Let your heart live forever" (Ps. 22:26; cf. 69:32) is to wish for that person to enjoy good health.

The heart is the place where physical and psychological traumas are felt. In serious illness, the heart becomes "faint" or weak (Isa. 1:5). Overwhelmed by sickness and guilt, the psalmist lamented, "My heart throbs, my strength fails me" (Ps. 38:10). Along the same lines, Jeremiah, apparently suffering a heart attack over the coming devastation of Jerusalem, cried out, "My inward parts, my inward parts! I am in anguish! The walls of my heart! My heart is pounding in me" (lit., Jer. 4:19; cf. 23:9). The fact that physical and psychological traumas are felt in the inaccessible area of our heart underscores the notion of the heart as the seat and powerhouse of human life.

But human life for the biblical writer was much more than complex physiological and psychological life. It is a life lived responsibly before God.

What defines us most as human persons is that each of us is a self, created in God's image with the capacity of personhood that enables us to have a relationship with him and with people. It is this inner self to which the word "heart" in Scripture overwhelming refers. The heart is the seat of our desires, intentions, and will (e.g., Isa. 10:7; 2 Cor. 9:7), our various intellectual activities such as knowing and thinking (e.g., Deut. 8:5; Matt. 9:4), and our feelings and passions (e.g., Isa. 1:5; Acts 2:26). The impressions from everything that we encounter along life's journey all meet together in our heart—impressions from various circumstances, contacts with people, and especially our relationship with God. Our responses to these circumstances likewise come out of our heart. The bottom line is that *human life is heart life.*

What We See Is Not Always What We Get

As there are different levels in our self—from the external surface self, seen by others all the way to the deep inner hidden self—so there are also levels of the heart (more on this in chap. 4). The real "you" is not what you are on the surface. The saying, "It's what's inside that counts," is true of persons. Indeed, the real person is found on the inside.

Overwhelmingly, heart refers to that deep core of the person—"the point at which a person finds that he is most basically, radically, and immovably himself."[10] Thus the apostle Peter encouraged godly women to make their beauty the qualities of the "inner person of the heart" (1 Peter 3:4 NET)—who they are as persons "at the deepest and most private level."[11]

This hidden person of the heart has an unfathomable depth that according to the Scripture cannot be plumbed—except by God. In amazement at the clever conniving schemes of the wicked, the psalmist exclaimed, "For the inward nature and the human heart—how deep they are!"[12] (Ps. 64:6). Similarly, the writer of Proverbs declared, "The purposes of a person's heart are deep waters" (20:5 NIV). The heart's depth is comparable to the immeasurable depth of the underworld: "Sheol and Abaddon lie open before the LORD, how much more the hearts of men!" (Prov. 15:11).

Thus the deepest thoughts and emotions of our life are buried in the recesses of our heart. The thoughts we keep from others, we hide in our heart. When Abraham doubted God's promise of a son, Scripture tells us that he "fell on his face and laughed, and said in his heart, 'Will a child be born to a man one hundred years old?'" (Gen. 17:17). Dreams that rise from the depth of our person play out in our hearts. The beloved in Song of Solomon says, "I was asleep but my heart was awake" (Song 5:2).

We can hide the deep hurt of our real person with outer joy, as the writer of Proverbs notes, "Even in laughter the heart may be in pain" (Prov. 14:13). We may do this as deliberate camouflage to keep others from knowing what is really going on inside of us. But even if we would like to communicate the contents of the depths of our heart to others, Scripture suggests that it is not possible: "The heart knows its own bitterness, and a stranger does not share its joy" (Prov. 14:10). We are called to rejoice with those who rejoice and to weep with those who weep (Rom. 12:15). But as Waltke explained, the writer of Proverbs believed that "one's emotional-intellectual-religious-moral motions are too complex, too inward, and too individualistic to be experienced by others or even to represent them adequately to others (cf. 1 Cor. 2:11)."[13] The deep person of our heart is uniquely us with our own experience.

The truth that the inner person of the heart is our real identity is evident also in our uneasy and often distressful experience of duplicity—of "putting on a front" so people do not see who we really are. At one time or another we have all felt like the young woman who admitted, "I don't like to be around people because they will see my real self under my outgoing personality. I feel so alone."

This distinction between what a person does and says—and what is in his or her "heart"—is frequently noted in Scripture. The psalmist said, "His speech was smoother than butter, but his heart was war" (Ps. 55:21). They "bless with their mouth, but inwardly they curse" (Ps. 62:4; cf. Jer. 9:8–9).

We will consider the pretentious dichotomy between our public persona and the real person more fully in a later chapter, but note here that because we usually desire to appear better than we are, this phenomenon is a particular problem in our moral and spiritual life.

God Relates to the Inner Person of the Heart

God Knows Your Heart

The real person of the heart that is hidden from others—and to some extent even from ourselves—is never hidden from God. The psalmist declared, "O LORD, You have searched me and known me" (Ps. 139:1; see vv. 1–5). Everything about our actions and our thoughts, "behold, O LORD, You know it all" (v. 4). God knows us truthfully and exhaustively—that is, he knows who we really are—because he knows our hearts.

We are reminded of this again and again in Scripture, apparently with the hope that we will never lose sight of it. A few of these reminders may be noted:

+ "Would not God find this out? For He knows the secrets of the heart" (Ps. 44:21).
+ "The refining pot is for silver and the furnace for gold, but the LORD tests hearts" (Prov. 17:3; cf. 1 Chron. 29:17; Ps. 17:3; Jer. 12:3).
+ "Render to each according to all his ways, whose heart You know for You alone know the hearts of the sons of men" (2 Chron. 6:30).
+ "I, the LORD, search the heart, I test the mind [lit. kidneys*], even to give to each man according to his ways, according to the results of his deeds" (Jer. 17:10).
+ "O LORD of hosts, You who test the righteous, who see the mind [lit. kidneys] and the heart" (Jer. 20:12; cf. 11:20).
+ "You are those who justify yourselves in the sight of men, but God knows your hearts" (Luke 16:15).
+ "You, Lord, who know the hearts of all men" (Acts 1:24; cf. 15:8).

---

* Kidneys are used in the Old Testament figuratively for the inner being, especially the deepest feelings of the emotional life.

+ "We speak, not as pleasing men, but God who examines our hearts" (1 Thess. 2:4).
+ "All the churches will know that I am He who searches the minds [lit. kidneys] and hearts; and I will give to each one of you according to your deeds" (Rev. 2:23).

In examining our hearts, God probes beneath the surface. He always knows what is really there. The individual whose life appears all together and peaceful on the surface may in the real person of the heart be coldly, even rebelliously, distant from God—like those Jesus described as whitewashed graves, beautiful on the outside, but inside full of "dead men's bones and all uncleanness" (Matt. 23:27–28).

God Deals with Us in Our Heart

God not only looks at our heart to see who we are, he meets us as persons in our heart. As Paul Minear said, "God fashions the heart as a forum for dialogue with him."[14] He puts thoughts into the heart (e.g., Ezra 7:27; Eccl. 3:11) and speaks words of comfort and love "to the heart" of his people (Hos. 2:14; cf. Isa. 40:2). He opens the heart of people to receive his Word (Acts 16:14) and shines "the Light of the knowledge of the glory of God in the face of Christ" in the heart (2 Cor. 4:6; cf. Eph. 1:18). Christ and the Spirit dwell "in the heart" (e.g., Eph. 3:17; Gal. 4:6), and the heart is the place where his love is "poured out" (Rom. 5:5).

God deals with us according to his knowledge of our heart. When the prophet Samuel went to the house of Jesse to anoint one of his sons as king, he saw Eliab, the firstborn, and thought, "Surely the LORD's anointed stands here before the LORD" (1 Sam. 16:6 NIV). He was quickly informed, however, that "The LORD does not look at the things people look at. People look at the outward appearance, but the LORD looks at the heart" (v. 7 NIV). Similarly, Jesus told the Pharisees, "You are those who justify yourselves in the sight of men, but God knows your hearts; for that which is highly esteemed among men is detestable in the sight of God" (Luke 16:15).

Most importantly, God judges us according to what is in our heart. We are often told he judges us according to our deeds or works. But our deeds are not only the acts that are seen or the words that are heard; they include the hidden thoughts and motives behind them. Thus God declared, "I, the LORD, search the heart, I test the mind, even to give to each man according to his ways, according to the results of his deeds" (Jer. 17:10; cf. 2 Chron. 6:30). Likewise, the glorified

Christ said, "I am He who searches the minds and hearts; and I will give to each one of you according to your deeds" (Rev. 2:23).

Speaking of the final judgment, Paul declared that God will "render to each person according to his deeds . . . when God . . . will judge the secrets [lit. hidden things] of men through Christ Jesus" (Rom. 2:6, 16; cf. 1 Cor. 4:5). In short, judgment according to our deeds is in reality the judgment of us as persons. For the deeds that come out of our heart actually disclose the real person of the heart.

Finally, God makes us new persons by giving us a new heart. Scripture speaks of the believer in Christ as "born again" (John 3:3, 5, 8), a "new self" (Rom. 6:6; Col. 3:9–10), and "a new creature" or "a new creation" (2 Cor. 5:17; NIV, NLT, etc.). As we will see later, all of this making us a new person is the result of receiving a "new heart" (Ezek. 11:19; 36:26; cf. Rom. 2:29).

Knowing the Real Person

The question of true self-identity is answered in the heart. As one Old Testament scholar expressed it, "The deepest sense of 'heart' is the genuine, the authentic man. . . . Man is made up of many layers. He who penetrates into the deepest layer (the heart) comes to know himself thoroughly."[15] This same concept of heart carries over into the writings of the New Testament.*

Now the knowledge of our self is part of the double knowledge that is vital to spiritual growth. As John Calvin, the great theologian of the Reformation, said, "Without the knowledge of self there is no knowledge of God." Conversely, "without knowledge of God there is no knowledge of self."[16]

To acknowledge that the deep hidden person of the heart is our true identity is thus vital for our relationship with God. Knowing that God has intimate knowledge of every thought and motive of our heart, we should be willing to walk openly and honestly before him. Trying to hide something from God is not only futile, but foolish. Like the prophet Isaiah who saw the vision of God and declared, "I am ruined! . . . I am a man of unclean lips" (Isa. 6:5), it is only as we come to know God that we clearly see ourselves. Without an awareness of our spiritual ills, we would never seek God but just gladly or perhaps sadly remain as we are.

God's intimate awareness of who we really are should also overwhelm us with the reality of his love. He knows everything about us. Yet he continues to love us

---

* Johannes Behm said, "The NT use of the word agrees with the OT use as distinct from the Greek [use which was primarily physiological]." "kardia," TDNT, 3:611.

with an infinite love and graciously works to transform our hearts so we might receive more and more of the life for which we were designed.

Recognizing that the real person is hidden in the depth of the heart is also meaningful in our relationships with other people. When we hear someone say or do something that we don't think is right, we are often quick to draw a conclusion about the person. What a difference it could make if we first stopped and asked our self, "Am I hearing or seeing the real person, the person in the depth of their heart?"

The character of the great German Reformer Martin Luther is often said to have been obstinate and irascible. He even said of himself, "I am rough, boisterous, stormy, and altogether warlike. I am born to fight against innumerable monsters and devils. I must remove stumps and stones, cut away thistles and thorns, and clear wild forests."[17]

No doubt this is the only Luther that many saw. They didn't see the heart of the Luther who wrote "A Mighty Fortress Is Our God" and many other hymns. Or the Luther whose sensitivity and struggle with his own sin is evident in the words of another of his hymns: "From the depths of woe I raise to thee / The voice of lamentation; / Lord turn a gracious ear to me / And hear my supplication."[18]

Someone once asked me whether an emotionally disturbed person could be a "good" Christian. I immediately conjured up in my mind the negative picture of a person who continually lived *under* life's circumstances bombarded with negative thoughts and responses—one who experienced considerable depression and couldn't cope well with life.

This picture didn't square well with my image of a believer walking in faith with the Savior. But I was also compelled to ask myself, "Do I really know the person behind who I see? Do I know the person's heart and what has shaped it this way? What traumatic wounds—perhaps in early childhood, perhaps continuing—have contributed to this outwardly dysfunctional life? Most importantly, do I know what is in the deepest part of the heart—the deep drives and passions that may be there battling against the powerful negative forces, but only occasionally and weakly breaking through?"

Paul said that no human being can know the heart of a fellow human being absolutely. That's why he wrote, "Therefore judge nothing before the time, until the Lord comes, who will both bring to light the hidden things of darkness and reveal the counsels of the hearts. Then each one's praise will come from God" (1 Cor. 4:5 NKJV, etc.).

The emotionally disturbed person who has difficulty coping may, underneath all of the outward dysfunction, have a heart that is genuinely seeking God—even more than the person who outwardly seems on top of things. There are times, of course, when we can't avoid making some kind of judgment about people. But caution should always be in order since the real person is the hidden person of the heart.

Directing the Inner Person

The heart of the person directs his or her life, but the person is also the one directing his or her own heart. Just like a man skiing down a mountain slope, the ski is like the heart—strapped firmly on to the skier, it takes him according to the pull of gravity. Slipping through the snow, the skier goes where his skis go. The person goes wherever his heart goes through his life of constant movement and change. Yet, it is the skier who puts on and takes off weight on his skis that determines the direction and speed down the slope. In the same manner, the person controls what goes in and out of his or her heart, which then determines the person's activities and responses in life.

Our Heart Directs Our Life

Since our heart is our real person, it is not surprising that God's Word teaches that we live life from our heart. Everything that comprises our life as persons—our thoughts, attitudes, feelings, our impulses and desires, our speech and actions—all spring from our heart. In short, our heart is the director of our life.

Proverbs 4:23, which we have already mentioned, is one of the most significant texts of Scripture for understanding life: "Watch over your heart with all diligence, for from it flow the springs of life." In other versions of this verse the heart is said to be the place from which "everything you do flows" (NIV); the "source of all life" (NEB); "where life starts" (MSG). Literally, the Hebrew text says: "Above all guarding, keep watch over your heart. For out of it are the *issues* of life" (emphasis added).

Identifying the heart as the source of "the issues of life" is not simply saying that the heart is the fountain or primal source of life. It also says that the heart *controls* the course of life. The same the Hebrew word for "issues" is used in other places to describe the boundaries of a territory. It delineates the point where the boundary begins and the course that the boundary follows from there—in other words, it begins here and goes from here to there and to there and so forth.

What God tells us in Proverbs 4:23, then, is that our life not only has "its fountain in the heart, but also the direction which it takes is determined by the heart."[19] In other words, our heart is not only the spring from which our life flows, it also directs the stream of our life in all of its bends and turns (note the plural "issues") as it continues its flow. In sum, the heart is the spring and director of all of our living.

The heart's control of our life is a constant theme of Scripture. "A wise man's heart directs him toward the right, but the foolish man's heart directs him toward the left," declared the preacher of Ecclesiastes (10:2). Our obedience or disobedience toward God is determined by the condition of our heart: "If your heart turns away and you will not obey" (Deut. 30:17). The people of Jeremiah's day rebelled in apostasy because they "walked, each one, in the stubbornness of his evil heart" (Jer. 11:8; cf. 7:24; 24:16; 16:12; 18:12; 23:17). The lie of Ananias and Sapphira was spawned in their heart as Peter's question indicates: "Why is it that you have conceived [lit. set, placed] this deed in your heart" (Acts 5:4).

No one taught that the heart is the source of life more plainly than Jesus. In response to those who were accusing him of casting out demons by the power of the Devil, he said, "How can you, being evil, speak what is good? For the mouth speaks out of that which fills the heart. The good man brings out of his good treasure what is good; and the evil man brings out of his evil treasure what is evil" (Matt. 12:34–35).

The implications of his teaching are clear: good words and good behavior do not spring from mere resolutions—"I *will* be good"—but from our being. Evil things come from evil persons. Good things come from good persons. What defines a person's character and the activities of his life is the content of the storehouse of his heart where he has treasured up either evil or good.

As Jesus' words attest, our speech is the primary way that we reveal who we are, and that revelation can sometimes be surprising. As a young teenager, I enjoyed driving a tractor to cultivate an orchard. I always tried to pull the disk cultivator as close as possible to the trunks of the trees so that I would catch all of the grass and weeds. On one occasion, I got too close and hooked the end of the disk on the tree, bringing me to an abrupt halt.

With the setup of the tractor and disk there was no way that I could back up and maneuver the disk away from the tree. So hot and annoyed (I thought I could handle the equipment better) I got off the tractor and tried to pull the disk away from the tree. I tugged and jerked at the heavy disk, but could barely move it a few fractions of an inch. In the midst of this angry agonizing struggle I suddenly found myself blurting profanity. It took me aback as I couldn't remember ever having said things like this before. Raised in a Christian home and a fundamental church all of my years, I wasn't in the habit of using such language. But there it was. Where did it come from?

Some years later William Newell's comments on the apostle's words in Romans 3:13—"The poison of asps is under their lips"—helped me understand this incident and a whole lot more about my life. Newell explained that when the serpent strikes, its fangs, ordinarily folded back in the upper jaw, drop down. And in the process of actually biting, serpents press a sack of deadly poison hidden "under their lips" at the root of the hollow fangs thereby injecting the venom into the wound.[20]

I realized from this and other Scriptures that what came out of my mouth on that hot afternoon was already in me, lying hidden in my heart. It just took the pressure of stress to spew it out. As F. Dale Bruner points out in his comment on Jesus' teaching: "Speech . . . is the overflow of our being; it is the main way we express what we 'are'; it is the major fruit of our personhood; speech is the self *ex*-pressed out ('pressed out')."[21]

This reality explains the common advice to count to ten before responding in a stressful situation. Unlike Jesus, who could respond immediately from a holy, loving heart, we need to be careful about letting the contents of our heart display themselves spontaneously. C. S. Lewis's testimony relates to all of us.

> When I come to my evening prayers and try to reckon up the sins of the day, nine times out of ten the most obvious one is some sin against charity; I have sulked or snapped or sneered or snubbed or stormed. And the excuse that immediately springs to my mind is that the provocation was so sudden and unexpected: I was caught off my guard, I had not time to collect myself. Now that may be an extenuating circumstance as regards those particular acts: they would obviously be worse if they had been deliberate and premeditated. On the other hand, surely what a man does when he is taken off his guard is the best evidence for what sort of man he is? Surely what pops out before the man has time to put on a disguise is the truth? If there are rats in a cellar you are most likely to see them if you go in very suddenly. But the suddenness does not create the rats: it only prevents them from hiding. In the same way the suddenness of the provocation does not make me an ill-tempered man: it only shows me what an ill-tempered man I am. The rats are always there in the cellar, but if you go in shouting and noisily they will have taken cover before you switch on the light. Apparently the rats of resentment and vindictiveness are always there in the cellar of my soul.[22]

We try, though not always successfully, to intercept the heart's expression, tweaking it with what is more appropriate for a good appearance and reputation.

But even these modifications stem from our mixed heart. We seek to hide what is in our heart, and to some extent are able to succeed in not exposing all of its contents. But as we've already seen, the issues of life flow out of the heart. In one form or another, the contents of our heart inevitably make their presence known in the experiences of our life. More on this in later chapters.

On one occasion, in a discussion over washing hands and utensils—an issue that was considered important for religious purity by some Jewish leaders—Jesus said, "There is nothing outside the man which can defile him if it goes into him . . . That which proceeds out of the man, that is what defiles the man. For from within, *out of the heart of men*, proceed the evil thoughts, fornications, thefts, murders, adulteries. . . . All these *evil things proceed from within and defile the man*" (Mark 7:15, 20–21, 23).

It was not certain food or eating with dirty hands or dirty utensils, according to Jesus that defiles the person. Only one's personal actions can thus defile—what comes out of his or her heart.

This discussion concerned dietary matters and ritual washing, but the principle applies to all things. Nothing can simply intrude in from outside and defile us—not even what we see or hear. For all of these things can become lodged in the heart only through our personal response to them. We either reject them or welcome them as treasure in the heart.

Jesus expressed the same priority of the heart in the activities of life when he said, "First clean the inside of the cup and dish, and then the outside also will be clean" (Matt. 23:26 NIV; cf. Luke 11:41). In other words, what is outside is determined by what is inside—deep within one's heart.

The heart, therefore, has rightly been described as "the mission control center" of human life.[23] Our thoughts, our motives, the words that we speak, our feelings and attitudes, and all of our actions originate from our heart. In the words of Herman Ridderbos, "Man is led and governed ultimately from one point"—the heart.[24] For this reason, God calls to us through the teacher of Proverbs: "Give me your heart, my son, and let your eyes delight in my ways" (Prov. 23:26). To give our heart to God is to give him control over all of our lives.

Directing Our Own Heart

Scripture teaches not only that our heart is the director of our life, but that *we also direct our heart*. To put it another way, it is our responsibility to direct the director of our life. Thus we are exhorted: "Direct your heart in the way" (Prov. 23:19). "Watch over your heart with all diligence" (Prov. 4:23). Our oversight of our heart is seen also in the Lord's command, "Do not store up for yourselves treasures on earth . . . . But store up for yourselves treasures in heaven . . . for where your treasure is, there your heart will be also" (Matt. 6:19–21).

We will consider the nature of our control over our heart more in future chapters. But it will be helpful here in order to understand Jesus' words to note that as beings created in God's image it is our very nature to love. And love's dynamic is to seek its object and cling to it with binding force. Thus it is our very nature to continually seek out and join to ourselves what we really value or treasure.

What Jesus is telling us therefore is that the treasure we choose to love and store up will finally control us—our heart will be where our treasure is. As D. A. Carson explained, "The things most highly treasured occupy the 'heart,' the center of the personality, embracing mind, emotions, and will . . . and thus the most cherished treasure subtly but infallibly controls the whole person's directions and values."[25]

The Bible's teaching that the heart is the real person—and the source and director of all personal activities—surely means that *the care of our heart is to be the supreme task of our life*. The heart deserves to be guarded "more than any treasure," for it is our treasure of greatest value—our own self (see Mark 8:36–37).

What we bring into it, what we allow to slip out from it, what we expel from it—all determine who we are, the direction of our life's journey, and finally, our ultimate destiny.

Questions for Thought

1. How does the biblical concept of the heart differ from our usual concept of the heart? Why is our heart so important for our living in the Bible?
2. Have you ever given any thought about the characteristics of your own heart? What characteristics do you see there? Is there a difference between your outward person and the inner person of your heart?
3. Do you usually try to consider the heart of another person rather than simply evaluating him or her on what is displayed outwardly? If so, what effect did this have on your attitude and judgment of the person?
4. What do you think about the reality that God knows everything in your heart fully? How does this truth affect your relationship with him?
5. Explain how our heart directs our life and we also direct our heart. What does our heart do in directing our lives, and what do we do in directing our heart? How does this reality relate to Proverbs 4:23?

■■ 3 ■■

The Real Problem in Life

Our Deviant Heart

The intent of man's heart is evil from his youth.

GENESIS 8:21

I loved to excuse myself and to accuse some other mysterious "thing" inside me that was disconnected from the real me. In truth it was wholly me and my wicked heart that divided me from myself.

AUGUSTINE

I will give you a new heart and put a new spirit within you.

EZEKIEL 36:26

Of all the ills of human beings, a "heartache" is one that is most written in prose and song—take for instance the country rock hit from the late seventies "It's a Heartache" (or for that matter most country songs) or the popular song "Heartache," and so on. A heartache means deep sorrow or anguish. It is not relieved instantly nor cured by potions. It is not isolated to a body organ nor is it a chronic condition but something that affects the whole person at one time. Hence, it is often associated with brokenness in romantic relationships, but also of other, equally important sources of grief and anxiety. Such a notion of "heartache" befits the biblical truth about the human heart.

If our heart controls the "issues of life"—our thoughts, attitudes, aspirations, feelings, talk, and behavior—we can only conclude that the problems of our life are ultimately problems of the heart. We don't experience the abundant life of love, joy, and peace for which we were created because something is seriously amiss in our heart.

Our Creator graciously does not leave us in the dark about our problem. In plain words and numerous examples of human life and experience he surgically diagnoses the fatal disorder of the human heart that is alienated from him. He also tells us of the sound heart that he desires and is willing to create anew in us—the kind of heart that is the spring of true human life. Both hearts are described so we might understand the real problem of our life and its solution in a transformed heart.

The Condition of the Natural Heart

According to God's Word, the entrance of sin into the world through the disobedience of the first man and woman affected all of their progeny—the entire human race (Rom. 5:12–19; 1 Cor. 15:22). We all came into this world estranged from God and consequently with a heart that suffers from serious irremediable problems. No one is exempt—"all have sinned and come short of the glory of God" (Rom. 3:23).

A Propensity to Moral Failure
Evil

The first reference to the human heart in Scripture is negative. Speaking about the judgment of the flood, Scripture says, "The LORD saw that the wickedness of man was great on the earth, and that every intent of the thoughts of his heart was only evil continually" (Gen. 6:5). The Lord not only saw the wicked (or "evil")* behavior of humankind, he also saw its source—a heart so dominated by sin that its "every" intention or inclination was "only evil continually."

To describe something as evil is basically to say that is it something "harmful."[1] The term encompasses a wrong relation to God and all of the hurtful effects that result from this wrong relationship. The real character of evil is revealed in the light of its opposite—good—which in Scripture means that which makes something desirable. What is pleasant, delightful, right, and most importantly, beneficial, is good. In the final analysis, the good is what makes for the enjoyment and fullness of life. When God looked at his creation and saw that it was "very good" (Gen. 1:31), he saw that it perfectly suited and was ordered for abundant life—a life of shalom.

Evil is the contrary to all these good qualities of life. It is unpleasant, bad, hurtful, and as such is associated with death. Evil entails all kinds of external

---

* "Wickedness" (*ra'a*) and "evil" (*ra'*), different forms of the same Hebrew root word meaning "evil," are both used in this verse, emphasizing the evil of mankind.

Evil: Whatever Hinders the Good Life

The wide uses of the Hebrew word for "evil" (*ra'*) do not always refer to the sin or the effects of evil persons, such as Abraham's "distress" (lit. "is evil in your eyes") over having to drive away his son through Hagar (Gen. 21:11–12), Hannah's "sadness" (lit. "is evil to your heart" because of her childlessness (1 Sam. 1:8), and the "days of trouble" (Eccl. 12:1 NIV) in old age (lit. "evil days"). But these and other instances of "evil" do reflect conditions that are the effect of sin and would not be present if sin were not in the world. They all detract from the well-being of life. This is also the meaning of "evil" when God is said to create "evil" (Isa. 45:7) or bring it upon people (Amos 3:6). He brings calamity or the disruption of the "good" life in retributive judgment, and also in chastisement that is designed to crush sinful hearts and stir them to repentance that they may experience the "good."

hurt and ugliness, but also various life-robbing mental states—troubled, down-hearted, distressed, anger, and displeasure.[2] Thus Moses set before God's people the choice of "life and prosperity [lit. the 'good']" and "death and adversity [lit. the 'evil']" (Deut. 30:15). And God pleaded, "Seek good and not evil that you may live" (Amos 5:14).

Drawing on the interesting tidbit that *evil* is *live* spelled backward, psychiatrist M. Scott Peck aptly summed up its meaning: "Evil is in opposition to life. It is that which opposes the life force. It has, in short, to do with killing."[3] Thus Satan, the personal embodiment of all of the negativity of evil and its radical opposition to God, is rightly called "the evil one" and "a murderer from the beginning" (Eph. 6:16; 1 John 2:13–14; John 8:44).

Because the person living apart from God today still has the remnant of the image of God as part of the "very good" creation, he or she still has a longing for the qualities of the *good* life. But at the depth of one's being, at the core of his or her person, Scripture says a person's heart is evil—it is bent against God and thus against the good.

We might think that the flood with its destruction of evil humanity (save for righteous Noah and his family) cured this problem, but the same description of the human heart is repeated after the flood: "the intent of man's heart is evil from his youth" (Gen. 8:21). The writer of Ecclesiastes affirmed this much later in his powerful description: "The hearts of the sons of men are full of evil, and insanity[*] is in their hearts throughout their lives" (9:3; cf. Jer. 7:24; 11:8; 16:12; Heb. 3:12).[†]

Like an insane or mad person lives irrationally or contrary to reality, the evil

---

[*] The verbal form of this word, which is primary in Scripture, "refers to irrational behavior" (H. Cazelles, "*holeloth*," *TDOT*, 3:411).

[†] While some of these texts concerning evil in the heart refer to specific people (see also 1 Sam. 17:28; 1 Kings 2:44; Pss. 28 ; 33; 140:4; 141:4 ; Prov. 6:14; 26:23 ; Eccl. 8:11; Isa. 32:6;

heart lives against the reality of God and his good ordered ways and thus suffers consequences. To live against reality is hard. Yet we often do it again and again, demonstrating the truth of the definition of insanity most frequently attributed to Albert Einstein—"doing the same thing over and over again and expecting different results."

Perverse

The natural heart bent away from God is also described as *perverse*—"the perverse in heart are an abomination to the LORD" (Prov. 11:20). The Hebrew word for "perverse" has the idea of not being straight forward or upright, not on the level, crooked, or twisted.[4] At its core, perversion signifies turning away from God and his "way" of life—"the wrong direction of the innermost being."[5] Cornelius Plantinga realistically portrayed the essence of this perverseness as "the turning of loyalty, energy, and desire away from God and God's project in the world: it is the diversion of construction materials for the city of God to side projects of our own, often accompanied by jerry-built ideologies that seek to justify the diversion."[6]

The diverted or perverse way is also not an easy path to walk. It is rightly called "crooked" and "twisting." The same word describes the "rough" places that are difficult to traverse—places that God makes smooth for his people (Isa. 42:16). Scripture lovingly warns us of the hurt and destruction that stems from a perverse heart. "Thorns and snares are in the way of the perverse" (Prov. 22:5). "The one whose walk is blameless is kept safe, but the one whose ways are perverse will fall into the pit" (Prov. 28:18 NIV).

The Hebrew describing the latter person whose ways are perverse may be more literally expressed as "the twisted one of double-dealing ways" or "the one who twists himself in double-dealing ways"[7]—he masks his real walk by pretending another. Diverted from the Lord's straightforward way of life, the many twists and diversions of the perverse ways make for a stressful taxing life. As the ancient philosopher Seneca noted, "Devotion to what is wrong is complex and admits of infinite variations."[8]

The writer of Proverbs forthrightly summed up the product of the perverse heart: "He who has a crooked mind [lit. heart] finds no good" (17:20), which is to say, he finds nothing of the pleasant prosperity of the "good" of life. The *Jerusalem Bible* simply reads: "The tortuous of heart finds no happiness."[9]

Jer. 3:17; 4:14; 18:12; Dan. 11:27), the characteristics of their evil hearts are common to all people to some extent pointing to the universality of evil in the heart.

Two Fundamental Defects

The moral failure of the natural heart—its propensity to evil and perversion—inevitably becomes obvious in our behavior. As a result, we tend to focus our attention on our conscious attitudes and actions. But God is not content simply to reveal the outward expressions of the fallen heart. He probes deeper to expose two fundamental defects that underlie our conscious thoughts, feelings, and actions: pride and deceitfulness.

Pride

"Everyone who is proud in heart is an abomination to the LORD," said the writer of Proverbs (16:5). To be "proud of heart" is literally in this verse to be "high of heart." Other places in the Old Testament speak of the heart "lifting up" the person (2 Kings 14:10) or the heart being "lifted up" (Deut. 17:20).[*] The arrogant heart is also pictured as "great" or "important" as well as "wide" or "broad" and in some cases simply literally "proud" or "insolent."[†]

Interestingly "pride" is never directly applied to the heart in the New Testament, but rather to persons (Rom. 1:30; 2 Tim. 3:2, 4; 1 John 2:16).[‡] Since the heart is the real person, however, proud persons obviously have proud hearts. Moreover, pride is sometimes indirectly associated with the heart as in the reference to people who are "proud in the thoughts of their heart" (Luke 1:51; cf. Mark 7:22).

The most fundamental characteristic of the proud heart is its belief in the first lie of Scripture, Satan's lie to Eve—"you will be like God" (Gen. 3:4). The essence of the proud heart is that it dethrones God and replaces him with self. The psalmist declared that the wicked "boasts about the cravings of his heart; he blesses the greedy and reviles the LORD. In his pride the wicked does not seek him; in all his thoughts there is no room for God" (10:3–4 NIV).

The person who lives his life without God may not consciously think of himself as being his own god. However, when one chooses to reject God's authority and follow his own will, in reality he is choosing himself as his final authority

---

* For other references using Hebrew terms meaning "high" or "lifted up" in relation to "heart," see Deut. 8:14; 2 Chron. 26:16; 32:25; Prov. 18:22; Jer. 48:29; Ezek. 28:2, 5, 17; 31:10; Dan. 11:12; Hos. 13:6.

† For references using a Hebrew term meaning "great, important" in relation to "heart," see Isa. 9:9; 10:12; Dan. 8:25. For references using a Hebrew term meaning "wide, broad" in relation to "heart," see Ps. 101:5; Prov. 21:4. The concept of a wide or broad heart is also used positively for a breadth of intellect or mental capacity as in the case of Solomon (1 Kings 4:29). For references using a Hebrew term meaning "proud, insolent," see 1 Sam. 17:28; Jer. 49:16; Obad. 3.

‡ See also 1 Cor. 4:18; 5:2; James 4:16; 1 Peter 5:5.

Pride versus Self-Esteem

The sin of pride, which traditionally is seen as the first of the seven deadly sins (Prov. 6:16–19), must not be confused with a proper self-esteem. As Augustine noted, there is a proper exaltation of our heart that comes through a right relationship of humility under God:

> And what is pride but the craving for undue exaltation? And this is undue exaltation, when the soul abandons Him to whom it ought to cleave as its end, and becomes a kind of end to itself. This happens when it becomes its own satisfaction. And it does so when it falls away from that unchangeable good which ought to satisfy it more than itself. . . . For it is good to have the heart lifted up, yet not to one's self, for this is proud, but to the Lord, for this is obedient, and can be the act only of the humble. There is, therefore, something in humility which, strangely enough, exalts the heart, and something in pride which debases it. This seems, indeed, to be contradictory, that loftiness should debase and lowliness exalt. But pious humility enables us to submit to what is above us; and nothing is more exalted above us than God; and therefore humility, by making us subject to God exalts us.[10]

"Before his downfall a man's heart is proud, but humility comes before honor." (Prov. 18:12)

As new persons in Christ, "We now have self shalom. We can say deep within our souls, *I am comfortable with who I am in Christ. I'm confident in who I am in Christ. I'm content with who I am in Christ.*"[11]

and thus his god, even as Adam and Eve did in the beginning. This is the charge that God brought against the arrogant prince of Tyre: "Your heart is lifted up. . . . Yet you are a man and not God, although you make your heart like the heart of God" (Ezek. 28:2, cf. v. 6).

Because pride directly opposes God, usurping his rightful place, classic Christian theology has rightly understood pride as the root and essence of all human sin.* C. S. Lewis expressed this classic view in his discussion of what he calls "The Great Sin": "The essential vice, the utmost evil, is Pride. Unchastity, anger, greed, drunkenness, and all that, are mere fleabites in comparison: it was through Pride that the devil became the devil; Pride leads to every other vice; it is the complete anti-God state of mind."[12]

Pride is the radical opposite of the first principle of a godly life, namely, the "fear" of or "awesome respect" for God (Prov. 8:13). Depicted as "haughty eyes,"

---

* For example, Augustine in his discussion of the origin of sin in Adam and Eve explains, "And what is the origin of our evil will but pride? For 'pride is the beginning of sin.'" *The City of God* trans. Marcus Dods (New York: Modern Library, 1993), 14.13, citing Ecclus. 10.13.

pride is at the top of the list of things that God hates (Prov. 6:16; cf. 8:13). And it is surely significant that humility ("poor in spirit") is the first characteristic of the "blessed" person according to Jesus (Matt. 5:3).

The centrality of pride in human sin is further evident in God's promise to future Jerusalem to eradicate pride through his salvation: "On that day you, Jerusalem, will not be put to shame for all the wrongs you have done to me, because I will remove from you your arrogant boasters. Never again will you be haughty on my holy hill. But I will leave within you the meek and humble. The remnant of Israel will trust in the name of the LORD" (Zeph. 3:11–12 NIV). The blessing of salvation is ultimately the removal of human pride. For as Paul asserts in Romans 1, the root of the sin and misery of humanity lies in the refusal to honor God as God, putting in his place the glory of the creature (Rom. 1:21–23).

The proud heart, living in antagonism to God, is also in opposition to itself. Pride brings the shattering or disintegration of the person as the writer of Proverbs declared, "Pride goes before destruction and a haughty spirit before stumbling" (Prov. 16:18). The proud person still bears something of the image of God that calls him to love and righteousness. But his arrogant heart urges to him to please self first and thus fights against the good that he still knows, tearing apart the wholeness or peace (*shalom*) of true life.

The proud individual actually becomes an enemy of everyone. As Pascal said, "The self is hateful. . . . In one word the self has two characteristics: It is unjust in itself, in that it makes itself the centre of everything; it is a nuisance to others, in that it wants to assert itself over them, for each self is the enemy, and would like to be tyrant to all the others."[13]

The numerous interpersonal problems of the prideful god-playing heart are often summed up in Scripture as "strife and envy" (e.g., Rom. 13:13; 1 Cor. 3:3).* For example, we are told not to "become boastful, challenging one another, envying one another" (Gal. 5:26). But pride causes us to disobey this command. In the areas of our strength, pride urges us to challenge others in order to display our superiority in power, knowledge, morality, or even religiosity.† When we feel inadequate, pride moves us to avoid competition and stand quietly on the sidelines simmering with envy. Pride can lead us to seek the destruction of the

---

* See also Phil. 1:15–17; James 3:14–16; cf. Prov. 13:10; 28:25.

† For a discussion of pride and its various forms, see Reinhold Niebuhr, *The Nature and Destiny of Man*, vol. 1, Gifford Lectures (New York: Charles Scribner's Sons, 1964), 186–240. See also C. S. Lewis's chapter titled "The Great Sin" in *Mere Christianity*, rev. ed. (New York: Macmillan, 1960), 94–99.

other person or to withdraw from people altogether—both actions for the sake of preserving our self-image.*

The distress that the proud heart brings upon itself is noted by psychologist Gordon Allport:

> Any neurotic is living a life which in some respects is extreme in its self-centeredness. . . . The region of his misery represents a complete preoccupation with himself. The very nature of the neurotic disorder is tied to pride. If the sufferer is hypersensitive, resentful, captious, he may be indicating a fear that he will not appear to advantage in competitive situations where he wants to show his worth. If he is chronically indecisive, he is showing fear that he may do the wrong thing and be discredited. If he is over-scrupulous and self-critical, he may be endeavoring to show how praiseworthy he really is. Thus, most neuroses are, from the point of view of religion, mixed with the sin of pride.[14]

Scripture rightly calls the proud heart a "foolish" or "senseless" heart (Rom. 1:21). As Cornelius Plantinga remarked, "The image of ourselves as center of the world is fantasy—perhaps, in its sheer detachment from reality, even a form of madness. . . . It's like pulling the plug on your own resuscitator."[15]

Living above and against other people, the proud heart is a lonely heart. It is also a frenzied, tired heart, attempting to live as God instead of living by God's wisdom and power as he designed for us to do. In the end, the proud heart with its undue exaltation is actually debased. As Augustine explained, "By craving to be more, man becomes less; and by aspiring to be self-sufficing, he fell away from Him who truly suffices him."[16] This is the truth of Jesus' words that "everyone who exalts himself will be humbled" (Luke 18:14).

Deceitfulness

The second major defect of the natural heart flows directly from the first. The proud heart is prone to deceit. The prophet Obadiah says of Edom, "The arrogance of your heart has deceived you" (v. 3; cf. Jer. 49:16). Human speech, so vital for human life with God and others, is defiled by deceit issuing from pride:

---

* For a good practical discussion of the effects of egoism in relation to others, see Earl Jabay, *The God-Players* (Grand Rapids: Zondervan, 1969), 50–61.

They lie to one another;
they speak with flattering lips and deceptive hearts. . . .
They say, "Through our tongues we have power;
our lips are our own—*who can be our master?*" (Ps. 12:2–4 HCSB)

Deception as "Double-Hearted"

The "deceptive heart" of Psalm 12:2 is literally the Hebrew metaphor, "double heart" (lit. "a heart and a heart"), which does not indicate different opinions or uncertainty but rather a double standard as in dishonest "differing weights" (Deut. 25:13, lit. "a stone and a stone"). In deception the very center of the person—the heart—is split resulting in a badly disintegrated existence.

The severity of the heart's problem of deceit is revealed in Jeremiah's words: "The heart is more deceitful than all else and is desperately sick; who can understand it? I, the LORD, search the heart" (17:9–10).* This language of Jeremiah must not be diminished. Aside from the great deceiver Satan (Rev. 12:9), who is not being considered here by Jeremiah, there is nothing in the world that is more cunning and crafty at attempting to make its pursuit of evil look good than the human heart. The deep fountain from which all of man's life flows is desperately sick, or as the Hebrew term suggests, it is "incurably ill" (cf. the same word in 15:18 and 30:12 where it is literally used for wounds that cannot be healed). Moreover, according to Jeremiah, the depth of this illness can never be plumbed by the person himself or any other human. Only the LORD, the searcher of human hearts, fully knows it.

The Incurable Deceitful Heart

The incurable nature of the deceitful heart is seen in Isaiah's comment concerning the foolish idolater who himself constructs the idol and then worships his own product: "He feeds on ashes; a deceived heart has turned him aside. And he cannot deliver himself, nor say, 'Is there not a lie in my right hand?'" (44:20). The idolater is so deceived that he is no longer able to detect the lie and is thus incapable of curing his own deceitful heart. That our deceitful heart is finally unfathomable even to ourselves also makes the task of its cure impossible for us. Perhaps the greatest self-deception of all is that we can cure our own deceiving heart. Only the entrance of God's truth into our heart can reveal and overpower our natural tendency to self-deception.

---

* For other references to the deceitful heart, see Pss. 12:1–2; 28:3; Prov. 12:20; 23:7; 26:24–25; Isa. 29:13; Jer. 14:14; 23:26; Hos. 10:2; Rom. 16:18; James 1:26.

The deceit in the heart is directly related to its pride. Despite the fact that the proud heart sets itself up as God, it is never able to fully convince itself that it is God. As a result it must continually "suppress the truth" that it is not God with self-deceiving lies (Rom. 1:18–23). By convincing itself that such self-serving lies are actually the truth—that is, by deceiving itself—the heart is now free to follow the agenda of itself—godhood. Thus Scripture warns against deceiving our own hearts by self-serving thoughts and the actions that flow from them (1 Cor. 3:18; James 1:26). Of course, the heart can also be deceived by others with similar lies that in various ways enforce our own deception of our supposed godhood.

The self-deceived heart, however, is never fully at rest. It cannot tune out the truth of reality—that we have not made ourselves, we cannot keep ourselves, we cannot control reality, we are not God. To aid itself in its self-deception, the deceived heart therefore seeks to deceive others who will then support its own pretensions. As Reinhold Niebuhr explained,

> If others will only accept what the self cannot quite accept, the self as deceiver is given an ally against the self as deceived. All efforts to impress our fellow men—our vanity, our display of power or of goodness—must, therefore be regarded as revelations of the fact that sin increases the insecurity of the self by veiling its weakness with veils which may be torn aside. The self is afraid of being discovered in its nakedness behind these veils and of being recognized as the author of the veiling deceptions.[17]

The deceitful heart thus blinds us to the truth of who we really are.* Studies in social psychology reveal the blindness of our proud deceitful hearts, showing that we all have a self-serving bent to consider ourselves better than we are. We take credit for good outcomes, viewing them from our effort and blame bad ones on other factors. We consider ourselves morally superior to others. Almost all of us "are above average."[18]

Most disastrously, our proud deceitful heart blinds us to the truth of its own condition so that if we do not turn our vices into virtues, we deceptively hide them from others and ourselves. The natural heart of man is allied with the enemy of our soul, the great deceiver of the garden of Eden.

Charles Schultz captured this reality humorously in a *Peanuts* comic strip

---

* For an interesting discussion of self-deceit, see Philip G. Monroe, "Exploring Clients' Personal Sin in the Therapeutic Context: Theological Perspectives on a Case Study of Self-Deceit," in *Care for the Soul: Exploring the Intersection of Psychology and Theology*, ed. Mark R. McMinn and Timothy R. Phillips (Downers Grove, IL: InterVarsity Press, 2001), 202–17.

in which Linus, looking forlorn, asks Lucy, "Why are you always so anxious to criticize me?" Lucy, looking very self-righteous, replies, "I just think I have a knack for seeing other people's faults." Linus becomes indignant. "What about your own faults?" he asks. Lucy replies, "I have a knack for overlooking them."

It is the deceptive propensity of the proud heart that helps us understand Jeremiah's description of the human heart as "incurably ill" (Jer. 17:9). For how can a heart that deceives itself concerning its own sickness ever cure itself?

Two Deadening Conditions

The tragedy of the proud deceived heart that wreaks so much devastation is compounded by two other deadening conditions that make it difficult to change. It is fat and hard.

Fat

Speaking of the arrogant, the psalmist said, "Their heart is covered with fat," or literally, "gross like fat" (119:70). In another instance, those who "speak proudly" are described as having "closed their unfeeling [lit. fat] *heart*" (Ps. 17:10). The people of Isaiah's day would not heed his exhortation because along with having spiritually "dull" ears and "dim" eyes, their hearts were "fat" (Isa. 6:10).

Fatness is figurative for the heart's insensibility, unreceptiveness, and consequent stubbornness. Noting that the Hebrew word for "fat" is derived from an original root that means "diaphragm" or "midriff," one Hebrew dictionary commented that the fat heart "is as unresponsive as the midriff-fat near it."[19] With no muscles and nerves, fat is impossible to move.

Scripture relates such fatness to the arrogance of prosperity. In his indictment of Israel, Moses declared, "[Israel] grew fat and kicked—you are grown fat, thick, and sleek—then he forsook God who made him, and scorned the Rock of his salvation" (Deut. 32:15).* The rich fat heart is also greedy and self-centered. Being unresponsive to God, such a heart is cruelly insensitive to the cares of people around it (cf. Ps. 17:10, "callous hearts" NIV; James 5:6).

Hard

More commonly than "fat," the unresponsive, obstinate heart is described in Scripture as a "hard heart," a "heart of stone," or a "stubborn heart."† Pharaoh's

---

* See also Neh. 9:25–26; Ps. 73:3–12; Jer. 5:28.

† The references to the hardness of heart and the various literal meanings of the original language used include: heart made strong or stout (Exod. 4:21; 7:13, 22; 8:15; 9:12, 33; 10:20, 27; 11:10; 14:4, 8, 17; Deut. 19:18; Josh. 11:10; Ps. 81:13; Jer. 3:17; 7:24; 9:14; 11:8; 13:10; 16:12;

adamant refusal to listen to God's word through Moses and the destructive consequences of this attitude in the plagues on Egypt provides a classic example of the hard heart (e.g., Exod. 7:13; 8:32). But the same hard-hearted stubbornness is found in God's people: "My people did not listen to My voice. . . . So I gave them over to the stubbornness of their heart" (Ps. 81:11–12). The psalmist echoing earlier voices warned, "Do not harden your heart, as at Meribah . . . When your fathers tested Me" (Ps. 95:8–9). Judgment came on the people of God because "they made their hearts like flint so that they could not hear the law and the words which the LORD of hosts sent by His Spirit" (Zech. 7:12). It was a hardness of heart in God's people, Jesus said, that caused Moses to permit divorce contrary to God's ideal in marriage (Matt. 19:8).

The hard heart arrogantly refuses to submit to God not only because it feels no need of him, but also because it stubbornly refuses to trust God that he is able to fulfill his gracious promises. Like the earlier people of Israel who in their fear of the Canaanites and lack of faith in the word and power of God refused to enter the Promised Land, some in Isaiah's day chose to look to foreign nations rather than God for deliverance from their enemies.

Rather than viewing this as the result of a weak frail faith, Isaiah sees it as the expression of a "stoutheart," or literally, "strong of heart"—an expression of the same arrogant obstinacy as hardness. Commenting on Isaiah's words, John Oswalt insightfully says, "Hard-heartedness . . . may be just as much . . . the response of those who recognize their need but cannot believe that God can meet it." They "presume to define what God can and cannot do."[20]

The various examples of the hardness of the human heart in Scripture demonstrate that there are degrees of stubborn resistance toward God and others. Pharaoh represents many unbelievers whom the apostle describes as "separated from the life of God because of the ignorance that is in them due to the hardening of their hearts" (Eph. 4:18; cf. Rom. 2:5).

But as we have seen, God's people can also have hearts that are stubbornly resistant to God's voice. Jesus' own disciples at times failed to comprehend his teaching or believe it because "their heart was hardened" (Mark 6:52; 16:14), or they were "slow of heart" (Luke 24:25). None of us is immune from this stony condition of the natural heart to resist God's transforming grace.

Hardness of heart is not always apparent as it was in the case of Pharaoh who was forced by God's power either into a humble submission or a steely

---

18:12; 23:17); heart made hard (Exod. 7:3; Ps. 95:8; Ezek. 3:7; Matt. 10:8; 19:8; Mark 3:5; 10:5; 16:14; Rom. 2:5); heart as stone (Ezek. 11:19; 36:26); heart as flint (Zech. 7:12).

The Petrification of Our Heart

In the process of petrification of wood—conversion of wood to stone—the organic material of the wood is replaced by inorganic minerals, the stuff of rocks. The fallen tree is buried in a wet sediment laden with stonelike minerals. As the tissues of the rotting tree break down, the mineral laden water seeps into the wood depositing the minerals which fill up the place of the original materials. Through this slow process the nonliving stony materials gradually replace the once-living organic materials of the tree leaving a stone mold in place of the original living form.

In the same way, we can and almost unconsciously harden our hearts by drifting through life without attention to the choices we are making every day—whether we are listening to God's voice or simply doing what we naturally desire. We can let the vitality of our spiritual life begin to decay and allow the nonliving materials of our environment to seep into our heart and very slowly replace the tissues of the soft, pliable new heart with the hard, lifeless—death-dealing—material of the world around us. The antidote to hardening is an awesome reverence for God and a heart that is open to his Word:

"Blessed is the one who always trembles before God, but whoever hardens their heart falls into trouble." (Prov. 28:14 NIV)

"Today if you hear His voice, do not harden your hearts." (Heb. 3:15)

resistance. Most of us rarely feel pressed in our relation to God to the kind of radical choice described by Solzhenitsyn that faced the prisoners in the Soviet Gulags—whether to save oneself *at any price* by selling out as a servile stool pigeon betraying fellow prisoners or refuse this path and risk the consequences. In the words of Solzhenitsyn this was "the great fork of camp life" where two roads diverge. "If you go to the right—you lose your life, and if your go to the left—you lose your conscience."[21]

Though not faced with such a stark choice that demands full exposure of the condition of our heart, we all continually come to forks in the path of life where we choose either to have open and receptive hearts to God's voice or closed resistant hearts that put up excuses and rationalizations to protect us from the humbling truth of who we really are.

The tragedy of the stony heart is that it not only resists God's desire to come in with life-giving grace, but it also encases the person within himself to live in a loveless tomb, unable to enjoy relationship with others.

This natural hardness of the proud human heart will only be cured when God's promise of a new heart is fully realized: "I will give you a new heart . . . and I will remove the heart of stone from your flesh and give you a heart of flesh" (Ezek. 36:26; cf. 11:19)—a heart that is living and sensitive, no longer dead and hard.

To summarize, the full comprehension of the condition of the natural human heart is beyond us as humans. It is evil, perverse, proud, deceitful, fat (insensitive), and hard. Other negative traits of the heart could be added, such as "adulterous" (Ezek. 6:9), "foolish" (Rom. 1:21), and "uncircumcised," that is, unconsecrated (Lev. 26:41; Acts 7:51). God alone knows the full depth of the mystery of evil in the natural heart. But we understand enough to know that the sinful heart is truly a "labyrinthine mass of lies and twisted motives."*

If we are honest with our own heart, we see all of these characteristics to one degree or another. We may not want to say it the same way, but we cannot deny the truth expressed by Chrysostom, the great fourth-century church father: "If indeed any one should tear open each man's conscience, many worms and much corruption would he find, and an ill savor beyond utterance; unreasonable and wicked lusts, I mean, which are more unclean than worms."[22]

The well-known former pastor of London's famous Westminster Chapel, D. Martyn Lloyd-Jones, confessed,

> Others see only that which is good in me; they see me only at my best. I shudder when I realize how unworthy I am and how ignorant they are of the dark and hidden recesses of my soul where all that is devilish and hideous reigns supreme, at times breaking through onto the surface and causing a turmoil that God and I alone know of.[23]

These traits of the natural heart that flow out in the issues of life provide the real explanation for the human condition in the world about us. Albert Einstein, the German-born Jewish theoretical physicist, lived through two world wars and therefore knew something of evil in the world. Fearful that the destructive force of the atomic bomb, which had recently been developed and used on Japan, could destroy all humanity, Einstein saw the real issue declaring, "Science has brought forth this danger, but the real problem is in the minds and hearts of men." At the same time he recognized that "it is easier to denature plutonium than it is to denature the evil spirit of man."[24]

Clearly the greatest need of humanity is a change of heart. This is all the more evident when we compare the picture of the heart that God commends.

---

* This is the description that psychiatrist M. Scott Peck applies to those particularly "evil" individuals with whom he struggled to help (M. Scott Peck, *People of the Lie: The Hope for Healing Human Evil* [New York: Simon & Shuster, 1983], 64). But Scripture teaches that to one degree or another, this same description is applicable to every heart. Also, some are better at hiding the display of these characteristics from outward behavior.

The Heart That God Desires

In total contrast to the hurtful ways of the natural heart, God sets before us the characteristics of the heart that he desires for us—qualities that yield an abundance of life. As we will see, many of these are found in the heart of David whom God described as "a man after My own heart" (1 Sam. 13:14; Acts 13:22). God's desire is that our heart in its deepest thought, affection, and will resemble his own.

A Heart of Integrity

In opposition to the evil perverse natural heart, David is frequently described as living and acting in "integrity of heart." He shepherded the people of Israel "according to the integrity of his heart" (Ps. 78:72; cf. 1 Kings 9:4). He testified that he walked within his house "in the integrity of my heart" (Ps. 101:2; cf. 1 Chron. 29:17). Integrity of heart was true of other believers as well (e.g., Ps. 119:80; Eph. 6:5).

The Hebrew word translated "integrity" means "completeness" or "perfection." The idea is not sinless perfection, but rather "sincerity of heart and motive, singleness of purpose, genuineness, truthfulness, uprightness."[25] In fact, it is those who profess this characteristic or are described by it in Scripture who are the most keenly aware of their own personal sin (e.g., David, Ps. 51:5; Job, 14:16–17). In short, integrity of heart marks the person who walks with pure motives, in good faith without guile and duplicity. Despite failures of sin, he is single-heartedly devoted to his Lord.

A Whole Heart

Closely related to a heart of integrity is the "complete" or "whole" heart. Variously translated as a heart "wholly devoted" (1 Kings 11:4; 15:3), "wholeheartedly" (2 Chron. 19:9), and even "blameless" (2 Chron. 15:17), the concept is derived from the Hebrew word for "peace" that we saw in chapter 1. Its root meaning signifies "completion and fulfillment—of entering into a state of wholeness and unity, a restored relationship."[26] The idea is of a heart that is sound, undivided with harmonious wholeness.

The call for an undivided, whole heart is a recurring theme of Scripture. Since God is *one*, his greatest command is to love him with "all" of our heart (Deut. 6:5; cf. 10:12; 11:13; 13:3; 30:2). He promises to let himself be found if one seeks him with "all" of his heart (Deut. 4:29; Ps. 119:2). Six times the psalmist in Psalm 119 writes of relating to God and his Word with "all" of his heart.

Nevertheless the godly person always recognized the need for greater wholeness of heart as is evident in David's prayer, "Unite my heart to fear Your name" (Ps. 86:11). David knew that the thoughts, affections, and desires of his heart were not yet fully brought together in the wholeness of God's *shalom*, his peace. He also recognized that the heart is unified only by a proper recognition of God. "His concern," as Derek Kidner says, "is not with unifying his personality for its own sake; the lines meet at a point beyond himself, the fear of the Lord."[27]

Such a completely unified harmonious heart would only come with the promised new heart when God would give his people "one heart and one way, that they may fear Me always"—a heart unified in awe and reverence toward God that would result in a unified way of life (Jer. 32:39; cf. Ezek. 11:19; Deut. 5:39).

A Pure Heart

The undivided heart is further characterized as a "clean" or "pure" heart, one that is unadulterated with moral impurity. Thus David also requests God to "create in me a clean heart" (Ps. 51:10). Only the person with "clean hands and a pure heart" can ascend the hill of the LORD and stand in his holy place and enjoy his blessing (Ps. 24:3–4). As the psalmist testified, "Surely God is good to Israel, to those who are pure in heart" (Ps. 73:1).

Similarly, Jesus said, "Blessed are the pure in heart, for they shall see God" (Matt. 5:8)—"now through the eyes of faith and finally in the dazzling brilliance of the beatific vision in whose light no deceit can exist."[28] The more our heart is assimilated to God's own heart in purity, the more we are able to see God in all of his characteristics and works and be conscious of his presence in our lives. And the more we see him, the more we are assimilated to his likeness (1 John 3:2).

An Upright Heart

In direct antithesis to the perversely twisted natural heart, God calls for an "upright" heart. Again, David is described as walking with God "in uprightness of heart" (1 Kings 3:6). God saves "the upright in heart" (Ps. 7:10) and extends his righteousness to them (Ps. 36:10). The Hebrew word literally means to be straight or level and describes a person's conduct as straightforward, on the level, right, honest, and upright.[29]

Instead of being crooked and twisted, David's heart was on the level and straightforward turning neither to the right nor to the left. As a result he walked on the straight and level path of God's way, a way not only of salvation, but of joy and thanksgiving as David exclaimed, "Let all the upright in heart exult!" (Ps. 64:10 ESV). "Shout for joy all you who are upright in heart" (Ps. 32:11; cf. Ps. 97:11: "Light is sown like seed for the righteous and gladness for the upright in heart.)"*

This last statement of David from one of his great psalms of confession (Ps. 51) again reveals the truth that the heart God desires for us is not necessarily sinless, although that is the final goal. David is described as having an upright heart because his heart was so bent toward the Lord and his ways that it kept him from holding on to his sin, keeping it covered in his heart. For the same covering that hid his sin would also block out the light of God's life for which an upright heart longs. Thus the upright heart as with David walks openly with God, acknowledging sin and rejoicing in cleansing and forgiveness.

A Steadfast Heart

We experience the fullness of life that flows from a heart with the qualities that God desires only to the extent that these qualities are constant and unwavering. Thus God also commends the heart that is "faithful" and "steadfast." Of Abraham, who is known in Scripture as the "friend" of God, we are told that God found "his heart faithful" to him (Neh. 9:8 NIV). In contrast, the "stubborn and rebellious generation" of Israel was one "whose heart was not steadfast" (Ps. 78:8 ESV).

The person with a steadfast heart trusts in God and is consequently upheld without fear. As the psalmist explained, he "will not fear evil tidings; his heart is steadfast, trusting in the LORD. His heart is upheld, he will not fear" (Ps. 112:7–8). The steadfast heart is also a joyful heart: "My heart is steadfast, O God, my heart is steadfast; I will sing, yes, I will sing praises!" (Ps. 57:7).

A Heart of Truthfulness

In place of the deceitfulness of the natural heart, God calls for a heart of truth. He desires "truth in the innermost being" (Ps. 51:6) or as Peterson's paraphrase pointedly says, "What you're after is truth from the inside out" (MSG). Life in the presence of God and the enjoyment of his fellowship belong to the one "who walks with integrity, and works righteousness, and speaks truth in his heart" (Ps. 15:1–2). God desires people who speak truth and live without the hypocrisy of pretending to be something on the outside that they are not in their heart. Such come only from hearts of truth.

---

* On the upright heart, see also Deut. 9:5; 1 Chron. 19:17; 2 Chron. 29:34; Job 33:3; Pss. 94:15; 125:4.

We are often told that it is important for us in life to listen to our heart. In doing so, however, it is vital to remember that the human heart is not the source of truth. If our heart is to know truth, it must receive it from outside of itself, from its Creator who is ultimate Truth. Thus after stating God's desire for us to have truth in our innermost being, David added, "In the hidden part You will make me know wisdom" (Ps. 51:6; cf. Ps. 40:8; Prov. 23:12).

We only gain a truthful heart by opening our heart to God's voice—by having a "hearing heart." When Scripture tells us that Solomon asked God for "an understanding heart," the Hebrews text literally says that he prayed for a "hearing heart"—a heart that would be constantly listening for God's voice of truth (1 Kings 3:9). God answered Solomon's prayer by giving him "wisdom and very great discernment and breath of mind [lit. breath of heart]" (1 Kings 4:29). What Solomon received was a large spacious heart filled with the truth of God's wisdom and discernment.*

Jesus himself spoke words of truth because he had a "hearing heart." "My teaching is not Mine," he said, "but His who sent Me" (John 7:16; cf. John 14:10; 17:8). The source of Jesus' ability to speak God's words of grace to the weary is revealed in Isaiah's prophecy of the Servant of the LORD—a prophecy of the coming Christ. There the Servant declares, "The Lord GOD has given me the tongue of those who are taught, that I may know how to sustain with a word him who is weary. *Morning by morning he awakens: he awakens my ear to hear as those who are taught*" (Isa. 50:4 ESV).

A few years ago a newspaper columnist suggested that "America has become a nation of blabbermouths." We are talking more and listening less. She cited a communications expert, who explained that "people think listening is boring; it's more fun to talk . . . . Talking is seen as active and dominant, listening is passive and deferential."[30] What a picture of the self-centered, prideful heart of man. There is a place to talk, but God calls first for a listening heart even in our communication with other people—"He who gives an answer before he hears, it is folly and shame to him (Prov. 18:13; cf. James 1:19), but especially in our relationship with him.

A Humble Broken Heart

The open receptive heart leads us directly to what is probably God's highest priority for our hearts. In order to have a heart formed after God's own heart, we must begin with a heart like that of Jesus who said, "Come to Me . . . and

---

* For the heart of wisdom, see also Ps. 90:12; Prov. 23:15; Eccl. 8:5.

learn from Me, for *I am gentle and humble in heart*, and you will find rest for your souls" (Matt. 11:28–29).

Humble is one of the Bible's great words that express our proper relationship with God. The basic sense of the Greek term for "humble" (*tapeinos*) is simply "low."[31] Jesus' submissiveness to his Father even to the point of death epitomizes the humble heart—a heart completely devoted and dependent on God.

To turn from the exalted arrogant position of the proud heart to the humble place is for the heart to return to its home. Far from a place of servile dependence, the humble heart is fully content with its place in the incomprehensible grandeur of life, attuned with God's own heart. J. R. R. Tolkien pictures such humbleness in his mythical story of God's original plan with his angels. Picking up the story immediately after God had revealed a glorious theme of music to his amazed angels, Tolkien writes,

> Then Ilúvatar [God] said to them [the Ainur, angels]: "Of the theme that I have declared to you, I will now that ye make in harmony together a Great Music. And since I have kindled you with the Flame Imperishable, ye shall show forth your power in adorning this theme, each with his own thoughts and devices, if he will. But I will sit and hearken, and be glad that through you great beauty has been wakened into song."

> Then the voices of the Ainur, like unto harps and lutes, and pipes and trumpets, and viols and organ, and like unto countless choirs singing with words, began to fashion that theme of Ilúvatar to a great music; and a sound arose of endless interchanging melodies woven in harmony that passed beyond hearing into the depths and into the heights, and the places of the dwelling of Ilúvatar were filled to overflowing.[32]

After further elaborating the wonderful music that would finally be made with the Children of Ilúvatar (humans), especially in eternity, Tolkien describes the tragedy that ensued when—because of dissatisfaction with the glorious place assigned to him—it "came into the heart of [the greatest angel] Melkor to interweave matters of his own imagining that were not in accord with the theme of Ilúvatar."

> Straightway discord arose about him . . . . Then the discord of Melkor spread ever wider, and the melodies which had been heard before

foundered in a sea of turbulent sound. But Ilúvatar sat and hearkened until it seemed that about his throne there was a raging storm, as of dark waters that made war one upon another in an endless wrath that would not be assuaged.[33]

As this story reveals, the humble hearts that willingly and joyfully take their place under God oriented to his grand themes find, as Jesus promised, "rest for your souls," and an unimaginable fullness of real life.

But such a humble heart is so radically opposite to the proud stony natural heart, that only when that heart is shattered can it begin to be formed into a heart like that of Jesus. Therefore we find God pleading with sinful people, "Return to Me with all your heart, . . . and rend your heart and not your garments" (Joel 2:12–13).

As David realized in his penitence, outward religious piety and good deeds are acceptable to a holy God only from a broken heart: "You do not delight in [ritual] sacrifice, otherwise I would give it; . . . The sacrifices of God are a broken spirit, A broken and a contrite heart" (Ps. 51:17). Literally, the "contrite heart" is a "crushed" or "pulverized" heart—the same Hebrew term describing Christ as "crushed for our iniquities" in Isaiah 53:5.[*]

God is delighted when the callous hardness of sin in our heart has been broken leaving it soft and "tender" toward him (2 Kings 22:19). His greatest desire is to come into our heart—the very center of who we are—and dwell there. He longs to restore its wholeness and straighten out its bent ways. Above all he wants to be at home there (John 14:23; Eph. 3:17). The most important thing that we can do to grow in our Christian life is to let God come in (Rev. 3:20).

There is a beautiful statement in the last chapter of Isaiah (66:1–2) where God says, "Heaven is My throne and the earth is My footstool. Where then is a house you could build for Me? And where is a place that I may rest? For My hand made all these things."

Following the human tendency to think that one can have God's presence through something they do, the people in Isaiah's day counted on God being with them because of their temple and rituals. But God said, "My resting place is not a building, it is not even the vast heavens and earth which I have created." Rather, "to this one I will look, to him who is humble and contrite of spirit, and who trembles at My word" (Isa. 66:2). The person with a humble and broken

---

* As verse 19 in this psalm indicates, David is not denying the value of the ritual sacrifices of the Old Testament, but rather indicating their repulsion to God without the sacrifice of the real person.

heart who stands open to his word is the person whom God regards and loves and comes in to be at home and bring renewal (Isa. 57:15).

A Glad Heart

A humble and contrite heart is the way to God's final goal for our heart— gladness and joy springing from fullness of life. In the same passage from Isaiah, noted above, the prophet goes on to depict the final restoration of his people. After describing the peace and comfort that would be theirs, he added, "You will see this, and your heart will be glad" (Isa. 66:14).

The same promise is found in the previous chapter: "Behold, My servants will shout joyfully with a glad heart, but you [who rebel against Me] will cry out with a heavy heart [lit. pain of heart], and you will wail with a broken spirit" (65:14; cf. 30:29).

This text reveals the great truth concerning our heart: If we come to God with a broken and contrite spirit, we will enjoy gladness of heart. If on the other hand we refuse to seek God with a broken heart, it will finally be broken by God.

Strains of the final bliss of heart already belong to the humble heart in this life amid all of its troubles. The thought of the presence of the Lord brought joy to David's heart: "I have set the LORD continually before me: Because He is at my right hand, I will not be shaken. Therefore my heart is glad and my glory [soul, NRSV] rejoices" (Ps. 16:8–9; cf. 33:20–21). God's word has the same effect: "The precepts of the LORD are right, rejoicing the heart" (Ps. 19:8). God continually desires to give himself to us so that we might be glad with his joy at the core of our being—our heart—and thus in all of life that stems from it.

The Christian's Heart

We have seen God's picture of the natural heart prior to God coming into it and also the heart that God desires and will ultimately give to his people. But what about the heart of the Christian in this life that seems to have traits of both hearts?

When we receive Christ a radical change takes place. We become "new persons" and "a new creation" (Col. 3:10; 2 Cor. 5:17). God gives us a new heart. The Old Testament prophets frequently spoke of God's promise to change the heart of his people. He was going to circumcise their heart (Deut. 30:5–6), and give them a new heart (Ezek. 11:19; 36:26), one that would know and fear him (Jer. 24:7; 32:40). He would write his law or instruction on the heart (Jer. 31:33). In the New Testament Peter speaks of God cleansing the heart (Acts 15:19). All of this is to say that since the heart is the real person, the believer is a new person.

But we still find life a struggle, sometimes worse than before we became a Christian. We still seem to be dealing with that old, twisted, fat, prideful heart. So what has really changed?

To answer this question we need to understand perhaps the most crucial feature of the heart. It does not live from itself. As we saw earlier, like all created life it lives by what it takes in from outside of itself. The heart is a treasure house that receives and stores the objects of its longing. It is, as Paul Minear said, "the hidden source of all desires, hopes and treasures."[34]

Most significantly, what the heart desires and takes in becomes its master, stamping the heart with its character.[35] It is the heart's desire, therefore, that shapes the heart itself and consequently the person. The momentous importance of this reality is explained by philosopher Peter Kreeft. Referring to the heart as "our center, our prefunctional root," Kreeft says,

> At this center we decide the meaning of our lives, for our deepest desires constitute ourselves, decide our identity. We are not only what we are but also what we want. This is not true of our surface desires. Wanting an ice cream cone does not make us an ice cream cone. But at our center the want decides the wanter rather than the wanter deciding the want.[36]

This deep want or desire of our heart that determines us is our love. As Augustine noted, "A body by its weight tends to move towards it proper place. . . . My weight is my love. Wherever I am carried, my love is carrying me" (*Confessions*, 13.9.10).[37] The love of our heart thus moves and determines the heart and finally who we are as persons. This reality that we are determined by the love of our heart is the key to understanding the "new heart" of the believer.

The deepest desire of our heart has been radically made new—our deep love has been reoriented 180 degrees. Before we were Christians, our old self-centered, god-playing heart was not only separated from God but actually antagonistic to him. Now it desires him as a loving Father. In the words of the apostle Paul, "God has sent forth the Spirit of His Son into our hearts, crying, 'Abba! Father!'" (Gal. 4:6).

What this means in relation to the believer's new heart is well summarized by Robert Jewett: "The center of man is thus his heart; the heart's intentionality [or desire] is determined by the power which rules it. In the case of Christian man, the direction of the heart's intentionality is determined by Christ's Spirit."[38] It is probably not going too far to say, as has been suggested, that if we could see the very center of the Christian's heart, we would find it always at prayer.

But the remnants of the old disordered love of self remain. While it is no longer the dominant bent at the core of our hearts, this old self-love is nevertheless still present. And as we grow toward maturity and the final perfection of our new heart in the presence of our Savior, the influence of the old heart often causes us to resonate with the thought of essayist Edward Martin's poem, "My Name Is Legion."

> Within my earthly temple there's a crowd;
> There's one of us that's humble, one that's proud,
> There's one that's broken-hearted for his sins,
> There's one that unrepentant sits and grins;
> There's one that loves his neighbor as himself,
> And one that cares for naught but fame and pelf.
> From much corroding care I should be free
> If I could once determine which is me.[39]

Questions for Thought

1. As a Christian, have you been disappointed with the thoughts, instincts, or reactions that come out of your heart? Is it any different than before you became one? What are the characteristics of your natural heart that still manifest themselves in your life even now?

2. What characteristic of the natural heart has been considered the fundamental root of all sins—"The Great Sin"? Do you agree? What is it about this sin that makes it lead to all other sins?

3. Do you feel challenged or comforted that God has given you a new heart when you put your faith in Christ? In what ways can you see this new heart at work?

4. What is the characteristic of the heart God desires that is most opposite of the fundamental root sin—"The Great Sin"? Why might this be God's highest priority for our hearts?

5. How do you reconcile the conditions of your natural heart with the new heart that God desires for you? When you look back, before and after you became a Christian, which one dominates in your life? According to Scripture, the strongest propensity or desire of the Christian's new heart is a love toward God, a love still toward sin, or equal toward both?

■■ 4 ■■

Living with Heart

Daily Dynamics of Our Heart

> Guard your heart above all else, for it determines the course of your life.
>
> PROVERBS 4:23 NLT

> Out of the abundance of the heart the mouth speaks.
>
> MATTHEW 12:34 NKJV

> ... Meditation here
> May think down hours to moments. Here the heart
> May give a useful lesson to the head,
> And learning wiser grow without his books.
>
> WILLIAM COWPER

> The theology of the heart is the theology of love, the theology of the person and that of the Holy Spirit.
>
> PAUL L. PEETERS

If all good people were colored blue, and all bad people were colored orange, what color would you be?" In honesty, we must all answer with the little girl in the Sunday school class, "I'd be streaky."

As we have seen our "streaky" hearts—a mixture of good and evil—account for the turmoil and confusion that we still experience in life. But this does not fully explain heart living. Life is not merely a struggle; it is a perplexing struggle. We all resonate at times with Paul's words, "What I am doing, I do not understand; for I am not practicing what I would like to do" (Rom. 7:15). We don't understand what is going on inside of us—why we feel the way we do, why

Heart Science Catches Up with Scripture

The results of recent scientific research are beginning to reveal the truth of the biblical teaching of the heart as the focal point of the personal functions of thoughts, emotion, and volition, or the central organ of the soul—a view of the heart that was also common in classical and Oriental antiquity (e.g., Greek, Indian, and Persian). But by virtue of the later elevated status of *nous* (cognitive mind) in philosophy and physiology, the brain gradually gained significance.[*]

Research in neurophysiology and the new discipline of neurocardiology is now demonstrating that the heart is more than a blood pump controlled by a nervous system from the brain. It has its own nervous system that processes information independently which is communicated to the brain. In sum, "the heart not only pumps blood, but transmits complex patterns of neurological, hormonal, pressure and electromagnetic information to the brain and throughout the body. As a critical nodal point in many of the body's interacting systems, the heart is uniquely positioned as a powerful entry point into the communication network that connects body, mind, emotions and spirit."[1]

Perhaps the suggestion of Franz Delitzsch more than a century earlier is not far off from the findings of neurocardiological research: "The heart is related to the head, as the hidden root to the manifest and outwardly-turned top of the tree. The root contains in itself all that is developed out of it."[2]

---

[*] For a brief discussion of the history of the relation of heart and brain as well as the biblical data, see Franz Delitzsch, *A System of Biblical Psychology*, 2nd ed., trans. Robert Ernest Wallis (1899; repr., Grand Rapids: Baker, 1966), 292–313.

we do things that we wished we didn't, or why we even say things that we do not mean.

The Heart: The Place of Personal Activities

The heart, as the deep center of our person, is the seat of all of the activities that we commonly associate with personality—self-conscious thought, emotion, and will. These personality functions are also at times related to our soul or spirit.[*] But most often Scripture portrays them as functions of the heart. As one biblical scholar noted, "Virtually every immaterial function of man" is attributed in Scripture to the heart.[3]

Most importantly for understanding biblical life, these functions of personality all coalesce in the depth of the heart into an inseparable unity. True living from our heart is living with our mind, emotions, and will in what might be termed a triune unity of function.

---

[*] See the discussion of the relationship of heart, spirit, and soul in chapter 2.

INTELECTUAL ACTIVITIES—
Thought, Belief, Memory, etc.

 EMOTIONAL ACTIVITIES—
Love, Hate, Joy, Sorrow, Fear, Courage, etc.

 VOLITIONAL ACTIVITIES—
Choosing, Desiring, Purposing, etc.

Thinking from the Heart

In contrast to our common association of heart with emotion, in Scripture the heart is most frequently related to *intellectual activities.* Thought, memory, understanding, attention, wisdom and other similar cognitive activities all take place in the heart.

In his valuable work, *The Anthropology of the Old Testament,* Old Testament scholar Hans Walter Wolff titled his chapter on the heart, "Reasonable Man," declaring that "in by far the greatest number of cases, it is intellectual, rational functions that are ascribed to the heart—i.e., precisely what we ascribe to the head and, more exactly to the brain."[4] Some scriptural examples will help us see this intellectual function of the heart. In Deuteronomy, Moses declared to the people of Israel: "Yet to this day the LORD has not given you a heart to know, nor eyes to see, nor ears to hear" (Deut. 29:4). Even as eyes are for seeing and ears for hearing, the heart is for knowing (Prov. 23:12: "Apply your heart to instruction and your ears to words of knowledge," NIV). In the future day of Israel's salvation, God promises to give his people "a heart to know me" (Jer. 24:7).

Declaring to his would be friends that he is not inferior to them in understanding, Job literally says, "I have heart as well as you" (translated in the NASB, "I have intelligence as well as you," 12:3; cf. 8:10). The "man of understanding" is literally "the man of heart" (Job 34:10, 34). Thoughts are in the heart (Judg. 16:17; Pss. 14:1; 15:2).

Insanity is therefore a problem of the heart (Eccl. 9:3), and to lack reason is to have the "heart" of a beast (Dan. 5:21; cf. Ps. 73:21–22). The lack of "sense" or "judgment" is to be without "heart" (Prov. 6:32; Hos. 4:11).

The crucial business of the heart is stated in Proverbs 15:14: "The mind [lit. heart] of the intelligent seeks knowledge." Significantly the word for "heart" occurs most frequently in what is known as the Wisdom Literature (e.g., Job,

Proverbs, and Ecclesiastes). It is also prominent in the book of Deuteronomy where teaching and instruction is emphasized.* These portions of Scripture instruct us in the ways of God so that we can come to know and understand them with our hearts (e.g., Prov. 2:2; 14:33; 16:21, 23) and gain the invaluable goal of "a heart of wisdom" (Ps. 90:12).

The heart as the place of mental function also continues in the New Testament. It is with the "eyes of the heart" that we come to "know" the riches of our salvation (Eph. 1:18). We "perceive" or "understand" with the heart (John 12:40; Matt. 13:15) and it is the place of our thoughts (Matt. 9:45; Luke 2:35; Rom. 10:6; Heb. 4:12). God's Word judges the "thoughts and intentions of the heart" (Heb. 4:12).

The New Testament does use, in addition to heart, some Greek terms that specifically denote mind and the related concepts of thought and reason (e.g., *nous*). These are very limited, however, and used primarily by the apostle Paul in his ministry in the Hellenistic environment where these terms were well known.† The mind in Greek philosophy and religion was thought to be the rational capacity of the human, which was a separate superior part of the inner life.‡ The perspective of the New Testament writers, however, remained in harmony with the Old Testament understanding of the intellect as an aspect of the whole personal life.§

The New Testament writers' terms for "mind" and related intellectual concepts therefore do not carry the same meaning that they had in Greek philosophy and religion, but rather a meaning similar to intellectual use of "heart" in the Old Testament. They were used, as John Laidlaw says, "to represent the contents or

---

* "Heart" (*lev, levav*) occurs 99 times in Proverbs alone, 42 times in Ecclesiastes, and 51 times in Deuteronomy. Hans Walter Wolff, *The Anthropology of the Old Testament*, trans. Margaret Kohl (Philadelphia: Fortress, 1974), 47.

† According to G. Harder, the *nous* word group "does not have a central part to play in the NT as a whole." *Nous* ("mind, understanding") is found only 24 times with 21 of these in the writings of Paul; *noeō* ("perceive, apprehend, understand") and *katanoeō* ("consider, contemplate") appear 14 times each, and other related terms even less often. G. Harder, "Reason, Mind, Understanding," *NIDNTT*, 3:126.

‡ There was also a popular use of these Greek terms with a broad, less technical meaning that made it easier to use in line with the Old Testament concept of the intellect and, in fact, was used at times to translate the Old Testament "heart" (*lev*) in the Septuagint (which is the Greek translation of the Old Testament, commonly abbreviated LXX) when intellectual activity was intended.

§ "The NT use of [*kardia*] coincides with the OT understanding of the term, just as much as it differs from the Gk. The meaning of heart as the inner life, the centre of the personality and as the place in which God reveals himself to men is even more clearly expressed in the NT than in the OT." T. Sorg, "Heart," *NIDNTT*, 2:182.

The Hebraic "Heart" of the New Testament

That the "heart" was still the important faculty of thinking in the New Testament and therefore "mind" represented the thinking aspect of the heart is evident when people are said to "understand" (*noeō* related to *nous*, mind) with their heart (John 12:40). They "think" in "their heart" (Matt. 9:4). The Word of God judges the "thoughts and intentions of the heart" (Heb. 4:12). "Futility of . . . mind" involves a "darkened . . . understanding [*dianoia*]" (Eph. 4:17–18), but also a "darkened" heart (Rom. 1:21). God's laws are put "upon their heart," and also written "on their mind" (Heb. 10:16).

This New Testament relationship of the intellectual terminology with the heart is well summed up in Robert Jewett's comment on Paul's reference to the peace of God "guarding your hearts and your minds in Christ Jesus" (Phil. 4:7). "Retaining the assumption of a unified personal center in the heart, Paul assumes that the thoughts flow from the heart and conceives of the mind as a constellation of thoughts and knowledge."[5] Thus, despite the New Testament's additional terms for intellectual activity, it is clear that they represent activities of the heart even as in the Old Testament.

products of the inner life, what the Old Testament calls the 'imagination of the thoughts of the heart.'"[6] The mind was simply the thinking aspect of the heart.

In sum, Scripture attributes all mental activities—including belief, meditation, memory, and concern or worry—to the heart.[*]

Choosing and Purposing from the Heart

The heart is also the seat of volition or activities of the will—our desiring, purposing, choosing, and so on. David rejoiced because God had given him the desire of his heart (Ps. 21:1–2). The apostle Paul's longing is his "heart's desire" (Rom. 10:1). Frequently God's people asked him to change the bent of their desire—"incline our hearts" (e.g., Ps. 119:36). Our choices are made in our heart. Scripture tells us that God tested his people "to know what was in your heart, whether you would [choose to] keep His commandments or not" (Deut. 8:2).

Resolve or purpose is also a matter of the heart. Barnabas encouraged the believers in the church at Antioch to remain true to the Lord with "resolute heart" (Acts 14:23, lit. "with purpose of heart"). Ananias and Sapphira "conceived" their deceitful plan in their hearts (Acts 5:4). Finally, the intentions and the drives of our life are in our heart. At the judgment, God will expose the "motives of men's hearts" (1 Cor. 4:5). These are only a few examples of the

---

* See the following Scripture references: for the heart's function of belief (e.g., Mark 11:23; Rom. 10:10; Heb. 3:12); for thought and consideration (e.g., Judg. 16:17; Pss. 14:1; 15:2; Dan. 2:30; Luke 12:45; Rom. 10:6); for concern or worry (e.g., 1 Sam. 9:20; Luke 21:14); for meditation (e.g., Pss. 19:14; 49:3); for memorizing (e.g., Deut. 11:18; Ps. 119:11; Prov. 6:21; Luke 2:51).

biblical teaching that all purposes and plans, all desires and cravings, all motives and intentions, and all resolutions take place in our heart.*

Emotions in the Heart

Finally, our emotions dwell in the heart. Love and hate, joy and sorrow, courage and fear, and all other emotions are in the heart.† We are commanded, for example, to love God with all our heart (Deut. 6:5), to shout joyfully to him with a "glad heart" (Isa. 65:14), and to keep our heart from being "troubled" or "afraid" by believing in Christ (John 14:1). The hearts of the disciples "burned" with strong emotion as their Lord, yet unrecognized, was explaining the Scriptures on the road to Emmaus (Luke 24:32).

Our emotions are not only experiences of the inner spiritual person of the heart, like a mental thought. They are also felt physically, especially in the physical heart.‡ The Old Testament in particular expresses emotions in vivid movements of the heart. If one loses courage, his heart quivers like leaves in the wind (Isa. 7:2); it is faint (Isa. 7:4; Deut. 20:8); it melts like wax (Ps. 22:14); or it turns to water (Josh. 7:5). In fear one's heart goes out (Gen. 42:28), leaves him (Ps. 40:12), or drops down (1 Sam. 17:32). On the other hand, courage is the strengthening of the heart (Ps. 27:14). Lack of love and responsiveness in both Testaments is a hard heart.

This relationship between the emotions and the physical is the reason why Scripture teaches—and modern medicine concurs—that our physical health is vitally affected by our emotional states. Proverbs 14:30 states, "A heart at peace gives life to the body, but envy rots the bones" (NIV). The power of positive emotions on the body is seen in Nehemiah's encouraging words to a grieving people: "The joy of the LORD is your strength" (8:12).

On the basis of his research and clinical experience related to the effect of the mind on the body, Bernie Siegel, a retired pediatric surgeon and clinical

---

* See these further references concerning the hearts desires or lusts (Ps. 39:3; Josh. 24:23; 1 Sam. 14:7; 2 Sam. 7:3; 1 Kings 8:58; Matt. 5:28; Rom. 1:24); purposes, resolves, plans, etc. (Gen. 6:5; Exod. 35:5; 1 Chron. 29:18; Prov. 10:21; 20:5; Isa. 10:7; Isa. 63:4; Dan. 1:8; Zech. 7:10; Luke 21:14; John 13:2; Acts 8:22; 2 Cor. 9:7; Heb. 4:12; Rev. 17:17).

† Further examples of various emotions in the heart include: love or hate (Deut. 19:6, lit. "his heart is hot"; Lev. 19:17; 2 Sam. 6:16; Rom. 5:5; 1 Peter 1:22); joy (Deut. 28:47; Prov. 15:15; John 16:22; Acts 2:46; 14:17); sorrow (Pss. 13:2; 34:18; 109:22; Prov. 25:20; John 16:6; Acts 2:37; Rom. 9:2; 2 Cor. 2:4); peace (Prov. 15:30; Phil. 4:7); courage or lack of it (Deut. 20:8; 2 Sam. 7:17; Dan. 11:25); anxiety or trouble (Prov. 12:25; John 14:27); fear (Deut. 28:67).

‡ The kidneys are also occasionally used metaphorically as the seat of emotions from joy (Prov. 23:16) to painful agony including pangs of conscience (Job 16:13; Ps. 73:21; Prov. 7:23; Lam 3:13).

professor at Yale University, wrote that "the state of the mind changes the state of the body by working through the central nervous system, the endocrine system, and the immune system. Peace of mind sends the body a 'live' message, while depression, fear, and unresolved conflict give it a 'die' message."*

Relating specifically to the heart, modern science reveals that "hardness" of heart is more than a psychological description. Researchers studying the movement of the heart between resting and beating found that "depressed, anxious, and chronically angry people had more rigid hearts—less able to respond to the changing demands for blood and oxygen."[7]

Increasingly, modern medicine is recognizing that the health of our heart—and therefore of us—is not only related to what we eat, but most importantly, to what eats us, a truth that Scripture pointed out centuries ago.

In summary, our heart is the place of our knowing, willing, and feeling. It is the center of our personality. Most importantly, our heart is the place where God addresses us and from where we respond to him as a whole person. This explains why the heart's function of knowing stands first. For the heart, above all, is designed to seek wisdom and knowledge by hearing God's Word.

The Heart: Where Intellect, Emotion, and Volition Unite

My wife once called me "cerebral" and I don't think it was meant to be a compliment. To be truthful, I do at times think, analyze, and debate things unprofitably. But few people, if any, are perfectly balanced in terms of thought, feeling, and action. We can probably all think of people who are weighty in reason but light on emotion or action. In fact, it is commonly believed that our thinking is clearer and more objective when we don't allow our emotions to get involved.

We also know people—and most of us are likely included—who know more truth than they actually practice. Their mind seems detached from their will. Finally, there are people who live from their emotions without thinking.

To be sure, these descriptions often accurately depict an individual's tendencies. But in truth the activities of our thought, emotion, and will cannot ultimately be separated. *True heart living, according to Scripture, takes place when thinking, feeling, and willing come together in holistic unity.*

A consideration of some key biblical words that denote the activities of *thought,*

---

* Bernie S. Siegel, *Love, Medicine, and Miracles: Lessons Learned about Self-Healing from a Surgeon's Experience with Exceptional Patients* (New York: Harper & Row, 1986), 3. See also, Norman Cousins, *Head First: The Biology of Hope* (New York: Dutton, 1989), and an older popular work that integrates the psychosomatic dynamic with Scripture, S. I. McMillen, *None of These Diseases* (Westwood, NJ: Fleming H. Revell, 1963).

emotion, and *will* show that, although the word "heart" in Scripture may emphasize one of these functions more than the others, it never sharply distinguishes them. Instead, the particular function emphasized merges with the others in various combinations.

Thinking and Knowing

To know something can, in some instances in Scripture, mean nothing more than possessing objective information about what is known. But the most significant use of "know" refers to knowledge derived from a personal encounter with the object, so what is known is actually experienced by the knower.[*]

As Johannes Pedersen explained, it is a knowledge that engages the *whole person*.[†]

> For the Israelite, thinking was not the solving of abstract problems. He does not add link to link, nor does he set up major and minor premises from which conclusions are drawn. To him thinking is to grasp a totality. He directs his *heart* towards the principal matter, that which determines the totality, and receives it into his *heart*, the *heart* thus being immediately stirred and led in a certain direction.[8]

The fact that thinking *stirs* the *heart* and *leads* it in a certain direction shows clearly that such thinking is not just an intellectual affair; it also involves emotions and will.[‡]

An interesting example of knowledge involving the will or actual behavior is seen in Isaiah's rebuke of the people of Israel: "An ox knows its owner, and a donkey its master's manger, but Israel does not know, My people do not understand" (Isa. 1:3; cf. Hos. 4:1–2; Jer. 4:22). In the ancient New East, the ox and

---

[*] Otto A. Piper explains this Old Testament *knowing* which extends into and is continued in the New Testament, saying, "For the Hebrews, 'to know' does not simply mean to be aware of the existence or nature of a particular object. Knowledge implies also the awareness of the specific relationship in which the individual stands with that object, or of the significance the object has for him." Piper, "Knowledge," *IDB*, 3:43.

[†] Pedersen makes the ensuing comments in relation to the "soul." But in his understanding the Hebrew concept of the "soul" and "heart" are closely related. The soul is man in his totality, while the heart "is the totality of the soul as a character and operating power, particular stress being laid upon its capacity" (p. 104). Thus what is said of the soul applies directly to the heart. For clarity "heart" has been substituted for "soul" throughout the citation. These substitutions are noted by italics.

[‡] The personal experience involved in this knowledge is seen in Rudolph Bultmann's comment on the knowledge of God in the Old Testament: it is "not thought of in terms of the possession of information. It is possessed only in its exercise or actualization" "*ginōskō*," *TDNT*, 1:698.

donkey were not considered very intelligent. Nevertheless, the prophet says that these animals had better knowledge than God's people because they knew to whom they belonged and who it was that put food in their manger, and they responded accordingly. In comparison, God's people lacked knowledge—"not theoretical ignorance, but rather failure to practice the filial relationship in which they stand with God."[9]

Jeremiah's scathing denunciation of Judah's king Jehoiakim is another example of knowledge including action. Pointing to Jehoiakim's godly father, Josiah, Jeremiah says, "Did not your father eat and drink and do justice and righteousness? . . . He pled the cause of the afflicted and needy; . . . Is not that what it means to know Me?" (Jer. 22:15–16). Knowing God, according to the prophet, includes *doing* justice and righteousness—in other words, appropriate action. *Without action, one does not have knowledge.* It's significant that all of the Hebrew words most commonly used for thinking include the idea of the movement of the heart toward activity.[10]

Emotion is also included in this experiential knowing. Expressing his delight for the Word of God, the psalmist exclaimed: "O how I love Your Law! It is my meditation all the day" (Ps. 119: 97). Your words are "sweet to my taste! Yes, sweeter than honey to my mouth" (v. 103). The emotion entailed in these last words is captured in Peterson's paraphrase: "Your words are so choice, so tasty; I prefer them to the best home cooking" (MSG). From his meditation on these words and the emotion which it included, the psalmist added, "I get understanding" and "have more insight than all my teachers" (vv. 104, 99).

Taken all together this testimony of the psalmist makes it clear that his understanding or knowledge involved an encounter with the Scripture that was more than intellectual. He *knew* with his total person—his mind, emotion, and willing commitment. The same portrait of total personality comes into view when Scripture tells us that "Adam *knew* Eve his wife, and she conceived and bore Cain" (Gen. 4:1).

The recognition of this essential unity of thought, emotion, and will in knowledge is critical when we consider our spiritual transformation. It is this kind of knowing that Scripture is talking about when it speaks of our knowledge of God and his knowledge of us. When Jesus said that he knows his sheep (John 10:27), but doesn't know those who were counterfeit disciples (Matt. 7:21–22), he is obviously not referring simply to an intellectual or cognitive knowledge. For on that level he knows both groups. In both instances he is talking about a holistic kind of knowledge that involves an experiential relationship.

Our relationship with God is expressed by Paul as a mutual knowing: "But now that you have come to know God, or rather to be known by God" (Gal. 4:9; cf. Ps. 1:6). We know God and he knows us. In both instances it is an experiential knowledge that involves the whole person: thought, emotion, and action. It is knowing by the *person*, which means knowing from the heart where all functions of personality reside in union.[*]

This is why eternal life can be described as knowing God through his Son Jesus Christ (John 17:3). This meaning of the word "know" also explains our Lord's promise, "you will know the truth and the truth will make you free" (John 8:32). We often "know" the truth, but don't experience the freedom that God offers us. In reality we don't know the truth deep in our heart, where it is known not only intellectually, but also emotionally and behaviorally—where it will affect the experiential issues of our life.

Hearing

Scriptural hearing in its full sense also includes the whole person. There are instances where *hear* denotes simply an auditory-cognitive activity—one simply hears words that convey meaning. But the most significant meaning of hearing in Scripture, especially in our relationship with God, like knowing, embraces much more of our person than simply the mind.

When God says to his people, "Hear, O Israel!" he is obviously asking for more than careful listening in the sense of cognitive understanding. Like a parent telling his child, "You better listen to me," God is exhorting his people to a hearing or "listening" that includes *willful obedience*. The same idea is in his words to the disciples on the Mount of Transfiguration: "This is my beloved Son . . . listen to Him" (Matt. 17:5).[†] Failure to hear is rebellion (Deut. 1:43).

---

[*] On the concept of our knowing with all of our personal functions rather than intellect alone, see Andrew Tallon, *Head and Heart: Affection, Cognition, Volition as Triune Consciousness* (New York: Fordham University Press, 1997). In this work Tallon argues for our experience as constituted by three meanings: felt meanings, cognitive meanings, and willed meanings leading to a "triune consciousness." See also essays by James H. Olthuis, "Introduction: Love/Knowledge: Sojourning with Others, Meeting with Differences," and Hendrik Hart, "Conceptual Understanding and Knowing *Other*-wise: Reflections on Rationality and Spirituality in Philosophy," in *Knowing* Other-*Wise: Philosophy at the Threshold of Spirituality*, ed. James H. Olthuis, Perspectives in Continental Philosophy 4 (New York: Fordham University Press, 1997), 1–15, 19–53, respectively; Esther Lightcap Meek, *Loving to Know: Introducing Covenant Epistemology* (Eugene, OR: Cascade Books, 2011).

[†] The same use of "hear" or "listen" is seen in relation to Jesus himself as the Servant of the Lord in Isa. 50:4–5: "The Lord God . . . awakens my ear to listen [and obey] as a disciple. . . . And I was not disobedient."

Spirituality through "Hearing"

Gerhard Kittel's comment related to the word "hear" is helpful in our understanding not only of the term itself, but of the holistic involvement of our person in biblical faith: "This prevalence of hearing points to an essential feature of biblical religion. It is a religion of the Word, because it is a religion of action, of obedience to the Word. The prophet is the bearer of the Word of Yahweh which demands obedience and fulfillment. Man is not righteous as he seeks to apprehend or perceive God by way of thought and vision, but as he hears the command of God and studies to observe it. It is thus that he 'seeks the Lord' (Jer. 29:13)."[11]

Thus the caution of Jesus, "So take care how you listen" (Luke 8:18), is echoed throughout Scripture. The religion of the Scripture, as has been noted, is not so much one of *seeing* God, but of *hearing* his Word, which calls for obedience. "It is a religion of action"[12] demanding a response from the whole person.

One does not really hear something unless it is heard with the heart, where thought, emotion, and will are inseparably united.

Love

The concept of love provides the clearest example of the unity of a human being's activities. Contrary to our culture, which tends to associate love with feelings, biblical love entails all of the functions of the heart. "I have loved you with an everlasting love," God told his people, "therefore I have drawn you with loving kindness" (Jer. 31:3).

The nature of God's love—and all genuine biblical love—is set forth in the words of the apostle John: "This is love: not that we loved God, but that he loved us and sent his Son as an atoning sacrifice for our sins" (1 John 4:10 NIV). Love is exhibited in God's act of giving the gift of his Son for our salvation.

As his love for us entails thought, emotion, and action, so also does our love for him and others: "But whoever has the world's goods, and sees his brother in need and closes his heart against him, how does the love of God abide in him? Little children, let us not love with word or with tongue, but in deed and truth" (1 John 3:17–18; cf. Deut. 11:22; 30:20).

As persons created in the image of God who is love, we were created to love. Human living is in a very real sense summed up in the two great commandments—love of God and love of our neighbor (Matt. 22:36–40).

It is not our reason or emotion or volition that defines our personhood. Ultimately, it is our love, and love entails all three of these capacities in an inseparable unity—in the person of the heart.

The Levels of the Heart in Spiritual Formation

We noted in chapter 2 that there was a deep hidden dimension of the heart. It is important to explore this matter further noting the different levels of the heart and the effect that this has on our life. Perhaps more correctly, we should speak of gradations of depth in the heart, extending from its surface to its deepest core (generally known as the unconscious). Recognizing this feature helps us understand something of the unrest and discord in our life. It is also a valuable key to discovering the process of how the heart is transformed.

The Various Levels of the Heart

The existence of levels in our heart is apparent in Jesus' parable of the sower in which seed fell on different types of soil (Matt. 13:3–9; 18:23). Some of the seed fell on the well-trodden pathway and was easily snatched away by the birds. From this picture we may think that this seed never got to the person's heart at all. But Jesus says it was "sown in his heart" (v. 19), obviously at what might be considered a surface level. The story proceeds to the final "good" soil that produces fruit. This is the person "who hears the word and understands it"—an "understanding" described as an "understanding with [the] heart" (v. 23, cf. v. 15).

Between the first hard-packed soil of the surface and the final productive "good soil," some seed fell on the rocky places where there was not "much soil." Here the seed sprang up quickly, but soon withered away because "they had no depth of soil" (vv. 5–6).

In his picture of the seed going to different levels—surface, shallow, and deep good soil—Jesus illustrates the truth that God's Word penetrates the human heart to various levels, with only the latter "good soil" receiving the Word at the deepest level where it brings forth the fruit of new life.[*]

The Hidden Levels of the Heart

Not only does our heart have different levels, but Scripture tells us that we do not fully know the contents of the deepest subterranean levels of our heart. Declaring that the heart is deceitful and incurably ill, Jeremiah posed the question: "Who can know it?" His answer, "I the LORD search the heart," plainly

---

[*] Similar heart levels also seem to be involved when we find the promise to write his Word on the heart in the future new covenant (Jer. 31:33), and yet Moses could already speak of the Word as being "in your heart" during his time (Deut. 30:14). As we will see in our discussion of the transformation of the heart, the Word clearly reaches a new depth with the finished work of Christ and the new age of the Spirit.

tells us that as humans we cannot fully know our hearts; only God has that knowledge (Jer. 17:9–10).

Without specifically mentioning the "heart," the psalmist similarly acknowledged an unconscious realm when he wrote, "Who can discern his errors? Forgive my hidden faults" (Ps. 19:12). He also implied that he doesn't know the depth of his heart when he prayed, "Search me and know my heart" (Ps. 139:23–24; see also Ps. 26:2; Prov. 16:2; 21:2).

Finally, the apostle Paul referred to an unconscious depth in the human heart when he testified, "I am conscious of nothing against myself," but then quickly added, "yet I am not by this acquitted." His final adjudication, he said, must wait "until the Lord comes who will both bring to light the things hidden in the darkness and disclose the motives of men's hearts" (1 Cor. 4:4–5).

The recognition of the various levels in our heart, including the unconscious level is vital to an understanding of our actual experience. Simply stated, *the deeper something is in our heart, the more it influences our life.*

Our heart, as we have previously noted, has a natural tendency to draw in outside influences and powers and be shaped by them. How much the heart and the life that flows from it is impacted by the elements that it takes in depends on the depth to which those elements are absorbed. Pedersen helps us understand this dynamic.

> Every time the *heart* merges into a new entirety, new centres of action are formed in it; but they are created by temporary situations, only lie on the surface and quickly disappear. There are other entireties to which the *heart* belongs, and which live in it with quite a different depth and firmness, because they make the very nucleus of the *heart*. Thus there may be a difference between the momentary and the stable points of gravity in the *heart*. But none of the momentary centres of action can ever annul or counteract those which lie deeper.
>
> The deepest-lying contents of the *heart* are, it is true, always there, but they do not always make themselves equally felt.*

What Pedersen tells us is that our encounters with various outside influences—such as people, circumstances—affect our heart. Some of these inter-

---

* Pedersen, *Israel*, 1:166. Pedersen makes these comments in relation to the "soul," but as they also apply directly to the "heart," *heart* in italics has been substituted for "soul." See explanation in footnote † on page 77.

changes affect us only at a surface level and have a temporary effect. Others go so deep that they become a more integral part of the very core of our heart, and as a consequence, significantly characterize the experiences of all of life. As in the ocean, there are surface waves, but also deep currents such as the Gulf Stream in the Atlantic. The former surface undulations may vary greatly with the winds, but they have no effect on the deep currents. Likewise, some influences affect the heart only at a surface level and have no lasting effect. Others penetrate to the core of the heart and bring change to its fundamental character.

How something is absorbed into the depths of the heart to bring about its transformation is therefore crucial to our spiritual growth as a person.

The Problem of the Hidden Heart Level

The reality of a hidden depth in our heart is also the answer to a common problem: our lack of understanding of why we behave or feel the way we do. We have certain conscious thoughts and attitudes, but our experience doesn't seem to correlate with them.

The truth is that other thoughts and attitudes deep in our heart—of which we are not fully conscious—are actually driving our life.[*] As psychotherapist Michael Bernard explains, we have conscious rational thought, but also deep internal thought not immediately accessible to us. It is this latter form of thought that often activates our life and contributes to "emotional and behavioral disorders."[†]

We often feel like we know and believe something as Christians, but in reality it is only a surface belief that has never reached the depth of the heart to activate our life. We may believe, for example, that we truly trust God. We know that he is trustworthy. He knows everything. He is all-powerful. And, he is infinite love. The combination of these attributes surely makes him trustworthy in every situation. We can rely on him. Yet when negative circumstances arise, we experience anxiety and fear.

The question we must ask ourselves is: do we really trust God in our hearts? Do we know that he is great and loving in the depth of our heart, or is it simply good theological doctrine lying on the surface, in our head?

---

[*] This is the same reality as the distinction made by some psychotherapists between an internal private realm of thought that activates life and an external realm.

[†] Michael E. Bernard, "Private Thought in Rational Emotive Psychotherapy," *Cognitive Therapy and Research* 5, no. 2 (1981): 127–28, doi: 10.1007/BF01172521. Bernard's entire essay is helpful in understanding the structure and function of human thought and the process of its change in the most significant internal realm.

Emotions: The Revelation of the Hidden Heart

If the thought of our heart affects our life, but it is hidden, the question arises: how we can come to know what we *really think* in our heart? Is there a way that our unconscious thought reveals itself to us? The answer to this question lies in the emotional life. Our emotions are the direct way that we—including the real person of our heart—experience reality.

As we go through life we are always experiencing the world around us, but this experience may not immediately become an object of our thoughtful reflection. It is, however, experienced in the realm of our affective or emotion.[13] In other words, our experience of something it is not first with thought, but with feeling. A smile from someone makes us feel good before we think about it. Watching newscasts of negative events and thought can bring depression without cognitively recognizing the connection.

There is, as the German philosopher-theologian Friedrich Schleiermacher recognized, an "original 'symbiotic' solidarity of self and the world in feeling."[14] Our emotions are like sensors that are always evaluating the situations of our life with feelings of pleasure or displeasure, with resonance or dissonance.

Feelings Have Meaning

"Feelings are the sensors for the match or lack thereof between nature and circumstance. And by nature I mean both the nature that we inherited . . . and the nature we have acquired in individual development, through interactions with our social environment, mindfully and willfully as well as not. Feelings, along with the emotions they come from, are not a luxury. They serve as internal guides, and they help us communicate to others signals that can also guide them. And feelings are neither intangible nor elusive. Contrary to traditional scientific opinion, feelings are just as cognitive as other percepts."[15]

We are drawn toward what is sensed as desirable with positive feelings like love, joy, or gratitude, and repelled from the undesirable with negative feelings like hatred, anger, fear, or grief.

Although, as we have noted, we may consciously experience these feelings before we think about them, we must always remember that our life, including our feelings, flows out of the heart where, as we have seen, *thought* is primary. The emotions that we feel therefore always reflect what we really think about the circumstances of our life in the depth of our heart.*

---

* We are thinking here of emotions that we generally consider in our emotional experience and not those that we experience instinctually, like animals do, such as a natural fright when confronted with unexpected danger.

What Is Important to Us Touches Our Emotions

"Our emotions depend on the import things have for us and what import things have for us is dependent on our interpretations of ourselves and our situations. In other words, because our emotions are essentially constituted by our self-understanding, the evaluations, desires, and aspirations that make up that self-understanding will be woven into our emotional lives. . . . It follows from this that we will not be able to fully account for self-understanding without reference to emotions, or our emotions with references to self-understanding."[16]

This relationship of thought and emotion will be considered more fully in chapter 7. But it is helpful here to briefly note philosopher Robert Roberts's definition of an emotion as "a *construal* of one's circumstances . . . in a manner relevant to some . . . concern."[17] Martha Nussbaum similarly says, "Emotions . . . view the world from the point of view of my own scheme of goals and projects, the things to which I attach value in a conception of what it is for me to live well."[18]

Defining our "concerns" as those things that we really care about—the things that we really value—Roberts explains an emotion as the result of the way we construe a situation in light of our values and passions, or the way we think about things. I feel shame, for example, because I believe I have done something dishonorable, or because there is something about me that I don't want others to see. The feeling of shame thus involves my perspective of myself, my dignity and worth, and how others view me.

Roberts thoughtfully applies this relation of thought and emotion to our Christian experience:

> To experience peace with God is to see God as a reconciled enemy. To experience hope is to see one's own future in the eternity and righteousness of God's kingdom. To be Christianly grateful is to see various precious gifts, such as existence, sustenance, and redemption, as bestowed by God. Because emotions are construals, and construals always require some 'terms,' and the 'terms' of the Christian emotions are provided by the Christian story, there is a necessary connection between the Christian emotions and the Christian story. . . . Emotions are no less tied to concepts than arguments and beliefs are.[19]

Our unexplained emotional feelings are thus the result of the unconscious thought deep in our heart. There is a *reason* why we feel the way we do about things. We feel that way because our heart thinks the corresponding way. Our emotions reveal the real thought of our life, what we are concerned about, our true set of values. In short, it is not what one says he believes, but what one *feels* that really indicates what he believes.

Therefore, if we would change our emotional life and the behavior that results from it, we must change the thought of our heart.

Being Honest with Our Heart

It is difficult to cure a physical illness without a proper diagnosis. The possibility of cure is even worse when one refuses to acknowledge the very existence of the illness. Such a person simply muddles along through life with lackluster health or until the problem becomes so troublesome that he acknowledges it and does something about it. The truth that solutions or improvements are achieved more readily when problems are known applies equally to our personal and spiritual growth.

One of the greatest hindrances to our healing and growth is leaving the issues that trouble our life and stifle our transformation hidden and unknown in the depth of our heart, split off from our conscious thought. *So long as we think that we believe something, but the real thought in the depth of our heart is different, we will never experience personal transformation.*

Attending to Our Heart

An honest appraisal of our spiritual condition—and that means the condition of our heart—is absolutely necessary for spiritual health and growth. The nineteenth-century English expositor Charles Bridges rightly said, "*The heart* must be known in order to be effectually *kept* [i.e., guarded]. Nothing is more difficult, while nothing is more necessary. If we know not our hearts, we know nothing to any purpose."[20]

With more explanation, John Henry Newman declared:

> It is in proportion as we search our hearts and understand our own nature, that we understand what is meant by an Infinite Governor and Judge; in proportion as we comprehend the nature of disobedience and our actual sinfulness, that we feel what is the blessing of the removal of sin, redemption, pardon, sanctification, which otherwise are mere words. God speaks to us primarily in our hearts. Self-knowledge is the key to the precepts and doctrine of Scripture. The very utmost any outward notices of religion can do, is to startle us and make us turn inward

and search our hearts; and then, when we have experienced what it is to read ourselves, we shall profit by the doctrines of the Church and the Bible.[21]

In like manner this kind of self-examination was of utmost importance for spiritual vitality in the Puritan tradition. As a member of that tradition John Flavel, in his little classic work *Keeping the Heart*, pleads with his readers: "O study your hearts, watch your hearts, keep your hearts! . . . All that I beg for is this, that you would step aside oftener to talk with God and your own heart; . . . that you would keep a more true and faithful account of your thoughts and affections."[22]

Keeping our heart in this way means opening our heart to God, to expose our heart to the truth of God's Word and quietly listen in prayer for the voice of the Spirit as he uses the Word to probe and search the recesses of our heart to reveal what is there. Other believers might also be used of the Spirit to enable us to see what otherwise we might have difficulty seeing or resist seeing.

To be sure, we cannot fully know the contents of our heart in this life.

Guarding the Heart through Heart Examination

It may be questioned whether such introspective examination of our hearts is called for in light of the fact that we do find any explicit biblical command to do so. But surely, as Charles Bridges' word cited in the text suggests, the command to watch over our heart with all diligence entails concern with its contents. The many teachings, especially from Jesus, about our heart and its contents, as well as the commands related to our speech and actions that flow from our heart, all suggest that we must attend to the source of our activities in our heart if we are to change our life. His exhortation to "take the log out your own eye" before we attempt to help another with the speck in his eye (Matt. 7:1–5) also suggests that we examine our own activities and attitudes, all of which flow from our heart.

A number of Scriptures likewise reveal God's people concerned with their hearts. The psalmist prayed, "Examine me, O Lord, and try me; test my mind and my heart" (Ps. 26:2; cf. 17:3; 139:23). He is asking God to "prove the state of his mind and, if it be not as it appears to his consciousness, to make this clear to him."[23]

Finally, the "living and active" Word of God pierces to the depth of our being, judging "the thoughts and intentions of the heart" (Heb. 4:12). God by his Spirit will continually reveal the content of the heart that is open to his Word—not necessarily all at once as that would be overwhelming, but perfectly according to our need for growth.

> Knowledge and wisdom, far from being one,
> have oft times no connection. Knowledge dwells
> in heads replete with thoughts of other men;
> Wisdom in minds attentive to their own[24]

Mercifully, this is no doubt for our own benefit as a clear view of its sinful distortions would be overwhelming. Nevertheless, failure to attend to our spiritual heart leads to failure in personal life in the same way that blindness about what is going on in our physical heart can lead to heart problems and the diminishing of physical life. On this point Bernard Lonergan wisely explains:

> It is much better to take full cognizance of one's feelings, however deplorable they may be, than to brush them aside, overrule them, ignore them. To take cognizance of them makes it possible for one to know oneself, to uncover the inattention, obtuseness, silliness, irresponsibility that gave rise to the feeling one does not want, and to correct the aberrant attitude. On the other hand, not to take cognizance of them is to leave them in the twilight of what is conscious [i.e., in vague negative feelings] but not objectified [i.e., cognitively understood]. In the long run there results a conflict between the self as conscious and, on the other hand, the self as objectified. This alienation from oneself leads to the adoption of misguided remedies, and they in their turn to still further mistakes until, in desperation, the neurotic turns to the analyst or counselor.[25]

A strong word of caution is needed at this point. As important as the knowledge of our heart may be for transformation, like diagnosis in medicine, the knowledge of our heart is not in itself the cure. We may take great pains to fully understand the darkness in our heart. Yet unless we appropriate the cure, this effort is not only fruitless, but can easily lead to depression as we focus on the ugly sinful distortions still residing in our heart. God's desire is that the recognition of our needy condition will increasingly lead us to his gracious remedy in Christ, and that with gratefulness we might experience the joy of growing in newness of life.

The Dangers of Living Detached from Our Heart

Unfortunately, there is a natural tendency in all of us to avoid the things in our heart that are difficult to face. These can include the pain of grief and loss or of other traumatic experiences such as horrible accidents or the violence of battle experienced by many in war.

But even more directly related to the issue of spiritual growth, we tend to suppress the gnawing pangs of conscience and the voice God's Spirit through his Word when he reminds us that we are not living the way we know we should.

Plutarch on Self-Examination

The ancient Greek philosopher and biographer Plutarch, in his essay *Of Curiosity*, portrays in strong language the unwillingness of some to reflect on their own failures, preferring to use their moral sense in relation to others. What Plutarch says of "some" is in reality natural to all of us.

"To some sort of men their own life and actions would appear the most unpleasant spectacle in the world, and therefore they fly from the light of their conscience, and cannot bear the torture of one reflecting thought upon themselves; for when the soul, being once defiled with all manner of wickedness, is scared at its own hideous deformity, it endeavors to run from itself, and ranging here and there, it pampers its own malignity with malicious speculations on the ills of others"[26]

Our reluctance to deal with the real state of our heart is forcefully expressed by another Puritan preacher, Richard Sibbes:

> It were an easy thing to be a Christian, if religion stood only in a few outward works and duties, but to take the soul to task, and to deal roundly with our own hearts, and to let conscience have its full work, and to bring the soul unto God, this is not so easy a matter, because the soul out of self-love is loath to enter into itself, lest it should have other thoughts of itself than it would have.[27]

The person who refuses to live in openness to the heart, however, lives a life that is disconnected from his heart. As long as he or she remains that way, there is no hope for change.

This disconnectedness can occur in various ways, no doubt related to our individual personality and the particular nature of the problem. We can become estranged from our heart by a sort of "willfulness" in which we simply override the heart. Rather than dealing with the dysfunction in our heart, we simply exert our willpower in determination to stop our wrongful behavior and be "good."[28] In our attempt to attain and sustain a good outward behavior, we compulsively focus on a list of "dos and don'ts" much like the Pharisees in Jesus' time.

If our will is strong enough, we may produce a rather respectable behavior, even a semblance of piety. At this point, however, our will is no longer the expression of the whole person of the heart. It has become a sort of detached power that we assert to force an outward order of life without dealing with the underlying disorder in the heart.

The apostle Paul describes this sort of life as having "the appearance of wisdom in self-made religion and self-abasement . . . , but . . . of no value against fleshly indulgence" (Col. 2:23). One remains like the Pharisees whom Jesus described as whitewashed graves—the outside looks in good shape, but inside the heart is putrid.

Life in this state is a rigid, compulsive, legalistic existence—anything but life flowing naturally from the heart. It may gain respect from others and even pride to the performer, but it is incapable of producing genuine joy and peace within the heart. Moreover, when there is a disconnect between our conscious outward life and our heart through this sort of willfulness, we are cut off from the possibility of transformation. Following the thought of Martin Buber that nothing hides the face of God more than religion, Cornelius Plantinga warns, "When we are most religious, we may be most at risk of losing touch with God."[29]

There is also another way that we can distance ourselves from the truth of our heart and that is through an irresponsible *absence of will*. Rather than exerting our will to control our behavior as with the pharisaical attitude above, we deal with the truth of our heart by simply giving up the struggle.

Tired of trying to live up to one's own high standards or those imposed by others, and feeling overwhelmed with guilt, we can abdicate responsibility for personal change and simply float along with the crowd, viewing ourselves as victims of circumstances beyond our control.

This abandonment of responsibility may seem passive at times, but it can also take a more active form of rebellion against the standards of one's ideal. Scripture doesn't give us the inner thoughts of the prodigal son who left his father and elder brother to squander his estate in "loose living" (Luke 15:11–32), but his story suggests that this may have been what was going on with him. The ideal of life set before him by his loving father and his apparently pharisaically "obedient" elder brother placed him under constant pressure to conform. Finding this burden too onerous, he responds by leaving home and plunging into a life of unrestrained sensuality.

The experience of the nineteenth-century Irish playwright Oscar Wilde—one of the greatest celebrities of his day and known for his sexual deviancy—may not have been as consciously deliberate as the prodigal son, but his lament in a letter written from prison to his friend Lord Alfred Douglas, who led him down the path of perversion, illustrates the same absence of will.

> I must say that neither you nor your father, multiplied a thousand times over, could possibly have ruined a man like me: that I ruined myself: and nobody, great or small, can be ruined except by his own hand. . . .

I let myself be lured into long spells of senseless and sensual ease. . . .
I ceased to be lord over myself. I was no longer the Captain of my Soul,
and did not know it. I allowed pleasure to dominate me . . . . I ended in
horrible disgrace.[30]

Whether someone passively surrenders to the tide of the crowd (though it's
still an active willingness to do so) or, like the prodigal son and Wilde, actively
defies moral restraints, the will-less person lacks the determination to do the
right thing. Such people simply give themselves over to sin as instruments of
unrighteousness (Rom. 6:13). By not attempting to live in integrity with the
moral law of their heart, they cut themselves off from their heart in their own
way—even as strong, willful people do in their heart.

These two ways of cutting off oneself from his or her own heart are summed
up well in Timothy Keller's description of the two forms of prideful sin: "One
form is being very bad and breaking all the rules, and the other form is being
very good and keeping all the rules and becoming self-righteous."[31] In both
instances, rather than face the truth of their heart and humbly look to God's
forgiveness and transforming grace to change, the person pridefully chooses to
live his own way.

Living with an Open Heart before God

All of this dysfunction is in sharp contrast to the spiritual life offered to us
by Christ. Instead of living life detached from our heart, God calls us to live
completely open to the truth at the depth of our being. "You desire truth in the
innermost being" (Ps. 51:6). This requires living with openness to the truth of
our own condition as well as the truth of God's remedy for our heart's disorders.
In short, God desires that we live honestly with our heart.

Throughout the Bible, one of the greatest problems for God's people was that
of living dishonestly with their heart. This should cause us to recognize that
the same weakness is present in each of us. This is obviously encouraged by the
natural tendency to hide what is on the inside and try to appear—in the eyes of
others and ourselves—that we are better than we really are. But it all stems from
the remnants of the sinful, "god-playing" pride that remain in us. After all, a god
cannot have bad attitudes, do bad things, or for that matter, fail in anything that
he or she attempts. When that attitude predominates, life is about justifying
ourselves before others and in our own eyes (Luke 10:29; 16:15).

While the root of this split between the heart and the external life lies in each
of us, this disconnect can also be nurtured by others. Through well-intentioned

encouragement and instructions people can unknowingly push others toward forms of mature behavior that are in reality beyond the actual situation of their hearts, thus causing a discord between the outward appearance and the heart.

Adrian van Kaam addresses this problem as a counselor, but what he says is pertinent to everyone who desires to help another person in spiritual growth, especially Christian parents in relation to their children.

> It is infinitely better that my counselee does a good thing in an awkward and deficient way but in a free and personal fashion than to perform such behavior in splendid perfection which is merely external and the fruit of my suggestion and encouraging approval . . . .
>
> Many people who come for religious counseling have lived their religion in an inauthentic way. Having heard or read about religious perfection, they started to imitate the perfect religious attitudes in their external religious behavior. Soon there came a split between their real personal inner life and the proliferation of perfect manners, customs, and devotions, which they had assumed to the great delight of their excited educators. The latter, animated by the best intentions, did not realize that they were producing a number of neurotics instead of saints.[32]

All Christians are vulnerable to living dishonestly with their heart. Leaders are particularly susceptible to this, since they are viewed as models (and rightly so). The uneasy feeling of spiritual failure—the sensing of an inner dryness—is often compensated by a pretense of spiritual vitality. Nothing is more dangerous to true spirituality and growth.

Testifying to having encountered this problem frequently among church people in his psychiatric practice, Paul Tournier, says, "Every discord between form and substance, between what others see and the reality of the heart, is a denial of the gospel and can only be a source of psychological trouble. . . . Everything becomes simple once again when this essential harmony is rediscovered, even if the outer facade then looks much less imposing."[33]

Because all of life is lived from the heart, Christian living and growth requires living before God in honesty of heart. This means a heart that is totally open to the searchlight of his truth—including our sinful disorders. Without God's grace of forgiveness, this is hard to face. But his grace is there.

God already knows fully what is in our hearts, and he longs for us to uncover it honestly and receive his cleansing. Only an open heart can be cleansed. And only an open heart can receive the presence of God's gracious power to nourish it toward greater maturity and fullness of life.

Questions for Thought

1. What are the personal activities from the heart? Was this biblical truth surprising to you? Why?

2. What is God's design for the relationship of the personal activities of our heart? Is one of the heart activities more prominent in your life? Is one weak in your life? How do these express themselves in your daily life?

3. Jesus said that eternal life is to "know . . . the true God, and Jesus Christ" (John 17:3). Given the real meaning of "know" in Scripture, how well do you think that you "know" God? How does this relate to your experience of him?

4. Have you ever said or done something that you really didn't intend to do? What was the source of this action? Is it good to recognize this reality; and think about it? Why?

5. If God looks at the heart including its depth, is it helpful in our spiritual growth to know more about what is in the depth of the heart? How can we come to know more of what is in the unconscious depth of our heart? Would you like to know everything that is in your heart right now? Why or why not?

6. Do you feel that you are living an outward life that is to a certain extent detached from what is in the depth of your heart? Of the forms of this mentioned in the chapter, what form or forms does it take in your life?

Radical Surgery

Changing the Heart at Its Deepest Level

A characteristic of the heart as the center of man is its inherent openness to outside impulses.

ROBERT JEWETT

I will obey thee eagerly, as thou dost open up my life [lit. enlarge my heart].

PSALM 119:32 MOFFATT

In December 1967 *TIME* magazine issued an article titled "Surgery: The Ultimate Operation." It was the story of the first human heart transplant performed by Christiaan Barnard in Cape Town, South Africa, on Louis Washkansky, who was dying of clogged arteries after surviving two heart attacks. The heart-lung pump assisting Washkansky through the four-hour surgery was switched off after fifteen minutes as his transplanted heart began to work. After thirty-six hours he was eating, and after a week he was joking around in a radio interview. Unfortunately the regimen of immunosuppressant drugs and treatment that he was placed on in order to ensure that his body would not reject the transplanted heart weakened his immune system so much that he died of pneumonia eighteen days after this pioneering surgery.[1] Today, with better methods of preventing and treating rejection, heart transplants are a relatively simple operation for a cardiac surgeon.

As a physical heart with clogged arteries needs a new heart, so if we would be genuinely transformed and not just spruced up on the outside or as Jesus accused the Pharisees, whitewashed, we must have a real heart change. But can our hearts really change? Can they change even if they are like bad physical hearts with clogged arteries that are old and rigid? Is there any hope for real and lasting change if our hearts are clogged with the plaque of engrained twisted patterns of life from a dysfunctional upbringing or simply from years of living a chaotic life? We will see in Scripture that God has clearly promised us "a new heart." To say that we need spiritual "heart transplant" surgery is really no exaggeration. But can this heart surgery already begin in this life to bring us greater fullness of real life? The Bible says yes. Even as people are born again to new life out of a variety of circumstances—young or old, rich or poor, dysfunctional or respectful life—so all who have life can grow no matter how deep our engrained attitudes and actions.

In this chapter and the next we will explore the changeable nature of the heart and the agents involved in that change, especially the two prime agents— God and ourselves. The all-important question of how that change actually takes place will then be our focus in the subsequent four chapters.

The Character of the Heart Determined by Its Content

The ability of the heart to change rests on what we have already seen in previous chapters—our heart is like a storehouse in which we store treasures that determine its character. Things come into our heart and go out of it. They can also be stored permanently. To understand the reality that our heart can be transformed and we can grow in the life that is ours in Christ, it will be helpful to probe this dynamic of the heart.

As we have seen earlier, we live from outside of ourselves. As God's creation we are all dependent beings. We did not cause our existence, nor can we maintain it without taking in sustenance from beyond ourselves. We require food, water, and air for our physical life—all from outside of us. The same reality is true of our spiritual life. As we live physically from our physical environment, so we are also designed to live spiritually through interaction with the spiritual environment that transcends us.

Like the digestive and respiratory systems in our physical nature that receive and process nourishment for our body, we also have a spiritual organ for receiving nourishment for our spiritual life, namely, our heart. Also like our natural systems, which we can use to ingest good substances that enhance our life or bad substances that cause sickness and rob life, our spiritual "system" can take good things into our heart that enhance our spiritual life or bad things that harm it. In short, our heart is "the work-place for the personal appropriation and assimilation of every influence."[2]

But the heart is more than an empty bucket waiting for things to drop into it. It passionately seeks for things to draw into itself. Like our physical nature hungers and thirsts for that which can satisfy and sustain physical life, our heart cries out for things to satisfy our spiritual nature. The popular writer Max Lucado vividly illustrates this comparison in his book *Come Thirsty*.

> Your body, according to some estimates, is 80 percent fluid. That means a man my size lugs around 160 pounds of water. Apart from brains, bones, and a few organs, we're walking water balloons.
>
> We need to be. Stop drinking and see what happens. Coherent thoughts vanish, skin grows clammy, and vital organs wrinkle. Your eyes need fluid to cry; your mouth needs moisture to swallow; your glands need sweat to keep your body cool; your cells need blood to carry them; your joints need fluid to lubricate them. Your body needs water the same way a tire needs air.
>
> In fact, your Maker wired you with thirst—a "low-fluid indicator." Let your fluid level grow low, and watch the signals flare. Dry mouth. Thick tongue. Achy head. Weak knees. Deprive your body of necessary fluid, and your body will tell you.
>
> Deprive your soul of spiritual water, and your soul will tell you. Dehydrated hearts send desperate messages.[3]

On one occasion Jesus used our eyes as an illustration of the heart's function of drawing in nourishment for life. After declaring that our heart will be where our treasure is, he went on to say, "The eye is the lamp of the body; so then if your eye is clear, your whole body will be full of light. But if your eye is bad, your whole body will be full of darkness (Matt. 6:21–22). Jesus says, the eye acts like a lamp in that, like a window, it takes in light for the whole person. In Scripture, light is the realm of our natural life (Ps. 56:13) and more importantly a metaphor of spiritual life (Pss. 36:9; 37:6). The condition of the eye therefore determines the condition of one's life. The "clear" or healthy eye receiving full undistorted light enables the person to see reality and function accordingly in fullness of life. The "bad" eye with blurred or double vision takes in only dim distorted light, thus curtailing (or diminishing) life.

Just as the eye is designed to take in light for the life of the person, so the heart is designed to draw in the true light of God for spiritual life. Thus Paul says the "eyes of our [the believer's] heart" have been "enlightened" (Eph. 1:18). Previously we lived in spiritual darkness (Eph. 4:18)—we all had "bad" eyes. Now as believers the eyes of our heart have been opened to draw in the light of God's truth, which brings life.

Eyes: The Gateway to the Heart

Jesus' movement from the heart to the eyes (Matt. 6:21–22) reveals the close connection of the eye and heart in Scripture. Eyes (along with ears) were considered "the gateway to the heart."[4] Their gaze could stimulate desire and spur the person to sin (e.g., Gen. 3:6; 2 Sam. 11:2; Matt. 5:28). Thus God's people were enjoined to remember God's commands and not follow the lusts of their "own heart and . . . eyes" (Num. 15:39). Contrariwise, the eyes could fasten on the things of God and incline the heart toward him (e.g., Ps. 119:18; Prov. 4:21). The close association of the eyes to the heart is seen in that the eyes "both send information to the heart (cf. [Job] 31:1, 7) and reflect the heart's disposition."[5] Even as the heart is the real person, the eye functions as "a concentrated expression of the personality" displaying one's disposition toward God, human beings, and the surrounding world.[6]

This spiritual thirst or appetite of our heart is best characterized as the desire of love. Created in the image of God who is love (1 John 4:8, 16), we are designed by nature to love. We are truly alive only when we are fulfilling the two great commandments—loving God and loving our neighbor (Matt. 22:36–40). The heart's love, of course, can be set on other things that are contrary to life. But no matter what it loves, whether healthful or harmful, the heart is always in the process of drawing into itself the objects of its love or desires.

The heart also responds to the love object that it has drawn in—clinging to it and longing to be united with it. In a very real sense the heart as lover gives itself to its beloved with the result that *it is changed through this interaction with its object of love.* Thus by its nature to love, the heart finally becomes *dominated* by what it loves.

Jesus didn't say, "Where your heart is, there your treasure will be," as if our heart dominates and determines our treasure. Rather, what he said was, "Where your treasure is, there your heart will be also" (Matt. 6:21)—our heart is finally dominated by our treasure. It is led by what it loves. In a nutshell, what the heart loves, it takes into itself and treasures—with the result that the heart and all of its activity take on the character and shape of the stored treasure (Luke 6:45).*

Plainly stated, our heart has a built-in "propensity to give itself to a master."[7] Jesus said, "No one can serve two masters; for either he will hate the one and love the other, or he will be devoted to the one and despise the other" (Matt. 6:24). What is clear from this statement is that *the heart will always serve a master,* which explains the religious nature of all human beings. Every person knows in his heart that he is not self-sufficient. We all depend on—and therefore trust

---

* See also Matt. 6:19–21; 12:34–35; Luke 12:34.

Drawing Treasures into the Heart and Storing Treasures in Heaven

The heart's drawing into itself its objects of love is not contrary to the truth that we are "to store up . . . treasures in heaven" (Matt. 6:20). For as the next verse indicates, "Where your treasure is, there your heart will be also" (v. 21). When our hearts are filled with the thoughts, emotions, and will of our heavenly Father, they are filled with the reality of "heavenly treasures." Scripture pictures this heavenly treasure as not only an inheritance reserved in heaven to be fully experienced in the future (1 Peter 1:4)—not only as an investment in heaven—but also something that we already taste in our present life. In Christ we already enjoy "every spiritual blessing in the heavens" (Eph. 1:3 HCSB). "All the treasures of wisdom and knowledge" are in Christ (Col. 2:3). The treasure of the "Light of the knowledge of the glory of God" (i.e., the true life of salvation) is "in the face of Christ," (2 Cor. 4:6; cf. v. 7)—and we are in Christ and he is in us. As Christ is increasingly formed in us by the Spirit through the Word (Gal. 4:19), we enjoy more and more of the heavenly treasures. Thus our spiritual transformation is at the same time bringing heavenly treasures into our heart and storing up treasures in heaven.

in—something beyond ourselves whether it is a personal deity, a vague spiritual "force," or a materialistic "Mother Nature." As Hendrik Hart rightly said, "Spirituality . . . interweaves human responsibility with realities that overcome us. It has to do with living consciously self-aware and responsibly in the face of transhuman powers."[8]

The manner in which our heart is changed is much like the popular young children's science experiment—changing a flower's color with food dye. The cut flower is placed in water with food coloring and amazingly within about twenty-four hours the flower's petals become the color of the dyed water. Flowers live by a process called transpiration, drawing water and nutrients up into the stems and leaves.[9] Placed in the colored water the plant pulls up that water through the stem and into the petals and leaves. There the water changes into vapor and evaporates. The dye is left behind in the tiny veins of the petals giving the flower the new color of the dye.

So our heart lives by that which it draws in. And like the dye in the flower, things that are drawn in can become part of the heart and manifest their color in the everyday experiences of our life.

Changing the Contents of Our Heart

Although our heart receives things that become its master and shape its character, it is important to remember that we are in a very real sense the director of our heart and have some responsibility for its contents. It is therefore helpful for us to consider what the Scriptures say about the kind of things that the heart takes in and who puts them there, and also the reality that things can go out of the heart or be stored permanently.

The Contents of Our Heart

The things that can be in our heart are in a word, everything that we experience, by way of thinking, feeling, willing, and doing. Here are just a few biblical examples of things that shape the heart . . .

Thoughts and Desires

After seeing the vision of the four awesome beasts, Daniel declared, "My thoughts were greatly alarming me . . . but I kept the matter to myself [lit. in my heart]" (Dan. 7:28; cf. Luke 1:66). The silent skeptics of Jesus sat there "reasoning in their hearts" (Mark 2:6, 8). God says his people are those "in whose heart is My law" (Isa. 51:7).*

Plans and desires fill our heart. The writer of Proverbs said, "Many plans are in a man's heart" (Prov. 19:21). Jonathan's armor bearer encouraged him to attack the Philistine garrison telling him, "Do all that is in your heart; . . . I am with you according to your desire [lit. heart]" (1 Sam. 14:7).†

Emotions and Passions

Our heart also contains our emotions and passions. The psalmist asked, "How long shall I take counsel in my soul, *having* sorrow in my heart all the day?" (Ps. 13:2). The writer of Proverbs declared, "Anxiety in a man's heart weighs it down, but a good word makes it glad" (Prov. 12:25; cf. James 3:14).

People

Finally, people can be in our heart. This is particularly significant in view of the nature of the heart's desire as love and the centrality of loving God and others in our life. Desiring to express his love for the Corinthian believers, the apostle Paul told them that his heart was open wide to them, or as eighteenth-century New Testament scholar Johann Albrecht Bengel puts it, "Our heart has enough room to contain you"[10] (2 Cor. 6:11). Later Paul added, "You are in our hearts to die together and to live together" (2 Cor. 7:3; cf. Phil. 1:7). We can also do the opposite and shut people out of our heart (1 John 3:17).‡

---

* See also Pss. 37:31; 119:11; Rom. 10:8.
† See also Deut. 8:2; 1 Sam. 2:35; 2 Sam. 7:3; 1 Kings 8:17; 2 Chron. 1:11; 29:10; Prov. 20;5; Isa. 63:4.
‡ The term that John uses here is the Greek word for "inward parts" or "bowels" (*splagchnon*), a term used figuratively for compassion, which is often associated with the heart as well.

Humans, of course, cannot be in our heart like Christ or the Spirit who are God and therefore can actually be *personally* present everywhere (omnipresent). But people do come into our hearts by the impressions that they make on our thoughts, emotions, and behavior through our relationship with them.

It is these contents in our heart—our thoughts, our emotions, our desires, our purposes and goals, and even the people who impact our lives—that determine the character of our heart and the experience of our daily life. *To change our heart and the experience of our life, therefore, we must change the contents of our heart.*

No matter what the present state of our heart is, this change is possible. We can receive new things into our heart and put old things out. The change may be more rapid for some than others due to the condition of their heart and life's circumstances. *But all believers, if they truly long for it, can see their lives change by changing the contents of their heart.*

Who Puts Things in Our Hearts?

According to the Scriptures things come into our heart through various agents. God and we ourselves are the primary agents. But other people as well as evil spirits also put things into our hearts.

God

God is said to place a wide variety of things into peoples' hearts, including skills and abilities such as the artistry and craftsmanship of the builders of the tabernacle (Exod. 31:6), the capacity to teach (Exod. 35:34), and Solomon's wisdom (1 Kings 10:24; 2 Chron. 9:23). Among other things that God puts into hearts are the law (Heb. 10:16; Jer. 31:33), the concept of eternity (Eccl. 3:11), the fear of himself (Jer. 32:40), various characteristics (e.g., gladness, Ps. 4:7; earnestness, 2 Cor. 8:16; faintness, Lev. 26:36), and direction in both good and evil hearts (e.g., Ezra 7:27; Neh. 2:12; 7:5; Rev. 17:17).

God also "makes" the heart have certain characteristics such as hardness (e.g., Exod. 14:8; Deut. 2:30), faintness (Job. 23:16), or strength (Ps. 10:17). He also turns the heart toward certain things (e.g., Ps. 105:25). These actions on the heart would also seem to be the equivalent of putting these things in the heart.

Some of the things that God puts into the heart clearly involve the cooperation of an open and receptive heart on the part of the recipient. When Solomon prayed for a wise heart, he literally asked for a "hearing heart" (1 Kings 3:9), that is, a heart that was open to receive God's instruction. And God graciously responded giving him great wisdom. On the other hand, things such as the concept of eternity, the fear of God (at least at times), faintness (in certain people), and even skills and abilities are apparently put into people's hearts by God without their invitation.

Ourselves

We also put things in (or lay them to) our heart by focusing our attention on them or, in the language of Scripture, by causing our heart to go after them. For example, when David was about to avenge himself against Nabal, Abigail—Nabal's wife—pleaded with David not to "pay attention [lit. set his heart] to" the foolish actions of her ungrateful, arrogant husband (1 Sam. 25:25; cf. 2 Sam. 13:20). In other words, "Don't focus your thoughts so much on Nabal's evil actions that they enter into your heart and cause it to lead you to do something foolish that you will regret."

On the other hand, the judgment of the Babylonian exile came on the people of Israel because they "paid no attention" to God's warnings and previous lesser punishments—literally, they did not "lay it to heart" (Isa. 42:25; cf. Jer. 12:11). Instead, "their heart continually went after their idols" (Ezek. 20:16). In contrast Daniel "made up his mind [lit. set upon his heart] that he would not defile himself" with the pagan king's food or wine (1:8).

God also commands us to "take to our heart," or pay attention to our own way of life. He warned the priests of Malachi's day, "If you do not take it to heart to give honor to My name, . . . then I will send the curse upon you" (Mal. 2:2). The prophet Haggai similarly admonished those who had built luxurious houses for themselves but were apathetic about rebuilding God's temple: "Consider [set your heart on] your ways" (Hag. 1:5, 7).

We often put the words of another person into our heart. For example, when David overheard the servants warning the Philistine king about the danger of having him live among them, Scripture tells us that "David took these words to [lit. in his] heart and greatly feared Achish king of Gath" (1 Sam. 21:12; cf. 2 Sam. 13:33).

Frequently God asks us to receive his words into our heart. His command to Ezekiel is typical: "Son of Man, take into your heart all My words which I will speak to you and listen closely" (3:10; cf. Job 22:22; Mal. 2:46; Exod. 9:21). To the one who searches and receives God's words the writer of Proverbs says, "Wisdom will enter your heart" (Prov. 2:1–10). We are commanded to put God's Word *on* our heart, which is essentially the same as putting it *in* the heart (Deut. 11:18; 6:6; Prov. 6:21; 3:3).

Other People

More often Scripture refers to other persons putting words into our heart. This, of course, requires that we also receive them. The pessimistic words of the ten spies returning from their reconnaissance of the Promised Land "restrained [discouraged] the heart" of the people from entering (Num. 32:8–9). Boaz spoke "to the heart" of Ruth, that is, he spoke kindly to her (Ruth 2:13; cf. Gen. 34:3). The godly father of Proverbs tells his son to "to let your heart keep my commandments" (Prov. 3:1; cf. 4:4). Deception—which usually involves words—is literally to "steal the heart" of a person (Gen. 31:20; 2 Sam. 15:6). Solomon's wives obviously put something into Solomon's heart when they turned it away from God (1 Kings 11:4).

Evil Spirits

Finally, along with God and people (including ourselves), it is sobering to realize that Satan can put things into our hearts. The thought and desire to betray Jesus was "put into the heart of Judas Iscariot" by Satan (John 13:2). He actually entered Judas's heart later to energize him to perform the act (v. 27; Luke 22:3). David's thought and subsequent desire to number his army—motivated by the pride of human strength rather than by reliance on God—were incited by Satan (1 Chron. 21:1). Similarly, Satan prompted Ananias to lie about the sale money of his property by "filling" (taking control of) his heart (Acts 5:3; see also Matt. 16:23 where Satan influences Peter's thought).

Scripture also tells us that Ananias "put this deed" into his own heart (Acts 5:4). This is no doubt true in all of the cases when Satan puts things in human hearts. He places them at a more surface level of the heart as a tempting thought. But we must then *actively receive them into the depth of our heart* before they can affect any real change of heart and life.[*] By God's grace we can choose to "resist the devil" and the further penetration of his evil thoughts in our heart (James 4:7; 1 Peter 5:9).

Letting Things Exit the Heart

Our heart is changed not only by what comes into it, but also by what goes out of it. To "forget" God's words and actions (Deut. 6:12; 8:11, 14, 19), Scripture says is to let them "depart from . . . [our] heart" (Deut. 4:9). The numerous

---

[*] Other examples of Satan apparently putting things in the heart of individuals include his deception of Eve (Gen. 3), the thoughts of Peter that Jesus recognized as from Satan (Matt. 16:23), and temptations in general, which by their nature always include thoughts and corresponding emotions and desires (1 Thess. 3:5).

commands to "remember" things in our heart also imply that these things can be forgotten or go out of our heart (e.g., Isa. 46:8, lit. "Remember this . . . recall it to heart").* Along with letting things slip out of our heart through inattention or forgetfulness, we can actively remove things from our heart. For example, we are told "remove grief and anger from your heart" (Eccl. 11:10).

Storing Things in the Heart

Many things come in and go out of our heart. But some things are stored with lasting effect on our life. Traumatic events, such as a disastrous accident or the tragic death of a loved one, can come into our life with strong emotional impact and impress themselves deep in our hearts, overwhelming any resistance to their presence that we might put up. This is especially true of young children who have not yet developed the personal strength to withstand strong influences.

But we can also deliberately, with resolute intent, store things in our heart—things that we treasure and value (Luke 6:45). God commands us to "keep" his words of wisdom "in the midst of your heart" (Prov. 4:21; cf. 2:1) and to bind his commandments "continually on . . . [our] heart" (Prov. 6:21). Binding the Lord's words on our heart entails "memorizing [them] in such a way" that they become permanently impressed on our "essential mental and spiritual being" and prompt all of our actions."[11] Because we do this with the things that we value, the binding of God's words on our heart has also been described as taking our "most highly prized personal treasure" and placing it so that it rests "on [our] heart like a costly locket or signet ring that hangs on a necklace."[12]

In obedience to such commands the psalmist declared, "Your word I have treasured in my heart" (Ps. 119:11; cf. Ps. 40: 8; Prov. 2:1; 7:1; Job 23:12). Mary similarly "treasured" in her heart the events of Jesus' early life (Luke 2:51). To our hurt, we can also "cherish" (NIV) and store sinful things in our heart (Ps. 66:18).

In summary, our heart is a storehouse where we are continually taking in materials from the experiences of our life. Some go in no further than the surface level and have no lasting effect on our life. Some things go out of the heart and no longer have any impact. Others, however, penetrate more deeply, and some are stored in the deep vault of the heart from where they shape the form of the heart and consequently the life.

---

* See also Isaiah 57:11, lit. "When you lied, and did not remember Me, You did not set it upon your heart"; and Jeremiah 51:50, lit. "Remember the LORD from afar, and let Jerusalem come upon your heart."

The Battle in the Storehouse

"When we think of the heart as the hidden source of all desires, hopes, and treasures, another feature emerges. The heart becomes the scene of death conflicts, for one desire competes with the others and one treasure must be chosen over many rivals. The heart cannot avoid choosing one lord over others. In fact, each desire represents a lord; many lords are therefore at work in the same heart, each soliciting obedience. So the parable of the seeds pictures the heart as soil on which God sows wheat and Satan sows weeds (Mt 13:18–30; Lk 8:9–15)."[13]

Our heart is thus always changing as long as we live, sometimes slowly, sometimes rapidly, but never remaining the same. Either it is growing in likeness to God's own heart or it is disintegrating into the disorder of death.

Questions for Thought

1. Do you believe that it is possible for your heart to be changed to experience more and more of true life in the world no matter what the present condition of your heart is?
2. Describe how our heart in relation to our spiritual life is like our physical digestive systems that receive and process nourishment for our body?
3. As with our physical body we can take in things that are detrimental, so in our spiritual realm we can take into our heart things both harmful and healthful. What is it that determines the nature of the things that we draw into our heart?
4. What things are in your heart right now—thoughts, desires, passions, emotions, objects, people, etc.? How do they define your overall heart? How do they determine the way you relate to other people and to God?
5. According to Scripture, who can put things into our hearts? Can you give examples in your life that this has happened?
6. After these things are put in our hearts, what are the ways we can store them up or let them exit from our heart?

▪▪ 6 ▪▪

God and Us

The Two Direct Agents of Heart Change

Only God . . . makes things grow.

1 CORINTHIANS 3:7 NIV

Therefore, my dear friends, . . . continue to work out your salvation
with fear and trembling, for it is God who works in you to will and
to act in order to fulfill his good purpose.

PHILIPPIANS 2:12–13 NIV

We cry to God in the words of David, "Create in me a clean heart,"
and He answers back, "Keep thy heart." Keep it with the keeping of
heaven above, and of the earth beneath—God's keeping bespoken in
prayer, and man's keeping applied in watchful effort.

WILLIAM ARNOT

In our desire for heart change it is important to know who really has responsibility for the content and consequent changing of our heart. A Chinese
proverb says, "You can't prevent the birds of sorrow from flying over your
head, but you can prevent them from building nests in your hair." So it is with
our heart.

The Devil, as we saw in the previous chapter in the case of Judas's betrayal
of Jesus and Ananias's and Sapphira's lying to the Holy Spirit, can put things
into our heart. The Bible never suggests that evil spirits have direct access to the
depth of the believer's heart to store something there without our own involvement.* Their input would be on the surface level in the form of temptations or

---

* The situation of unbelievers is somewhat different. The apostle who declared that God is "at

105

thoughts and emotions that would divert our love away from God and his way. But without our active reception they do not penetrate deeply to be stored in the heart with transforming effect. The same principle expressed in the Chinese Proverb is applicable to temptation. We cannot prevent a tempting thought from entering our mind, but when it does, we have the option of either rejecting it or entertaining it—welcoming it into our heart.

This truth applies as well to the input of other people and even the thoughts that arise in our own mind. Every day many things enter our heart at a surface level—thoughts both positive and negative, true and false. We can reject them and turn to other thoughts that cancel them out.* Or we can welcome and nurture these surface thoughts drawing them deeper and deeper into our heart, effectively letting them "build a nest"—or perhaps better, a mountain—that comes to have dominating power over our life.

Thus while other created agents—people and spirits—can exert influence on our heart, it is only God and we ourselves who directly manage our hearts and its contents. It is vital for our spiritual transformation to understand something of what these two agents do and how their work is related. In the first instance, both God and we ourselves appear to be involved in the same activity. For example, God put wisdom into Solomon's heart. But Solomon also asked for a hearing heart that was open to receive that wisdom. Thus, both God's and Solomon's actions were involved in putting things into his heart. This raises the related question of how God's sovereign working is related to our free actions as humans—a question that has never been solved to everyone's satisfaction and will not be here.

What is clear in all of this is that God is the ultimate heart-changer. Everything that we do in our transformation, although necessary, is always secondary in terms of ultimate causation and always dependent upon his work in

---

work . . . [in believers] both to will and to work for His good pleasure" (Phil. 2:13) uses similar language to say that "the prince of the power of the air . . . is now working in the sons of disobedience" (Eph. 2:1). This should not be interpreted to mean that Satan and evil spirits control the unbeliever without the concurrence of his receptive will. But in line with the total teaching of Scripture concerning the heart of the unbeliever, which we have seen in chapter 3, it is naturally dominated by sin so that it (the heart, including the will) is described as in bondage to sin. That is, the heart naturally wills in accord with its own sinful self-godhood propensity and thus is receptive to Satanic input against the will of God.

* This *active reception* in the case of small children might in certain instances be described more as a *passive reception* due to the overwhelming power and perceived authority of the initiating agent, e.g., a parent. But there is reception nonetheless. If resistance were possible, the matter could be kept from lodging in the heart.

us.* We will therefore consider first what God does in spiritual transformation and then look at our part.

The Ultimate Heart-Changer

As the creator and sovereign ruler of his creation God exercises ultimate control over the hearts of all people. As we have already seen he puts things in the hearts of both believers and unbelievers and causes their hearts to have certain dispositions, all of which signify a certain control of the heart. Although sin is never caused by God, its manifestations or the ways in which it expresses itself are nevertheless under God's control as many Scriptures demonstrate.

God "deprives the leaders of the earth of their reason [lit. heart]; he makes them wander in a trackless waste" (Job 12:24 NIV). In the last days, he will "put it in [the] hearts" of the ten evil kings "to execute His purpose . . . by giving their kingdom to the beast, until the words of God will be fulfilled (Rev. 17:17). He maneuvers the hearts of leaders in relation to his people. "He turned . . . [the Egyptians'] heart to hate His people, to deal craftily with His servants" (Ps. 105:25). Positively, he "turned the heart of the King of Assyria [Darius] toward them [God's people] to encourage them in the work of the house of God" (Ezra 6:22).

More generally, the writer of the Proverbs said, "In the LORD's hand the king's heart is a stream of water that he channels toward all who please him" (Ps. 21:1 NIV). "Just as the farmer leads water along the irrigation channels in pursuance of his agricultural projects; Yahweh directs the mind of the king and makes him the agent of his designs."[1]

Scripture, however, has much more to say about God's work in the hearts of believers than unbelievers, *no doubt because he does more in hearts that are open to receive him and his Word.*

The New Heart in the Believer

The description of the natural sinful heart that we saw in chapter 3 makes it clear that the transformation of our life requires nothing less than a radical change of heart. We need precisely what God promised to give us—a "new heart."

Throughout the Old Testament God's people had his righteous laws directing them in the path of life. They also had his gracious activity working to help them in their walk. Despite all of these divine provisions, their story is a sad mixture

---

* The priority of God's activity in the change of our heart will further discussed in chapter 13 where we will see that all spiritual transformation is totally by grace through faith.

of faith and unbelief, obedience followed by more disobedience. This continual cycle of repentance and rebellion made it obvious that if sinful humans were ever going to enjoy the blessing of life that flowed from walking with God in righteousness, something more was necessary.

So, at the very time when the disobedience of God's people brought the wrath of his judgment in the destruction of Jerusalem and their exile to Babylon, God promised to one day make a "new covenant" with them—a covenant that would finally bring about the newness of life that he desired for his people. On the basis of an ultimate forgiveness of sin that he would provide through the work of his own Son, he would enable the people to have direct intimate relationship with him. They would no longer have to be represented by a human priest who alone could enter God's presence in the Holy of Holies, first in the tabernacle and then the temple. God would come into the very core of the believer's heart through the Spirit, and in so doing he would create a new heart.

The Old Testament Believers and the Promised New Heart

The promise of a "new heart" for believers through the future new covenant brought by Christ does not deny that there were people in the Old Testament that sought to obey God and walk in the integrity of their heart, like Abraham and David. Such believers obviously had some change of heart worked by the Spirit in comparison to those who rebelled against him. But the old covenant of the Law of Moses never promised to give anyone a "new heart." The change of "heart" that took place in the Old Testament was thus not as radical so as to be called a "new heart." Scripture teaches that the Old Covenant could not make anyone "perfect." The writer to the Hebrews declares, "The Law is only a shadow of the good things that are coming—not the realities themselves. For this reason it can never, by the same sacrifices repeated endlessly year after year, make perfect those who draw near to worship" (10:1 NIV; cf. 7:19). The superiority of the new covenant rests upon the superiority of the once-for-all sufficient sacrifice of Christ for the ultimate forgiveness our sins (Heb. 10:4, 11–14; Acts 13:38–39).

Listen to the predictions of the prophets in the midst of Israel's failure:

"Behold, days are coming," declares the LORD, "when I will make a new covenant with the house of Israel and with the house of Judah. . . . I will *put My law within them and on their heart* I will write it; and I will be their God, and they shall be my people. . . . they will all know Me, . . . for I will forgive their iniquity, and their sin I will remember no more." (Jer. 31:31–34; also note related to Ezek. 36:26 below)

"I will *give them a heart to know Me*, for I am the LORD, and they will be my people, and I will be their God, for they will return to Me with their *whole heart.*" (Jer. 24:7)

"I will make an everlasting covenant [i.e., new covenant] with them that I will not turn away from them, to do them good; and I will *put the fear of Me in their hearts* so that they will not turn away from Me." (Jer. 32:40)

"Moreover, I will *give you a new heart* and put a new spirit within you; and I will *remove the heart of stone* from your flesh and *give you a heart of flesh*. I will put My Spirit within you and cause you to walk in My statutes, and you will be careful to observe My ordinances." (Ezek. 36:26–27; note the effect of the new heart in obedience here and in 11:19–20 below)

"And I will *give them one [undivided*, NIV] *heart*, and put a new spirit within them. And I will take the heart of stone out of their flesh and *give them a heart of flesh*, that they may walk in my statutes and keep My ordinances and do them. Then they will be my people, and I shall be their God." (Ezek. 11:19–20)

Since the heart is the real person, to receive a "new heart" is nothing less than to be made a "new" person. In New Testament language, the person is "born again" (John 3:2–8), "regenerated" and "renewed" (Titus 3:5). He no longer belongs to the old creation dominated by sin and corruption. He is a "new creation" (2 Cor. 5:17; cf. Eph. 2:10). Scripture declares that one day God will make "all things new"—"a new heavens and a new earth" (Rev. 21:5, 1; Isa. 65:17). The believer at the core of his heart is already part of this miraculous new creation.

The New Heart in the Believer's Experience

The provision of a new heart making us new persons is one of the great blessings of Christian salvation. But daily experience makes us wonder what having a new heart really means. We have a new relationship to God through Christ, but has anything really changed in us?

Despite the fact that our life often seems little different than life with the "old heart," Scripture tells us that a real transformation has in fact taken place in us when we received a "new heart"—a transformation that can only be termed "radical," for it goes to the very root (radix) of our existence. Because of the presence of God now dwelling in it, the new heart is radically reoriented. The love or desire of the heart that draws things into itself has undergone a 180-degree polar change.

The old, self-focused heart loved anything that propped up self as god, anything that brought significance and security to *me*—such as power, wealth, knowledge. The love of the new heart, in radical contrast, is now directed toward God in fulfillment of his promise that he would "circumcise* your heart . . . to love the LORD your God with all your heart and with all your soul, so that you may live" (Deut. 30:6).

This love of the new heart is nothing less than God's own love kindled in us. As Paul wrote, "The love of God has been poured out within our hearts through the Holy Spirit who was given to us" (Rom. 5:5). The old self-love cut us off from others; this love flows out to others. Through this love of the new heart, the new person becomes a new self that begins to live life as intended by God—life in relationship with God and others.

The heart's new love establishes an intimate relationship with God even as he promised: "I will put the fear [awesome reverence] of Me in their hearts so that they will not turn away from Me" (Jer. 32:40). To fear God in the sense of this promise means to live with the recognition of God for who he really is—the one who created us and loves us enough to bring us back to himself. As Old Testament scholar Hans-Joachim Kraus explains, "For those who fear Yahweh, God is a living reality. They look for the self-disclosure of God and are always alert to receive him."[2]

God further declared, "I will give them a heart to know Me"—to know me personally and experientially, "and they will be My people, and I will be their God" (Jer. 24:7; 31:33). They will be my own "sons and daughters" (2 Cor. 6:18; Rom. 8:16).

This new orientation of love toward God in a re-created heart also brought a new freedom from the bondage to sin. Jesus taught that "the whole Law and the Prophets" are encompassed in the two great commandments: love of God and love of neighbor (Matt. 22:36–40). Paul similarly said, "Love does no wrong to a neighbor; therefore love is the fulfillment of the law" (Rom. 13:10). Philosopher Peter Kreeft helps us understand why these things are true.

---

* Circumcision of the heart indicated a spiritual purification that made the heart open and obedient to God as opposed to closed and stubbornly rebellious (Deut. 10:16, "So circumcise your heart, and stiffen your neck no longer"; also Jer. 4:4).

One of the things we mean when we say that love is the fulfillment of the law is that when we do not love a person, it is difficult or impossible to fulfill the moral law with respect to that person; but when we love someone, it is possible, even easy, even inevitable, and positively delightful to do what the moral law commands us to do to him [or her]. It is hard to do good deeds to one you despise, but joy to do the same deeds for one you love.[3]

The orientation of our heart's love toward God gives us the ability for the first time to live according to what he desires—to live righteously with him and our neighbors, and even with ourselves. Prior to our new heart, we lived out of the love of our old heart, which was ultimately turned in upon itself. We lived against God and others because we saw them as threats to the citadel of our god-playing ego. There was no way that we could fulfill God's law of love. In the words of Scripture, we were slaves to sin.

All of this was radically changed when we became new persons with a new heart. Our faith not only united us with Christ, it also united us with his death and resurrection. Joined to Christ we died as the old person that we were, and were resurrected a new person. This had a profound effect on our relationship to sin. As Paul explained, "Our old self was crucified with Him, in order that our body of sin ['myself in all my sin-prone faculties'[4]] might be done away with [rendered powerless], *so that we would no longer be slaves to sin*" (Rom. 6:6).

Living from the old heart meant bondage to sin. Even our actions that were in some sense "good" were always conditioned by a deep—and perhaps deceptively unconscious—motive in the heart that ultimately ended in some way on enhancing self rather than God and other people.

As new persons with new hearts, we have been set free from this slavery. This is not to say that we no longer sin or that we are incapable of sinning. But rather that we are no longer slaves to sin—*we don't have to serve sin*. By the power of God living in us, we can resist temptations. Our old heart which was controlled by the sin of self-godhood has been fundamentally re-created. In the words of John Stott, we "have been decisively rescued out of the lordship of sin into the lordship of God, out of the dominion of darkness into the kingdom of Christ."[5]

Freed from sin's bondage, we can now serve God. Our new heart *not only makes us able* to serve God and his righteous ways, but it *gives us a positive inclination or propensity* toward them. "Thanks be to God," the apostle exclaimed, "that though you were slaves to sin, *you became obedient from the heart* to that form of teaching to which you were committed, and *having been freed from sin, you became slaves of righteousness*" (Rom. 6:17–18). This new propensity flows from a heart that has been "cleansed" through faith (Acts 15:9; Titus 3:5; cf. John 15:3).

To be sure, we have not yet attained perfection; impurity remains in our heart. But our new heart is continually being cleansed by God's gracious forgiveness (1 John 1:7), and a new seed of purity has been implanted in the depth of the new heart due to the abiding, indwelling presence of God's Word and Spirit (James 1:21; 1 John 3:9).

This change of heart means nothing less than a change of our nature as is evident in the apostle's words to the Ephesian believers: "You were once darkness, but now you are light in the Lord" (Eph. 5:8 NIV). He didn't merely say that they now lived in the realm of light or that they did works of light—realities which of course are true of believers. He said, "You *are* light in the Lord." What our heart loves comes to control it and finally determine what we are. With its orientation of love toward God and his Son, our new heart takes on the very qualities of their nature, which is light (John 8:12; 1 John 4:8), or as Jesus says using a Hebrew idiom, we become "sons of light" (John 12:36)—that is, spiritually genetically related to light.

Darkness and Light as Spiritual Powers

"For you were once darkness, but now you are light in the Lord. Live as children of light" (Eph. 5:8 NIV). Darkness and light are more than metaphors for the ethical or moral qualities of "good" and "evil." They refer to realities of opposing spiritual powers that are outside and above us as human beings. God is Light (1 John 1:5), the power that brings life (Ps. 36:9; John 1:4; 8:12). The power of darkness—that is, sin and death—fights against the light, but cannot overcome (John 12:35; cf. 1:5). Through faith we are joined to Christ who is God's light of the world (John 8:12). Because he is in us and we are in him, we participate in the Light and its life-giving power, becoming in reality "children of light." Partaking of the light in our very nature we become vessels of light, lighthouses through which light and its power of life radiate to overpower the remaining darkness in us and about us.

The concise list of the characteristics of the new heart below helps us grasp something of the scope of the transformation that took place in the creation of our "new heart." The magnitude of the change is enhanced when we realize that just the *opposite* of these traits characterized our natural heart apart from God.

+ We now have a clean (forgiven) heart (Acts 15:9).
+ We now have love toward God (Deut. 30:5–6).

+ We are sensitive and pliable in relation to God (Ezek. 11:19; 36:26).
+ We possess a new living force that drives life; we have a "new spirit" that is dominated by God's own Spirit dwelling in us (Ezek. 36:26).
+ We experience a personal knowledge of God (Jer. 24:7; 31:33).
+ We enjoy a filial relationship with God (Jer.24:7; 31:33).
+ We have received an orientation and power to do God's righteous will (Ezek. 36:26–27; 31:33, God's law written on our heart).*

These qualities of the Christian's new heart obviously raise questions in relation to life experience: "If life flows out of the heart as the Bible teaches, why don't I experience these characteristics of the new heart?" "Why isn't love for God and others always dominant in my life?" "Why do I so often still seem to be in bondage to sin?"

The truth is that any believer who would claim to be fully experiencing the traits of his new heart all of the time, and so be without sin, would be deceiving himself (1 John 1:8). Even when we walk openly in the light of God's truth, we still sin, for according to Scripture we are constantly being cleansed from sin even as we walk in the light (1 John 1:7).

Having a new heart, therefore, does not mean that all remnants of the old, disordered love of self are gone. But these remnants now stand at the periphery of the new person. The center of the person in the depth of his heart is now God-oriented and bent toward righteousness. And, as the Puritan Henry Scougal explains, it is the orientation or bent of our love that determines who we really are as persons.

> Love is that powerful and prevalent passion by which all the faculties and inclinations of the soul are determined. . . . The worth and excellency of a soul is to be measured by the object of its love. He who loveth mean and sordid things doth thereby become base and vile, but a noble and well-placed affection doth advance and improve the spirit into a conformity with the perfections which it loves.[6]

John Calvin, the great Reformed theologian, put it this way: "God begins His good work in us . . . by arousing love and desire and zeal for righteousness in

---

* The qualities of the new heart are also seen in the characteristics of the new person "born of God." These include love for God and his Son (1 John 5:1), love for "the brethren" or fellow believers (3:14; 4:7), practicing righteousness (2:29; 3:9), overcoming the world (5:4), and a "living hope" (1 Peter 1:3). In sum, it is evident again that the fundamental transformation is a change of loves. The new heart loves God and all that God loves—his people and his ways.

our hearts; or, to speak more correctly, by bending, forming and directing, our hearts to righteousness."[7]

Although this deep core of our new heart is not always evident in our conscious life, it is still the dominating aspect of our being. As we saw in the previous chapter, the heart takes things into itself at various levels. Some things lie on the surface leaving little permanent effect on the heart and life. Others, as Pedersen explains it, "live in it with quite a different depth and firmness, because they make the very nucleus of the soul [or heart]." The surface elements come and go in me in the conscious experience of life. But the deep contents, while not always felt, remain as "the stable points of gravity in the soul [or heart]."[8]

This reality is illustrated in Paul's explanation of the believer's struggle with sin in Romans 7:14–25. These verses are probably talking more directly about an Old Testament believer living under the Mosaic Law prior to the coming of the new covenant that came with Christ. Nevertheless, this picture of the experience of the Old Testament believer in his struggle with sin gives us some insight into our own experience with sin even as new persons with a new heart living under the new covenant in Christ.

Describing the situation in the first person, Paul says, when I sin, "I do not understand what I do" (v. 15).* It's contrary to my "mind" (v. 25). It is also something "I hate" (v. 15), and something that "I do not want" (vv. 19–20). In essence Paul says, "my mind, my emotion, and will—the very faculties of my heart—are all on God's side and against sin." He even goes so far as to say, "I am no longer the one doing it, but sin which dwells in me" (vv. 20, 17).

In this last statement, he is not denying that he commits sin and is responsible for it. He is pointing to the power that dominates him when he sins, much like when he says concerning his good work—"I worked harder than all of . . . [the other apostles]—yet not I, but the grace of God that was with me" (1 Cor. 15:10).

In brief, what the apostle teaches us about the believer and sin is that our new heart at its core—our real "I"—is opposed to sin. Sin is still present, but it lies at a more surface level of the heart. Delitzsch captures Paul's thought when he says, "The Ego is no longer one with sin—it is free from it; sin resides in such a man still, only as a foreign power."[9] It can and does at times temporarily overwhelm the good propensities at the core of our new heart. But this does not

---

* The Greek term for "understand" (*ginōskō*) is the common word for cognitively knowing or understanding. But it can also have the meaning of "acknowledge" or "approve," which some interpreters see here in Rom. 7:15. Cf. Douglas J. Moo, *The Epistle to the Romans*, NICNT (Grand Rapids: Eerdmans, 1996), 457.

Who Is Struggling in Romans 7:14–25?

That the believer's struggle in Romans 7:14–25 is best understood as referring directly to a believer living under the Mosaic Law is evident by the statements declaring that the believer is in "bondage to sin" and "a prisoner of the law of sin" (vv. 14, 23). Such is no longer true of the believers "in Christ." In Christ we are "free from the law of sin and death" (Rom. 8:3). At our conversion we "died to sin" (Rom. 6:2) and are thus "freed from sin" as slaves (Rom 6:6–7, 18, 22). The context prior to 7:14–15, which deals with the New Testament believer's freedom from the law, also supports this conclusion (Rom. 7:1–12). Lest freedom from the law suggest that the law is our problem, the apostle Paul in this description of the believer's struggle provides an apology or defense for the law explaining that the problem was never the law that the believer acknowledges as good. The culprit is rather sin that dwells in us.

negate the characteristics of the new heart residing at its core. The dominant traits of the new heart will again inevitably assert themselves in impulses toward God through the working of the indwelling Spirit.

In conclusion, two important truths should be remembered when thinking about the significance of the new heart in our daily experience of transformation. *First, our new heart is not fully grown or mature.* Spiritual life in this heart begins when the *seed* of God's living Word is planted at the deepest core of the heart, and with it, the presence of the living God—who brings life where once there was death, which results in a "new creation."

A seed has the genetic structure of the eventual plant, but growth must take place for the full nature of the seed to be manifest in maturity. Similarly, the new heart is not created fully mature. Its genetic propensities of godlike characteristics are designed to grow, reaching final maturity only with our glorification in the presence of our Lord (1 John 3:2).

Scripture compares new believers to "newborn babies" (1 Peter 2:2). All of the properties that characterize mature human personhood are inherent in a baby, but they are not yet fully mature. The weaknesses of immaturity are seen in many ways: (self-centeredness, desire for instant gratification, being easily deceived, etc.). So along the path to growth and maturity, the newborn person stumbles frequently. But as he or she grows to adulthood, the qualities of mature human personhood in the image of God become more and more dominant over the ways of childhood. The new heart increasingly manifests the inherent traits of its "new" nature in actual life.

The fact that our heart is designed for growth leads naturally to the second important truth: *the propensities of the new heart are the most powerful force in the believer's life.* There is a life principle within the new heart that is stronger than the contrary principle that leads to death. The new heart is designed to *grow*. This doesn't mean that the propensities of the new heart predominate at all points in the believer's experience. But rather that over time there is an *increase* in the display of these propensities. In short, the direction of the believer's life is up rather than neutral or down.

Although we will never be perfectly mature in this life, the new heart denotes a radical change in the believer. Jewett's comment, cited earlier, is worth hearing again, "The heart's intentionality is determined by the power which rules it. In the case of the Christian man, the direction of the heart's intentionality is determined by Christ's Spirit."[10] The words of John Flavel in the opening words of his little classic, *Keeping the Heart*, are true. "The heart of man is his worst part before it is regenerated, and the best afterward."[11]

God's Work in Growing the New Heart

After planting the seed of his new life in the heart, God continues to nurture its growth. Having made our new heart his home through the indwelling Spirit, he now works in various ways to form it, decorating it with the beauty of the characteristics of his own heart.

Looking at everything that God does in relation to the new heart would involve tracing out all of his dealings with the believer—for dealing with the person is dealing with his heart. For the sake of brevity we will simply note those actions of God that are explicitly said to be related to the believer's heart:

- He inclines or directs the heart toward himself (Josh. 24:23; 1 Kings 8:58), toward his life-giving word (Ps. 119:36), and toward an appreciation of his own love (2 Thess. 3:5; cf. 2 Cor. 13:11–14).
- He opens the heart to greater knowledge and understanding of the revelation of his Word and thus himself (Eph. 1:18; 1 Kings 3:9).
- He increases the heart's fundamental propensity of love. Having poured his own love into the new heart through the Spirit, he continually focuses the hearts of the believers on his own love for them, and works to produce in the believer's life the fruit of that love and the spectrum of godly traits that radiate from it (Gal. 5:22).
- He strengthens or establishes the heart in faith and godly living (Ps. 10:17; 1 Thess. 3:13; 2 Thess. 2:17; James 5:8), encouraging it when crushed and down (Isa. 57:15; cf. 2 Thess. 2:17).
- He sets the heart free (lit. enlarges or makes the heart wide), liberating it from the bondage of sin and consequent stifling constraints and enlarging

it with wisdom, joy, and inner freedom for true human life (Ps. 119:32; cf. v. 45).

+ He directs the heart in various ways in the believer's personal life (Neh. 2:12; 2 Cor. 8:16).

In sum, God works in the new heart to stimulate and strengthen all of the new characteristics implanted at its creation. This finally encompasses all of our life. For when God comes into our heart to make it new, he comes not to patch it up but to make it his home. Along with our mind, emotion, and will, the powerful presence of the Almighty God is at work to transform all of our life—from the inside out.

Our Human Responsibility for Heart Change

Although the heart can be transformed only by God—for he alone has the power to free our heart from slavery to sin and create it anew, our heart will never be transformed without our own activity. In fact, *Scripture tells us to perform many of the very same activities that God performs in changing our heart.*

The necessity of our participation in our transformation is obvious when we realize that we are talking about changing our heart or our essential person, which includes our mind, emotion, and will. For me to change, it is necessary that my thinking, my emotions, and my willing change. But how are these changed? If God simply programmed my thinking, feeling, and willing without me doing the thinking, feeling, and willing, the real me would no longer be functioning, and thus my heart would remain unchanged. The only way that our personal capacities can be transformed is when they are freed to be exercised in a new orientation.

In other words, God can change my mind, emotions, and will only by working through them, which means that they must be active. For example, there is no way to renew a will other than through the exercise of that will. It is impossible to grow in love without actually loving. *Thus we are called to be part of the transformation of our heart by our active thinking, feeling, and choosing.* Some of the commands explicitly calling for our activity in relation to our "heart" include:

+ Renew our heart (Ezek. 18:31, "make yourselves a new heart") and keep our heart clean (Ps. 73:13).
+ Incline or direct our heart toward God and his things: toward God (Josh 24:23; 1 Sam. 7:3; 2 Chron.19:3; 30:19), toward the right way (Job. 11:13;

Prov. 23:19), God's Word (Ezra 7:10; Ps. 119:112), and toward wisdom
(Prov. 2:2).

+ Watch, or guard, our heart through various activities (Prov. 4:20–27).
+ Let Christ rule in our heart (1 Peter 3:15; Col. 3:15).
+ Assure our heart (conscience) or set it at ease before God through loving
  behavior (1 John 3:19).
+ Pray for God's activity to change our heart—for enlightenment of the eyes
  of the heart to the knowledge of God (Eph. 1:18) and the work of the
  Spirit so Christ may be at home in our heart (Eph. 3:16–19).

In reality all of our Lord's commands and instructions for life call us to activities that shape our heart. When we obey such commands as "renew your minds"
(Rom. 12:2), "do good to all people" (Gal. 6:10), or "rejoice always" (1 Thess.
5:17), we are doing heart-changing work.

God is the ultimate heart-changer, but he does not change it apart from our
active participation. It's like an old story of a pastor who loved his flower garden.
Finding him working in it one day, a deacon commented, "My, the Lord sure
gave you a beautiful garden." To which the pastor responded, "Well, thank you
very much, but you should have seen it when God had it to Himself!" There
would have been no flowers without God's creative and sustaining activity. But
the garden would not have looked the way it did without the pastor's work.

So it is with our heart. God's sovereign design for heart transformation
involves both his work and our work. Heart-change does not occur without
our active pursuit of obedience to our Lord's instructions for living. Only as we
actively "work out" our salvation in reality will we experience change in our daily
lives (Phil. 2:12).

The Relationship of Divine and Human
Activity in Heart Change

If God and the believer are both agents in the transformation of the heart,
how does this work? The answer to this question about the relationship of divine
and human activity in our growth is probably beyond our full comprehension.
But two principles are clear, and understanding them and putting them into
practice are crucial to effect genuine heart change.

First, *our work and God's work are present in all spiritual growth.* We readily
believe that our Christian life begins with God's work. We are born again with
a new heart simply by receiving Christ (John 1:12–13). We are justified or given
a right relation with God by faith alone (Rom. 5:1; 3:21–30). The Holy Spirit

comes in to dwell in our hearts solely by faith in Christ (John 7:38–39; Gal. 3:14). As believers we accept all of these truths that essentially teach that by grace God through Christ has forgiven our sins and given us eternal life through faith alone.

But what about Christian growth? After all that our Savior has done for us, we know that we should obey him. We also believe that as a new creation we are no longer slaves of sin. We now have the ability to obey and do good works pleasing to God.

In our determination to make progress in living the Christian life, however, we must never forget that even as we began by God's activity, so we also grow by his activity. We constantly need to hear Paul's rebuke to the Galatian believers who, although they acknowledged that they began their salvation through faith alone, sought to grow in that salvation through various rituals and works.

"How did your new life begin?" the apostle asked, "Was it by working your heads off to please God? Or was it by responding to God's message to you? Are you going to continue this craziness? For only crazy people would think they could complete by their own efforts what was begun by God. If you weren't smart enough or strong enough to begin it, how do you suppose you could perfect it?" (Gal. 3:2–3 msg).

We also need to remember the same apostle's words written to the believers at Philippi—"he who began a good work in you will carry it on to completion until the day of Christ Jesus" (Phil. 1:6 niv). God gave us a new heart by planting the seed of his own life in it, and he continues his transforming work in our heart until it is finally perfect in the presence of Christ.

In the same Philippian letter, Paul gives perhaps Scripture's clearest answer to the question of the relationship of the divine and human activity in the believers' life and heart: "Work out your salvation with fear and trembling; for it is God who is at work in you, both to will and to work for His good pleasure" (2:12–13). The Greek term translated "work out" means to "bring about, produce."[12] Its present tense signifies that as believers, we are to exert *"continuous, sustained, strenuous effort"* to bring our salvation to reality in our daily life.[13]

But all the while we are active with our responsibility of working out our salvation, God is also "at work" in us. In short, our transformation takes place when both God and we are continually active in the process. As John Murray explains it, "God's working in us is not suspended because we work, nor our working suspended because God works. Neither is the relation strictly one of co-operation as if God did his part and we did our so that the conjunction or

The Priority of God's Love

The priority of God's activity in our relationship with him including our activity is seen also in Galatians 4:9: "But now that you have come to know God, or rather to be known by God . . . ." The "knowing" in this text refers to an experiential knowledge of relationship and declares that our relationship with God "does not have its basis in man's seeking (mysticism) or doing (legalism) or knowing (gnosticism), but it originates with God himself and is carried on always by divine grace."[14] The same priority of God's activity is seen in 1 Corinthians 8:3: "But if anyone loves God, he is known by Him." We love him because he first established a relationship with us. In the words of Paul Peeters, "Our whole rational and spiritual activity must be inspired and finalized by divine love. Stirred to consciousness and love by revelation and the love of God who loves us first (1 Jn. 4:10), the heart becomes active."[15]

co-ordination of both produced the required result. God works in us and we also work."[16]

The importance of never forgetting God's activity along with ours in heart change is found in the second principle: *our activity in transformation is totally dependent on God's.* Paul says, "Work out your salvation . . . for it is God who is at work in you." We work "for" or "because" God is at work in us. Our work is totally dependent on the "the dynamic and ongoing activity" of God in us.[17] In other words, we are totally powerless to change our heart without the work of God. Ethelbert Stauffer says it well: "We are capable of active orientation on God only to the extent that we are passive before Him."[18]

We will explore further in a later chapter the biblical teaching that our transformation is an essential part of our salvation, which is all by grace through faith. Here we simply want to emphasize the truth that while we are called to be active agents, only God *can* change our heart.

Spiritual growth always entails victory over the power of sin. Prior to coming to Christ we lived in bondage to sin. Sin reigned over us with a power stronger than any human power. This same sin that is all around us and even in us as believers has not lost its power. Only by a power greater than our own—God's power in us—can we overcome sin and make any progress in the transformation of our heart.

We cannot cleanse our hearts by our own actions. Rigorous disciplines or scrupulous observance of religious practices have no power over the defilement of sin in our heart and life. As the apostle put it, "They are of no value in checking self-indulgence" (Col. 2:23 NRSV). An alternate translation of this text favored by some interpreters actually makes our self-transforming practices destructive—"they are of no value, serving only to indulge the flesh"—that is, our own attempts to conquer sin in our life actually promote it.[19]

We may, as the ancient philosophers taught, develop virtues that make our life better through knowledge and training. Such changes, however, do nothing to transform the heart and thus the real person in relation to the root problem of sin—from self-centeredness to God-centered living.

The well-known Scottish Presbyterian minister John Witherspoon, who later served as president and professor at Princeton University where he influenced many of the founders of the United States, rightly declared in a sermon delivered in 1776, "The fear of man may make you hide your profanity; prudence and experience may make you abhor intemperance and riot; as you advance in life one vice may supplant another and hold its place; but nothing less than the sovereign grace of God can produce a saving change of heart and temper, or fit you for his immediate presence."[20]

Scripture does encourage us to discipline and training for spiritual growth (e.g., 1 Tim. 4:7; 1 Cor. 9:27; 2 Tim. 3:16). But these actions are useful only as they open our hearts to God's powerful activity. Even reading and studying the Scripture is fruitless unless God opens our eyes and illumines its truth to our hearts (Ps. 119:27, 73). The command for us to cleanse our hearts is obeyed only with the cry of David: "Create in me a clean heart, O God" (Ps. 51:10). And only through God's power can we faithfully "guard" our heart from defilement (Prov. 4:23).

In a word, our activity in the transformation of our heart is totally and continually dependent on the powerful energizing activity of God in us. As Jesus taught, we are branches who are commanded to actively bear fruit. But the possibility of our doing so rests wholly on abiding in the vine: "Apart from Me you can do nothing" (John 15:5).

To carry the illustration a bit further, the branch not only depends on the vine for its *ability* to bear fruit. It depends on the vine for its very *existence*. So it is with us. Our life as believers is first and foremost a relationship with God through Jesus Christ. Accordingly, in our pursuit of the transformation of our heart, growth in a personal relationship with God must be preeminent. All heart-changing activity flows from this.

Questions for Thought

1. Why are God and we ourselves the only agents who can directly change or manage the contents of our heart if, as we saw in chapter 5, there are a number of agents who can put things into our heart?

2. Describe the characteristics of the "new heart"? What is its basic radical newness (difference) as compared to the old heart? Are you aware of this radical newness in your daily experience as a Christian?

3. If you have a new heart and if the issues of life flow from the heart (Prov. 4:23), why do you still experience characteristics of the old heart? Which heart (old or new) characteristics are most prominent in your present experience? How does Paul's discussion of the believer's struggles in Romans 7:14–25 relate to your experience? Is the dominant power of your heart oriented toward God? What evidence do you have?

4. What are some of the important things that God does in growing or changing our new heart? What are some of the things that we are told to do in changing our heart?

5. Can God change our heart without our activity? Can we change our heart without God's activity? What do your answers to these last questions suggest that a believer should be doing if he or she desires heart transformation?

6. Why do you think God is the ultimate heart-changer? Why can't it be we ourselves?

Minding the Mind

Initiating Spiritual Transformation through Renewal of Mind

> Let God transform you into a new person by changing the way you think.
>
> ROMANS 12:2 NLT

> [The Scripture] is not an herb, but a tree, or rather a whole paradise of trees of life, which bring forth fruit every month, and the fruit thereof is for meat, and the leaves for medicine. It is . . . as it were, a shower of heavenly bread . . . and, as it were, a whole cellar full of oil vessels. In a word, it is a panary of wholesome food against fenowed [moldy] traditions; a physician's shop (as St Basil calls it) of preservatives against poisoned heresies; a pandect [complete code] of profitable laws against rebellious spirits; a treasury of most costly jewels against beggarly rudiments; finally, a fountain of most pure water springing up unto everlasting life.
>
> TRANSLATORS OF THE KJV BIBLE (1611)

It's all in the mind." So say many famous entertainers, professional athletes, and coaches with reference to self-confidence or performance anxieties, asserting the primary importance of mental state or way of thinking in achieving one's goals or potential. Could it be the same for Christians, who live with a nagging thought that we can be so much better? Is it really all in our mind?

We have seen that God is the ultimate heart-changer, but our spiritual transformation also requires our activity. God works in us *to will and do* his good pleasure, but we must *actually will and do* his good pleasure in working out our salvation (Phil. 2:12–13). We draw life and nourishment from the vine, but fruit bearing is our activity. So what must we do to actually will and do God's good pleasure in our life or in other words bear spiritual fruit, all of which flow from a transformed heart?

As we probe this question of what we must do in the process of heart change in this and the following three chapters, we need to be mindful of two important features of the heart. First, the heart is where we think, feel (experience emotion), and will the actions of our life. And second, these three personal functions are joined together in inseparable unity in the depth of the heart. Thus there is an inevitable interchange between our thought, emotion, and will in our heart. For example, a change in our thought will bring change in our emotion and will, or behavior. The same is true with our emotion and will. A change in any one of the three functions brings change in the other two. This is only natural if all three are united in the core of our heart.

Understanding of the process of heart change and what we can do to bring change therefore requires that we unpack this relationship. Since our thought, emotions, and will are ultimately connected, can we break into this triad and begin to change any of them directly and thus the whole heart? Or is there a relationship between thought, emotion, and actions that would indicate a beginning point for change?

Spiritual Transformation Begins with Our Thoughts

Interestingly God's commands and instructions address all three of our heart's functions—our thought, emotion, and will. God tells us to believe certain things, to change our thoughts from the lies of the world and Satan to God's truth—to "take every thought" captive to the obedience of Christ (2 Cor. 10:5). He challenges us again and again to change our actions or behavior—to turn away from sinful practices in favor of the ways of God. And finally, he commands our emotions—Rejoice! Love! Don't fear! Put all bitterness and wrath and anger away from you!

It is clear from our experience that we can't obey God's instructions concerning our emotions by simply commanding them directly. When we are depressed, we can't simply command ourselves to be joyful and expect to experience joy. We can't calm ourselves when we are afraid by telling ourselves to stop fearing. In short, we can't change our emotions by directly willing them to change. We can only change our emotion by changing our thoughts or actions.

In the case of our thoughts and actions, however, we do have some direct control over them. While it may be difficult at times, we can change our thoughts by deliberately turning them to something different. Rather than dwelling on what is negative about a person, we can focus on his or her good qualities. Rather than pining over what we don't have, we can follow the psalmist, telling our self to "Bless the Lord, O my soul, and forget none of His benefits" (Ps. 103:2).

To some extent, we can also control our actions. We can decide and determine to do something different. But with the exception of instinctive actions of raw stimulus response, which occur without conscious thought such as instantly running from a large ferocious animal, we always decide or think before changing our actions.*

Thinking about the relationship of our thought, emotion, and will in our daily experience therefore suggests that thought has a certain priority in changing these heart functions. We can change our thought directly, but our emotions and even our actions depend on our thought. In short, we ultimately live according to the thought of our heart. This truth is confirmed by the important teaching of Scripture that our transformation begins with the renewal of our mind or thought. It is also coincides with what we saw in chapter 4, namely, that the primary function of the heart is to think, or reason.

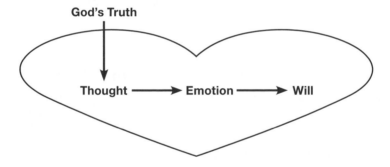

At least three lines of biblical evidence demonstrate the priority of thought in transforming our heart: (1) clear biblical teaching (2) the primacy of truth versus lies in spiritual warfare, and, (3) truth as the source of life and growth.

Clear Biblical Teaching

At the beginning of the last major section of Paul's letter to the Romans in which he urges them to live out their beliefs in practical daily life, he sets forth the fountain from which all Christian living and spiritual growth springs:

---

* Although there is no conscious thought before emotion and action in the case of stimulus response, there is always an appraisal of the stimulus that triggers the emotion and action. See further discussion later in this chapter under "The Relation of Thought and Emotion."

Therefore, I urge you, brothers and sisters, in view of God's mercy, to offer your bodies as a living sacrifice, holy and pleasing to God—this is your true and proper worship. Do not conform to the pattern of this world, but be transformed by the renewing of your mind. Then you will be able to test and approve what God's will is—his good, pleasing and perfect will. (Rom. 12:1–2 NIV)

Fundamental in the process of our transformation, according to the apostle, is the renewing of our "minds"—our thoughts and attitudes, our way of thinking. He says essentially the same thing again in Ephesians 4:23: "Be renewed [continually, Greek present tense] in the spirit of your mind." The "spirit of your mind" refers to the believer's reborn spirit, which is the operating force of all of one's personal capacities and is indwelt by the Holy Spirit.[1] The spiritual renewal that Paul commends takes place in relation to the mind.*

We see the same principle of transformation through the mind when Paul tells the believers at Rome: "You became obedient from the heart to that form of teaching to which you were committed" (Rom. 6:17). Their heart obedience was the result of commitment to truth.

"Mold" the Heart to Obedience

Some interpreters have noted that the Greek word for "form" (*typos*) in "form of teaching" (Rom. 6:17) in many instances includes the idea of a pattern or a mold. Derived from the word meaning "to strike," this Greek term *typos* refers to the impression made by the strike that actively molds or imprints its shape on an object—a "form-giving form."[2] Paul is then suggesting in this verse that the Christian teaching to which believers were committed at their conversion "molds" and "forms" their heart to obedience.[3]

These clear statements on the priority of thought in our spiritual growth are buttressed by Scripture's emphasis on the importance of hearing and attending to the words of God, which of course come to us through the means of our mind. The great Jewish Shema,† which is the central part of the Jewish prayer services,

---

* The priority of "mind" in the spiritual life is also suggested in Paul's statement that "those who are according to the flesh [i.e., live according to the flesh, or apart from God] set their minds on the things of the flesh, but those who are according to the Spirit [i.e., live according to the Spirit], the things of the Spirit" (Rom. 8:5). The crucial difference between the person living apart from God and the one living by the Spirit is one's mind-set.

† The Shema consists of three Old Testament passages: Deut. 6:4–9; 11:13–21; and Num. 15:13–41.

is so named after its initial Hebrew word *shema'*, "hear": "Hear, O Israel, The LORD is our God, the LORD is one!" (Deut. 6:4). Immediately following this command to "hear" we find the "greatest" of all commandments—"You shall love the LORD your God with all your heart and with all your soul and with all your might" (v. 5). Obviously, obedience to this great commandment depends on first *hearing* God's Word. Moses later commands the priests to read the law "in front of all Israel in their *hearing* . . . so that they may *hear* and *learn* and *fear* the LORD your God" (Deut. 31:12).

As persons who are designed to live in relationship, our primary means of communication is speaking and hearing—*and hearing comes first*. As we saw earlier, Solomon's great wisdom came from a "hearing heart" (1 Kings 3:9–12).* Proverbs 18:13 tells us that it is our folly and shame to respond to another before we hear the person out. If this is the case with our fellow human being, how much more so in relation to God? According to Hans Walter Wolff, hearing others and God is "the root of true humanity. . . . The man who, having closed his ears, takes himself as starting point and never moves away from himself not only loses his humanity among men; he also sets himself up as God in opposition to God."†

The supreme importance of hearing, especially the voice of God, is also evident in Isaiah's prophecy of Jesus as the Servant of Yahweh. In one place we hear the Servant himself speaking through the prophet: "The LORD God has given me the tongue of those who are taught, that I may know how to sustain with a word him who is weary. Morning by morning he awakens; *he awakens my ear to hear as those who are taught*. The LORD God has opened my ear, and I was not rebellious; I turned not backward" (Isa. 50:4–5 ESV).

Even as Jesus' life and ministry flowed from a heart that listened to his heavenly Father, so we live and grow in our relationship with God through receiving the communication of God's truth into our hearts. As we immerse ourselves in God's truth it changes the thinking of our heart and consequently the way we live.

As humans, we are the most unfinished at birth of all God's earthly creatures. Unlike the animals around us, we are not totally controlled by instincts in our interactions with our environment. We also have a spiritual nature with the

---

* See discussion under "A Heart of Understanding" in chapter 3.

† Hans Walter Wolff, *Anthropology of the Old Testament*, trans. Margaret Kohl (Philadelphia: Fortress, 1974), 74, 76). Gerhard von Rad similarly expressed the primacy of hearing for human life when he said, "Constitutive for man's humanity is the faculty of hearing." *Wisdom in Israel*, trans. James D. Martin (Nashville: Abingdon, 1972), 314. God is also known through seeing his acts (Exod. 14:13–31; Deut. 29:2–4; Isa. 43:8). But as Wolff notes "the opening of the eye comes through the Word (Exod. 14.13f., 30f., Isa. 43.8–13 [note esp. v. 12]; 30.2f.)"

capacity of freedom, which allows us and in fact requires us (we cannot avoid it) to actively take part in the unfolding of our life. To a great extent our life experiences are determined by the choices we make along the way.

The great question is therefore, how can we make the right choices and choose the right path? Not being ourselves the source of truth and goodness, Scripture tells us to look outside of ourselves, to our Creator, for the way of true human life. In other words, we are created and called to be a dialogue partner with our Lord, listening to his voice and responding in loving obedience. This is where transformation begins, by receiving God's truth and making it the thinking of our own heart.

Again and again, the writer of Proverbs tells us that walking in God's way comes from listening to his wisdom. "Listen, my son, and be wise, and direct your heart in the way" (23:19). "Give me your heart [in the sense of mind], my son, and let your eyes delight in my ways" (v. 26). "My son, if you will receive my words and treasure my commandments with you, make your ear attentive to wisdom, incline your heart to understanding . . . then you will discern the fear of the LORD and discover the knowledge of God. . . . For wisdom will enter your heart and knowledge will be pleasant to your soul; discretion will guard you, understanding will watch over you to deliver you from the way of evil" (Prov. 2:1–2, 5, 10–12; cf. 4:20–23).* Statements such as these lead Bruce Waltke to say that "the ear [which is designed to receive truth] is the key to the heart."[4]

The principle of transformation through the mind is also echoed by the psalmist when he says, "Your word I have treasured in my heart that I might not sin against You" (119:11). As Derek Kidner wisely comments, "The mind which stores up Scripture has its taste and judgment educated by God."[5]

The characteristics of our new heart also reveal the priority of thought. God gave us a heart to "know" him (Jer. 24:7). He puts the "fear" of himself in our heart—which of course we cannot have without knowledge of him (Jer. 32:40). He writes his law on the heart, which leads to a new life (Jer. 31:33). These divine activities, which continue throughout our life, are not worked in us apart from our own mental activities of repentance and faith.†

---

* Commenting on the concept of the "way" of life in the book of Proverbs, Koch says, "He who binds the Torah upon his *lebb* [*lev*], 'heart,' and acts accordingly, experiences it as an illuminating revelation of the way of life ([Prov.] 6:20–23; 4:10f.; 28:6–10; cf. 7:1–5). Thus the Torah of the wisdom teacher . . . brings the instruction that a man needs and must understand if his *derekh* [way] is to be successful." K. Koch, "*derekh*," TDOT, 3:287.

† M. Scott Fletcher notes that there are "the two Scriptural states or processes through which the human personality passes in conversion. The consciousness of sin leads the individual to

The prayers of the apostle for the eyes of the heart to be enlightened in order to "know" certain truths (Eph. 1:18–23), and for the inner person (i.e., the heart) to be strengthened in order "to comprehend" and "to know" the truth of the love of Christ (Eph. 3:18–19) also point to the priority of the incorporation of truth in the process of our transformation.

Primacy of Truth versus Lies in Spiritual Warfare

The priority of thought in our transformation is also evident in the struggle with our spiritual enemy, who does everything he can to hinder the growth of our new life. When we become a Christian, we become engaged in a "warfare" against our enemy's fortresses, which the apostle Paul described as "speculations [thoughts, reasonings, arguments] and every lofty thing ['high-minded thing,' HCSB] raised up against the knowledge of God." Paul's goal—which must also be ours if we would grow spiritually—was to tear down the fortresses of lies against God's truth and bring "every thought captive to the obedience of Christ" (2 Cor. 10:5). The battle that is raging in this spiritual warfare is a battle of thoughts. As Philip Hughes explains, the prisoners taken are "the thoughts—the cogitations and intentions—of man's mind, and they are led captive, every one of them, into the obedience of Christ. . . . The rebellion of the human heart is quelled, the truth of God prevails."[6]

This is the same battle of mind evident in the conflict waged between the flesh and the Spirit in the life of the believer—"the flesh sets its desire against the Spirit, and the Spirit against the flesh; for these are in opposition to one another" (Gal. 5:17). The crucial issue in the struggle that results in the radically diverse outcomes, either the deadly "deeds of the flesh" or the living "fruit of the Spirit" (Gal. 5:19–23), is seen in the apostle's explanation: "For those who are according to the flesh set their minds [mind-set or attitudes] on the things of the flesh, but those who are according to the Spirit, the things of the Spirit (Rom. 8:5).

We have no trouble recognizing that good and evil are at war in the world and even in our own lives. Our experience tells us that growth requires struggle. But we tend to think of the conflict in terms of will and not as a battle of thought. We engage our spiritual enemies with resolve and willpower, but often to no avail because we don't recognize that our will is the servant of our thought.

The real power at work is the thought of our heart. The will is involved, to

---

repentance. The consciousness of divine grace inspires the man with faith." *The Psychology of the New Testament*, 2nd ed. (London: Hodder and Stoughton, 1912), 210.

be sure, but according to the Scripture the primary battlefield is the arena of thought that directs the will. Jesus pointed to the real issue when he said, "You will know the truth, and the truth will make you free" (John 8:32). The battle is between the truth that frees from sin and lies that enslave.

The devil is usually seen as the powerful evil spirit who perpetrates ungodly attitudes and all kinds of immoral deeds, and so he is. But according to Scripture his primary activity is deception and his weapon, the lie. Jesus told those who wanted to kill him, "You are of your father the devil, and you want to do the desires of your father. He was a murderer from the beginning, and does not stand in the truth, because there is no truth in him. Whenever he speaks a lie, he speaks from his own nature; for he is a liar, and the father of lies" (John 8:44). The desire to kill Jesus was motivated by Satan the original murderer. *But he is a murderer because he is a liar.*

This is the lesson from the beginning of sin in the garden of Eden (Gen. 3:1–7). After bountifully supplying Adam and Eve with every good food, God asks them to obey him by prohibiting any eating from the tree of the knowledge of good and evil. If you eat, he warned, "you will surely die" (Gen. 2:17).

Satan enters the picture not with fearful threats of punishment if they refuse to follow him, but simply with the lie—"You surely will not die" (3:4). As a result of believing this lie, death came to Adam and Eve and the entire human race even as God said. At the root of this death and every other human misery is the lie of Satan against the truth of God's Word.

The lie as Satan's primary tactic is also revealed when in the future he is cast into the abyss for a thousand years (Rev. 20). The restriction of his activity on earth as a result of this imprisonment is tellingly summarized by the purpose statement "so that he should not deceive the nations any longer" (Rev. 20:3). When he is later loosed for a time we are told that he goes forth again "to deceive the nations in the four corners of the earth" (vv. 8, 10).

Satan directly and by means of his demonic minions, along with humans under his sway and the present world system with its idolatrous values, continually attacks the minds of unbelievers, blinding them to the light of the gospel (2 Cor. 4:4). But he also assaults the believer's mind.

At least two dozen references in the New Testament alone warn believers against being deceived by others (e.g., Eph. 5:6; Col. 2:8; 2 Thess. 2:3), or by self-deception (e.g., 1 Cor. 3:18; Gal. 6:3; James 1:26)[*] The apostle Paul warns

---

[*] See also Matt. 13:22; Mark 4:19; Rom. 16:18; 1 Cor. 6:9; 15:33; 2 Cor. 11:3, 13; Gal. 6:7;

Deceit: The Most Dangerous Weapon of Our Enemy

That God wants us to be on the alert for deceit and its deadly effect on human life is evident by the many times it is mentioned in his Word. Frequently the term is used simply to characterize the wicked in contrast to the righteous, for example, "The thoughts of the righteous are just, but the counsels of the wicked are deceitful" (Prov. 12:5); "The wisdom of the sensible is to understand his way, but the foolishness of fools is deceit" (14:8); "You have rejected all those who wander from Your statutes, for their deceitfulness is useless" (Ps. 119:118; see also Pss. 17:1; 32:2; 34:13; Isa. 53:9; Zeph. 3:13). Again and again believers are warned against being deceived by others or deceiving ourselves with at least 175 references to deception and its various cognate forms ("deceive," "deceit," "deceitful," etc.) found in the total Scripture (NASB). Protection from this deadly threat to our spiritual life comes only through the truth of God's Word.

us that deceptive spirits will be at work in the "last times" (i.e., the present time between Christ's first and second comings; 1 Tim. 4:1). He fears that the minds of the Corinthian believers are already being "led astray from the simplicity and purity of devotion to Christ" even "as the serpent deceived Eve" (2 Cor. 11:3).

When we understand that our spiritual life and its growth flows from our relationship with God and is communicated to us through his truth, the significance of deception as the key tactic of our enemy becomes clear.

Our heart naturally loves and is drawn toward what we believe to be true and good. For example, no person ever desires to be lied to. No one deliberately does what he knows is hurtful to himself unless he also believes that somehow he can escape the full harm, for example, taking harmful drugs. Even intentional actions of self-destruction such a taking one's own life are somehow deemed good by a despairing person—better than any alternative at the moment. The only way that we can be turned away from God's life, therefore, is to be deceived into believing that something other than what God says is true and good.

Thus Scripture warns us against being "hardened by the deceitfulness of sin" (Heb. 3:13; cf. 2 Thess. 2:10). That the power of our spiritual enemy—the power of sin—attacks us fundamentally through deceit is clear from the apostle's own testimony. After Paul acknowledged that "sin produced in [him]

Eph. 4:14; 1 Tim. 4:1; 2 Tim. 3:13; Titus 1:10; Heb. 3:13; James 1:16; 1 John 1:8; 2:26; 3:7; 2 John 7.

coveting [lusting or wrong desires] of every kind" (Rom. 7:8; cf. Eph. 2:3; Rom. 1:24),* he then explained how this happened: "Sin . . . deceived me and through [the commandment not to covet] killed me" (Rom. 7:11).

The connection between sin and deception is also seen in the command for us to "lay aside the old self, which is being corrupted in accordance with the *lusts of deceit* [or deceitful desires, NIV]" (Eph. 4:22).† The primary weapon of the enemy of our spiritual transformation is exposed in this command. As Andrew Lincoln explains, "A false perspective on reality generates a confusion of desires which can never be satisfied because they have lost touch with what is true."[7]

From Adam and Eve on, the immense destructive power of Satan's lie is evident in human history and in our own personal experience. But the lie retains its power only so long as it can continue masquerading as truth. Once it is unmasked and exposed by the truth of God, its strength drains away and its power over us is broken. Martin Luther captured this power of truth over the enemy in his well-known hymn "A Mighty Fortress":

> And though this world, with devils filled,
> Should threaten to undo us,
> We will not fear, for God hath willed
> His truth to triumph through us.

All of this is to say that the front line of spiritual warfare is the mind—whether it will be filled and thus controlled by God's truth or whether the deceitful lies of the enemy of our soul will dominate.

Not that the battle is simply intellectual. As we have seen, our thoughts are linked with the whole personal life of the heart including our emotion and will. Thus when Scripture refers to the "mind" it is not only referring simply to our mental capacities, but includes our whole attitude or moral orientation. Our mind is our "way of thinking."[8] This is what needs to be renewed for transformation. But since the first purpose of our mind is to hear the word of our Creator, our thoughts or beliefs are determinative for our way of thinking.

One of the most helpful things we can do for our spiritual life therefore is to examine our thoughts. Too often we live our life completely unaware of the thought that is driving it. When we are depressed or feel like a failure, when we

---

* The Greek term translated "coveting" (*epithymia*) in Rom. 7:7, 8 is the same as that for "lusts" in Eph. 2:3 and Rom. 1:24.
† The "lusts of deceit" in v. 22 are the antithesis of the "righteousness and holiness of the truth" (i.e., that come from the truth) in v. 24.

The Ultimate Struggle: The Word of God against Satan

"Indigenous in this world of thought is the idea that God is able to write his laws on the heart, so that a Christian's knowledge of God becomes superior to any knowledge received from relatives or teacher (Rom 2:15; Heb 8:8–12). It is such knowledge that enables the recipient to discern the fateful difference between one hope and others, one treasure and others. With His Word God initiates the struggle with Satan. It is the function of the prophet to penetrate the secrets of the heart and to disclose the strategies of these two prime evil enemies. By responding to this prophetic disclosure, the self determines the community to which it belongs and discovers within that community the strongest of family ties."[9]

feel guilty or anxious, we need to ask ourselves, what am I really thinking in my heart that makes me feel this way?

Unknowingly, we are defeated on the spiritual battlefield because we believe the lies of the enemy. We may have imbibed the world's criteria of success and failure—my identity and significance comes from what I accomplish, or how many things I have, or how well people like me. We may believe the enemy when he tells us that we are basically sinners, that there is no hope for change this side of heaven—we are simply spiritual failures. Or we might think our sins have put us beyond God's love and forgiveness.

In all of these and similar situations when we have negative emotions, we need to ask, are the thoughts that are driving my life and fostering my experience right now really true, or are they lies from the enemy? Am I looking at my life and circumstances through God's eyes, or unwittingly viewing myself and the situation through the lens of a world apart from God dominated by the false values of the Deceiver?

Truth as Source of Life and Growth

The priority of the mind in our transformation rests ultimately on the foundational principle of Scripture that genuine life is lived in accord with truth. Truth in Scripture refers to that which is reliable or faithful, genuine, and real. Depending on the context, sometimes the idea of faithfulness is uppermost. In other places the focus is on the genuineness or reality of the objects, such as the "true" God, emphasizing that God is the genuine God as opposed to all impostors. But all of these aspects of truth come together comprehensively in the God of the Bible who is ultimate truth—he is the genuine God, the ultimate reality, who is absolutely trustworthy in word and action.

Jesus taught that eternal life is found in coming to know "the only true

God" (John 17:3), and this knowledge is found in himself who is "the way, and the truth, and the life" (John 14:6). Jesus is the *way* because he embodies *truth* and *life*. Significantly *truth* comes before *life* as Jesus says in another place, "He who hears my word and believes Him who sent me, has eternal life" (John 5:24).

Spiritual life and its growth in all of it aspects thus flows from the knowledge of truth found in the revelation of God. In the words of Jesus—words by which he lived in his own life: "Man shall not live on bread alone, but on every word that proceeds out of the mouth of God" (Matt. 4:4; cf. Deut. 8:3). To seek spiritual transformation apart from a steady diet of God's Word is like trying to gain physical strength without eating. Both are impossible.

The life-giving property of God's Word permeates all of Scripture. While other people in the ancient Near East sought the forces of life from their gods through magical incantations and rites, God's people were to find it in their relation to God through his living written Word. The acceptance or rejection of the Word of God would determine the path they walked—the way of life and prosperity or the way of death and adversity (Deut. 30:15–20). The Word of God is "not an idle word for you; indeed it is your life," Moses told the people (32:47). God's words of "instruction" taught by the father to his children are "life to those who find them" (Prov. 4:22, cf. v. 13). Similarly the gospel of Christ is the "word of life"—the word that brings life (Phil. 2:16). Scripture reveals the priority of God's "word of life" for every facet of our spiritual journey and transformation.

+ *The Word is the seed of life.* Our spiritual journey began by being "born again . . . through the living and enduring word of God" (1 Peter 1:23), "through the word of truth" (James 1:18 NIV; cf. 2 Thess. 2:13). Our faith through which we are saved came "from hearing, and hearing by the word of God" (Rom. 10:17). Jesus compared the Word of the kingdom to a seed planted in the ground. Just as a seed has life in it to produce a living plant, so the living Word of God implanted in the soil of the human heart creates new spiritual life (Matt. 13:19–23; cf. Ps. 119:144, "Give me understanding that I may live").

+ *The Word is the nourishment of life.* Our new life was not only conceived by the Spirit through the Word of God's truth, it grows by the same Word. The apostle Peter says, "Like newborn babies, long for the pure milk of the word, so that by it you may grow in respect to salvation" (1 Peter 2:2). We were "created in righteousness and holiness of the truth," that is, a righteousness and holiness *that comes from the truth* (Eph. 4:24), so it is from the truth that we grow in righteousness and holiness.

Jesus witnesses to the nourishing power of the Word in his prayer for his disciples shortly before leaving them to go to the cross. Declaring that they had become his disciples by receiving the words of his Father that he had given them (John 17:8, 14) he goes on to say, "Sanctify them by the truth; your word is truth," (John 17:17 NIV), or as Peterson says in his paraphrase of Jesus' words: "Make them holy—consecrated—with the truth; Your word is consecrating truth" (MSG). D. A. Carson rightly comments, "No-one can be 'sanctified' or set apart for the Lord's use without learning to think God's thoughts after him, without learning to live in conformity with the 'word' he has graciously given."[10]

- *The Word is the protection in battle.* The Word of God also has priority of place in the battle with our spiritual enemies. The first action in putting on the armor of God is girding your waists with truth (see Eph. 6:14). This probably refers to the leather apron worn by the Roman soldier under his armor to protect his thighs and to fasten other clothing securely around his waist in preparation for rapid movement in battle. So girding ourselves with truth—receiving it into the depth of our heart so it becomes our very life and character—is the foundational requirement for victory in spiritual battles. Truth shows up again in our warfare as the only offensive weapon mentioned—"the sword of the Spirit, which is the word of God" (v. 17).

- *The Word is the medicine for sin's "sickness."* The presence of sin around us and in us makes us vulnerable to its debilitating "disease" of sin. But God's Word is our powerful prescription. Like a preventative medicine, it can ward off sin. "How can a young person stay on the path of purity? By living according to your word. . . . I have hidden your word in my heart that I might not sin against you" (Ps. 119:9, 11 NIV). "As for the deeds of men, by the word of your lips I have kept from the paths of the violent" (Ps. 17:4).

When sin does get in to bring its infection, the Word is also the remedy. Like a spiritual mirror or as we might think today a spiritual X-ray, the word exposes our sin (James 1:23–25; cf. Lam. 2:14). And like a surgeon's scalpel it dissects our heart so everything about us is "uncovered and laid bare before the eyes of him to whom we must give account" (Heb. 4:12–13).

But it is also the healing balm for the open wounds of sin, beginning with the cleansing of forgiveness. As Jesus told his disciples, "You are already clean because of the word which I have spoken to you" (John 15:3). We are "cleansed . . . by the washing of water with the word" (Eph. 5:26).*

The Word heals the misery of sin. Suffering sickness that brought them "near to gates of death" because of their sinful rebellion, the psalmist tells us that the people finally cried out to the Lord. In response, "He sent his word and healed them" (Ps. 107:17–20). The Word gives new strength and refreshes life in all of our weakness no matter what the cause. Elated over the Word of God, the psalmist declared, "The Law of the LORD is perfect, restoring [or reviving] the soul," (Ps. 19:7), or as Peterson puts it in his paraphrase, "The revelation of GOD is whole and pulls our lives together" (MSG; cf. Ps. 119:50).

The cleansing and renewing power of the Word is illustrated by the Old Testament ordinance of the red heifer (Num. 19). According to the Old Testament law, anyone who had become defiled or unclean had to be purified before they could resume their place in society and take part in the worship of God. One of the ways to be cleansed from the defilement that occurred through contact with death, such as touching a corpse or a human bone or a grave—one of the worst forms of defilement—was through the ritual of the red heifer.

This involved taking a red heifer outside the camp and killing it. Some of its blood was then sprinkled seven times toward the front of the tabernacle as a sacrifice to the Lord. The entire animal was then burned to ashes, which were gathered up and stored in a clean place for use whenever someone became defiled. When defilement occurred some of these ashes were mixed with water, which was known as the "water for cleansing" (Num. 19:9 NRSV). This purifying water was then sprinkled on the defiled person making him once again clean.

What gave this water its cleansing effectiveness was the fact that it contained the ashes of a sacrificial death. The application of the water was therefore the application of the benefits of that death. In the same way the Word of God contains the message of the sacrifice of Christ for the cleansing of our sin (Heb. 9:13–14). When we first came to Christ, we received an initial cleansing through that message. As we walk through life and become defiled by sin, we need repeated cleansing by the application of the truth of Christ's sacrifice for our sins through reading and meditation on the Word.

---

* All that was said above concerning spiritual growth through the Word also relates to the cleansing power of the Word.

The powerful effect of God's Word in our spiritual transformation is simply part of Scripture's teaching that God works his will in all of creation through his Word. Eight times in the creation story of Genesis 1, we read the words, "Then God said, 'Let there be . . .'; and it was so" (cf. Ps. 33:6; Heb. 11:3). The psalmist declared, "By the word of the LORD the heavens were made . . . . He spoke, and it was done" (Ps. 33:6, 9). The vast universe, created by God's Word, is also sustained by the same "word of his power" (Heb. 1:3). His Word controls nature, including the weather. "He sends forth His command to the earth; His word runs very swiftly. He gives snow . . . He scatters the frost . . . He casts forth His ice . . . He sends forth His word and melts them" (Ps. 147:15–18).

Wherever his Word goes it works powerfully and effectively: "My word . . . which goes forth from My mouth . . . will not return to Me empty, without accomplishing what I desire, and without succeeding in the matter for which I sent it" (Isa. 55:11). The power of the Word lies in the fact that it is "living and active" (Heb. 4:12). "Is not my word like fire," God says, "and like a hammer which shatters a rock?" (Jer. 23:29; cf. 5:14).

God's Word Has the Power to Change Us

The awesome power of God's Word to change even our deepest desires is seen in the comments of the great fourth-century preacher and Bible expositor Chrysostom on Jesus' teaching against laying up treasure on earth. Acknowledging that we all have a natural desire of greed and love of money, Chrysostom goes on to say, "Even this cloud may be easily scattered and broken, if we will receive the beam of the doctrine of Christ; if we will *hear* Him admonishing us, and saying, 'Lay not up for yourselves treasures upon earth.' 'But,' said one, 'what avails the *hearing* to me, as long as I am possessed by the desire?'" Chrysostom's answer: "There will be power in the continued *hearing* to destroy even the desire."[11]

God's Word is powerful because he is actively present in it. To be sure a person is surely more than his words, but his words cannot be separated from him. The most significant means through which we reveal ourselves to one another as persons is through our words. Our words reveal our heart, for "the mouth speaks out of that which fills the heart" (Matt. 12:34). God's Word is thus God speaking to us from his heart.*

---

* God speaks through his Son (Heb. 1:1–2), who in turn speaks by the Spirit through the inspired Scripture (John 16:12–15). See the letters to the seven churches in Rev. 2–3. They are spoken by Christ, yet each letter concludes with the statement, "He who has an ear let him hear what the Spirit says to the churches" (2:7, 11, 17, 29; 3:6, 13, 22).

Being by nature relational beings, our personal identity comes from inter-action with other persons. We have all taken into our hearts something of our parents, and others with whom we have had significant relationship, so that they are part of who we are today. Since we communicate primarily through words, this "indwelling" of the other person in us has taken place particularly through verbal dialogue—we are shaped by that other person's words.

Thus we are not simply reading the words of God in the Scriptures. We are encountering and incorporating the living Word himself. The Scriptures give us life and healing because they give us Christ, the living personal Word of God, and all that he is for us. Both Scripture and Christ are living and active. Thus the ancient biblical scholar Jerome rightly said, "Ignorance of Holy Scripture is ignorance of Christ."[12] By continually consuming the Word we are nourish-ing ourselves through communion with Christ. We taste of the goodness of the Lord himself (1 Peter 2:2).

The apostle Paul expressed this same truth to the Ephesians when he told them, "You did not learn Christ in this way, if indeed you have heard Him and have been taught in Him, just as truth is in Jesus" (Eph. 4:20–21). Hearing the message of Christ was not only being taught "in Him," but it was in reality *hear-ing* and *learning* Christ himself.*

Communion with the person of Christ through the Word thus brings Christ into our heart so that as the apostle put it, he becomes "formed" in us (Gal. 4:19). Alexander MacLaren beautifully expressed this: "A soul habitually in contact with Jesus will imbibe sweetness from him, just as garments laid away in a drawer with some . . . perfume absorb fragrance from that beside which they lie."[13]

The power of God's Word to transform our lives rests in the truth that it is more than theological doctrines and instructions for life. It is not teaching and learning like that of the philosophies in the Greek academies. It is the powerful voice of the risen Lord—the truth in Person—communicating himself to us today.

J. I. Packer, the highly respected evangelical theologian known especially for his classic work *Knowing God,* was recently asked in an interview what it was that keeps his faith fresh after decades of being a pastor and biblical scholar. His response echoes the teaching of Scripture and the experience of God's people throughout history: "I suppose [that it's] the fact that I know God, the

---

* The same relation of Christ to the Word is seen in Jesus' teaching concerning the way to freedom from the slavery to sin in John 8. In v. 32 Jesus says, "The truth will make you free," while in v. 36 he says, "If the Son makes you free, you will be free indeed." Receiving the Word is obviously receiving the powerful person of the Son.

Father, the Son and the Holy Spirit, and God remains alive. That is testified to in Scripture, and it comes through when I read the Bible. Understood in that way, it's reading the Bible that keeps me fresh. The living God keeps coming through in all sorts of ways. You're always in [the] process of seeing things that you never saw before."[14]

Only in such a personal relationship with our Savior through hearing and responding to his Word can we grow spiritually. If the Word does not lead to a relationship with the person, we are misusing it with the consequence that it has no transforming effect.

The Relation of Thought and Emotion

Experience sometimes causes us to question the idea that transformation of the heart begins with thought. Counselors regularly see Christians who have faithfully read the Bible and attended church for years, but their lives have changed very little, if at all. What is needed, it is frequently argued, is not truth, but love; not a change of mind, but a change of emotion.

Clearly as we will see later, emotion plays an important role in our life. In fact, thought that does not touch emotion produces no change. Emotion even changes our thinking. According to research from psychology and neuroscience, our emotion and thought "interact, . . . making important contributions to the guidance and organization of the other."[15] For example, past experiences that had a strong emotional impact on us can impact our thinking in similar experiences in the present. A terrifying encounter with an angry dog can make us see all dogs as fearful objects rather than as man's best friend.

Similarly, if a child develops feelings of rejection and anger in response to persistent unloving criticism, these same feelings may be aroused at a later age when any criticism is received. No matter how helpfully intended and graciously given, all criticism will tend to be interpreted or misinterpreted as unfair and demeaning. While the emotions connected with past experiences do not have to determine the meaning that we give to a similar situation in the present, they clearly arise in us to influence how we presently understand our world.

But in such scenarios is emotion really prior to thought? When we analyze them closely we find that even in these instances any change that takes place in the person actually begins with thought. According to researchers who study the functions of the human mind and brain, all of our emotional experiences begin when something arouses the attention of our brain. Immediately a complex appraisal system in the brain—which includes our past experiences, the present situation, and our state of mind—assesses this stimulus of the brain as "good" or "bad," desirable or hurtful, something to move toward or away from. This initial or primary appraisal of good or bad is then further differentiated into the various categories of positive and negative emotions, such as fear, anger, and sadness; or joy, peace, hope, and contentedness.[16]

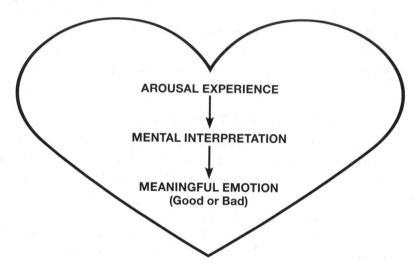

Feelings are the result of the mind's appraisal of an experience.

This analysis tells us that our emotions are not simply feelings, but feelings that result from our mind's appraisal of that which has aroused our attention. In other words, they are feelings freighted with meaning—feelings that have meaning to us.*

As Richard Bondi said, "Emotions and feelings are epistemological; they are sensors relating us to the world, needing interpretation to find significance."[17] David Burns further explains, "Your emotions result entirely from the way you *look* at things. It is an obvious neurological fact that before you can experience any event, you must process it with your mind and give it meaning."[18]

This is not to say that "giving it meaning" is always conscious. We come into this world with some of our appraisal system already preprogrammed in us. Infants seem to express positive and negative emotions before they are consciously aware of their situation. Nevertheless this appraisal is a function of the mind.[19] Some of this intuitive appraisal system no doubt remains with us throughout life. But as we mature we develop increasingly complex mental

---

* See also the discussion of emotions in chapter 4.

Emotions: The Effect of Cognitive Evaluation of Life's Happenings

"Cognitive activity is a necessary precondition of emotion because to experience an emotion, people must comprehend—whether in the form of a primitive evaluative perception or a highly differentiated symbolic process—that their well-being is implicated in a transaction, for better or worse. A creature that is oblivious to the significance of what is happening for its well-being does not react with an emotion."[20]

processes with which we are able to consciously appraise a situation with deliberate evaluations and thus alter our emotional reactions in our relationships with people and situations.*

To return to the questions of the priority of thought or emotion in the process of our transformation, it is obvious that for us to experience love from another person and be changed by it, we must first interpret an action of love directed toward us as love. If someone lovingly puts their arms around us, depending on various circumstances, we could interpret that act as an attempt to manipulate us, see it as insincere, or even mockery. Even if loving words are spoken, these could likewise be misinterpreted as something else. Children have been known to reject the love of their parents. People reject God's love. Both do it for some reason, perhaps misinterpretation or even deliberate refusal. The point is that an emotion is always interpreted before it has any effect upon the person.

To be sure the trigger for change may be an emotional experience. The experience of love rightly interpreted can help us become loving persons. But the change in us does not begin until the interpretation is made. Our internal change thus actually begins with our thought about the emotional experience. So it is with the change of our heart in spiritual growth. It begins, as Scripture teaches, with the renewal of the mind, replacing the false thinking of the old deceiving heart—the false interpretations of our experiences—with the truth of the mind of Christ.

The reality of thought-inspired emotions is illustrated in the gospel account of the confrontation between Peter and Jesus. After Jesus had just told his disciples that he must suffer many things and be rejected and finally killed, we are told

---

* Daniel Siegel said, "Consciousness may be necessary for an intentional alteration in behavior patterns beyond 'reflexive' responses. Without the involvement of consciousness and the capacity to perceive others' and one's own emotions, there may be an inability to plan actively for the future, to alter ingrained patterns of behavior, or to engage in emotionally meaningful connections with others." Daniel J. Siegel, *The Developing Mind: How Relationships and the Brain Interact to Shape Who We Are* (New York: Guilford Press, 1999), 136.

that Peter "took Him aside and began to rebuke Him" (Mark 8:32). Nothing is said about Peter's emotion, but he must have been stirred up emotionally to challenge his Lord's words after he had just recognized him as the Messiah of Israel (v. 29). Jesus counters by explaining Peter's actions: "You are not setting your mind on God's interests, but man's" (v. 33). Peter's response including the accompanying emotion was, according to Jesus, the result of incorrect thinking—his "mind" was filled with human thoughts and not God's thoughts on the matter.

We can also surmise with Matthew Elliott that our Lord's emotion at this point was also due to his thinking. Rather than strong negative emotions that would naturally come from letting his mind dwell on his future suffering, Jesus appears calm, apparently choosing to dwell on accomplishing his mission and the positive results that it would bring.[21]

Sources of Truth for Our Thoughts

The truth of God by which we are transformed is all around us, for he is the source of all reality.[*] Even as we who are created in the image of God reveal our self and come to know one another through what we do and say, so God reveals his truth through his works and his words. Thus the truth that nourishes our heart is everywhere. We only need to train our eyes to see and our ears to hear.

God's Words

As in our personal communications it is our words through which we most clearly and deeply communicate with one another. So God communicates his truth most fully and personally through his revealed Word. As we will see below, the creation around us tells us truth about God, but these are also revealed more explicitly in the written Scriptures. Through the biblical record of history and prophecy and especially in the story of his redemptive acts for his people, God reveals his presence as the sovereign Lord of all history, including the days and years of our personal lives.

The Scriptures contain truth that we cannot know from any other source. We come to know God's plan of salvation only through the Scriptures. For only through words can he reveal his heart of love for us and the meaning of his

---

[*] God, of course, is not the source of sin, which is also a "reality" in at least some sense of the word. But its "reality" is in fact more a disordering or disturbance of the reality that God created rather than an additional creation analogous to the created reality of God. Sin is more a retreat into nothingness, a parasitic perversion of everything created good, true, and beautiful, yet in its twisting and distorting of reality it results in incredible destruction to life, relationships, and the world.

historical acts of redemption. No doubt many who witnessed God's historical interventions—such as the miraculous escape of Israel through the Red Sea or the miracles of the prophets and Jesus—explained them away as the result of natural coincidences or evil powers. But God lets us know through his prophetic word that he was personally acting in and through those events and persons.

Most importantly, the great acts of redemption in Christ, could not be understood but for the written Word of God. That he died is an historical fact. But that the one who died was the Son of God, the God-man, and that his death was substitutionary (in our place) as the satisfaction for our sins that we might be reconciled to a holy God—all of these truths concerning God's action for us are revealed only in the Scriptures. In brief, it is only through his words written in the Scriptures for us that God has chosen to communicate the thoughts of his heart. This includes the church's witness to and record of the words and acts of Jesus, the Revealer of God himself, as conveyed to us and preserved in the New Testament writings of the Gospels and Acts, the Epistles, and in the Revelation to John.

To this we would add, that Scripture alone—as God-breathed words (2 Tim. 3:16) written by men who spoke "from God" because they were "moved by the Holy Spirit" (2 Peter 1:21)—reveals truth without error and thus normatively. The thoughts that arise in us from our intuitions of God and from our experience of reality about us are susceptible to being confused by the influence of our sinful desires. Only the words of Scripture reveal God's truthful thoughts directly and reliably.

God's Works

Although the Scriptures are the primary and normative avenue through which God communicates himself and his truth to us for the renewal of our minds and heart, his created reality surrounding us also conveys his truth for our transformation. As a work of art tells us something about the artist, so God's work reveals God.

The wonders and beauty of creation with their awesome majesty and unfathomable intricate designs reveal his wisdom, eternal power, and divine glory. Thoughtful consideration of God's creation will lead us to say with the psalmist, "The heavens are telling of the glory of God; and their expanse is declaring the work of His hands" (Ps. 19:1; cf. vv. 2–4; Rom. 1:19–21). The provision of food through rain and fruitful seasons also witnesses to his goodness (Acts 14:17). And our own nature as humans with reason and a conscience that witnesses to a sense of right and wrong (Rom. 2:14–15) tells us something of the God who made us and in whom "we live and move and have our being" (Acts 17:24–29 ESV).

Simply looking at people around us as well as looking at the man or woman in the mirror shows us something of God. The creativity of the artist and musician and other forms of art are all his gifts and all reveal something about him however incomplete in themselves. Most significantly God's truth is revealed in the fellowship of his people as they minister spiritual gifts to one another (1 Cor. 12:7: Eph. 4:15–16) and embody truth in concrete form in their lives (2 Cor. 3:1–3; 1 Thess. 1:6–7), especially in the examples of Christian leaders (1 Cor. 11:1; Heb. 13:7).

God's truth revealed in the reality around us helps us to see and assimilate his truth revealed in the Word. Scripture tells us of the glory of God, including his mighty power and wisdom in nature. Gazing at the majesty of snowcapped mountains or meditating on the grandeur of a sunset increases our understanding of that glory and arouses our imagination toward the glory and beauty of the promised new creation. Trying to understand the complexity of a single cell or the staggering amount of information stored in human DNA or the vast expansiveness and mysteries of the unexplored galaxies within our universe causes us to wonder at the wisdom of the Creator.

And yet right here on planet earth we can fellowship with God through meditating on his Word and gain a sense of his love and peace. But experiencing that love through another believer amplifies it and causes us to grow not only in the reception of God's love, but in letting that love flow through us to others.

As we live surrounded by the truth of God revealed in his Word and work, we must remember that the lies of Satan and our world in its captivity to sin and its rebellion against God are also all about us. To use the metaphor of Proverbs, both woman wisdom and woman folly are speaking to our hearts. The one to which we attend, the one to which our heart is open, determines the nature of our heart and our life.

The First Requirement of Spiritual Transformation

Because God in his love shines his transforming truth into our world so we might come to him and live in fullness of life, heart change is possible for all who desire it. The crucial question facing each of us therefore is, do we really want to change?

Eve saw the forbidden fruit in the garden as something "delightful" and "desirable." So also sin has created in all of us desires for things that bring short-term satisfaction and pleasure but no ultimate fulfillment, no real life— things like material possessions, accomplishments, even the smug satisfaction of a good payback to someone who has hurt us. Do we truly want to change if it means changing the appetites we might have for the "passing pleasures of sin"?

No doubt everyone wishes at times that they were different. But many are insufficiently motivated to do anything to bring about change. If we are basically content with our thoughts, emotions, and actions the way they are, it is certain that there will be no change.

Change requires an openness to receive something beyond what I presently have. It involves a confession of my own inadequacy and a purposeful openness of my heart to receive what is needed for change. Only those who are "weary and heavy-laden"—those who are tired of their present life and long for a change—are invited by Jesus to come to him and find rest (Matt. 11:28). It is the "thirsty" who will be given drink (John 7:37; cf. Ps. 63:1).

Scripture repeatedly affirms that "the fear of the LORD is the beginning of wisdom" (Ps. 111:10; cf. Prov. 1:7; 9:10; 15:33; Job. 28:28). What this Scripture tells us is that wisdom—true life according to God's pattern—begins and is continually controlled by the fear of God, which is "that affectionate reverence by which the child of God bends himself humbly and carefully to his Father's law."[22] Stated another way, wisdom or spiritual transformation belongs to those who "glorify Him as God"—those who let God be God in their lives, who are ready for heart change in contrast to the pagans who refused to do so and consequently suffered with foolish, darkened hearts (Rom. 1:21).

The first activity in the change of our heart is therefore to open our heart to the transforming activity of God. Even this initial activity is dependent on the gracious activity of God who speaks his powerful Word and opens hearts. Thus we need to pray, "Lord, take away my appetites for the deceitful things of this world and give me an appetite for you and your truth." "Open my heart to your Word and give me ears to hear your voice speaking the life-changing truth." "Give me eyes to see you and your truth in all of creation around me and in the lives of your people." "Remove anything in me that hinders me from receiving your truth."

Along with our prayer, we have the responsibility of actively directing our hearts toward God, deliberately and consciously seeking to keep our heart open toward him, and exposing ourselves to all of the sources of his truth. Finally, as we will see in the next chapters, we must by his gracious Spirit use God's instructions that tell us how to incorporate that truth with its transforming power into the depths of our heart.

God is willing and able to change our heart and thus our life. No matter how old we are or how long we have been a believer, by God's grace we can be "renewed day by day" (2 Cor. 4:16). Growth rate will vary, but growth there will be if we sincerely desire it and are willing to open our self to the transforming grace of our Lord.

Questions for Thought

1. What does it mean that we "ultimately live according to the thought of our heart"? What scriptural teaching supports this principle of life? Does this concur with your thinking and experience? Do you believe that your emotions flow from your heart's thought? Give evidence.

2. Why do we as human beings need to listen to God's voice and receive his truth in order to live the life for which we were created? Do you believe that a person at any given time is living according to God's truth or Satan's lie?

3. Have you experienced any of the ways that helps us on our spiritual journey? Which ones have been most prominent to you?

4. Do you believe that when you read the Word of God you are encountering the living God himself? Has this been your experience in reading the Bible? Why or why not?

5. What is the first requirement from us if we truly desire to be transformed? How are you meeting this requirement?

■■ 8 ■■

Meditation (Part 1)

Getting God's Truth into Our Hearts

To know much and taste nothing—of what use is that?

BONAVENTURE

There is only one way of reading that is congruent with our Holy Scriptures, writing that trusts in the power of the words to penetrate our lives and create truth and beauty and goodness . . . . This is the kind of reading named by our ancestors as *lectio divina*, often translated "spiritual reading," reading that enters our souls as food enters our stomachs, spreads through our blood, and becomes holiness and love and wisdom.

EUGENE PETERSON

I know Christians who have gone to church all of their lives. They have heard hundreds of sermons, attended Sunday school classes, and home Bible studies. But you should see them in a church business meeting or during the week at their workplace. If God's Word really has the power to transform our life, why doesn't it work?" We wonder about these questions, sometimes even in relation to ourselves. Why is God's Word seemingly ineffective in bringing about change in so many lives, causing many to seek transformative experience through other means?

The answer lies in the biblical teaching that life is lived from the heart. *For the Word to have a transformative effect in our life, it must reach the depth of the heart and touch our whole person. Knowing it in our mind is not enough.*

We saw from Jesus' parable of the sower that the heart has layers or variations of depth.* God's Word—the seed—can rest on the surface of the heart or only

---

* See discussion in chapter 4 under "The Levels of the Heart in Spiritual Formation."

The Word Must Be Treasured in the Heart— Deeper Than the Intellect

The comment by Dietrich Bonhoeffer in his "Meditation on Psalm 119" (1939–40) on verse 11 is instructive concerning meditating on Scripture:

I do not treasure God's promise in my understanding but in my heart. It is not to be analysed by my intellect, but to be pondered in my heart. It is like the word of a dear friend which lives in my heart even when I do not think about it at all. . . . If I have God's Word only in my mind, then my mind will often be busy with other things and I will sin against God. Therefore, it is never sufficient simply to have read God's Word. It must penetrate deep within us, dwell in us, like the Holy of Holies in the Sanctuary, so that we do not sin in thought, word or deed. It is often better to read a little in the Scriptures and slowly, waiting until it has penetrated within us, than to know a great deal of God's Word but not to treasure it in our hearts.[1]

shallowly penetrate, soon to be lost without producing anything but disappointment. The problem is not with the Word but in penetrating the depth of our heart.

Spiritual transformation does indeed come from knowing God through his Word, but the knowledge is a personal experiential knowledge. It is a knowledge that knows the other person so intimately that the relationship actually impacts your life. It is a knowledge that involves our entire person—our mind, emotions, and actions. In short, it is a knowledge of the heart where these personal capacities are inseparably united as the source of our life.

But how do we gain this knowledge in which our mind, emotion, and actions work together to bring about a change of heart and life? In the previous chapter we saw that change begins with renewal of our mind. In this chapter and the next we will build on that and will explore how we change the thought and consequent emotions of the heart. How our will or action is involved in forming our heart will be the subject of chapter 10.

Meditation: The Key to Getting Truth into the Heart

If transformation requires God's truth to reach the heart and replace the lies that reside there, the crucial question is, How do I get that truth into the depth of my heart?

Reading the Bible is frequently mentioned as an important means of spiritual growth. In a number of texts, the Bible does encourage reading, especially public reading as all people did not have their own copies of Scripture as we can today (e.g., Col. 3:16).* Scripture also makes it clear, however, that transformation doesn't come simply through reading the Bible or hearing it read or even taught.

Change comes only when the truth of Scripture is truly heard in the biblical sense of "hear" or "heed." It's possible for us to hear truth, but not really *hear* it. Talking about some people of his day, Jesus said, "while hearing they do not hear." They hear with their ears, but do not "understand with their heart" (Matt. 13:13–15; cf. Mark 4:9, 23; Luke 8:8). The risen Christ's repeated exhortation to the churches implies the same truth that hearing must be more than hearing words—"He that has an ear, let him hear" (Rev. 2:7, 11, 17, 29; 3:6, 13, 22).

According to Scripture, the "hearing" that receives the Word of God into the heart does not come simply through reading or even studying the Word but through *meditating* on it. Unfortunately for many Christians the word *meditation* conjures up the recitation of mantras and other mystical practices often associated with Eastern religions. It is therefore to be avoided. But Scripture tells us again and again that meditation on God's truth is vital to spiritual life and health.

When Joshua was assigned the awesome task of leading the people of Israel, he not only had to step into the shoes of the great Moses who led God's people out of the slavery of Egypt; he also immediately faced the daunting challenge of leading the people in their conquest of the Promised Land. Just forty years earlier the people had refused to go into the land in fear of its great fortified cities and giants of people (Num. 13:25–14:10). These same cities and giants were still there.

Graciously, along with the mission, God also gave Joshua the key to its successful fulfillment. After encouraging him to "be strong and courageous" and promising to be with him and give him victory (Josh. 1:3–6), God told him, "Be careful to do according to all the law of which Moses My servant commanded you . . . so that you may have success wherever you go. This book of the law shall not depart from your mouth, but you shall meditate on it day and night, so that you may be careful to do according to all that is written in it; for then you will make your way prosperous, and then you will have success" (vv. 7–8).

The key to successfully fulfill your mission, God told Joshua, is to be "careful

---

* Examples of the public reading of Scripture are also found in Neh. 8:2; Luke 4:16; Acts 13:15; 1 Thess. 5:27; Rev. 1:3.

Real "Prosperity" and "Success"

The basic idea of the Hebrew word for "make . . . prosperous" (Josh. 1:8) is "to accomplish satisfactorily what is intended."[2] In the words of Johannes Pedersen, this word "designates the efficiency as an inner power to work in accordance with its nature, and at the same time success, prosperity and the carrying out of that for which one is disposed [i.e., one's intentions]."[3] The somewhat synonymous Hebrew term translated "have success" has the primary meaning "to have insight" (note the alternate translation, "act wisely," NASB, ESV). It refers to "the process of thinking through a complex arrangement of thoughts resulting in a wise dealing and use of good practical common sense" and therefore can also denote the resultant success or prosperity.[4] It denotes both the gaining understanding and wisdom and the success or prosperity that result from them—as one commentator translates it, "prudently prosperous."[5] Together these words describe the power, knowledge, and resultant success in life that God gives through absorbing his Word (of power and wisdom) into our lives through meditation.

to do according to all that is written" in the book of the Law. This is easy to understand and makes perfect sense to us—live obediently to God's Word and you will prosper. But the hard part and thus the real question is, How can we do this? How can we live in obedience to God's Word and as a consequence prosper in spiritual growth?

The answer to these all-important questions lies in God's further instructions: "This book of the law shall not depart from your mouth, but *you shall meditate* on it day and night, *so that* you may be careful to do." Successful doing or living is the result of meditating on the Word of God.

We find the same truth in the first psalm. Setting the tone for the entire book of Psalms, the writer of Psalm 1 describes the "blessed," or "happy," person who walks in "the way of righteousness" as one who avoids evil (v. 1) and lives a fruitful and prosperous life. He is "like a tree firmly planted by streams of water, which yields its fruit in its season and its leaf does not wither; and in whatever he does, he prospers" (v. 3).

How he comes to such a blessed and prosperous existence is revealed in verse 2: "His delight is in the law of the LORD, and in his law he *meditates* day and night." As with Joshua, successful living results from absorbing and assimilating God's Word into your heart and life through meditation. This principle is echoed throughout Scripture. Words denoting the concept or activity of meditating or meditation are found at least nineteen times in the Old Testament,[*]

---

[*] See Josh. 1:8; Job 15:4; Pss. 1:2; 19:14; 49:3; 63:6; 77:6, 12; 104:34; 119:15, 27; 48, 78, 97, 99, 148; 143:5; 145:5.

eight of which are in Psalm 119, which has well been described as the "'The Rich and Precious Jewel' of the Word."[6]

Meditation is also implied even when the term is not used. For example, along with the great commandment to love God "with all your heart and with all your soul and with all your might," God said, "these words, which I am commanding you today, shall be on your heart" (Deut. 6:5–6). He then goes on to explain how these words would come to be on their heart: "You shall teach them diligently to your sons and shall talk of them when you sit in your house and when you walk by the way and when you lie down and when you rise up. You shall bind them as a sign on your hand and they shall be as frontals on your forehead. You shall write them on the doorposts of your house and on your gates" (vv. 6–9; cf. 11:18–20). Through various means, God says, meditate on the words of the Law and they will come to dwell in your heart and in the hearts of your children.

The wisdom teacher in Proverbs also alludes to meditation when he says, "Bind . . . [the teaching] continually on your heart" (Prov. 6:20–21), "bind them around your neck, write them on the tablet of your heart" (3:1–3), "treasure my commandments within you" (2:1). The result of such actions, as the context shows in each of these instances, is a life of wisdom—a life that leads to the knowledge of God and his ways in successful blessed living (Prov. 2:1–11; 3:1–26; 4:4–9; 6:22–23). As Derek Kidner says, "The call to think hard about the will of God is not merely for the recluse, but is the secret of achieving anything worthwhile."[7]

The many commands throughout Scripture for us to *remember* God or his wondrous works also involve the concept of meditation. The psalmist declared, "I shall *remember* the deeds of the LORD; surely I will *remember* Your wonders of old. I will *meditate* on all Your work and muse on Your deeds" (Ps. 77:11–12). As the parallelism of the words "remember" and "mediate" in these verses indicates, to remember something involves meditating on it. When Jesus at the institution of the Lord's Supper commanded, "Do this in remembrance of Me" (Luke 22:19), he was instructing his disciples to meditate on him and his saving activity.[*]

These instructions on meditation—which as we will see continue in the New Testament, along with numerous biblical testimonies of its actual practice—make it abundantly clear that meditation on God's truth is vital for the life of

---

[*] In addition to the parallel between remembering and meditation, remembering is also found parallel to the expression "placing on the heart," which also suggests meditation ("placing on the heart" is the literal Hebrew wording in Isaiah 47:7 for "consider" and for "give . . . a thought" in Isaiah 57:11).

God's people. The vital place of meditation for the believer is seen in David's experience recorded in Psalm 63.

As the title of the psalm indicates, it took place "when he was in the wilderness of Judah"* —a dreary wasteland along the western shores of the Dead Sea, which David himself pictures as "a dry and weary land where there is no water" (v. 1). Because he was away from the comforts of royalty in Jerusalem, David could easily have found this physical environment alone depressing. But the reason for his being there was far worse than his bleak surroundings. Absalom, his son, had formed a conspiracy and was attempting to wrest the kingdom from him. It is difficult to conceive of more disheartening circumstances—fleeing for your life from your own son.

We can only imagine what thought might have been flooding David's mind in this situation. Perhaps he was laden with guilt, thinking, "God is punishing me for my sin." Perhaps he was angry at God for allowing this to happen to him, the anointed king. What happened to all of the great promises God had given to him? Or perhaps, he was simply stoically resigned to the situation in hopelessness.

But far from any of these negative thoughts and emotions, we find David's heart strong toward God. With his entire being ("soul" and "flesh") he declares his longing for the fellowship of his God (v. 1). His thoughts of happier experiences in the "sanctuary" in Jerusalem (v. 2) move him to praise the faithful love of God, which he testifies is better than life itself to him (vv. 3–5). Somehow in the midst of this dark disheartening situation, David can say, "My soul is satisfied as with a rich feast" (v. 5 NRSV).

How could David possibly respond this way? I would suggest that a critical part of the answer lies in the very next verse where he says, "When I remember You on my bed, I meditate on You in the night watches" (v. 6). Despite the bleakness of his situation both physically and psychologically, David had a vital relationship with his God and was fulfilled and satisfied in the Lord because he meditated on God and his wonderful works.

But what is meditation, and how does it work to bring about transformation in our lives?

What Does It Mean to Meditate?

Meditation in the Old Testament is expressed primarily through two interesting Hebrew words. The first word for "meditate" is *haghah*, which is the term

---

* This title actually appears in the Hebrew text.

used for David's meditation mentioned above. This verb and its related nouns are also used in Scripture to describe the cooing of doves (Isa. 38:14; 59:11), the growling of a lion over its prey (Isa. 31:4), moaning or sighing (Isa. 16:7; Ps. 90:9), the rumbling of thunder (Job 37:2), reverberating music (Ps. 92:3), and muttering or whispering (Isa. 8:19; Lam 3:62)—all of which suggest some form of repetitive action.

Haghah can refer to silent musing or pondering (Prov. 15:28; Ps. 19:14). But its basic idea seems to involve some kind of utterance such as muttering or whispering, like talking to oneself. It is interesting to note that along with telling Joshua to meditate, God also said, "Do not let this word depart from your mouth," suggesting that "this could indicate softly spoken oral recitation in connection with the study of the law."[8]

The emphasis of the word *haghah*, however, is not so much on speaking— there are other commonly used Hebrew terms used for speech—but rather on engaging in deep thought to the extent that it touches one's whole being.* As one Old Testament scholar explains, *haghah* "means that a man 'is lost in his religion,' that he is filled with thoughts of God's deeds or will."[9]

The other prominent Hebrew word for "meditation" is *siakh*, which has a similar meaning—rehearsing or going over something in one's mind, either outwardly talking or musing silently. This meaning is illustrated in the parallel questions of Proverbs 23:29: "Who has contentions? Who has complaining [*siakh*]?" Here *siakh* is used for repeated complaining or what we might call "nagging." Applied to meditation on God's Word, *siakh* refers to pondering on God's Word so that it dominates our mind and heart and becomes the perspective through which we view all of life and the world around us.†

Although the words *meditate* or *meditation* are not found in many modern translations of the New Testament (e.g., NASB, NIV), the concept is. Paul instructs the believers at Philippi to "dwell on" [*logizomai*] positive things— things that are "true," "honorable," "right," "pure," "lovely," and "of good repute" (Phil. 4:8 NKJV, "meditate on these things"). The Greek term simply means to "to give careful thought to a matter, *think (about), consider, ponder, let one's mind dwell on*" something.[10] By using it in the present tense, Paul is telling these believers to *think continually* about these things so their mind is saturated with them, with the result that they shape their life.

---

* References where various forms of *haghah* are used for meditation include: Josh. 1:8; Pss. 1:2; 5:1; 19:14; 49:3; 63:6; 77:12; 143:5.

† References where various forms of *siakh* and the related verb *suakh* are used for meditation include Gen. 24:63; Pss. 104:34; 119:15, 23, 48, 78, 97, 99, 148.

Again in Colossians 3:2, Paul says, "Set your mind [*phroneō*] on the things above," that is, on the realm of their new resurrection life, which should already impact their life. The Greek word means "to keep on giving serious consideration to something—'to ponder, to let one's mind dwell on, to keep thinking about, to fix one's attention on.'"[11]

Meditation in God's truth is also apparent in Paul's instructions to young Timothy concerning the Scriptures and his own teaching: "Take pains with these things; be absorbed in them" (1 Tim. 4:15), or as one commentator translated the verse, "Immerse yourself in them."[12] "Consider [or "reflect on," "contemplate"] what I say, for the Lord will give you understanding in everything" (2 Tim. 2:7).

To sum up the biblical teaching, we can say that meditation means to think, to think to yourself, even to talk to yourself, or sing, about some concept until it gets into your inner being and your behavior.

We have all practiced meditation without calling it such. When we learned a skill such as typing or driving a car—especially one with a stick shift, we began with much conscious thought. We focused intently to learn the keystrokes for different characters. We thought and practiced again and again how to release the clutch and press down on the accelerator in exactly the right synchronized motion. We repeated the actions sufficiently until our thoughts became part of our heart. Now we can type an email or drive to the store without consciously thinking about the motions. The thoughts have become part of our life; the knowledge has embedded in our mind and muscles.

Mindful Attention (Meditation?) Rewires the Brain

Interestingly, modern neuroscience through brain imaging is finding that mindful attention has powerful effects on the brain. Psychiatrist Jeffrey Schwartz, who has utilized this newly recognized phenomenon of the power of attentiveness on the brain with patients diagnosed with obsessive compulsive disorder, said concerning mindful awareness, "When you pay attention to something, the part of your brain that processes that something becomes more active." Furthermore "once you muster the appropriate focus, you can literally direct your brain to filter out . . . unwanted information." Such willed attention not only "redraws the contours of the mind," but "in so doing can rewire the circuits of the brain."[13] The import of this truth in relation to biblical meditation is evident in the words of neuroscientists Michael Merzenich and R. Christopher deCharms: "This leaves us with a clear physiological fact . . . . : moment by moment we choose and sculpt how our ever-changing minds will work, we choose who we will be the next moment in a very real sense, and these choices are left embossed in physical form on our material selves."[14]

Some years ago (before the breakup of the Soviet Union) I heard a sports psychologist discussing the practice of the East German luge riders in the Winter Olympic Games. Watching the games on TV, I had noticed that these luge competitors stopped at the top of the run, closed their eyes, and seemed to be in a kind of trance. What they were doing according to the psychologist was mentally going over the whole luge run visualizing every grade and turn in their mind. They were practicing the truth that psychologists have learned and which the Bible told us long ago—we get something into the depth of our being and consequently into our actions by continually thinking about it.

When Solomon asked God for wisdom, he literally asked for "a hearing heart." He wanted to hear God's words of wisdom so that he could rule the people with justice (1 Kings 3:9). Meditation is simply hearing God's Word and pondering—thinking about its meaning and import for our life. On occasion, we find the psalmist talking to his own soul (e.g., "Why are you in despair, O my soul? . . . Hope in God," Ps. 42:5; cf. 103:1–2).* In a very real sense our meditation functions as a teacher of our heart as we repeatedly think and ponder God's truth, even reiterating scriptural soliloquies such as Psalm 42:5 in our own voice. It is as God teaching a "hearing heart."

On What Should We Meditate?

Healthy spiritual life, like good mental health, requires living in touch with reality—if we get too far away from reality we may be institutionalized. But it must be God's reality—reality that is genuinely real and not the skewed, limited perspective of our own mind or the lies of our culture and the worldly system in which we find ourselves. Scripture richly prescribes the content for our meditation, which if followed will plant the understanding and living of God's reality into our hearts and lives. The benefit comes not from the practice of meditating itself. In various ways we meditate on many things. It has often been said, "If you know how to worry—think about negative things to the point of anxiousness— then you know how to meditate." So it is not meditation per se that changes us, but the content of our meditation—*the truth of God*—that brings life.

Meditating on God Himself

The primary focus of biblical meditation is on God himself. In the bleak Judean wilderness, David testified, "I meditate on You in the night watches" (Ps. 63:6). This must have been his common practice as he recalled his past

---

* See also Pss. 42:11, 43:5; 62:5; 104:1, 35; 146:1.

experiences of gazing on God's power and glory in the temple (v. 2). The truth that God is the one "in whom we live and move and exist," (Acts 17:29), the source of all that we are, should make him the supreme object of our thought. God, in fact, commands us to keep him in our minds. Declaring his superiority over all idols and false gods, God says, "Remember this, and be assured; recall it to mind [lit. heart] . . . . For I am God, there is no other; I am God and there is no one like Me" (Isa. 46:8–9).

To contemplate on our God so that the vision of him in all of his majestic unsearchable greatness and goodness is embedded in our heart is life changing.* To grasp the truth that God is present everywhere with unlimited knowledge and power—that there is nothing that he does not know or anything outside of his control—and that he is infinitely good and loving, is to find adequacy for our finiteness, strength for our frailties, peace from anxiety and guilt, and balm for all of our hurts.

To know our own heart as much as possible is vital in our spiritual growth, but to know God is primary. For, as Isaiah experienced, it is only when we see God as the awesome Holy One† that we see the truth about ourselves as woeful sinners desperately in need of salvation (Isa. 6:1–5). David saw both God's power and glory (v. 2) and the grace of his lovingkindness (v. 3).

Seeing the God of the Bible as a real living presence in our life also enables us to view our circumstances in their true reality. Focusing our mind only on our troubles or enemies causes them to grow all out of proportion with reality. But their seemingly awesome power is broken when we turn our gaze toward God. Remember the spies that Moses sent to reconnoiter the Promised Land, how they returned overwhelmed with fear. They had seen the walled cities "fortified to heaven" and the giant people of the land that made them and feel like "grasshoppers" in comparison (Deut. 1:28; Num. 13:31–33). Sadly their vision did not include the God in comparison to whom all of the inhabitants of the earth, including these giants, were "like grasshoppers" (Isa. 41:22). In contrast, Joshua and Caleb were ready to take the land, declaring, "The Lord is with us; do not fear them" (Num. 14:9).

Psalm 3, ascribed to David during his flight from Absalom (similar to Ps. 63),

---

* For a brief but excellent discussion on the mental health benefits of contemplating on some of the attributes of God, see Eric L. Johnson, "How God Is Good for the Soul," *Journal of Psychology and Christianity* 22, no. 1 (Spring 2003): 78–88.
† The "holiness" of God refers first to the truth that he is distinct from everything else, i.e., everything that is not divine. For Isaiah this also denoted God's otherness in sinless character, e.g., his absolute purity, uprightness, and truthfulness, etc.

is often described as a "morning prayer" because of the reference to awaking after sleep (Ps. 3:5). If such is the case, David seems to begin his day with disheartening thoughts of increasing adversaries and the painful comments of those who said, "There is no deliverance for him in God" (vv. 1–2). But then turning his thoughts to God, he exclaims, "But you, O LORD, are a shield about me, my glory, and the One who lifts my head" (v. 3). Often our day begins with a fresh awareness of our problems from which we were briefly relieved by sleep. Purposely turning our gaze toward God and contemplating the greatness of his reality and his everlasting love for us inevitably makes these threats to our peace take on a different size and hue.

Referring to another instance where David turned his thoughts from the terror of his enemies to focus on his God, Kidner vividly says, "David wrests the initiative from his enemies and deliberately turns in a new direction."[15] The writer of Psalm 119 similarly found encouragement and strength through meditation in response to attacks of his enemies (see vv. 23–24, 52, 78). So we also can wrest the initiative from our enemy who constantly seeks to defeat us through negative thoughts by deliberately turning our minds to our God and his gracious works on our behalf.

Meditation on God and his characteristics not only changes our perspective on life's circumstances; it transforms our heart. As the young Puritan preacher Henry Scougal wrote, "The true way to improve and ennoble our souls is by fixing our love on the divine perfections that we may have them always before us and derive an impression of them on ourselves, and *beholding with open face, as in a glass, the glory of the Lord, we may be changed into the same image, from glory to glory*."[16]

Meditating on the Works of God

David's meditation in Psalm 63 also included remembering how God had helped him personally in the past—"For You have been my help" (v. 7). He could think of the victory God gave him over Goliath when he was a youth, or the many times God had rescued him from the grasp of King Saul. He may have also thought of many less miraculous blessings such as the friendship of Jonathan and even the rebuke of the prophet Nathan that prompted him to acknowledge his sin and receive God's forgiveness and peace. God is at work in every believer's life providing grist for fruitful meditation.

David, no doubt, also thought of the great redemptive acts of God in the history of his people—how he freed them from slavery with awesome miraculous works as he guided them to the Promised Land, and how he continued to deliver them from their enemies.

Meditating on the works of God was a regular practice of God's people. The psalmists declare, "On the glorious splendor of Your majesty and on Your wonderful works, I will meditate" (Ps. 145:5). "I shall remember the deeds of the LORD; surely I will remember Your wonders of old. I will meditate on all Your work and muse on Your deeds" (Ps. 77:11–12).* Remembrance of the works of God was, in fact, commanded by God (Deut. 8:18),† because it was "forgetting" the deeds of God that resulted in Israel's sinful behavior in the wilderness (Ps. 78:11, 42).

Prolonged thought on God's works is also seen in the psalmist's declaration that the great works of God are "studied by all who delight in them" (Ps. 111:2) or as Peterson puts it in his paraphrase: "GOD's works are so great, worth a lifetime of study—endless enjoyment" (MSG).‡

Remembering God's great historical saving acts is far more than simply mentally recalling something buried in the past. *To remember* in biblical thought is to think and contemplate on something (i.e., taking it to heart) so that we have an active relationship with it. With reference to a past event, it means to bring the event into the present so that its original dynamic and vitality are experienced afresh in our present lives.§ As Old Testament scholar Brevard Childs explains, remembering "serves to actualize the past for a generation removed in time from those former events in order that they themselves can have an intimate encounter with the great acts of redemption. Remembrance equals participation."[17]

Such remembrance is illustrated in the incident of the widow of Zarephath blaming the prophet Elijah for the death of her son: "You have come to me to bring my iniquity to my remembrance and to put my son to death" (1 Kings 17:18). She was accusing Elijah of causing her past sin to be remembered, which brought it actively into the present with its punishment—the death of her son.

For us to remember God's historical redemptive acts is thus not only to

---

* See also Deut. 7:18; 8:2; 1 Chron. 16:12; Pss. 78:35; 111:4; 143:5, 7; Isa. 63:11.

† See also Deut. 32:7–8; 1 Chron. 16:12.

‡ The Hebrew term *darash* translated "study" (NASB) has the primary meaning of "seek" and is used in relation to God's people seeking him, his law, or an abstract idea such as justice, peace, good. The term suggests "research, investigation, study," "being occupied with" the object of the seeking. S. Wagner, "*darash*," *TDOT*, 3:298–99.

§ Of the Hebrew term *zakhar*, "to remember," Schottroff said it "connotes an active relationship to the obj[ect] of memory that exceeds a simple thought process. . . . Memory pertains to past events that the memory awakens to realization because of their present significance (Gen 42:9; Num. 11:5; 2 Kings 9:25), to places and objects to which the one remembering clings (Jer. 3:16; 17:2; Pss. 42:5, 7; 137:1, 6)." W. Schottroff, "*zkr* to remember," *TLOT*, 1:383–84. Similarly Eising said biblical remembering "denotes an active cognitive occupation with a person or situation. . . . Recollection concerns not only past events, but also the consequences their memory entails." Eising also cites from P. A. H. de Boer: "To speak of the past is to make it effectual, authoritative for today." H. Eising, "*zakhar*," *TDOT*, 4:66–68.

recognize that our own spiritual life is grounded in them, but to bring their saving significance and original dynamic into our present life. In the tradition of the Jewish Passover the head of the household takes bread in hand and recites a formula based on the explanation of Deuteronomy 16:3: "This is the bread of affliction which our fathers ate when they came out of Egypt." In this Passover remembrance, the historical bread of affliction is linked to the present bread allowing the participant to relive the original historical experience of Passover and make it his own. As the Jewish Passover tradition states: "In every generation a man must so regard himself as if he came forth himself out of Egypt."[18]

For Christians this remembrance includes God's wondrous works on behalf of his people in the history of the Old Testament, but most importantly his acts of final redemption for all people in Jesus, climaxing in the cross and resurrection. It was for this purpose that our Lord at the institution of his Supper instructed his disciples to "do this in remembrance of Me" (Luke 22:19). Jesus asks us to meditate on the meaning of the bread and the cup that symbolize his sacrifice for our salvation until the dynamic of his historical actions become present to us.

An old African American spiritual asks, "Were you there when they crucified my Lord? / Oh, sometimes it causes me to tremble, tremble, tremble. / Were you there when they crucified my Lord?" It goes on to ask in the same way, "Were you there when they nailed him to the cross? / . . . Were you there when they laid him in the tomb? / . . . Were you there when God raised him from the tomb?"[19] In asking us to remember him through the Lord's Supper, Jesus is telling us to be "there." To meditate on the meaning of the bread and cup until we experience afresh the reality of his saving power that frees us from the bondage of sin and gives us eternal life.

This biblical idea of remembrance relates not only to the past but also to "present realities that have a formative character for existence . . . or demand observation as an obligation."[20] God's truth present in his Word is to be remembered or made active in our lives (Rom. 15:15; 2 Peter 1:12).* Above all, the apostle proclaims: "Remember Jesus" (2 Tim. 2:8)—make the living Lord alive in your present life.

Along with the great saving actions Christ accomplished for us through the cross and his resurrection, we are to "know" through remembrance and meditation that which is true of us "in Christ." God calls us to know that our old

---

* See also 1 Cor. 4:17; 2 Tim. 2:14; 2 Peter 3:1–2; Jude 17. The gospel itself is the result of the Spirit's work of causing the disciples following Christ's resurrection to "remember" (i.e., to understand the significance of) the words of Jesus (John 14:26) and no doubt his works as well.

sin-enslaved self has died, and we are a new person with a new heart, free from sin's bondage so we no longer have to sin (Rom. 6:3–11). He wants us to know that our victorious Savior lives in us through the Spirit who dwells in our heart (Gal. 2:20). As the seventeenth-century Puritan preacher Jeremiah Burroughs reminds us, Christian believers' "sanctification comes not so much from their struggling, and endeavors, and vows, and resolutions, as it comes flowing to them from their union with him."[21] A vital means of appropriating this flow of transforming grace is through meditation on him and his saving work for us.

Scripture encourages us also to ponder the works of God in creation around us. Psalm 104 is essentially the meditation of one who has considered nature in all of its variety and dynamic in relation to the reality of God. The writer can only conclude with words of praise: "O LORD, how many are Your works! In wisdom You have made them all" (v. 24), and thus express his desire that this "meditation be pleasing to Him" (v. 34).

Most of us no longer share the same direct contact with nature experienced by the psalmist and those of his time. God's glory displayed in the heavens (Ps. 19:1) is often dimmed by earth's electric-powered or artificial lights. But photos of the stars taken by modern space explorers as well as new scientific knowledge of the amazing intricate designs of living cells provide us with new cause for meditation on the wondrous works of God.

Looking down on earth from 250,000 miles away, Frank Borman, the commander of the first space crew to travel beyond the earth's orbit, radioed back the message of Genesis 1:1: "In the beginning, God created the heavens and the earth." He later explained, "I had an enormous feeling that there had to be a power greater than any of us—that there was a God, that there was indeed a beginning."[22] God calls us all to take time to consider and meditate on the wonders of creation in all of its majesty, beauty, and mystery that we might come to know and stand in awe at the greatness of our God.

Meditating on God's Instructions

The revelation of God through all his works including his present activity in our lives and among his people is truly understood only in the context of God's historical saving actions—most importantly in the miraculous liberation of his people in the exodus and in the ultimate redemptive act of the cross and resurrection. Therefore, so that we might grasp our own participation in God's redemptive story and meditate on all of his works and words throughout history, God has given us the record of his historical saving acts in the Scriptures.

But Scripture is more than an historical record; it is instruction for life—the

Torah with a capital *T*. Because the Hebrew word *torah* is frequently used for the Law given through Moses at Sinai, we tend to think of it as "law." But the term *torah* has a much broader denotation than law.* The basic meaning of the word is "instruction" or "teaching."[23] In this more comprehensive sense, Torah as divine instruction encompasses all of God's revelation and can be a synonym for his Word. For example, to "walk in the *law* of the LORD (Ps. 119:1) is equivalent to "keeping . . . [one's way] according to Your word" (v. 9). All of the writings that make up the Psalms and the Prophets can be called "law" in this sense (John 10:34; 15:25; 1 Cor. 14:21).

Thus the Scriptures in all of their diversity—whether specific directives, wisdom teachings, prophetic messages, historical records, or theological discourses—are Torah. They are "the instruction which God gives to mankind as a guide to life,"[24] his "gracious gift which points out or shows the way through life's twisted highways and byways."[25] In sum, through his great historical acts of salvation God redeemed us from sin and death and gave us life. By his Word, the Scriptures, God explains these actions and instructs us on how to live that life.

It should not surprise us therefore to learn that the blessed life comes from knowing and obeying God's Word as Torah, and this comes from making it the object of our meditation and joy. According to Psalm 1 the "blessed" person finds "delight . . . in the law of the LORD" and meditates on it "day and night" (vv. 1–2). As Peter Craigie explains, "The prosperity and happiness of the righteous depends upon their finding 'delight' in the Lord's Torah. But how is such delight to be found? In practical terms, it is achieved by constant meditation upon the Torah (v. 2b), which is God's *instruction*."[26]

Several key Scriptures telling us of the blessing and success in life that flows from meditation on God's Word have already been mentioned at the beginning of this chapter (i.e., Josh. 1:7–8; Deut. 6:6–9, and Prov. 6:20–21. But this meditation on the Word is most fully described in Psalm 119 (see also Ps. 19:7–14). As in Psalm 1, Psalm 119 begins by declaring the blessedness of those who live according to the Word of God—those "who walk in the law of the LORD, . . . who observe His testimonies, . . . who seek Him with all their heart" (v. 1–2). The psalmist then proceeds to express his love and trust in God's law (*torah*),†

---

* In Judaism Torah has "a wide range of connotations, from Pentateuch (Torah par excellence) [i.e. the first five books of the Bible], to all divine revelation in biblical and postbiblical literature" (J. A. Sanders, "Torah," IDB [Supplementary volume, 1976], 909).

† Some eight synonyms are used for "law" (*torah*) in Psalm 119 (e.g., "testimonies," "precepts," "statutes," "ordinances," etc.), but they are all encompassed in the comprehensive use of law for the totality of God's instruction in this psalm.

extolling its virtue and supreme value, letting us know from A to Z that real life is found through incorporating God's Torah into life.

In the midst of this devotion to the Word of God, the psalmist mentions meditation at least eight times, along with related concepts such as "remembering" or "not forgetting" the Word. "I will meditate on Your precepts and regard Your ways. I shall delight in Your statutes: I shall not forget Your word" (vv. 15–16). "O how I love Your law! It is my meditation all the day. Your commandments make me wiser than my enemies, for they are ever mine [or "ever with me"]. I have more insight than all my teachers, for Your testimonies are my meditation" (vv. 97–99, see also vv. 23, 27, 48, 78, 148).*

Other Scriptures also encourage meditation on the law or instructions of God, some of which we have noted above (e.g., Josh. 1:7–8; Deut. 6: 6–9; 11:13, 18–22; Prov. 6:20–21).† Ultimately, all references to meditation on God's Word finally involve meditating on his Torah, as the apostle Paul told his young son in the faith, every part of Scripture—"all Scripture"—is intended for our instruction (2 Tim. 3:16).

For the psalmist, meditating on God's instruction—including the commandments—was far from the boring task that we sometimes find it. The Torah was his love and delight—"sweeter than honey to my mouth" (v. 103; cf. Ps. 19:10). By thinking hard and long on God's instructions he had come to understand and experience them as his guide and power for walking in the "way" of the wise life. This walk brought satisfaction because it was in harmony with God's created order for human life. Even as we find certain foods that "agree" with us, the psalmist found God's way congenial to the deepest desires of his heart, and through it he had come to experience something of God's promised shalom, the peace of well-being.

Meditating on Positive Things

When we focus our thoughts on God and his works and Word, we are practicing Paul's instruction to have our mind dwell on positive things, things that lift and inspire the mind and heart. "Finally, brethren, whatever is true, whatever is honorable, whatever is right, whatever is pure, whatever is lovely, whatever is

---

* The psalmist also no doubt is expressing his meditation when he says, "I seek your precepts" (v. 45, cf. v. 94), even as Ezra did earlier when he "set his heart to study [lit. seek] the law of the Lord" (Ezra 7:1). See footnote ‡ on page 158 for the meaning of the Hebrew term for "seek."
† The early chapters of Proverbs 1–7 are filled with exhortation to listen to and receive instructions through the teachings of father and mother, which are in truth God's wisdom (cf. 2:1 and 6).

of good repute, if there is any excellence and if anything worthy of praise, dwell on these things" (Phil. 4:8).

Of course, we must live in touch with all reality—the good and the bad. We have to give some thought to the negative circumstances of our life so that we understand them and respond accordingly. We need to acknowledge our own sins and think about their hurt to God and to others and deal with them in genuine repentance.

But for the believer in God's Word, there is no negative—not even the worst—for which there is not a positive that triumphs over it. When we are weighed down with guilt and shame, God invites us to meditate on the truth that "there is now no condemnation for those who are in Christ Jesus" (Rom. 8:1). Overwhelmed with fear, our hearts can be calmed by pondering God's promise: "Do not fear, for I am with you. Do not anxiously look about you for I am your God. I will strengthen you, surely I will help you, surely, I will uphold you with My righteous right hand" (Isa. 41:10).

When we are simply tired and stressed out, we can hear the words, "He gives strength to the weary, and to him who lacks might he increases power. . . . Those who wait for the LORD will gain new strength; they will mount up with wings like eagles, they will run and not get tired, they will walk and not become weary" (Isa. 40:29, 31). Or the words of our Lord, "Come unto Me all who are weary and heavy-laden, and I will give you rest" (Matt. 11:28).

The reality of evil is fully revealed throughout the Scriptures, climaxing in the cruel suffering and death of our Lord. But the overshadowing message is *gospel*—good news. Meditation on the Scriptures will enable us to face all of reality truthfully.

I remember vividly one December morning in 1991 receiving a phone call about 8:30 in the morning from the principal of the school where our youngest daughter was teaching. She informed my wife and me that Becky had been found by her teaching aid lying unconscious on the floor in her classroom. No students had arrived yet. The paramedics were there and still working to revive her, but she was not responding and thus the call. We were greatly concerned and began to pray, hopeful that she would respond. The school was some thirty miles away. After a short time we received another call letting us know that Becky still had not regained consciousness and that the paramedics had taken her to the hospital where they could continue to try to revive her.

When Nancy and I arrived at the hospital, hoping and praying all the way for her recovery, we were informed that she was gone. By that time we knew that this was a possibility, but to see her lifeless body on the gurney was devastating.

Her heart had failed, but no heart problems had ever shown up in medical exams or in her experience, and she had been very active in sports. Her sudden and unexpected passing was a shocking blow to us. As one of my colleagues put it, it's like being struck in the chest with a .45 caliber slug.

In the heaviness of my grief, I remember frequently retreating to my study and sitting in my reading chair with God's Word open usually to the Psalms. I found great comfort in the truth of the gospel that Becky was now with the Lord. Yes, from one perspective she had missed out on a great deal of life. She had been married for three years, but had no children at this point. Yet I was reminded that our Lord lived on this earth for only thirty some years, and we don't usually think that he missed out on life by going back to his heavenly Father in glory.

Meditating on the thought that Becky was now experiencing a fullness of life beyond anything that we here yet knew and that we would join her someday— all because of the reality of the gospel of Jesus—seemed to bring a certain joy. But beyond thinking of these particular truths, by faith I simply wanted to meet God, to see him in his Word, to be open to him so that he could come in and do what he knew I needed at the time—I figured that he knew what I needed better than I did. No matter how bitter the sorrow, there was always a sweetness from these times. I felt the arm of God buoying me up with a deep joy even in the midst of a sea of grief.

No matter what hard realities come in life, if we hear God's ultimate message, we will always end by dwelling on his triumph in Christ over all of the negatives we must endure. We will come to know and experience the reality of the apostle's words, "In all these things we overwhelmingly conquer through Him who loved us" (Rom. 8:37). The words of Charles Wesley's hymn "Thou Hidden Source of Calm Repose" will increasingly become our reality in life.

> Jesus, mine all in all thou art;
> My rest in toil, my ease in pain,
> The medicine of my broken heart,
> In war my peace, in loss my gain,
> My smile beneath the tyrant's frown,
> In shame my glory and my crown:
>
> In want my plentiful supply,
> In weakness my almighty pow'r,
> In bonds my perfect liberty,

My light in Satan's darkest hour,
My help and stay whene'er I call,
My life in death, my heav'n, my all.[27]

Meditating Prominently on the Gospel

When we mediate on truth, whether in creation or in his Word, we are opening our heart to all of his truth—his laws and instructions for life, our sinful condition, and his gracious saving actions of the gospel. No aspect of God's truth can be ignored.

But as the "gospel" (from the Greek word *euangelion* meaning "good message") dominates the biblical story, so the gospel must be foundational in our meditation. Christianity is not first and foremost biblical ethical and moral principles. It is the gospel of God's triumph over sin and all its destructive effects through Christ's death and resurrection, and our participation in this through our faith union with him. Thus our transformation rests on the gospel.

Referring to life-robbing fears, anger, and lack of self-control, Timothy Keller rightly says, "You cannot change such things through mere will-power, through learning Biblical principles and trying to carry them out. We can only change permanently as we take the gospel more deeply into our understanding and into our hearts. We must feed on the gospel, as it were, digesting it and making it part of ourselves. That is how we grow."[28] In his often-plain speaking, Martin Luther expressed the same opinion: "The truth of the Gospel is the principle article of all Christian doctrine. . . . Most necessary is it that we know this article well, teach it to others, and beat it into their heads continually."[29]

We grow through incorporating God's truth into our heart, and the foundational truth that needs to be "beat" into our hearts is the gospel—"the power of God for salvation" (Rom. 1:16). The words of Katherine Hankey's old hymn "Tell Me the Old, Old Story" capture our continual need to meditate on this truth:

Tell me the story slowly,
That I may take it in—
That wonderful redemption,
God's remedy for sin;
Tell me the story often,
For I forget so soon,
The "early dew" of morning
Has passed away at noon.[30]

Questions for Thought

1. Have you ever felt that the Word of God is not working in your life as the Bible says that it does? If so, what did you think was the reason? What do you think the reason is according to the Scripture? Can you think of an experience when the Word of God touched your whole person? What made it stick?

2. What is biblical meditation? How does it compare with other forms of meditation commonly recommended today? Taking the basic meaning of biblical meditation, do you think that everyone meditates on something? Are there things in your life that you have meditated on? As you think about the real nature of the things that you have meditated on, would you say that you meditate more on things that belong to God's truth or things that belong to the lies of the world? If worry is meditation, is God's truth involved in this kind of meditation?

3. We should acknowledge all reality, both good and evil. But what should be the focus of our meditation according to the Scriptures?

4. In order to experience triumph in the negative times of our life, during suffering of all kinds, what should be our focus in meditation? Have you ever tried to deliberately change from meditating on negative things to positive things? Did you succeed, and if so, what were the effects?

5. Do you believe that the good news of the gospel of salvation in Christ triumphs over all of the pain and suffering—the "bad news"—of life in this present world? Do you believe therefore that meditating on the gospel and all that Christ is to you can help you experience triumph over the suffering and pain that you experience in life? Why do you think that we don't do this more?

Meditation (Part 2)

How Meditation Transforms Us

I pray that the eyes of your heart may be enlightened, so that you may know . . . .

PAUL, THE APOSTLE

Now I saw, that the most important thing I had to do was to give myself to the reading of the Word of God and to meditation on it, that thus my heart might be comforted, encouraged, warned, reproved, instructed; and that thus, whilst meditating, my heart might be brought into experimental communion with the Lord.

GEORGE MÜLLER

In the prologue of *The Return of the Prodigal Son*, Henri Nouwen spoke of how he greatly anticipated seeing the Rembrandt painting that inspired his book. He had previously seen only copies of it, but at long last he finally came to the Hermitage in Saint Petersburg. Upon seeing the masterpiece, he said, "So there I was; facing the painting that had been on my mind and in my heart for nearly three years. I was stunned by its majestic beauty."[1] Nouwen gazed at the majestic painting—eight feet high and six feet wide—for more than four hours over several days, taking notes on its details, what the different light conditions reveal, what he heard from guides and tourists passing by, and what he described as "what I experienced in my innermost being as I became more and more part of the story that Jesus once told and Rembrandt once painted."[2] Nouwen admired that painting until it moved his emotions, and until it became a part of him and how he looked at others. To be sure, as he was leaving the museum, he wished to express his gratitude for putting up with his long stay there, so he went over and looked into the eyes of the young Russian guard and in those eyes he "saw a man like myself: afraid, but with a great desire to be forgiven."[3]

Nouwen's reflection on the story and the painting, *The Return of the Prodigal Son*, enriched his spiritual life, encouraged him in his difficult ministry, and even resulted in a book that has inspired many. This is the power of meditation. The same is true when we meditate on God's Word.

When we meditate on God's Word something does happen in our lives. But what is it that happens in such meditation? Exploring how meditation actually functions to transform our heart will be the subject of this chapter. We will also suggest some basic principles for its practice.

The Operation of Meditation

Looking again at David in Psalm 63 we notice that certain things happen in his life after he mentions meditating on God and his great works. He first experiences a change in his attitude or emotion, then an increase in faith, and, finally a fresh working of God in his life. These experiences of David, I would suggest, provide insight into the dynamic of meditation and its effects in our life. In a word, through meditation, we experience the presence and power of God.

A Change of Emotion

After declaring that he meditates on God and his works including his personal help, David exultantly exclaimed, "In the shadow of Your wings I sing for joy" (Ps. 63:6–7). His meditation affected his attitude. When we come to know something in our heart, that knowledge is "always accompanied by an emotional reaction"—either positive or negative.[4] The writer of Psalm 104 appears to share David's experience when he declares, "Let my meditation be pleasing to Him; as for me, I shall be glad in the LORD" (v. 34).

The "remembering" of God and his acts also produced changed emotions. Taunted and derided by his enemies and in danger for his life, the psalmist said, "I have remembered Your ordinances [i.e., your just judgments[*]] from of old . . . and comfort myself" (Ps. 119:52; cf. Pss. 42:6; 137:1, 6). The emotional effect of focusing on God's love and gracious acts is also evident in the psalmist's assertion:

---

* The Hebrew term *mishpat*, "ordinances," refers to the just judgments of God in terms of his laws, just decisions, or acts of just judgments. In this verse the emphasis is probably on the past saving judgments of God for the deliverance of his people. A. A. Anderson, *The Book of Psalms: Psalms 73–150*, New Century Bible Commentary (1972; repr., Grand Rapids: Eerdmans, 1992), 2:824.

It is good to give thanks to the Lord
And to sing praises to Your name, O Most High;
To declare Your lovingkindness in the morning
And Your faithfulness by night . . .
For You, O Lord have made me glad by what You have done,
I will sing for joy at the works of Your hands. (92:1–2, 4)

Numerous Scriptures also reflect the emotional power of God's Word. It "restores the soul," lifting the flagging spirit, and rejoicing the heart (Ps. 19:7–8). The writer of Psalm 119 can scarcely contain the delight and joy that he receives from God's Torah: "I have rejoiced in the way of Your testimonies, as much as in all riches . . . I shall delight in Your statutes" (vv. 14–16); "Your testimonies . . . are the joy of my heart" (v. 111, cf. vv. 24, 47, 77, 92, 143, 174).

Even more frequently the psalmist declares his love for the Word: "O how I love Your law! It is my meditation all day long" (v. 97, cf. vv. 47, 48, 113, 119, 127, 140, 159, 163, 165, 167). This love, as all biblical love, also included knowledge and the corresponding response—in this case, obedience to the instructions in God's revelation. But these expressions of the psalmist's love for God's Word cannot be read without hearing a strong emotion.

To be moved by the Word, we must also be moved toward it. And it is the Word that accomplishes both movements. We come to know God and his gracious love for us through the Word, and his love in turn woos us to respond in love. The growth of our responsive love, which is the essence of our spiritual growth, takes place through the same process. We love God more as we increasingly come to know and experience his loving heart and actions toward us through meditating on his Word.

This reality is much like the dynamic impact of a love letter (or email) from one's absent beloved. After eagerly reading the letter with a picture of the one we love in our mind (or on our screen), we reread it more slowly, probably more than once, until the next letter arrives. When the letter is not before us, we contemplate some of the things in it that particularly speak to our heart, lifting our soul with joy and delight.

The love that was already there is refreshed and enlarged as we hear the voice of our beloved again through the letter and come to know that one even better. In the case of God's letter (Scripture) he is actually present speaking his words of love through his Spirit to the heart of the believer so we might grow in our love for him and listen even more eagerly to his voice as we meditate on his words.

Commenting on the godly man whose "delight is in the law of the LORD" (Ps. 1:2), Martin Luther said, "It is the nature of all who love to chatter, sing, think, compose and frolic freely about what they love and to enjoy hearing about it. Therefore this lover, this blessed man, has his love, the Law of God, always *in his mouth, always in his heart and if possible always in his ear.*"[5]

Meditating on the truth of Scripture, of course, will at times produce negative emotions. Jesus himself was angry and sorrowed as he saw the evil and its effects around him (e.g., Mark 3:5; John 11:33). The more we are renewed in mind and heart and Christ is formed in us (Gal. 4:19), the more these same emotions should be felt in us as we look at reality through the truth of Scripture.

The revelation of our own sins by God's convicting voice as we meditate on his Word ought also to evoke a measure of hurt and sorrow. As the apostle Paul told the Corinthian believers who were made sorrowful by his rebuke for their sin, there is a "sorrow according to the will of God" that leads to genuine godly repentance (2 Cor. 7:7–10).

Even meditating on God, when we see no response to our cries for help, can produce painful emotions like that expressed by the psalmist: "In the day of my trouble I seek the Lord; in the night my hand is stretched out without wearying; . . . I think of God, and I moan; I meditate, and my spirit faints" (Ps. 77:2–3 NRSV).

But as Scripture's message is ultimately positive, so the emotions produced

Godly Sorrow versus Worldly Sorrow

Sorrow over our sin is normal for the Christian. In sinning we "grieve the Holy Spirit of God" (Eph. 4:30). And since the basic meaning of the Greek word translated "grieve" (*lypeō*) is "to cause pain,"[6] when we sin we hurt or give pain to God's Spirit or God himself. It is impossible not to feel bad when we hurt anyone whom we love. How much more when we hurt the One whom we know loves us and gave his precious Son to die as payment for our sins that we may have eternal life? Our sin should thus bring a "sorrow that is according to the will of God" and lead to repentance and salvation (2 Cor. 7:9–10; cf. also Ezekiel's prophecy of the negative feeling of repentant Israel as a result of their sin, 6:9; 16:61–63; 20:43; 36:31). But it is vital to distinguish godly sorrow from "the sorrow of the world" that leads to death (2 Cor. 7:10). Worldly sorrow focuses on self. To be sure, we may sorrow for the hurt we have brought on someone, but primarily worldly sorrow is because of the consequences to our self—self-accusation and guilt, a tarnished self-image bringing shame and self-hatred, and a spoiled reputation in the eyes of others. Godly sorrow, on the other hand, is experienced in relation to God, acknowledging our sin as first against him as well as against others, turning from it in repentance, and receiving his forgiveness and restoration with humble gladness. Such sorrow is God-willed for our spiritual growth.

through meditation on it are overwhelmingly positive. God's faithful presence and his continual working on our behalf for our final salvation triumph over all of the power and work of evil, including the sin in our own life. The depressed writer of Psalm 77, mentioned above, goes on to lift his heart in praise as he turns from staring at the darkness to "meditate" on the deeds of the Lord and "remember" his "wonders of old" (Ps. 77:11–20). There is always truth in Scripture to bring comfort and even joy in our most depressing times.

Meditation on God's Word thus means dwelling on it until it reaches our heart. There it touches our emotions, which in turn energize our beliefs to action. How meditation reaches our emotion is aptly described by seventeenth-century Puritan writer Richard Baxter in his work on heaven: "Meditation holds reason and faith to their work, and blows the fire until it thoroughly burns. Though a sudden occasional thought of heaven will not raise our affections to any spiritual heat, yet meditation can continue our thoughts till our hearts grow warm."[7]

The truth that transforms is thus not only heart-believed as we have seen earlier in our study, it must also be heartfelt truth. It is truth that is received into the whole person of our heart where our thought, emotions, and will combine in inseparable unity. Noting Psalms 1 and 119 as expressions of other Old Testament teaching, Gerhard von Rad concludes that the revelation of God's will in the Torah is to be "the subject of ceaseless meditation and ceaseless joy. Man is unremittingly busied with it alike in the sphere of his emotional life and in his mental capacities." The result is "a man whose spiritual life is completely filled by God's addressing him and who for his action too derives every power from the word of God: for where a man so lays himself open to 'the Torah,' all will be well."[8]

Unless God's truth touches our emotions, it will not change our lives. The great eighteenth-century American theologian Jonathan Edwards, in his work *Religious Affections*, rightly declared, "The Author of the human nature has not only given affections to men, but has made 'em [them] very much the spring of men's actions." He goes on to say this:

> Such is man's nature, that he is very inactive, any otherwise than he is influenced by some affection, either love or hatred, desire, hope, fear, or some other. These affections we see to be the springs that set men agoing, in all the affairs of life, and engage them in all their pursuits . . . . Take away all love and hatred, all hope and fear, all anger, zeal and affectionate desire, and the world would be, in a great measure, motionless

and dead; there would be no such thing as activity amongst mankind, or any earnest pursuit whatever.[9]

Failure to think about God's truth long enough—and in a way that illuminates meaning for us personally and actually affects our emotions—is no doubt a great reason for our failure to experience its transforming power. We simply don't receive it into our hearts. Edward's comment on people's failure to let the truth of the gospel and God's instruction reach their emotion is still valid today:

> They often hear these things, and yet remain as they were before, with no sensible alteration on them, either in heart or practice, because they are not affected with what they hear; and ever will be so till they are affected. I am bold to assert, that there never was any considerable change wrought in the mind or conversation [conduct or behavior] of any one person, by anything of a religious nature, that ever he read, heard or saw, that had not his affections moved.[10]

But why is it, as Edwards says, that the truth of God's Word often fails to touch our emotions and thus produces no change in our life? I would suggest that the answer lies in philosopher Martha Nussbaum's explanation that our emotions are tied to something that we deem valuable and important to us personally. They "have to do with me and my own, my plans, and goals, what is important in my own conception . . . of what it is for me to live well." *The intensity of the emotion* is therefore directly related to the degree of importance or value that I place on the object of my emotion. In Nussbaum's words, "*Differences of intensity . . . involve object-related intentionality* [i.e., what the emotions are

True Understanding Involves Affections

The great Puritan pastor Richard Baxter said of meditation, "It is not bare thinking that I mean, . . . but a business of higher and more excellent nature. When truth is apprehended only as truth, this is an unsavoury and loose apprehension; but when it is apprehended as good, as well as true, this is a fast and delightful apprehension. As a man is not so prone to live according to the truth he knows, except it do deeply affect him, so neither doth his soul enjoy its sweetness, except speculation [i.e., thinking] do pass to affection. The understanding is not the whole soul, and therefore cannot do the whole work. As God hath made several parts in man to perform their several offices for this nourishing and life, so hath he ordained the faculties of the soul to perform their several offices for his spiritual life."[11]

about]: they are explained by the importance with which I invest the object (or what befalls it) among my own goals and projects. If the importance is below a certain threshold, I will not have an emotion at all."[12]

The degree with which the truth of God touches our emotions and thus brings change in our life depends on how much we truly value that truth in relation to our personal life and well-being. This perhaps explains why a person who has been delivered from a reckless profligate life of sin that ended in despair and hopelessness often demonstrates more emotion in relation to his or her redemption and new life than the person who grew up in a Christian community and basically lived in outward conformity to that culture.

The truth is that God's salvation in Christ has delivered us all from a desperate plight—slavery to sin and its consequence of an eternity of eternal death apart from God—and made us his own sons and daughters with a new life of love, joy, and peace for which we were created. Meditation on the biblical picture of our natural heart, seeing who we were before God's gracious salvation no matter what our outward facade may have been, and then gazing at the God who loved us and in pure grace called us to himself and made us new person on the way to a glorious eternity should indeed touch us emotionally.

Augustine, the great fourth-century church father, saw emotions as the feet of the soul. On our journey they either lead us closer to God or farther from him, but without them we cannot travel the way at all.[13] Biblical meditation that makes the transformative power of the Scripture active in our lives is thus more than an intellectual understanding of its truth. There must be a dwelling on that truth—thinking, talking, singing about it—until it is known personally with the whole heart including our affections.

An Increase of Faith

Again in Psalm 63, we see that beyond changing David's emotions, meditation on God and his work goes on to strengthen his faith. After mentioning his joyful singing, David declared, "My soul clings to You" (Ps. 63:8). By remembering and contemplating God and his past help, David experiences the presence of God in the midst of his bleak situation.

Praise of God and his works often accompany the remembrance of God in the Scriptures. Thus David, along with his joyful singing—and no doubt its primary lyrics, declared, "My lips will praise You. . . . I will bless You as long as I live; I will lift up my hands in Your name" (Ps. 63:3–4). Similar are the words of another psalmist: "I will cause Your name to be remembered in all generations; therefore the peoples will give You thanks forever and ever" (Ps. 45:17).

Praise and thanksgiving are not only the result of meditation and remembrance, they are part of it. Just as we are commanded to remember God and his works, so we are called again and again to praise and thanksgiving (e.g., Pss. 135:1; 148; 150). "Hallelujah" [i.e., "praise the Lord"] occurs some twenty-four times in the Psalms.

The very act of praising God requires us to focus on who he really is and what he has done—all of the characteristics of his greatness and goodness, and his mighty acts in creation and redemption. The psalmist speaks of God as "enthroned upon the praises of Israel" (Ps. 22:3). Our praises are like the wings of the cherubim in the Holy of Holies of the temple upon which God's presence hovered in Israel.[14]

As David joyfully mediated on God and his works, the presence of God and his power become more real to him. His faith is bolstered so that he "clings" to his God even in the midst of painful circumstances and heartache. John Oswalt's words aptly describe David's experience and what is true for every believer: "What is the antidote to unbelief? Memory. . . . Remember those moments [God's great historical acts] . . . , for as you do, you will see reality. You will see God as he really is and know that you can entrust yourself to him."[15] Like Moses of whom it is said, "By faith he left Egypt, not fearing the wrath of the king; for he endured, as seeing Him who is unseen" (Heb. 11:27). Through meditation, David, living in the wilderness, gained the eyes of faith to see the reality of God's invisible realm in which he also lived.

The Working of God in Our Lives

Our faith opens our lives to God's working. Jesus told the two blind men as he healed them, "It shall be done to you according to your faith" (Matt. 9:29).* The greater our faith, the more we experience the working of his grace.† Thus, as a result of the meditation that energized his faith and caused him to cling to God, David experienced the present working of God in him—"your right hand upholds me" (Ps. 63:8).

Meditation thus brought more than a psychological experience of joy and bolstered confidence. It brought the powerful presence of an objective working of God's grace into David's open heart and life. As Psalm 112:7–8 describes it,

---

* See also Matt. 9:22; 15:28; Acts 3:16; 14:9.

† This is not to deny that our faith itself is due to the working of grace in our hearts (Eph. 2:8–10), nor to deny that even when our faith is weak, God continues to work in us toward our growth (Phil. 2:13). But Scripture also teaches that it is through our faith that God works in and through us. It was "by faith" that the heroes of Heb. 11 accomplished their feats (v. 33).

Faith Brings Firmness in Life

The powerful effect of faith in all situations of life is evident in Isaiah's statement to the unbelieving King Ahaz: "If you will not believe, you surely shall not last" (Isa. 7:9). There is a word play in this verse in that "believe" and "last" or "be established" are both from the same root word meaning "to be firm" (*'aman*). The translation could therefore read something like, "Unless you hold firm (in faith) you will not be made firm (in life)."[16] Faith in God is thus "a holding on to God through which man gains a firm hold for his life."[17]

"His heart is steadfast, trusting in the LORD, His heart is *upheld*, he will not fear" (cf. Ps. 28:7, "My heart trusts in Him and *I am helped*"; see also Isa. 26:3).

The realization of God's presence and work in our life changes things. Life is different. There is power to live, to grow spiritually, no matter what the circumstances. There may not always be outward joy. In all of our lives there will be times of sorrow and pain. But there is always the sustaining presence of God providing the deep inward joy and peace of our Lord that he promised to give us (John 15:11; 16:33).

In addition to changing us when we practice it, meditation also stores up God's truth in our heart for all of life. By talking to our heart in meditation, we are storing up truth that our heart can speak back to us. In his exhortation to young people to heed the commands and instructions of their parents, the writer of Proverbs says, "Bind them continually on your heart; Tie them around your neck. When you walk about, *they will guide you*; When you sleep, *they will watch over you*; and when you awake, *they will talk to you*" (Prov. 6:21–22). What we have bound on our heart through meditation will become the guide, protector, and counselor of our life.

The story is told of a woman who had been critically injured in an accident and lay semiconscious in the hospital for weeks. During that time she heard one of the hospital personnel refer to her as having only a short time to live. But she also heard at the same time other words speaking to her from her inner being: "I sought the LORD, and he answered me, and delivered me from all my fears." Years before, this lady had memorized these words from Psalm 34:4. Now in her dim awareness they came to her, giving her comfort and strength. After her recovery she looked back on these words as that which gave her the hope she needed in her battle for life.

Not only words of comfort and strength, but words of instruction and correction will also come to us through the Spirit because we have put them in our heart through meditation. As the psalmist testified, "Your word I have treasured in my heart, that I may not sin against You" (Ps. 119:11).

The Practice of Meditation

Biblical meditation, as we have seen, is essentially rehearsing, thinking about, and pondering the truth of God's Word until it reaches the depth of our heart and affects our lives. Some who have thought deeply on the subject add further insight into the nature of this type of meditation. According to seventeenth-century English Puritan William Bridge, meditation is "the vehement or intense application of the soul unto something, whereby a man's mind doth ponder, dwell and fix upon it, for his own profit and benefit."[18] A good brief definition of meditation is provided by Donald Whitney, a contemporary writer on the spiritual disciplines: "Deep thinking on the truths and spiritual realities revealed in Scripture for the purposes of understanding, application, and prayer."[19] Some additional helpful insights are found in Peter Toon's explanation of meditation as "a reasoned application of the mind to some supernatural truth in order to penetrate its meaning, love it and carry it into practice with the assistance of divine grace."[20]*

As for the actual practice of meditation, various suggestions have been offered, some more helpful than others.† In reality, it is not any particular technique that is important. But rather that we grasp and practice the fundamental elements of meditation so we are truly hearing and incorporating the truth of God's Word into our heart. The following are some general suggestions for attaining this goal.

+ *Pray that God will speak his life-giving Word into your life, that he would give you understanding and an open heart to receive what he desires to say to you at this point* (Ps. 119:18, 33–36).
+ *Deliberately open your heart.* To the best of your ability turn aside from distracting things and thoughts and focus on your relationship with the living God who still speaks his creative Word.

---

* Cf. also Campbell McAlpine's clear definition of meditation: "The practice of pondering, considering, and reflecting on verses of Scripture in total dependence on the Holy Spirit to give revelation of truth and meaning, and by obedient response and reception of that Word, having it imparted to the inner being." *Alone with God: A Manual of Biblical Meditation* (Minneapolis: Bethany House, 1982), 81.

† For an excellent discussion of the method (and benefits) of meditation, see Whitney, *Spiritual Disciplines for the Christian Life*, 43–59; see also Simon Chan, *Spiritual Theology: A Systematic Study of the Christian Life* (Downers Grove, IL: InterVarsity Press, 1998), 158–71; Richard J. Foster, with Kathryn A. Helmers, *Life with God: Reading the Bible for Spiritual Transformation* (New York: HarperCollins, 2008), especially chapter 4; McAlpine, *Alone with God*; Toon, *Meditating as a Christian*, and Peter Toon, *The Art of Meditating on Scripture: Understanding Your Faith, Renewing Your Mind, Knowing Your God* (Grand Rapids: Zondervan, 1993).

+ *Read the portion of Scripture slowly with a listening heart prayerfully asking the Spirit to speak his Word to you.* If you are open to him, he will speak. As a recent student of mine said in the opening of her report on a meditation assignment: "Wow, God's Word is powerful. While I was reading this passage slowly, my heart was penetrated by God's Word. These thirteen verses are packed with God's redemption plan, grace, hope, holy living and obedient life."

  God often speaks softly like the gentle blowing of God's presence with Elijah. He will not speak everything of his Word to you all at once. That would be overwhelming. Rather he will speak what he wants you to incorporate into your heart at this time, what he knows you can receive at this point in your spiritual life. Listening for God's voice shapes our life, which in turn aids our ability to hear more clearly.

+ *Understand the text.* Hearing God's Word for us today requires that we understand its meaning in its original context. Because it is the inspired record of God speaking to his people over a period of some 1,500 years, not everything is directly applicable to us today as it was to its original hearers. For example, God called Abraham to leave his home and kindred and go to another land. We are not all called to do the same today (although some may be called as missionaries). Nevertheless, God can use the truth of his historical instructions to Abraham to speak to you about leaving some things and pursuing others, or leaving some security and stepping out in another direction with the faith of Abraham. A good study Bible can be very helpful in understanding the original meaning and the meaning that is applicable to us personally.

  As we will see in chapter 11, our understanding of the text and its meaning for us is enhanced through various ministries of others in the community of believers, especially gifted teachers. What we hear from our pastors and other ministries of God's Word should also be something on which we meditate in addition to our own reading and studying of the Bible.

+ *Apply the truth to yourself personally.* Seek the meaning of the text for your own personal life, not just the meaning that it had for its original hearers. All of Scripture is given for our instruction (2 Tim. 3:16; see also Rom. 4:23; 1 Cor. 10:11). In God's Word to his people, there are always spiritual truths and principles that the Spirit can bring to your thought and make applicable to you personally.

◆ *Meditate or ponder on the word that God speaks to you.* Make it personal. Place your own name in the text where applicable. In Romans 5:5, for example, "The love of God has been poured out within our hearts" can be read "within *my* heart." See yourself in the text. See yourself in the place of the Virgin Mary as she responds to God's message through the angel that she is to bear his Son: "May it be done me according to your word." Envision yourself in the historical encounters with Jesus in the Gospels and the many word pictures of Scripture: "The Lord is *my* Shepherd. He makes *me* lie down in green pastures; He leads *me* beside quiet waters" (Ps. 23:1–2).

By spending time, repeatedly mulling over God's truth and seeking its varied application to our own life, we are allowing it to penetrate into our heart and interact with our thoughts, our memories, desires, and hopes, impacting them with God's truth and consequently diminishing the power of the lies that have been influencing our lives. We are allowing God's life-transforming Word to become his word for us, to become part of our heart and thus the issues of our life.

◆ *Respond to the truth you hear from God.* If we truly hear God's voice, we cannot but respond. If the truth that he speaks calls for praise, stop and praise him in word and/or in song. If it calls for confession and repentance, do so. If it calls for action, do it. Meditation, as Peter Toon writes, "is not speculative study of a truth from the Bible or a Creed but a pondering in faith of that truth with the aim of loving God and the neighbor: thus it includes the making of resolutions to put into practice what has been understood and felt."[21]

In the final analysis meditation is not complicated, requiring a certain schema. It is simply understanding and doing the essence of meditation. Dietrich Bonhoeffer, the German Christian leader and theologian who was noted for his meditation on Scripture, especially on the Psalms, captures meditation's heart in the following instruction:

> In the same way that the word of a person who is dear to me follows me throughout the day, so the Word of Scripture should resonate and work within me ceaselessly. . . . *Accept the Word of Scripture and ponder it in your heart as Mary did. That is all. That is meditation.* . . . Ask what it tells you! Then ponder this word in your heart at length, until it is entirely within you and has taken possession of you.[22]

Although time spent with the Scriptures in a deliberately focused, interactive relationship with God provides the foundation of the process, it is evident from Bonhoeffer's illustration of Mary that meditation does not only apply to a certain special time. The truth of God spoken to us through the Word should reverberate in our minds and hearts throughout the day. Even as the people of Israel were instructed to talk about God's Word when sitting in your house, when walking along the way, when laying down to sleep, and rising up (Deut. 6:7), so the truth that God has impressed on us through our special time with him that day, or any truth that comes to mind, can continue to be in our thoughts throughout the day, especially when we retire and get up to enjoy a new day with him. As Luther commented, "Learn this Word diligently and betimes. Hear God's Word often; do not go to bed, do not get up, without having spoken a beautiful passage—two, three, or four of them—to your heart."[23]

Our waking minds are always filled with some thought. For the believer who desires to grow in the knowledge of God and his kind of life, God's Word should have a prominent place in his or her thoughts.

The Absolute Necessity of Meditation

It is difficult to overemphasize the importance of meditation for the transformation of our lives. George Müller, remembered as one of the greatest men of faith and prayer, tells of the profound impact that meditation brought to his life and ministry. Müller ministered as a pastor, educator, and later as a missionary proclaiming the gospel around the world. He is best known, however, as the founder and director of a vast orphanage in Bristol, England, for which he never asked for support. Every need was supplied by God through faith and prayer. Although somewhat lengthy, this selection from a booklet Müller wrote about his experience is worth hearing for our own spiritual formation today.

> I saw more clearly than ever, that the first great and primary business to which I ought to attend every day was, to have my soul happy in the Lord. The first thing to be concerned about was not, how much I might serve the Lord, or how I might glorify the Lord; but how I might get my soul into a happy state, and how my inner man might be nourished. For I might seek to set the truth before the unconverted, I might seek to benefit believers, I might seek to relieve the distressed, I might in other ways seek to behave myself as it becomes a child of God in this world; and yet, not being happy in the Lord, and not being nourished

and strengthened in my inner man day by day, all this might not be attended to in a right spirit.

Before this time my practice had been at least for ten years previously . . . to give myself to prayer, after having dressed in the morning. *Now* I saw, that the most important thing I had to do was to give myself to the reading of the Word of God and to meditation on it, that thus my heart might be comforted, encouraged, warned, reproved, instructed; and that thus, whilst meditating, my heart might be brought into experimental communion with the Lord. . . .

. . . The first thing I did, after having asked in a few words the Lord's blessing upon His precious Word, was to begin to meditate on the Word of God, searching, as it were, into every verse, to get blessing out of it; not for the sake of the public ministry of the Word; not for the sake of preaching on what I had meditated upon; but for the sake of obtaining food for my own soul.

The result I have found to be almost invariably this, that after a very few minutes my soul has been led to confession, or to thanksgiving, or to intercession, or to supplication; so that though I did not, as it were, give myself to *prayer*, but to *meditation*, yet it turned almost immediately more or less into prayer. When thus I have been for a while making confession, or intercession, or supplication, or have given thanks, I go on to the next words or verse, turning all, as I go on, into prayer for myself and others, as the Word may lead to it; but still continually keeping before me, that food for my own soul is the object of meditation. The result of this is, that there is always a good deal of confession, thanksgiving, supplication, or intercession mingled with my meditation, and then my inner man almost invariably is even sensibly nourished and strengthened and that by breakfast time, with rare exceptions, I am in a peaceful if not happy state of heart.[24]

More recently, the importance of meditation for spiritual life was demonstrated through research conducted by the Christian psychiatrist Paul Meier. Working with seminary students Meier did a study in which he sought to find a correlation between a person's psychological state and spiritual life.[25] Each student was asked to complete a standard psychological test and a spiritual life questionnaire. Meier acknowledges that his first response to the results of his research was surprise and disappointment. The students who had been Christians for many years were only slightly healthier and happier than those that had just recently become Christians. The difference was not statistically significant. Obviously transformation was not simply a matter of time.

Disappointment, however, turned to joy when he found the crucial factor that made a difference—daily or almost daily meditation in the Scripture. All of the students who had meditated on Scripture daily or almost daily for three years or longer were in the two groups with the highest mental health and maturity—most in the top group. None of the students in the third or lowest group were presently meditating daily, although some were reading and studying the Scriptures for classes.

Several conclusions that Meier drew from his research are profoundly important for our spiritual transformation:

+ "Even though trusting Christ is all that is needed to obtain eternal life, experiencing the abundant life Christ promised (John 10:10) and experiencing the fruit of the Spirit (love, joy, peace) rather than bitterness, depression, and anxiety are dependent upon a renewing of the mind."
+ "Renewing of the mind is a continual process, a progressive sanctification requiring continual, preferably daily, input from God's Word."
+ Daily meditation on Scripture, with personal application, is the most effective means of obtaining personal joy, peace, and emotional maturity."
+ "On the average, it takes about three years of daily Scripture meditation to bring about enough change in a person's daily thought patterns and behavior to produce statistically superior mental health and happiness."[26]

Horatius Bonar, the great nineteenth-century Scottish hymn writer, captures the reality of transformation demonstrated in Meier's research when he says,

He that would be like Christ . . . must *study* him. We cannot make ourselves holy by merely *trying* to be so . . . . Men *try* to be holy, and they fail. They cannot by direct effort work themselves into holiness. They must gaze upon a holy object; and so be changed into its likeness "from glory to glory" (2 Corinthians 3:18). They must have a holy being for their bosom friend. Companionship with Jesus, like that of John, can alone make us to resemble either the disciple or the Master.

He that would be holy must steep himself in the Word, must bask in the sunshine which radiates from each page of revelation. . . . Exposing ourselves constantly to this light we become more thoroughly "children of light."[27]

Conclusion

The transformation of our heart and life comes through the presence of God and his truth in our heart. This takes place, according to Scripture, through meditation on the Word of God. If we are serious about spiritual growth and life change, we will regularly practice what earlier believers called *lectio divina*, the "divine reading" of the Bible—reading not solely for information but for transformation. We will not simply get into the Word. We will get the Word into us through meditation that touches our mind, emotion, and finally our will.

Lectio Divina

"In classic form, *lectio* comprises four elements, although there are many variations on them with different wording and emphasis: *lectio* (reading with a listening spirit), *meditation* (reflecting on what we are 'hearing'), *oratio* (praying in response to this hearing), and *contemplatio* (contemplating what we will carry forward into our lives [i.e., obeying])."[28]

It is a fundamental truth of Scripture that we live by the Word of God. We are born again by the Word, and we grow by the Word. The Word is the food of our soul. Like food for our bodies, we must eat the Word *and digest* it for it to have any benefit in our spiritual life. Meditation is the process by which we digest the Word, incorporating it into our hearts—the wellspring of our life.

It is not always easy to keep our minds focused on the things of God. Our spiritual enemy knows the importance of incorporating God's truth into our hearts, and he will do everything that he can to distract us and make meditation on Scripture difficult. But we can, by God's enablement, turn our thoughts to him in all situations. As John Calvin affirmed,

> The thoughts of the godly are never so stayed upon the word of God as not to be carried away at the first impulse to some allurements, and especially when dangers disquiet us, or when we are assailed with sore temptation, it is scarcely possible for us . . . not to be moved by the enticements presented to us, until our minds put a bridle upon themselves, and turn them back to God.[29]

May the psalmist's prayer be our own:

> Let the words of my mouth and the meditation of my heart
> be acceptable in Your sight,
> O LORD, my rock and my Redeemer. (Ps. 19:14)

Questions for Thought

1. From the example of David's meditation in Psalm 63, what happens in our life when we meditate? Have you experienced this effect through your times with God and his Word? How is this similar or different from your ordinary Bible study and prayer time? Is there anything that you need to do differently to practice biblical meditation?

2. Do you think that Bonhoeffer captured the essence of the practice of meditation when he simply said, "Accept the Word of Scripture and ponder it in your heart"?

3. Of the suggestions for the practice of meditation suggested in the chapter, which ones have challenged you the most to put into practice during your time with God and his Word?

4. From the analogy of taking in food to enhance the growth and health of the body, what place does meditation play in the process of receiving spiritual food for our transformation? How does this relate to the fact that we so often know more biblical truth than we practice in life?

■■ 10 ■■

Habits of the Heart

Changing Our Hearts through Action

"Everyone then who hears these words of mine and does them will be like a wise man who built his house on the rock. . . . And everyone who hears these words of mine and does not do them will be like a foolish man who built his house on the sand."

MATTHEW 7:24, 26 ESV

Man changes one way or another with all his actions and with all that happens to him: both these forms of the dynamism . . . make something of him and at the same time they, so to speak, make somebody of him.

KAROL WOJTYLA (JOHN PAUL II)

If I am not participating in the reality—the God reality, the creation/salvation/holiness reality—revealed in the Bible, not involved in . . . obedience . . . , I am probably not going to be much interested in reading about it—at least not for long.

EUGENE H. PETERSON

According to some social psychologists, "We are as likely to act ourselves into a way of thinking as to think ourselves into action."[1] If this is true, how does it harmonize with what we have seen both from Scripture and psychology that it is what we think or believe in the depth of our heart—how we really construe things—that determines our emotions, which in turn drive our conduct? How does it fit with the biblical teaching that our heart must be formed by the truth of our Creator in order to experience the true human life for which we were created?

The strong belief that it is God's truth that transforms our lives often leads us to emphasize biblical preaching and Bible studies, and well it should. But we may conclude from what we have seen of the primary sequence of thought → emotion → action, and the biblical teaching that transformation takes place by the renewing of our minds, that the flow of transforming activity is only uni-directional—from teaching to behavior. We may take the apostle's words "the goal of our instruction is love (1 Tim. 1:5)" to mean that we become more loving simply through more instruction.

Such thinking, however, overlooks a crucial element in the dynamic of heart transformation. Our actions are not only the result of the change of heart that has taken place through the change of our thought and emotion. Our actions contribute to heart change and, in fact, are necessary to it. This should not be surprising when we remember that in the depth of the heart, thought, emotion, and will are joined together in inseparable unity.[2] There is therefore, along with the primary flow noted above (thought → emotion → action) also a mutuality in which these personal activities all affect one another.

In this chapter we will see from scriptural teaching and human experience that our actions significantly impact our thinking and feeling and that what we do is therefore a vital aspect of our spiritual transformation and not merely the result of it.

Our Actions Affect Our Feeling

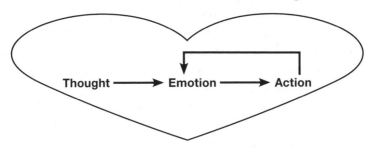

Thought ⟶ Emotion ⟶ Action

Human Experience

That our actions affect our emotions is recognized and utilized in our common experience. Deliberately putting a broad smile on our face really does soften and lift our spirit when are down. Whistling in the dark to bolster courage is an old adage because it works. Singing can help us feel good even as is suggested in the popular old song, "Singing in the Rain." Even a change of posture can affect our emotions. Walking at a quickened pace with shoulders back and head high, or sitting up straight, do invigorate our emotional state.

The reality that our actions affect our emotions is verified by social psychology research. Observers found that when some industrial workers were promoted to shop steward (a union position) and others to foreman (a company position), these different behaviors required of them in their new positions resulted in *new attitudes*. The ones who were promoted to shop stewards became more sympathetic toward the union, and those promoted to foremen more favorable toward the company.[3]

The same principle functions in morality. We may have strong feelings against certain actions, such as cheating. But if we can suppress these feelings enough to actually cheat (and get away with it), our original feelings will gradually subside. Our belief against cheating will also weaken since our feelings represent our thought. The observations of social psychologists on the effects of immoral acts lead to the conclusion that "evil acts not only reflect the self, they shape the self." The same principle, of course, would apply to good actions.[4] To deliberately engage in good actions that we don't really feel like doing will strengthen the emotions associated with that action and make it easier and easier to do.

Biblical Teaching

When we turn to the Scriptures, we find the interesting phenomenon that God commands us to have certain emotions. Again and again we are commanded to rejoice and be joyful—injunctions that unfortunately we often disobey. We are also told to love, to mourn, to have peace, and not be afraid or anxious—all of which involve emotions.

How can we obey these biblical commands, since it is impossible to change our emotions directly by commanding them to change? We can't say to ourselves, "self, be happy," and thereby become happy, or become calm when fearful simply by telling ourselves to be calm. Scripture's primary answer for changing emotion, as we have already seen, is that we do so by changing our thought or perspective regarding our situation. But Scripture also tells us that there is another avenue for changing emotions: through our actions.

Interestingly we find in Scripture that commands for particular emotions or attitudes are often connected with certain behavioral actions, suggesting that the emotions that are commanded are to be attained through certain actions.[5] The commands to love God and to love your neighbor as yourself provide an obvious example. Although emotional experience is the root meaning of the Old Testament term for "love" (*'ahav*), love also clearly entails "a conscious act in behalf of the person who is loved or the thing that is preferred."[6] The same is true of love throughout Scripture. To love someone is to have both certain emotions toward that person and to perform certain actions in relation to him or her. But again the emotion of love cannot be directly commanded. So how can we attain the emotional element of love?

We may, of course, arouse the emotion of love for someone by causing our mind to contemplate characteristics of that person that naturally evoke the feeling of love. We might stir up the emotion of love toward God by contemplating his abundant goodness toward us. We could think of the help that another person provided us in our time of need and as a result begin to experience a sense of love toward that person.

But Scripture tells us that we can also generate the emotion of love by overt actions that are part of love. Simply put, the doing of an action of love from our heart can incite the emotion of love in the heart.

To love our enemies by finding something in them that naturally stimulates loving affection toward them may be difficult (although we can always remember that they are bearers of God's image and he loves them). But significantly, Scripture joins the command to love our enemies with commands for behavioral actions toward them. Along with his command to "love your enemies," Jesus tells his disciples "do good to those who hate you, bless those who curse you, pray for those who mistreat you" (Luke 6:27–28; cf. Rom. 12:14).

God commanded his people to return the lost or stray animals of their enemy and to give aid to any helpless animal of the enemy that they came across (Exod. 23:4–5). They are also to give their enemies food and drink when they were hungry and thirsty (Prov. 25:21; Rom. 12:20). Although these last commands are not directly linked with verbal commands to love our enemies, their purpose is no doubt "to serve the practical inculcation of love for enemies, not being concerned directly with the disposition towards them, but making obligatory a specific line of conduct."[7]

In other words, these commands for acts of love are not directed immediately toward the emotion of love but to actions that belong to love. And since our emotion is connected to our will in the depth of our heart, a sincere volitional act will inevitably effect a change in our emotion. In short, the doing of a loving act from the heart incites the emotion of love in the heart.

In the story of *Fiddler on the Roof*, Tevye asks his wife, Golde, "Do you love me?" She responds with a very biblical answer: "For twenty five years I've washed your clothes, cooked your meals, cleaned your house, given you children, milked your cow." Acting toward another person is part of love, and in fact, as was no doubt true with Golde and Tevye, actions encourage the corresponding emotion.

C. S. Lewis expresses scriptural teaching when he said in *Mere Christianity*,

Though natural likings should normally be encouraged, it would be quite wrong to think that the way to become charitable is to sit trying to manufacture affectionate feelings. . . . The rule for all of us is perfectly simple. Do not waste time bothering whether you "love" your neighbor; act as if you did. As soon as we do this we find one of the great secrets. When you are behaving as if you loved someone, you will presently come to love him.[8]

The connection between action and emotion is even more explicit in relation to joy and grief. On one anniversary of the Feast of Trumpets when the people were weeping out of remorse over their sins, Nehemiah and others encouraged them saying, "This day is holy* to the LORD your God; do not mourn or weep. . . . Go, eat of the fat, drink of the sweet, and send portions to him who has nothing prepared . . . . The joy of the LORD is your strength" (Neh. 8:9–10). In response to this exhortation, we are told that the people went away "to eat, to drink, to send portions and to celebrate a great festival" (v. 12).

The phrase "to celebrate a great festival" is literally "to *make* a great joy [or gladness]." So also in 2 Chronicles 30:23, the statement "they celebrated the seven days with joy" is literally, "they made the seven days with joy." The emotion of sadness is similarly said to be "made" as in the report that Joseph "observed" [lit. made] seven days mourning for his father" (Gen. 50:10). This language of "making" or "doing" a joy or sadness clearly suggests that the command to have a certain emotion entailed some behavioral action. They were not only to think about these emotions, but to do something related to them.

The same concept is suggested by the frequent association of actions in relation to emotions even where there is no specific reference to *making* the emotion. For example, as in the Nehemiah reference above, joy is often associated with eating and drinking. Deuteronomy 12:5–7 states:

> But you shall seek the LORD at the place which the LORD your God will choose. . . . There you shall bring your burnt offerings, your sacrifices, your tithes, the contribution of your hand, your votive offerings, your freewill offerings, and the firstborn of your herd and of your flock. There also *you and your households shall eat before the Lord your God,*

---

* The day was the new moon of the seventh month, which was the New Year's Day of the civil calendar celebrated as the Feast of Trumpets (Num. 29:1–6), also known in modern times as Rosh Hashanah (lit. "head of the year").

and rejoice in all your undertakings in which the LORD your God has
blessed you.

The command to rejoice is obviously linked here to the offering of sacrifices
and other offerings. Burnt offerings, of course, were totally burnt up to the
Lord. But in the case of the other sacrifices, apart from the fat portions which
belonged to the Lord and certain portions for the priest, the rest of the sacrificial
animal went back to the person who brought the offering to share it with family
and friends. The rejoicing that the Lord called for therefore was to take place in
connection with a sacrificial feast (see also vv. 11–12).

Moses' instruction to the people just prior to their entrance into the Promised
Land provides another example. Telling them to build an altar on Mount Ebal,
Moses added, "You shall sacrifice peace offerings and *eat there, and rejoice* before
the LORD your God" (Deut. 27:7).*

Scripture also associates the emotion of joy with singing, dancing, and praising
God.† Nehemiah tells us that at the dedication of the city's walls the joy of Jerusalem was "heard from afar" (12:43). This most certainly entailed activity, and the
context speaks of singing to the accompaniment of musical instruments (v. 27).

The connection of joy and the action of praising God is especially prominent
in the Psalms. David declared, "I will be glad and exult in You; I will sing praise
to Your name, O Most High" (9:2). "Let them shout for joy and rejoice, who
favor my vindication; and let them say continually, 'The LORD be magnified'"
(35:27). "I will also praise You with a harp . . . ; to You I will sing praises with
the lyre. . . . My lips will shout for joy when I sing praises to You" (71:22–23).
Singing and shouting praises to our God inevitably lifts one's spirit.

Joy was also linked to anointing with oil. Scripture tells us that the coming
Messiah would anoint his people with the "oil of gladness" bringing an end to
their period of mourning (Isa. 61:3; cf. Ps. 45:7). This is more than a metaphor.
In the ancient biblical world scented oil was used to express festive joy. The
writer of Proverbs says, "Oil and perfume make the heart glad" (27:9; cf. Eccl.
9:8; Amos 6:6). During mourning, such anointing was suspended (2 Sam.
12:20–21; 14:2; cf. Dan. 10:3). Something of this same connection is still with
us in the delight of some women with a good fragrant perfume.

---

* For other instances where eating and joy are associated, see Deut. 14:26; 16:11, 14–15; 26:10–
11; 27:7; 2 Sam. 6:12; 1 Chron. 12:41; 2 Chron. 30:21, 23, 25; Ezra 6:22; Neh. 12:43; Esther
8:15–17; 9:17–19, 22; Joel 1:16.
† See Anderson, *A Time to Mourn, a Time to Dance*, 37–45. On dancing associated with
rejoicing, see Pss. 30:11; 87:7; 149:3; 150:4.

A joyful experience was also associated with the donning of certain clothing. Describing the end of his lament, the psalmist said, "You have turned for me my mourning into dancing; You have loosed my sackcloth and girded me with gladness" (30:11). Even as sackcloth was worn during mourning, so "gladness" here includes the festal apparel appropriate to this emotion.[9] Whether with school children or corporate executives, we know that the way one dresses impacts the way one feels.

In contrast to these actions related to joy, there are corresponding opposite actions connected with the experience of mourning. Where eating and drinking are connected with joy, fasting is associated with mourning. Mourning called for lamentation as opposed to singing and dancing in praise of God. Instead of donning festal clothing and anointing with oil in gladness, mourners put ashes or dust on their heads and wore sackcloth. Finally having sexual relations between spouses was associated with joy while abstinence was practiced in mourning.[10] Many of these corresponding actions are evident in the prophecy of the Messiah's work in bringing comfort to all who mourn. He will give "a garland instead of ashes, the oil of gladness instead of mourning, the mantle of praise instead of a spirit of fainting" (Isa. 61:3).

All of this demonstrates that emotion in Scripture is not simply an inner feeling; it is integrally related to action. Furthermore, the fact that emotions were often commanded and obligatory as in the case of rejoicing and mourning suggests that the relationship was not always from the inside out, that is, not always from the feeling to the action. The flow was also from the outside in. The action related to the emotion gave rise to the actual feeling of that emotion.

The reality that our actions affect our emotions might seem to contradict or at least seriously modify the fundamental relationship of thought $\rightarrow$ emotion $\rightarrow$ action that we saw earlier. However, an analysis of the place of thought, emotion, and action in the experience of acting to change our emotion, demonstrates that we are still functioning according to this underlying relationship.

In order for me to change my emotion by taking action I must first know the connection between action and emotion that we have seen, and believe it with my mind. I must also desire to perform the action for some reason that I hold with sufficient passion or emotion that actually moves me to act on my knowledge. For example, in the case of the people of Israel, although they may not have felt joyful, they could desire to obey God with a sufficient depth of passion to move them to obey his command to "do a joy." In this instance, most likely the feeling to please God would also be accompanied with some feeling of desire for the pleasure of joy.

Am I Inauthentic If I Do Something I Don't Feel Like Doing?

The argument is sometimes raised that to do something that we don't feel like doing is to be inauthentic or phony. But such is not the case, for even in this scenario the basic flow—thought → emotion → action—is still present. For example, our apathy toward obedience to God's commands (e.g., faithfully attending church) is always driven by some thought and emotion. For us to change these by taking actions, we must have other thoughts and emotions that override these. The overriding truth may be the command of God, the realization that not obeying will bring the chastisement of God, or we know that it is and has been good for us. No doubt we have all experienced this with exercising. We don't always feel like exercising, but we do so anyway because we realize its value and remember the consequences of not doing so. Thus, we force ourselves to put on the shoes and go out running or go to the gym.

Thus when we do something that we don't really feel like doing we are not inauthentic or phony. What we do is still finally the result of our strongest belief at the time and its accompanying emotion that enables our action. As Charles Taylor points out we may have a strong feeling with corresponding thought to act spitefully toward a person, yet we hold back on the basis of a moral assessment that spite is a base motivation. But such cognitive moral assessments are also "anchored in feelings, emotions, aspirations . . . and could not motivate us unless they were [so anchored in emotions]."[11]

In the end, while the emotion for obedience might be somewhat of a different emotion than the emotion that was prompting disobedience, we finally do feel like doing what we do. In all of this, especially the struggle of emotions, it is helpful to think about what thoughts (lies) are actually driving our apathy to obey. In the final analysis, it is the question of truth and lies about human reality.

Thus, even though a person was not presently experiencing the emotion of joy, the knowledge that doing something could enable them to experience joy and that their God had commanded them to do it would evoke emotions corresponding to these thoughts (but not yet joy). These thoughts with their emotion are then what drives them to actually do the action that would give rise to the experience of joy, like singing or praising God.

Our emotions play an immense role in our life. The experience of love, joy, and peace gives energy and zest for life. "A joyful heart is good medicine," says Proverbs 17:22. Experiencing grief and mourning helps us to know the reality of sin's hurt, enabling us to know with greater joy the greatness of God's redeeming love and grace that frees from sin's power.

God wants us not only to know his thoughts, but to experience his emotions—he even commands them. Thus in addition to changing our emotions by filling our minds with God's truth so that we view our circumstances through his eyes, God tells us to change our heart's emotions *through* actions.

It goes without saying that Scripture doesn't command us to perform all of the same emotion-related actions that were practiced in biblical times. We don't have to put ashes or dust on our head at a funeral. And we cannot rejoice with the same feasts related to the sacrifices of the old covenant now that Christ has given himself as the final sacrifice.

But many of the biblical practices or practices analogous to them are still pertinent to us. Who of us does not associate joy with feasting with family and friends? The believers in the New Testament churches commonly enjoyed a fellowship meal, often termed the agape (love) meal, in connection with partaking of the Lord's Supper (1 Cor. 11:20–34; Jude 12).

Various biblical postures of prayer still unite the body with the heart, thus strengthening the inner attitude. We feel a sense of humility and adoration when kneeling before God. Lifting one's hands in prayer extends the inner person toward God, energizing heartfelt praise (e.g., Pss. 63:4; 134:2), and—often with palms open—intensifies the longing of the heart in supplication and the anticipation of receiving his gracious response (e.g., Pss. 28:2; 88:9; Isa. 1:15; 1 Tim. 2:8).

The sacraments or ordinances of baptism and the Lord's Supper with their bodily actions impact and strengthen our emotions (and thoughts) related to the truths that these rites symbolize. Finally, we all know the feeling of joy and satisfaction that comes when we have been able to serve others in practical actions of love whether fellow believers or others in need. The underlying principle in all of this is that our external actions are united with the internal person of our heart. They *flow from* the emotion of our heart and *in turn have an effect upon* the heart's emotion.

It should be noted that any action that is designed to shape our emotions like those of our Lord must be done in relation to him. It is not enough simply to eat a hearty meal or have a party. As God's people ate the sacrificial meal with family and friends and rejoiced in the blessing of God, so our acts must be done in relation to God with the recognition that all of life and its bounty are from him. Moreover, while our action can certainly be done privately, much of the actions in Scripture were done before others—either in the general public as was no doubt true of the baptism of the three thousand at Pentecost or in the believing community. Acts before and with others tend to enhance the emotional impact of the action.[12]

Our Actions Affect Our Thought and Belief

Our actions not only impact our emotions, they also affect our thoughts and beliefs. Again this is seen both in Scripture and in our human experience. As we consider this relationship of actions to thoughts it will be evident that our emotion or attitude is also involved, demonstrating again the unity of our personal functions in our heart.

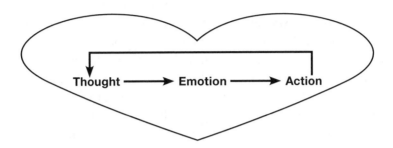

Human Experience

In light of the strong emphasis of Scripture on transformation through the reception of biblical truth, we might not want to go all the way with the psychologists cited earlier who say that we are as likely of changing our way of thinking through action as we are to change it through thought. But there is much evidence indicating that our behavior does affect our beliefs and attitudes.[13] One explanation for this dynamic is that our intentional actions cause us to construe the situation in terms or our actions. For example, if we deliberately stir up a feeling of grief by weeping, this action of weeping will cause us to think of our situation in grief-terms.[14]

Psychologist Roger Brown explained this further in terms of how we can be changed through living out a new role:

> In the playing of roles in society I think we function . . . first with conscious technique, later living the part. Try to remember a time when you had newly assumed some role that made a sharp break with your previous life. The first days of the freshman year in college or the first days in the Army will serve. At such times one is keenly alert to a new set of prescription and one tries to learn them and to satisfy them. The talk of college students or soldiers, their routine, their tastes and values are alien at first. You can still distinguish between that which is really you and that which you have undertaken to become. There is a feeling of "walking through the part," but this usually passes and one becomes a student or a soldier. . . . Important roles leave a residue in the personality, indeed personality is largely an integration of all the roles that have been played.[15]

This transforming effect of acting out a role is confirmed by evidence. Researchers found that young women smokers who played an emotional role in the life of a lung cancer victim reduced their smoking more than those who were simply given information about the hazards of smoking. The claim of the Marines to "make a man out of you" is not accomplished essentially by intellectual study, but "by active practice of the new role requirements."[16]

Experiments show that when people willingly and freely commit themselves to a public action, they come to believe more strongly in that action. California housewives, for example, were more apt to allow a large ugly "Drive Carefully" sign to be placed in their front yard if they had first been asked to sign a safe driving petition.

The same principle applies to morality. Our actions in relation to good or evil influence our moral beliefs and attitudes. When older children are asked to teach or enforce moral behavior in younger children they themselves follow that behavior more than if they are simply taught the same moral behavior. The savage harshness of war sometimes makes soldiers capable of committing cruel acts on an enemy that their prior beliefs would never have allowed them to do.

These psychological studies and experiments tell us that our actions not only reflect the thought and emotion of our heart, they shape the heart. As John Paul II explained in his encyclical *Veritatis Splendor*, our moral actions do not simply produce a change outside of us. Rather, "to the extent that they are deliberate choices, they give moral definition to the very person who performs them, determining his *profound spiritual traits*." In this John Paul II is echoing the fourth-century church Father, Gregory of Nyssa, who in noting that our human life is constantly subject to change that occurs through free choice concludes, "Thus *we are* in a certain way our own parents, creating ourselves as we will, by our decisions."[17]

Willful deliberate action is therefore necessary for spiritual growth. As James Burtchaell explains, "People have somehow got it into their heads that the evil in their lives will evaporate at will. But we are born in selfishness and nurture that infection within us by years and years of action for our own convenience. The way to purge the evil of years of action is by action."[18]

Biblical Teaching

The reality that our actions affect our thoughts is also taught in Scripture. A number of significant biblical words combine both thought and act, clearly indicating that the two functions are united and mutually affect each other. We also find explicit teaching of this relation between our actions and thoughts.

Biblical Words That Include Thought and Act

The most significant meaning of the word "know" in Scripture is not objective knowledge but rather experiential knowledge. In this full biblical sense of knowing, I can know a great deal about a person, but unless I have a personal relationship with that person so that he or she actually impacts my own experience in some way, I do not really know that person.

This kind of knowledge is not only thoughts in the mind, but thoughts embodied in the whole person. It has been likened to the knowledge of a typist, which is not simply a theoretical knowledge of the keyboard but a knowledge embodied in the typist's hands and fingers as well. As Bruce Waltke explains, in the knowledge of God "the notions of cognitive response to his revelation and existential intimacy and obedience are inseparable."[19] As a result, "the person who does not act in accordance with what God has done or plans to do has but a fragmentary knowledge [of him]."[20]

Yale University Old Testament theologian Brevard Childs similarly said, "To know God is to know his will. In the Old Testament to know God is not a mystical experience or merely an inter-personal relationship. Nor is it a feeling of spirituality. Rather, the knowledge of God is defined throughout as obedience to his will which has a content."[21]

The profound connection between thought and action is seen also in biblical wisdom. Waltke's explanation of wisdom in Proverbs is true of all biblical wisdom.

> In Proverbs *hokma* [wisdom] mostly denotes mastery over experience through the intellectual, emotional, and spiritual state of knowing existentially the deed-destiny nexus—that is, to act on moral-spiritual knowledge out of its internalization . . . , thereby enabling its possessor to cope with enigma and adversity, to tear down strongholds, and thus to promote the life of an individual and/or community.[22]

Biblical wisdom is thus not—as we often surmise—profound deep thought but the combination of internalized knowledge along with its emotional element acted out in experience.*

The Hebrew verb "to learn" or "to instruct" (*lamad*), also joins intellect and action. Its underlying meaning is "have experiences" or "accustom oneself to

---

* See also Georg Fohrer's definition of *wisdom*: "The reference [wisdom] is to prudent, considered, experienced, and competent action to subjugate the world and to master the various problems of life and life itself." "*sophia*," *TDNT*, 7:476.

something."[23] This active behavioral dimension of learning is evident in its use for training one's hands in the use of a bow for battle (2 Sam. 22:35) or taming an unbroken calf (Hos. 10:11).

Other words that we might think refer only to the intellect also contain something of the will. When the apostle says "set your mind on things above" (Col. 3:2), he uses the verb *phroneō*, which signifies both thought and movement of the will—"both interest and decision at the same time."[24] The same is true of the verb *logizomai* translated "dwell on" in the exhortation "let your mind dwell on these things" (Phil. 4:8). The idea is both "thoughtful contemplation" and "an admonition to action," exhorting us to make what our mind thinks about part of our life.[25]

Most significantly, all of our personal functions—mind, emotion, and will—are joined in the word that should most characterize us as followers of Jesus—*love*. Previously we saw the connection of action and emotion in love—how loving acts can induce loving feelings. Here we will simply note that love requires the union of all of the dimensions of the heart including the will. If I love someone, I obviously hold thoughts about them. Moreover, to love with genuine biblical love requires that I hear God's words concerning the nature of such love with understanding.

But love is more than thought. It's a strong unifying power with a passionate desire that impels the lover to be close to the object of love. The one who loves someone or something cleaves to that person or thing (Deut. 11:22; 30:20; Prov. 18:24; cf. 1 Kings 11:2), runs or goes after him (Isa. 1:23; Jer. 2:2), or seeks him (Prov. 8:17; Pss. 4:2; 40:16). Love also has "a strikingly pragmatic character" that produces benevolent actions toward the object of love (Jer. 31:3; Hos. 11:4).[26] Thus love, as the sum of all of God's commandments, is a single reality composed of thought, emotion, and action in mutual interaction.

Biblical Teaching on the Effect of Action on Thought

In addition to words that join thought and action, Scripture directly teaches that our actions affect our thoughts. Knowledge of God's truth obviously begins with thought as we hear his Word. But according to Scripture we don't really know God's truth without doing it. As Calvin put it, "all right knowledge of God is born of obedience."[27]

This truth is clear in the apostle's prayer request for the Colossian believers: "that you may be filled with the knowledge of his will in all spiritual wisdom and understanding, so that you will walk in a manner worthy of the Lord, to please Him in all respects, bearing fruit in every good work and increasing in the knowledge of God" (Col. 1:9–10). The apostle desired that these believers be filled with an initial knowledge that would lead to the activity of "bearing fruit in every good work," which in turn would lead them to "increasing in the knowledge of God."*

The knowledge of God, which is the essence of our spiritual life and growth, thus entails intellect and action. It "ensues from risking oneself to obey the specific teaching that pertains to all sorts of human behavior in full reliance on God to keep his promises coupled with them."[28]

The intertwining of thought and action is also evident in the biblical teaching that we are to *do* truth and *walk* in it (John 3:21; 1 John 1:6; 2 John 4; 3 John 3–4). Jesus said, "He who *practices* the truth comes to the Light" (John 3:21). Practicing the truth enables us to understand it and be further drawn to it, even as Jesus also declared, "If any man is willing to do His will, he shall know of the teaching" (John 7:17). Likewise "ignorance" and a darkened "understanding" is due to "hardness of . . . heart" or willful refusal to walk in truth (Eph. 4:17–19).

The interplay between knowledge and action is also involved in gaining wisdom, that is, experientially living God's pattern for human life. The "fear of God," Scripture says, is the beginning and first principle (foundation)[29] of wisdom, or as Bruce Waltke explains, "What the alphabet is to reading, notes to reading music, and numerals to mathematics, the fear of the LORD is to attaining the revealed knowledge of this book [Proverbs]"[30] (See Ps. 111:10; Prov. 9:10).

Now we may understand this as simply saying that wisdom or successful living results from fearing God or acknowledging him with reverential awe. But the "fear of God" itself is more than knowledge and reverence. It includes a life of active obedience to God's instructions.

Israel's king was commanded to read God's Law so "that he may learn to fear the LORD his God, *by carefully observing* all the words of this law and these statutes" (Deut. 17:19; cf. 31:12–13). Thus we see that doing—living wisely—does not only flow from the fear of the Lord; doing contributes to that fear.

After declaring that "the fear of the LORD is the beginning of wisdom," the psalmist added, "A good understanding have all those who do His commandments" (Ps. 111:10). In the words of one commentator, the psalmist tells us that "he who practices the fear of Yahweh as practical piety [i.e., wisdom] . . . has valuable insight . . . , so that the most important knowledge of life is attained

---

* The same truth that activity leads to knowledge is seen in Paul's prayer for Philemon: "I pray that the sharing of your faith may become effective for the full knowledge of every good thing that is in us for the sake of Christ" (v. 6 ESV); cf. Peter T. O'Brien's translation: "I pray that your generosity, which arises from your faith, may lead you effectively into a deeper understanding and experience of every blessing which belongs to us as fellow-members of the body of Christ." *Colossians, Philemon*, WBC 44 (Waco: Word Books, 1982), 275.

The Fear of the Lord and Living Righteously

The connection between the fear of the Lord and righteous living, making them virtually synonymous, is evident in several biblical texts as the following examples indicate:

"So you shall not wrong one another, but you shall fear your God; for I am the LORD your God." (Lev. 25:17, 36; cf. 19:14, 32)

"If you are not careful to observe all the words of this law which are written in this book, to fear this honored and awesome name, the LORD your God." (Deut. 28:58)

"He who rules over men righteously, who rules in the fear of God." (2 Sam. 23:3)

"You have given me the inheritance of those who fear Your name." (Ps. 61:5)[*]

---

[*] For a good discussion of the fear of the Lord showing that it combines both the nonrational numinous emotional fear and the cognitive dimension of knowing and obeying God's will, see Bruce K. Waltke, "The Fear of the Lord: The Foundation for a Relationship with God," in *Alive to God: Studies in Spirituality Presented to James Houston*, ed. J. I. Packer and Loren Wilkinson (Downers Grove, IL: InterVarsity Press, 1992), 17–33.

---

in the sphere of right action rather than in that of the cultus [i.e., external religious practices] or of thought."[31] Psalm 119:100 expresses the same reality: "I have more understanding than the elders, for I obey your precepts" (NIV). Leslie Allen aptly remarks on this verse, "The secret of human understanding of [the Torah] is practical obedience."[32]

David Williams echoes these thoughts when he reminds us that real knowledge is not simply the *mirroring of reality* in conceptual thoughts in our mind; it entails our *participating in reality* through actions.[33] In other words, to truly know something, we must not only know it intellectually, we must act on that knowledge or live it out practically in our lives.

Not only our knowledge but our faith, which surely includes thought, is also impacted by our actions. James tells us that when Abraham offered his son Isaac on the altar, "his faith and actions were working together, and *his faith was made complete by what he did*" (2:22 NIV). We tend to think of faith as producing works—as Paul expresses it, "faith working through love" (Gal. 5:6; 1 Thess. 1:3). But James tells us that the relationship between faith and actions goes both ways—faith produces works (2:17, 20) and works "complete" or "perfect" faith (v. 22).

By saying that works "complete" faith, James does not mean that what we do adds something to an incomplete or defective faith as if some part of our faith is missing and works add that part. Nor is he saying that works simply

Our Actions Change Our Heart

According to philosopher Robert C. Roberts, the truth that actions effect change in our life including thought and perception is also entailed in the apostle Paul's exhortations for us to "walk" according to our new life. Walking, Roberts says, "suggests that one way to get into the new self and out of the old is just to start performing the kind of actions, or emitting the kind of behaviors, that are characteristic of the new self. . . . It seems to be common wisdom that changed behavior sometimes leads to changed perceptions, changed patterns of thinking and changed desires and emotions. Significant and deep-going changes in life and personality may be precipitated in this way."[34]

demonstrate faith. The idea is rather that our actions cause our faith to grow, to be strengthened and matured.[35] All faith is born complete in the sense of having all of its parts like a healthy baby. But also like a baby, newborn faith is immature and needs to grow. James is simply teaching that actions done in faith have a maturing and strengthening effect on that faith.

This maturing of faith relates not only to the elements of will and emotion that are part of faith, but also faith's intellectual component. By exercising our faith we grow in the understanding of God and his activity or deepen the conviction of our present understanding. We can only imagine the maturing effect on Abraham's faith that resulted from his actions of faith in taking the steps toward sacrificing his son Isaac. The exercise of faith in Peter when he let go of the boat to walk on the water no doubt also matured his faith in many ways.

Finally, our knowledge of love comes from practicing love. The apostle John said, "And we have come to know and have believed the love which God has for us" (1 John 4:16). More literally, John says that we have come to know "the love which God has *in* us."* The apostle is not thinking merely "of the love for us shown by God in the cross but also of the personal experience of his love in our hearts."[36] In other words, we know God's love because it is operating in us—in our experience of love. As John continues to say, "God is love and the one who abides in love abides in God, and God abides in him. . . . If someone says, 'I love God,' and hates his brother, he is a liar; for the one who does not love his brother . . . cannot love God" (1 John 4:16, 20). All of this is to say that our knowledge of God and his love is inherently connected with actively loving.

---

* The comment on this verse in the NET Bible argues that the apostle John is emphasizing interiority here, i.e., God's love is "in us," and not simply that God has done something for us. The only other uses of the same verb "has" (*echō*) and preposition "in" (*en*) in 1 John (3:15; 5:10) both mean something *in* someone (see 1 John 4:16a NET, translator note 40, https://net.bible .org/#!bible/1+John+4).

It is meaningful that the exhortation to "watch over your heart with all dili-gence" in Proverbs 4:23 is connected not only to the previous verses that tell us to hear and keep God's words in our heart (vv. 20–22), but also to the following verses that instruct us on the practical conduct of life—what we say, what we look at, and where we go (vv. 24–27).

Attending to our heart so that it grows in likeness to our Lord requires both taking in God's Word and living it out in practical life. What Derek Kidner says in connection to our speech applies to all of our actions: "*Superficial habits* of talk react on the mind [i.e., heart]; so that cynical chatter, fashionable grumbles, flippancy, half-truths, barely meant in the first place, *harden into well-established habits of thought.*"[37]

Heart Transformation Requires Putting God's Truth into Action

If our actions affect our emotions and thought, as we have seen both from Scripture and our experience, then it follows that action is vital to heart trans-formation. Change of intellect and emotion alone cannot bring deep change of heart. Our active will must be engaged. In plain language, the transformation of our heart requires our active obedience to God's truth. The truth of God is living and powerful, but for that truth to effect life in us it must reach the depth of our heart—the place from which our life flows. And for that to happen, it must be lived out.

When we hear truth and receive it in our mind and emotions, it enters our heart, but only to a certain depth. Resisting the further impulse of the Spirit—in whatever way—blocks truth from penetrating deeper into our heart and thus

Christianity Is Rightly Received Only When It Is Practiced

John Calvin rightly explained that Christianity "is a doctrine not of the tongue but of life. It is not apprehended by the understanding and memory alone, as other disciplines are, but it is received only when it possesses the whole soul, and finds a seat and resting place in the inmost affection of the heart. . . . We have given the first place to the doctrine in which our religion is contained, since our salvation begins with it. But it must enter our heart and pass into our daily living, and so transform us into itself that it may not be unfruitful for us."[38]

Scripture is like a musical score that is designed to be sung or played, like a recipe that is designed to be produced and eaten. Scripture is a performative document. It doesn't just move the mind and emotion to spiritual visions and awe. It is rightly received when it is inculcated in daily life.

hinders real heart change. For example, I may strongly believe with emotion that the Lord's commission to evangelize the nations is incumbent on me as a Christian. But if I don't actually do anything in relation to this belief (e.g., witness, pray, give), my belief will weaken and the attached emotion will fade. Or I may be convicted that I need to change some behavior—excessive anger, for instance. If my conviction does not lead me to actually do something to overcome this destructive attitude such as trying to understand why I feel and act this way, meditating on truth that counters the motives that drive my anger, or seeking the help of others, I will not really change.

Jesus clearly taught that our spiritual life is built on the practice of truth and not merely profession of belief. The person who "hears my words and *puts them into practice*," he said, "is like a man building a house, who dug down deep and laid the foundation on rock. When the flood came, the torrent struck that house but could not shake it, because it was well built." In contrast, the person who hears and *does not practice* the Lord's words is like building a house without a deep foundation which is easily destroyed when the torrent strikes (Luke 6:46–49 NIV). A deep stable foundation of life comes only from a deep transformation of heart through *hearing* and *doing* God's truth.

Jesus also taught that our heart and life are shaped both by things in the heart and activity that comes out of the heart. Referring to the human-devised traditions of the Jewish religious leaders concern about defilement by eating with unwashed hands, Jesus said, "Whatever goes into the man from outside [i.e., foods] *cannot defile him, because it does not go into his heart*, but into his stomach . . . . *That which proceeds out of the man, that is what defiles the man. For from within, out of the heart of men, proceed the evil thoughts, fornications, thefts, murders. . . . All these evil things proceed from within and defile the man*" (Mark 7:18–23).

Jesus is not denying here what we have seen earlier, namely, that we *can receive things into our heart that do bring defilement*. But in this instance, as Jesus said, the things that are taken in do not go into the heart. What our Lord is pointing out in this teaching is the reality that what proceeds out of our heart—our activities of thought and deed—is what changes us. Although his reference here is only to sinful activity, it would seem to follow by good and necessary inference that if evil actions have a defiling effect upon the person, contrariwise good actions would have a positive effect. Thus all of our actions—good and bad—change our heart ever so much.

The transformation of our heart thus depends not only on feeding our heart on the truth of God's Word, but also exercising it by living in accord with the pattern of the way of life revealed in that Word. It is no doubt true in our spiritual life as in our physical life—the greater our activity, the greater appetite and capacity we will have for nourishing food. Spiritual transformation thus requires actively obeying God's voice as he speaks to us through his Spirit so that the propensity of our heart grows increasingly toward God's will.

Growth in this obedience requires training and discipline. Paul's exhortation to young Timothy is for all believers: "Discipline [or train] yourself for the purpose of godliness" (1 Tim. 4:7). "Mature" believers, as the writer of Hebrews points out, are those who "because of practice have their senses trained to discern good and evil" (Heb. 5:14).

We can even expect our heavenly Father to help us in this process with his loving discipline, a discipline that at the time "seems not to be joyful, but sorrowful; yet to those who have been trained by it, afterwards it yields the peaceful fruit of righteousness" (Heb. 12:11).

The training in obedience to God's truth covers the entire process of our heart's transformation—from the disciplines necessary to incorporate God's truth into our hearts to training in learning to practice it. The absolute necessity of such training is emphasized by the writer of Proverbs when he says, "Hold on to instruction [the Hebrew term signifies a chastening or disciplining[39]]; do not let go. Guard her, for she is your life" (Prov. 4:13).

As we have noted before, growth in the way of life is learning a skill—the skill of living wisely. Any skill—whether making fine furniture or playing basketball—requires repetition of correct actions. As has been said, "If you want to get things right, you have to practice doing things right."[40] So progress in the transformation of our heart and growth in the skill of living requires the continual practice of God's Word, or in Peterson's words, "a long obedience in the same direction."* Henry Drummond's words concerning love relate to all heart transformation:

> Is life not full of opportunities for learning love? Every man and woman every day has a thousand of them. The world is not a play-ground; it is a schoolroom. Life is not a holiday, but an education. And the one eternal lesson for us all is *how better we can love*. . . . What makes a man a good

---

* Friedrich Nietzsche, *Beyond Good and Evil*, trans. Helen Zimmern, Modern Library of the World's Best Books (1886; repr., New York: Boni and Liveright, 1917), 98, sec. 188. Although Nietzsche opposed such disciplinary training of the human heart, Eugene Peterson used these words from Nietzsche in a positive way for the title of his excellent work, *A Long Obedience in the Same Direction: Discipleship in an Instant Society* (Downers Grove, IL: InterVarsity Press, 1980).

artist, a good sculptor, a good musician? Practice. . . . What makes a man a good man? Practice. . . . Love is not a thing of enthusiastic emotion. It is a rich, strong, manly, vigorous expression of the whole round Christian character—the Christlike nature in its fullest development. And the constituents of this great character are only to be built up by ceaseless practice.[41]

But the practice of obedience brings more than learning correct behavior; it also enhances strength and stamina. Living the Christian life means being engaged in a struggle—described in terms of an athletic event (e.g., 1 Cor. 9:24–29; Phil. 3:4), or more often warfare (e.g., Eph. 6:12; 1 Tim. 6:12; 2 Tim. 2:3; 4:7). The more we exercise our will to act in obedience to God's voice, the more strength we will have to resist the attack of the enemy of our soul, and the more stamina we will have to persevere through the trying circumstances that tempt us to give in.

Perhaps even more important, our actions are not simply shaping our heart as if we are independent agents who are totally in control of ourselves. By our actions we are actually binding ourselves over as slaves to other powers. The apostle Paul wrote, "Don't you know that when you offer yourselves to someone as obedient slaves, you are slaves of the one you obey—whether you are slaves to sin, which leads to death, or to obedience, which leads to righteousness?" (Rom. 6:16 NIV). Obedient actions increasingly enslave us to righteousness and life; disobedient actions do the same toward sin and death. What we actually do impacts the shape of our hearts, increasing either the order of a heart after God and the attendant experience of genuine life or the disorder of death.

Conclusion

The transformation of our heart involves the whole heart. God calls us to love him "with all your heart and with all your soul and with all your might" (Deut. 6:5). While the precise meanings of "heart," "soul," and "might" in this verse are not easy to determine, in general the *heart* may be said to refer to the central innermost person including the personal functions of thought, emotion and volition out of which human life flows (see chapter 4), *soul* to the expression of heart in the personality of the whole self-conscious being, and *might*, the vigor and strength with which the expression of the heart is performed in the total person.[42]

Our love relationship with our Lord thus entails the inner person of the heart and the outer person of our physical being where the heart flows out in the activity of life. The actions of our life and our heart are inseparably united so we function as a holistic or integrated person. The inner person of our heart—our thoughts, emotions, and propensities of will and desire—lead to outward activity, and the outward activity in turn strengthens and enhances the inner contents of the heart. The application of this principle in all areas of our life is necessary for the transformation of our heart.

As we have already noted, the thoughts and emotions of our heart toward our God can be enhanced through bodily actions such as lifted hands, kneeling, or even singing. But most of all our hearts take on the form of love through loving actions. The psychiatrist Karl Menninger was once asked, "What would you advise a person to do if that person felt a nervous breakdown coming on?" His answer: "Lock your house, go across the railroad tracks, find someone in need and do something for him."[43] When we don't feel like loving (often in a bleak and downcast spirit), we can restore the vitality of love and live by deliberately doing an act of love.

God has given each one of us as his people abilities or "spiritual gifts" for the purpose of being a channel of his grace and love to others. Growth in biblical knowledge even to the point of allowing it to touch our emotions is vital for heart change. But without allowing God's life to flow through us to others, our transformation will be seriously stifled.

It is of vital importance for every believer to move away from being turned in on himself and seek avenues of loving service for others. The ministry of the church must help all people to be more than spectators or Bible students by aiding them to become active participants, developing and giving opportunity for the ministry of the various gifts of the people. The ultimate characteristic of our heart—love—is dynamic, requiring both receiving God's love and letting it flow out in love for others.

In all of this, our actions train our heart. They enhance the heart's thoughts, emotions, and activities, developing patterns of behavior or life—either good or bad. As someone has noted, Jesus did not say, "Take my chair and learn from me," but "take my yoke and learn from me." A yoke is not a sitting instrument but a walking instrument. It is not as we hear Jesus' words but as we *live* in obedience to them that we learn from him and come to find his promised "rest for your souls."[44]

In his thoughtful discussion of "putting on Christ," C. S. Lewis wonderfully portrays the place and power of actions in growing as a Christian. He explains that our growth always entails actions that extend beyond what we really are—what we might think of as actions of faith. When we believe in Christ and become united with him, we become sons and daughters of God who is now our heavenly Father. We, of course, are far from living fully as the children of God that we are.

Thus Scripture challenges us to "put on Christ" (Rom. 13:14), or put on our "new self [lit. man]" (Eph. 4:24; Col. 3:10). In obeying this command, we purpose in our heart and try to live out the example of Jesus and the new person in practical life. Lewis describes this as pretending to be what we are not yet in reality and goes on to explain how this active pretense actually transforms us unto the real thing.

> Very often the only way to get a quality [of character] in reality is to start behaving as if you had it already. That is why children's games are so important. They are always pretending to be grown-ups—playing soldiers, playing shop. But all the time, they are hardening their muscles and sharpening their wits, so that the pretense of being grown-up helps them to grow up in earnest.
>
> Now the moment you realize "Here I am, dressing up as Christ," it is extremely likely that you will see at once some way in which at that very moment the pretense could be made less of a pretense and more of a reality. You will find several things going on in your mind which would not be going on there if you were really a son of God. Well, stop them. Or you may realize that, instead of saying your prayers, you ought to be downstairs writing a letter, or helping your wife to wash up. Well, go and do it.
>
> You see what is happening. The Christ Himself, the Son of God who is man (just as you) and God (just like His Father) is actually at your side and is already at that moment beginning to turn your pretense into a reality. . . .
>
> . . . He is beginning to turn you into the same kind of thing as Himself. He is beginning, so to speak, to "inject" His kind of life and thought, His *Zoe* [life], into you; beginning to turn the tin soldier into a live man.[45]

Questions for Thought

1. Do you agree that by deliberately doing some action, we can change our emotions and thoughts? Can you remember a time when the way you acted toward someone or something changed the way you think or feel about them? How did your thoughts or feelings change?
2. What biblical evidence mentioned in the chapter do you think is the strongest support for actions changing emotion. For actions changing thought?
3. We have seen in earlier chapters that our heart is the seat of our thought,

emotion, and will, and that in the depth of the heart these three personal functions are unified. From this understanding of the heart why does it make sense that what we do would affect our emotions and thought?

4. If the transformation of our heart takes place as we incorporate God's Word in the depth of our heart, how does failure to exercise our will to actually practice God's Word affect the Word getting into the depth of the heart?

5. According to Jesus' teaching in Luke 6:46–49 about a person who heard the Word (probably with emotion) and put it into practice, and another person who heard the Word (also possibly with emotion) but didn't go on to practice it, what effect does practicing or not practicing God's Word have on our life? How would you describe the real life experiences of the two men in this illustration? How does this teaching of Jesus apply to your own experience?

▪■ 11 ■▪

No Man Is an Island

The Necessity of Community for Spiritual Transformation

No man is an island, entire of itself; every man is a piece of the
continent, a part of the main. . . : Any man's death diminishes me,
because I am involved in mankind, and therefore never send to know
for whom the bell tolls; it tolls for thee.

JOHN DONNE, "FOR WHOM THE BELL TOLLS"

So we, who are many, are one body in Christ, and individually members one of another.

PAUL, THE APOSTLE

The individual . . . is not self-sufficing, and therefore he is like a part
in relation to the whole. But whoever is unable to live in society, or
who has no need of it because he is sufficient for himself, must either
be a beast or a god.

ARISTOTLE

We have seen that the transformation of our heart is very personal. My heart is
who I am as a person. Changing my heart is therefore changing my real *self*. It
involves engaging my mind, emotion, and will in the truth of God, which in essence
is receiving the living God himself—the ultimate changer of hearts.* This personal
nature of spiritual transformation may lead us to think of the process of change as
a matter of individual inwardness—such things as contemplation, solitude, fasting,
and various other disciplines that are for the most part individual spiritual practices.

---

* While this is the basic process, there are many helpful details concerning this process of transformation and especially its application to individual lives that could be added but which are
  beyond the scope of this work.

The history of the church tends to lend support this idea. The Eremites (hermits) withdrew from society to seek closer relationship with God in solitude. We admire the Hesychasts (named after the Greek word meaning "quiet" or "stillness") who pursued union with God through silence of the heart via inner prayer aided by certain particular bodily postures and controlled breathing.[1] Guides in spirituality both past and present are prominently those who explored the interior life with little emphasis on our social nature as human beings and the place of communal relations in our spiritual transformation.

To be sure, God's command to guard or watch over your heart (Prov. 4:23) is directed to us as an individual person. I must know and guard *my own* heart. But human life according to the Bible is more than a private personal affair between me and God. It also involves relationship with fellow humans. Our transformation as human beings therefore involves both a personal relationship with God and with other people as part of a new community of God's people.

In this chapter we will lay the foundation for the need of community in our spiritual transformation by considering: (1) the reality of our communal nature as human beings and (2) the unique nature of the biblical community that transforms. How communal life actually effects change in us will be the subject of the chapter that follows.

The Reality of Our Communal Nature

The biblical perspective of human nature is concisely summarized by Orthodox professor Oliver Clément when he says, "Human nature . . . cannot belong to a solitary being. . . . It resides in the great interchange of life by which each exists for and through all the others."[2] This communal nature of human beings is seen both in our creational design as relational beings and in the instructions that God has given us for practically living human life.

Relational by Creation

Spiritual transformation is in essence becoming the being that God created us to be. It is progressing toward being fully human. But what does it mean to be human? What is our real nature as human beings? The most fundamental answer to these questions is found in Genesis 1:26 where our Creator said, "Let us make man in Our likeness." This statement along with other biblical teaching on God's design for human life clearly tell us that we are by nature relational beings designed to live in community—a reality that we will see is increasingly being supported by psychological and neurobiological studies.

We Desperately Need Each Other

"It is true that we are called to wholeness. But the reality is that we can never be completely whole in and or ourselves. . . . There is a point beyond which our sense of self-determination not only becomes inaccurate and prideful but increasingly self-defeating. It is true that we are created to be individually unique. Yet the reality is that we are inevitably social creatures who desperately need each other not merely for sustenance, not merely for company, but for any meaning to our lives whatsoever."[3]

Created in the Image of God: A Trinitarian Relationship of Mutual Love

Being created in God's image, of course, does not mean that we are like him in every aspect. As spirit, God does not have a physical body as we do. More importantly, we are created and therefore finite beings who are totally dependent for our existence on God who in contrast exists eternally and has life in himself—"who alone possesses immortality" (1 Tim. 6:16). Despite all of the differences, however, God defines us as creatures made in his image, and it is this truth that most centrally defines our human nature.

What it means for humans to be in the image of God has been the subject of much discussion. There is general agreement, however, that a central factor is the crucial distinction between humans and the lower creation, including animals. Humans are *personal* beings even as God is *personal*. As Walther Eichrodt states,

> For Man to be created in the likeness of God's image can only mean that on him, too, personhood is bestowed as the definitive characteristic of his nature. He has a share in the personhood of God; and as a being capable of self-awareness and self-determination he is open to the divine address and capable of responsible conduct. This quality of personhood shapes the totality of his psycho-physical existence; it is this which comprises the essentially human, and distinguishes him from all other creatures.[4]

But what does it mean to be personal? When we consider the personal nature of God, we are immediately confronted with his uniqueness—he is a plurality of persons and yet one personal God. Against the polytheism that surrounded his people Israel, God declared, "The Lord is our God, the Lord is *one!*" (Deut. 6:4). The concept of the "one" entails both unity and exclusivity—the Lord is the "*one* and *only*" God.

But God is also three persons. This is seen most clearly in God's revelation of himself on the stage of history in the work of redemption. First, the Father sends the Son to accomplish the work of redemption (John 17:3). Then the Father and the Son send the Spirit to apply that redemption to creation (John 15:26). The Father, Son, and Spirit communicate with one another as distinct persons (e.g., Matt. 11:27; Rom. 8:26–27), mutually sharing themselves with the other and glorifying one another (John 17:1, 4–5; John 16:13–14). Each of the three persons of God fully lives in the other two without loss of personal identity, even as Jesus declared, "The Father is in Me, and I in the Father" (John 10:38; cf. 14:10–11; 17:21, 23).

The full understanding of God who is three persons in one personal being is beyond our comprehension as we know nothing analogous to God among created beings. He is unique. What is clear, however, is that in his basic nature, God is a relational being eternally existing in a communion of love even as Jesus said to his Father, "You loved Me before the foundation of the world" (John 17:24). This relationality of love is the very nature of God, for "God is love" (1 John 4:8).

As God's image bearers we also are relational beings. We are like him in being persons who are designed to love and share ourselves with one another.

Our relational nature is immediately evident in the first biblical uses of the word "man." After God declared, "Let Us make *man* in Our image, according to Our likeness," we are told that "God created *man* in His own image, in the image of God He created *him*; male and female He created *them*" (Gen. 1:27).

Notice that the term "man" ('*adam*) in this foundational creation statement refers both to the singular ("him") and the plural or collective ("them"). It can therefore be used individually as the name of the first person, Adam (2:20: 3:17), and also for mankind as a corporate unity. Thus, while not Trinitarian like God, *man* does bear the image of God in being both individual and corporate, one and many; man is a social being whose fundamental nature is relational.

We Are Truly Ourselves Only in Relation to Others

Theologian Karl Barth's words concerning man and woman reflect the relational nature of mankind created in the image of the relational God. "The life of man is ordered, related and directed to that of the woman, and that of the woman to that of the man. . . . This connection is summed up in . . . [1 Cor. 11:11]: 'Nevertheless neither is the man without the woman, neither the woman without the man, in the Lord.' This is true of man and woman in marriage, but not only of them. We remember that to say man *or* woman is also, rightly understood, to say man *and* woman. . . . Man proceeds from woman and woman from man, each being for the other a centre and source. This mutual orientation constitutes the being of each. It is always in relationship to their opposite that man and woman are what they are in themselves."[5]

Our relational nature as humans is also revealed in the story of the first marriage. After he had created Adam and charged him with responsibilities in the garden, God still saw that something was missing. "It is not good for the man to be alone" (Gen. 2:18). Up to this point, like a craftsman who has finished his work, God looked at what he had created and pronounced it all "good," signifying that it was complete and perfectly suitable for its purpose (Gen. 1:4, 10, 12, 18, 21, 25). Now for the first time, he declares that something is not "good," namely, the individual man alone.

As a result he creates another human, someone corresponding to the man who can be his helper, someone with whom he can relate in reciprocal love, someone with whom he can become one. Only after the creation of woman to be with the man does God declare that all of his created work is "very good" (Gen. 1:31). Only as we exist in relationship with our Creator and other humans are we fully complete as human beings and able to fulfill our purpose for life.

The creation of the woman therefore tells us not only that "mutual help is an essential part of human existence,"[6] but also that human life is patterned after the life of God—a life of mutual love. In the words of Derek Kidner, man is "a social being, made for fellowship . . . ; he will not live until he loves, giving himself away to another on his own level."[7] The deepest desire of the human heart—the desire of love—is satisfied only as it lives in a community of love with God and other people.

Persons Only in Relations

We image God's communal nature in yet another way. Like the persons of the Trinity, we are *persons* only in relation with other persons. Without a relation to the Son the Father would not be the Father, nor would the Son be the Son apart from the Father. So with each person of the Trinity: they are who they are as persons—Father, Son, and Spirit—only in their mutual relationships with one another.

Interestingly, history reveals that the very concept of *person* arose in human thought through the early discussion of God as Trinity.[8] Recognizing that personhood entailed relationship with others it was concluded that the "*concept of person implies a plurality of persons.*"[9]

The Human Communal Nature in Empirical Studies

Despite the popular emphasis on individualism with its teaching of finding one's *self*, being true to *self*, *self*-actualization, *self*-fulfillment, *self*-esteem, and *personal* rights, the biblical picture of human nature as relational is increasingly being supported by psychological and neurobiological studies. During the last half of the twentieth-century, psychologists began to speak of an attachment system that was inherent to our nature. John Bowlby, the early pioneer of this concept, wrote:

> Intimate attachments to other human beings are the hub around which a person's life revolves, not only when he is an infant or a toddler or a schoolchild but throughout his adolescence and his years of maturity as well, and on into old age. From these intimate attachments a person draws his strength and enjoyment of life and, through what he contributes, he gives strength and enjoyment to others. These are matters about which current science and traditional wisdom are at one.[10]

The deepest yearning of every child is for communion with his or her mother and father. "When a child feels it does not belong to anyone, it suffers terrible loneliness and this is manifested in anguish."[11] This emotional hurt stems from something that is actually taking place in the structure of the child. The relationship between child and parent literally works to form the child's brain and mind, or in biblical language, the heart.

Daniel J. Siegel, known for his work in interpersonal neurobiology, states that "attachment establishes an interpersonal relationship that helps the immature brain use the mature functions of the parent's brain to organize its own processes."[12] He further notes that "genetic potential is expressed within the setting of social experiences, which directly influence how neurons connect to one another. Human connections create neuronal connections."[13]

It is also recognized that like the persons of the triune God, our identity as a person is dependent on relationships. We enter this world without self-consciousness. As a newborn infant, we don't see ourselves as an "I" in distinction from another person as a "you." But as our human nature unfolds, somewhere around eighteen months to two years old, the self-consciousness of personhood becomes actualized and we begin to use pronouns like "me" and "mine."

However, it is only in relation to another person that this actualization of personhood takes place. As philosopher W. Norris Clarke explains, "We come to awareness of ourselves as 'I' through the reaching out of another to us who is already an 'I' and appeals to us to respond as another self, a 'Thou.' . . . Unless someone else treats me as a 'Thou' I can never wake up to myself as an 'I,' as a person."[14] Like the persons of the Trinity, our person entails relations with other persons.

Relational Persons from Conception

The truth that normal human development of self-consciousness entails a relationship with other persons should not be understood as saying that the infant is not a person from conception. For personhood does not require that all human capacities are always functioning, else when one is asleep or in a coma he or she would no longer be fully a person. To be a person is to have the capacities that belong to a human being and normally develop into human functioning capacities. Thus even though the infant develops a sense of "I" through self-consciousness he or she is a person. Even as an acorn has oak-treehood and develops into an oak tree, so the zygote and fetus has the personhood of a person. Moreover, the person created in the image of God as a relational being, is from conception already related to God (Ps. 139:13–16; Jer. 4–5; esp., Luke 1:41–42). It is simply that in God's design, the unfolding of that person is intended to involve human relationships.*

---

* On the personhood of humans as established on a relationship with God as person, see Robert A. Connor, "The Person as Resonating Existential," *American Catholic Philosophical Quarterly* 66, no. 1 (1992): 39–56; Thomas F. Torrance, *Reality and Scientific Theology*, Theology and Science at the Frontiers of Knowledge 1 (Edinburgh: Scottish Academic Press, 1985), 178–80.

The primary emphasis of attachment research has been on the effects of the relations between children and their parents and other primary caregivers. But studies also demonstrate that the "capacity for attachment remains a central characteristic of human experience throughout life,"[15] although the nature of the relationships change. In early childhood parents and other adults tend to dominant the relationship. As we mature our part in the relationship becomes more active and consequently more responsible in the give and take with others. Through it all, our relationships are always forming our personalities, making us who we are. As Daniel Siegel says,

> If the capacity of the mind to adapt remains into adulthood [which is supported by contemporary evidence], then the emotional relationships we have throughout life may be seen as the medium in which further development can be fostered. These attachment relationships and other forms of close, emotionally involving interpersonal connections may serve to allow synaptic connections to continue to be altered, even into adulthood.[16]

Our hardwired nature for relations is also attested by research in social psychology that reveals the profound effect that others have on us.[17] For example, we see ourselves as *fat* or *thin* according to some ideal social standard around us. Our self-evaluation seems to be related to how we believe others perceive us. The standards by which we measure the success or failure of our performance are ideals or models developed through observation of others such as parents, friends, and even media characters. Moreover, we seem to have a chronic tendency to feel good about ourselves by comparing ourselves favorably with others.

Research also demonstrates that we tend to change our beliefs to fit our actions. Of course we do this in order to resolve our own inner conflict between our beliefs and our actions. But if our action is observed by others, our need to back it up with a consistent belief is heightened. All of this evidence showing the profound effect that our social environment has on us leads to the conclusion that "the 'inner self' is not an entity distinct from its social relation, but an entity whose identity is profoundly shaped by . . . relations."[18]

Being so significantly shaped by others might lead us to the conclusion that we are all becoming ciphers in the herd of a social mass—that our social nature is in conflict with our individual identity. In reality the opposite is true. Even as our identity as a person—an "I"—is called forth through relations with others, so our personal identity grows through relationship.

Referring to the first human relationship of man and woman, Karl Barth perceptively observes that their "mutual orientation constitutes the being of each. It is always in relationship to their opposite that man and woman are what they are in themselves. . . . Relationship to woman . . . makes the man a man, and her relationship to man . . . makes the woman a woman."[19] Thus rather than our

The More We Unite with Others, the More We Become Ourselves

On the seeming paradoxical relationship between individual and community Karl Rahner explains, "At first sight one is inclined to say that anything that exists possesses its own peculiarity (and difference) in inverse relation to its unity with, its bond with, what is other than itself; that, in other words, it decreases in selfhood the more it is bound up with something else, while any growth in distinguishing selfhood involves a decrease in unity with and relationship to anything other than itself. . . . And yet even at the lowest subhuman level, if we look at it properly, we see that it is not so. Something that is merely separated spatially and temporally from something else is neither really anything for itself (does not really possess anything for itself) nor really one with anything else. . . . Hence the true law of things is not: the more special and distinct in character, the more separated, isolated and discontinuous from anything else, but the reverse: the more really special a thing is, the more abundance of being it has in itself, the more intimate unity and mutual participation there will be between it and what is other than itself"[20] individual self being lost or even diminished through participation in a community of deep relationship, it is liberated and nourished "bringing us to know our own unique individuality even more keenly."[21]

In sum, both God's revelation and scientific observation of human nature affirm that we are designed by our Creator to live with others in community. In the words of James Beck and Bruce Demarest, "We are born as persons to connect, affiliate, and relate with other humans . . . . Humans clarify their identity, experience growth, and find fulfillment in the web of loving relationships."[22]

Relational by Divine Instruction for Human Life

The instructions that God gives us on how we should live also reveal that his design and goal for human life is life lived in community. On the basis of the covenant that God made with the people of Israel they became known as "the people of God." This language obviously expressed their relationship with God. But the Hebrew word for "people" (*'am*)—which carries the basic idea of kinship—also expressed their relationship with one another. They constituted a "kind of family" of God that was bound by covenant not only to God but also to one another.

This becomes clear in the Ten Commandments, which represent all of the laws of the covenant. The first five commandments express the vertical relationship of the people with God and the last five manifest the horizontal relationship between people. A violation of any of the commandments was not only sin against God; it was also a threat against the community that in some instances resulted in the violator being cut off.

Whether as punishment for breaking a commandment or for another reason such as persecution, to be separated from one's community was to exist in misery. According to Old Testament scholar G. Ernest Wright, "the greatest curse which can befall a man" was to be alone.[23] Thus Cain, who because of murdering his brother was condemned to be a wondering fugitive cut off from any community, bemoaned this banishment: "My punishment is too great to bear!" (Gen. 4:13).

The faithful also experienced loneliness as misery. Rejected by the people, Jeremiah complained to God: "Because of Your hand upon me I sat alone . . . Why has my pain been perpetual and my wound incurable, refusing to be healed?" (Jer. 15:17–18). The psalmist likewise lamented his loneliness in the midst of afflictions: "I am like a desert owl, like an owl among the ruins [unclean birds that were fond of the loneliness of the desert and ruined places]. I lie awake; I have become like a bird alone on a roof" (Ps. 102:6–7 NIV; cf. Ps. 42:4–5).

It should be noted in passing that there is a difference between loneliness and solitude. We can be alone and yet happy because we know that we are a part of a family or community. But with loneliness we feel cut off—that we are not part of anything.

Our communal nature becomes even more prominent in the New Testament where the corporate unity of God's people is expressed in various metaphors. Believers are *a temple* made of stones compactly fitted together (Eph. 2:20–22). They are members of *one body* who share a common life (1 Cor. 12:12–30), one *bride* of Christ (Eph. 5:25–33), and brothers and sisters in *the family of God*.

We are told that the members of the early church "devoted themselves . . . to *the fellowship,*" a term (*koinōnia*) that denotes sharing in something with another person in a close bond (Acts 2:42). Sharing together in Christ and the benefits of his salvation, bound these believers together both vertically with Christ and horizontally with one another. They enjoyed the fellowship pictured in the words of the apostle John: "What we have seen and heard we proclaim to you also, so that you too may have fellowship with us; and indeed our fellowship is with the Father, and with His Son Jesus Christ" (1 John 1:3, cf. v. 7).

God's communal design for human life is seen also in the numerous calls for the unity and oneness of God's people: "Be diligent to preserve the unity of the Spirit" (Eph. 4:3). "Make my joy complete by being of the same mind, maintaining the same love, united in spirit, intent on one purpose" (Phil. 2:2). "Love one another even as I have loved you. . . . By this all men will know that you are My disciples, if you have love for one another" (John 13:34–35). Perhaps Jesus' greatest desire for his disciples was expressed in his prayer shortly before going to the cross: "that they [his disciples] may all be one; even as You, Father, are in Me and I in You, that they also may be in Us, so that the world may believe that You sent Me" (John 17:21).

Such indications of God's desire for us to live life in community are echoed throughout the New Testament. If it is true that God seeks our good as his human creatures—and he does—then we must conclude that our true good is found in relational living.

The great value of relational living is confirmed by secular psychological and medical authorities who point to the debilitating effects of loneliness. According to Dean Ornish, who is well known for his work in relation to heart disease, "studies have shown that people who feel isolated have three to five times the mortality, not only from cardiovascular disease, but from all causes, when compared to people who don't feel isolated." Earlier, Ornish stated, "I am coming to believe that anything that promotes isolation leads to chronic stress and, in turn, may lead to illnesses like heart disease. Anything that promotes a sense of intimacy, community, and connection can be healing."[24]

The damaging psychological consequences of isolation are also noted by the renowned psychoanalyst Erich Fromm in his classic work, *The Art of Loving*. Referring to the gift of reason to human beings and thus self-awareness, Fromm said,

> This awareness of himself as a separate entity, the awareness of his short life span, of the fact that without his will he is born and against his own will he dies, that he will die before those whom he loves, or they before him, the awareness of his aloneness and separateness, of his helplessness before the forces of nature and of society, all this makes his separate, disunited existence an unbearable prison. He would become insane could he not liberate himself from this prison and reach out, unite himself in some form or other with men, with the world outside.[25]

Noting that the sin of Adam and Eve has led to human separateness and the accompanying anxiety, shame, and guilt, Fromm explains that the great question that confronts humankind of all ages and cultures is "the question of how to overcome separateness, how to achieve union, how to transcend one's own individual life and find at-onement."[26]

Summary

Both Scriptures and human observation tell us that our human nature is relational. Köhler's well-known statement is true: "Ein mensch ist kein mensch" ("*a* man is no man"[27] or "One human being is nobody"). We all came into this life generated through relationship, and we grow and experience genuine human life only in relations with others.

Affirming that it is God's plan for all people to live in covenant relationships, Johannes Pedersen asserted, "One is born of covenant and into a covenant, and wherever one moves in life, one makes a covenant or acts on the basis of the already existing covenant. If everything that comes under the term of covenant were dissolved, existence would fall to pieces, because no soul can live an isolated life."[28] The character in Jean Paul Sartre's play *Huis Clos* who says that hell is other people is radically in error. For Scripture teaches just the opposite: "hell is ultimate solitariness, the final triumph of our egocentricity and therefore our self-inflicted death."[29]

God's purpose to "create and sustain community, a community which is to exist in love and peace" stands at the center of the Bible.[30] It is often noted correctly that we are created with a God-shaped vacuum in our heart that only God can fill. But it should also be added that there is a God-created emptiness in each of us that can be filled only by our fellow humans. Given this truth, our spiritual transformation, which is designed to make us human, requires that we attend to the social dimension of our life.

This is not to say that one cannot commune with God with blessing as an individual. Our discussion of meditation on God's truth in chapters 8 and 9 surely entails a very personal conversation with our Lord. Furthermore, Scripture gives evidence of God meeting and blessing people who are actually cut off from any communal relationships. Paul recounts that "at my first defense no one supported me, but all deserted me. . . . But the Lord stood with me and strengthened me" (2 Tim. 4:16–17). So also God met Elijah alone in a cave at Horeb after fleeing from Jezebel (1 Kings 19:8–18). No doubt throughout history many believers have communed with God alone, either through solitary confinement in persecution or evangelistic forays into unevangelized territory.

But Scripture is clear that God's pattern for spiritual growth entails being part of his spiritual community. As we were designed by our Creator to be individuals and social beings bound together by love, so our transformation toward that goal is both individual and social. God commands us to "consider how we may spur one another on toward love and good deeds, not giving up meeting together, as some are in the habit of doing, but encouraging one another—and all the more as you see the Day approaching" (Heb. 10:24–25 NIV). To ignore or reject participation in the community of believers or the church is, as we have seen in chapter 10, to refuse to exercise our will in obedience to God and thus hinder the penetration of God's transforming presence in our heart. And, as we will see in this chapter and the next, it is to pridefully ignore and even reject the transforming presence of Christ's grace which he desires to give us through other members of God's community.

We will consider the various effects of communal relationships on our spiritual growth in the next chapter. But first, it is important to understand the unique nature of this new human community that God is creating (not every human community is transformational), and the vital place of this community in communicating God's life for our growth.

The Unique Nature of Biblical Community

Human communities are typically formed by people coming together around things they share—things like family ties, neighbors, work, hobbies, recreational activities, social concerns, political causes. People are bound together in a horizontal relationship around an interest or natural relationship. Such communities are valuable for satisfying some of our natural propensity for relationship. But they are not yet the human communities intended by God, and therefore not the place where spiritual transformation takes place. Genuine human community is a people united first by a common loyalty to God.

The Vertical Dimension: Relationship with God

Since we were designed to live in fellowship with God, it is only logical that "true human community is created only where the community between God and humans is restored."[31] Such community is depicted in G. Ernest Wright's description of the Old Testament community of Israel.

> It is a psychic harmony of individual souls, held together by mutual vows in covenant with its Lord and sharing the common blessing which he confers. The harmony of wills is not a simple agreement of a horizontal type, but a conforming of all wills to that of the Lord in a mutuality of commitment which results in a oneness of heart and life, in a psychic unity.[32]

A. W. Tozer captured the same principle when he noted that "one hundred pianos all tuned to the same fork are automatically tuned to each other."[33]

But it is not only community formed through common loyalty *to* God; it is community *in* God. It is *fellowship* or common participation in God through Christ by the Spirit. As Christians we no longer live simply as human individuals. We are alive with the life of Christ so that we can say with the apostle, "It is no longer I who live, but Christ lives in me" (Gal. 2:20). He is "our life" (Col. 3:4).

This presence of the life of God in every believer is what makes ordinary human relationships different and transforming. Receiving the unconditional love of God empowers us to love others with the same gracious love even when they are not loveable. Through the life of Christ in us we are enabled to gain victory over the great enemy of all community—our old god-playing ego, which in order to remain godlike must continually assert itself over or against others and at the same time hide behind a facade lest it be known for what it really is. Only through the self-emptying life of the One who gave up his own life for us are we able to deny this old self and give our self to others thereby entering into communion with them.

The Christian's Relational Nature Is Different

Our relationship with God transforms our relational nature as the following statements show:

Christ's call to repentance meant abandoning any absurd notion of isolated self-sufficiency and acknowledging instead one's poverty, one's need of God and others. Those Christ called had, like children, to be incapable of living alone and unaided in order to enter the kingdom.[34]

For face to face with God our monologue with ourselves is turned into dialogue with another. The circle of our subjectivity is breached. Our self-centredness, our selfishness, our introverted self-affirming existence are under attack, and we are taken captive in a transcendental relation to what is beyond us. But in this very movement of extroversion we find ourselves being healed of a damaged personal structure. . . . To retreat from that encounter with God into some encounter with ourselves is to abandon ourselves to the destruction of our essential personal structure, for it is to cut ourselves off from person-generating relations with God.[35]

Only as members of a community related to each other in God are we free to give ourselves to others for their good rather than cling to them to meet our own needs.[36] Genuine authentic relationship is between two individuals who are secure in their own self-identity, and as such are free to treat the other person as truly an *other*—one who is free to be who they are. Only when a person is secure in himself is he able to give himself for the other person's good and not in some way utilize the relationship for his own good.

Such personal security is found only in God. When I know that I am a child of God and trust him to meet all of my needs, I am free to genuinely relate to others. I can be open to others since my identity does not depend on them, but on my relationship to God. I can be vulnerable in both giving and receiving help without fear of losing my own self, which is attached securely to God and has its identity from him. Because our life is hid with Christ in God we can experience the power of God to become servants for the good of others even as Christ did on our behalf (Phil. 2:7).

Praying to the Father for his disciples, Jesus said, "The glory which You have given Me I have given to them, that they may be one, just as We are one" (John 17:22). The oneness of genuine human relationship comes through participating through the Spirit in the glorious nature of God manifest in Christ and his redemptive work—including a divine love that unites Father, Son, and Spirit together as one.

Jewish pilgrims—from various places, families, and walks of life—sang the following words from Psalm 133:1 as they made their way together to celebrate the annual feasts at Jerusalem: "Behold, how good and how pleasant it is for brothers to dwell together in unity." The psalm concludes with the words: "For *there* the LORD commanded the blessing—*life forever*" (v. 3). Whether "there" is understood as the fellowship itself or as the place of fellowship (i.e., Jerusalem), the psalmist declares that "'life' is enjoyed . . . in communion with the people of God."[37]

The transforming community united through the presence of God becomes reality primarily through the communal worship of God. In song and word God's people remembered and witnessed through confession and affirmation of faith the wonders of God's grace and his mighty acts of salvation. Individuals gave testimony of God's blessing in their personal lives "in the great congregation" (Pss. 35:18; 40:9–10).

Unitedly, they joyfully rehearsed God's wondrous works for their salvation through communal rites such as the Passover and the Day of Atonement and other Jewish feasts in the Old Testament and the Lord's Supper in the New Testament. It was in this united praise of the glory of their God above all that God's people experienced the community designed for human life. T. S. Eliot, a Nobel Prize winner in literature, captures this biblical teaching in his poetry:

God's People Were Transformed through a Transforming Community

"I have proclaimed glad tidings of righteousness in the great congregation; . . . I have not concealed Your lovingkindness and Your truth from the great congregation." (Ps. 40:9–10)

"I will tell of Your name to my brethren; in the midst of the assembly I will praise You." (Ps. 22:22)

"Let them give thanks to the LORD for His lovingkindness, and for His wonders to the sons of men! Let them extol Him also in the congregation of the people, and praise Him at the seat of the elders." (Ps. 107:31–32)

"I will give thanks to the LORD with all my heart, in the company of the upright and in the assembly." (Ps. 111:1)

"Sing to the LORD a new song, and His praise in the congregation of the godly ones." (Ps. 149:1)

Let the word of Christ richly dwell within you, with all wisdom teaching and admonishing one another with psalms and hymns and spiritual songs, singing with thankfulness in your hearts to God." (Col. 3:16)

What life have you if you have not life together?
There is no life that is not in community,
And no community not lived in praise of God.[38]

The Horizontal Dimension: Relationship with Neighbor

Joined together in God, believers are at the same time joined with one another. Becoming a member of the church is not something we *do* after becoming Christians; it is something we *are* by virtue of our union with Christ. For union with Christ, the Head of the church, inevitably means union with his body, the church. Emil Brunner rightly stated, "The fellowship of Christians is just as much an end in itself as is their fellowship with Christ."[39] Thus our fellowship with other believers even as our fellowship with our Lord is the matrix of our spiritual transformation.

An Organism: More Than an Organization

Like any human community, the fellowship of God's people in the church has the characteristics of an organization. But more deeply it is a living organism—"a living complex adaptive system of organs that influence each other in such a way that they function in some way as a stable whole."[40] To use the favorite metaphor of the apostle Paul, the community of God's people is a living body.

An organization is constructed through good structures and programs. But an organism or body is the product of life with order and function all coming from inside. Members of an organization do not have to be related to one another. But members of an organism must be related as they share a common life.

Members of an organization contribute their abilities and gifts to the cause of the group. In a body, they contribute their unique functions to one another. Every part of a body is mutually dependent on one another and each part is needed—there are no real vestigial organs—even as the apostle writes, "The eye cannot say to the hand, 'I have no need of you'; or again the head to the feet, 'I have no need of you'" (1 Cor. 12:21). The eye is a marvelous mechanism, but cannot go anywhere without the feet. And the feet don't know where to go without the eye, and so throughout the body.

The health of the entire body, including that of each part is thus dependent on the proper functioning of every part. A member of a body does not grow on his or her own, but only as the whole body grows. So our spiritual growth as members of Christ's body depends not only on a personal relationship with Christ, our Head, but on a vital relationship with fellow believers in his body.

We Live in Each Other

The organic affinity of God's people is highlighted in the apostle's teaching that as members of "one body in Christ" we are also "individually members one of another" (Rom. 12:5)—we actually *live in each other*. Because God has bestowed the Spirit with his gifts on each member of the body, all of the members "have property in one another and therefore in one another's gifts and graces." Each member is enriched "because they have communion in all the gifts of the Holy Spirit."[41]

Our sharing in one another is evident in the apostle's exhortation to truth-telling: "Therefore, laying aside falsehood, speak truth each one of you with his neighbor, for we are members of one another" (Eph. 4:25). In commenting on this text, the great fourth-century preacher Chrysostom points to the living relationship of the members of a body when he asks, "If the eye were to spy a serpent or a wild beast, will it lie to the foot? . . . And what again, when neither the foot nor the eye shall know how to distinguish, but all shall depend upon the smelling, for example, whether a drug be deadly or not; will the smelling lie to the mouth? And why not? Because it will be destroying itself also."[42]

This affinity of believers in the body of Christ underlies the apostle's statement that "if one member suffers, all the members suffer with it" (1 Cor. 12:26). It doesn't simply say that one member *should* suffer with the other, but that in the body they *do* suffer together. As Robert Banks points out, the body "has a common nerve."[43] Anyone who has suffered with a painful tooth or a sore toe knows this to be true. It is true also for the members of a close-knit family. What affects one member affects the others.

The reality that we can live in one another as a result of relationships is attested by contemporary clinical and neurobiological research. In his acclaimed work on how relationships with others interact with our brain to shape who we are, Daniel Siegel concludes that "the psyches of those who have been an intimate part of our development live on within us in both the details and the structure of the ongoing story of our lives." He says further, "Children carry those to whom they are attached inside of them, in the form of multisensory images (faces, voices, smell, taste, touch), a mental representation of the relationship with them."[44]

If such is the case in our natural relationships, how much more is it true in the community of God where we are related not only naturally, but supernaturally in the common life of the Spirit. Referring to the indwelling of one another in the church, Miroslav Volf writes,

In personal encounters, that which the other person is, flows consciously or unconsciously into that which I am. The reverse is also true. In this mutual giving and receiving, we give to others not only something, but also a piece of ourselves, something of that which we have made of ourselves in communion with others; and from others we take not only something, but also a piece of them. Each person gives of himself or herself to others, and each person in a unique way takes up others into himself or herself. This is the process of the mutual internalization of personal characteristics occurring in the church through the Holy Spirit indwelling Christians.[45]

God's Life Is Communicated to Us through Others

All life is communicated through relationship with others. As we saw earlier, we came into our natural life through the relationships of our parents and that life has continually been nourished by relationships with others—family members, teachers, members of groups to which we belong, and good friends. What is true in our natural life is also true in the human community of the new creation—we are nourished in our new life by relationships with others who are channels of God's life to us.

One of the most profound principles of spiritual growth is found in the apostle's words to the Ephesians believers: "We are to grow up in all aspects into Him who is the head, even Christ, from whom the whole body, being fitted and held together by what every joint supplies, according to the proper working of each individual part, causes the growth of the body for the building up of itself in love" (Eph. 4:15–16; cf. Col. 2:19).

The ultimate source of our growth is Christ—"the head *from whom*" the body receives everything necessary for its growth. But in this Scripture Christ is not the immediate or direct cause of the growth of each member. Rather we are told that the body *"causes the growth"* of *itself* as the members are "fitted and held together by what every joint [contact, or connection] supplies according to the proper working of each individual part."

In the previous context the apostle has just said that every member of the body has been given "grace . . . according to the measure of Christ's gift" (Eph. 4:7). As each member exercises this grace gift to minister to others in the body, he or she is contributing to the growth of the body. We are like the cells in our body. Although separate entities cells are not designed to live in isolation but rather to contribute to the growth of the entire body and with it their own growth.

One of the most important biblical terms for our growth is "edification" or "building up." All of the key uses of this concept (except for one debatable text*) speak of *building up one another* rather than directly *building up our self*. We are to edify or build up our neighbor (Rom. 15:2), mutually build up one another (Rom. 14:2; 1 Thess. 5:11), and speak for the edification of our hearers (Eph. 4:29). We are to use our spiritual gifts for the edification of the "other person" (1 Cor. 14:17), and the church (1 Cor. 14:4, 5, 26).

To sum up, the spiritual growth or transformation of the believer takes place as the life-giving grace of Christ flows through the members of his body through their fellowship with one another. As Montague explains the apostle's teaching in Ephesians 4:15–16 (cited above): "Christ diffuses His own eminent perfection in a myriad of different graces so that in and through their diversity, He may bring His members, and they may bring one another, to His own perfection *andra teleion* [one mature man, v. 13]."[46] Expressed another way, Chrysostom said: "If we wish to enjoy the spirit which comes from the head, let us cling to one another."[47]

Spiritual growth is nothing less than the Spirit producing his fruit in our lives—"love joy, peace, patience, kindness, goodness, faithfulness, gentleness, self-control" (Gal. 5:22). When we think about it, almost all, if not all, of these qualities by their very nature grow not when we are alone, but when we are in relationship with others.

Community Established in and through Christ

In our pursuit of spiritual growth through relationship it is important to remember that "we belong to each other only through and in Christ."[48] Apart from Christ the way of genuine mutual relationship is blocked by our own ego. He is our "peace" (Eph. 2:14)—our reconciliation with the other—that creates our fellowship and allows us to be open to Christ's word and touch through the other.

Only by the love of God through Christ in our hearts are we able to respect and value the other person as one created in the image of God and be open to each other as channels of God's transforming grace. In the community that

---

* The apostle Paul in 1 Cor. 14:4 mentions that the "one who speaks in a tongue edifies himself." This has been understood in a positive sense as the tongue speaker being personally edified through speaking in tongues. But it has also been taken negatively in the sense of a self-centered exalting of oneself and therefore contrary to the apostle's general teaching on spiritual gifts, which are for the edification of other believers or the church (cf. Otto Michel, "*oikodomeō*," *TDNT*, 5:141).

transforms, our concern is not in the first place to please the other person, or even to please the community as a whole, but rather to please Jesus the creator of the community and the one from whom it grows.

Questions for Thought

1. What does it mean to say that the human person is a relational being? What are some of the biblical and empirical evidences that it is human nature to be relational? Do you sense this reality in yourself? How have relationships with other people affected your life? Give examples.

2. If we cannot be true human persons according to God's design without relationships with other people, how do relationships with other people relate to our personal spiritual transformation? Do you think that a person can successfully grow spiritually outside of a community? Explain why, or why not?

3. How would you describe the impact of relationship with other believers on your own spiritual growth? How does the impact of relationships compare to the impact of your private times with God in terms of your growth as a Christian? Which has helped you grow the most?

4. What is the unique difference between biblical community and other human communities or fellowships, such as social clubs, service organizations, hobby clubs, or sports teams? What is the difference between an organization and an organism? Has your relationships with other believers in your church been more like the description of the biblical community or like an ordinary human community? If more like an ordinary community, in what way? Why?

5. Think about how God's design of us in his image harmonizes with his design that we grow in relationships as we minister to one another. Could we grow in the likeness of God's life and love apart from relationships?

6. How do you relate your personal life to the truth that we are relational beings and that transformation involves living in relationship with other believers? Is there anything that you need to change in your desires in order to grow in genuine life?

■■ 12 ■■

Love One Another

How Christian Community Transforms Us

> From . . . [Christ] the whole body, joined and held together by every
> supporting ligament, grows and builds itself up in love, as each part
> does its work.
>
> EPHESIANS 4:16 NIV

> Christ diffuses His own eminent perfection in a myriad of differ-
> ent graces so that in and through their diversity, He may bring His
> members, and they may bring one another, to His own perfection.
>
> GEORGE T. MONTAGUE

After hearing a clap of thunder one night, a little girl called out, "Mommy,
please come and stay with me!" Her mom rushed in to calm her. "Don't
worry," she told her. "You're never really alone because God is always with you.
God will take care of you, honey." To which the little girl replied, "But Mommy,
I want a God with skin on!"

Fellow believers, of course, are not really gods with skin on. But as we saw in
the previous chapter they are very visible and tangible humans through whom
God desires to manifest himself with grace for our spiritual transformation.

In this chapter we will explore how we help one another on our spiritual journey and what we contribute to each other's spiritual growth. We will see that it
is God's design for believers to actually bring Christ to other another through
our communal relationships. That is, what Christ is to us, we are called to be to
each other.

Stephen Greggo, a professor of pastoral counseling, suggests on the basis that
we are created in the image of God and since Christ is the perfect image that
all of the biblical names and metaphors used of Christ in relationship to us are

Being What Christ Is to Others

Without attempting to be comprehensive, Stephen Greggo lists fourteen word pictures of Jesus' relationship to people that are applicable to the relational ministry of believers to one another. Some of these, in addition to the ones mentioned in the text include: *Light*—wisdom/righteousness displayed; *Lamb of God*—sacrificial burden bearer; *Living water*—refreshment resource; *Gate*—watchman/security system; *True vine*—supply connection and lifeline; and *Advocate*—intercessor and ally.[1] Such suggestive pictures should stimulate us to think of all that Christ is to us and to realize that he is being formed in us by the Spirit (Gal. 4:19) so we can be instruments through which he can minister his transforming grace to others.

likewise applicable to our relationship with one another. As Christ is the Way, the Truth and the Life, so we are called to help one another navigate along God's way, to teach each other God's truth, and to nourish one another with the bread of life. As Christ is the Good Shepherd, so we are to care for and serve one another.[2] In short, every attitude or action that we are called to express toward one another is a manifestation of the ministry of Christ.

These mutual ministries, like the ministry of God through his Word and Spirit, transform our heart by impacting our mind, emotions, and actions. God uses other members of the body of Christ to shape and invigorate our thoughts, emotions, and behavior. Various ministries of our brothers and sisters in the body may be more related to one dimension of our heart, such as teaching with the intellect or comfort with emotion. But as all of our personal capacities are united in the depth of our heart, every ministry contributes to the transformation of the entire heart.

The Effects of Life Together

Many of the ministries that Christ works through his people are expressed in the biblical commands for actions and attitudes that they are to have toward one another. For example, believers are to:

+ Encourage one another (Rom. 1:12; 1 Thess. 5:11; Heb. 3:13; 10:25).
+ Serve one another through love (Gal. 5:13).
+ Bear one another's burdens (Gal. 6:2).
+ Build up one another (Rom. 14:19; 1 Thess. 5:11).
+ Admonish one another (Rom. 15:14; 1 Thess. 5:14; Col. 3:16).
+ Comfort one another (1 Thess. 4:18).
+ Care for one another (1 Cor. 12:25).
+ Be hospitable to one another (1 Peter 4:9).

+ Stimulate one another to love and good deeds (Heb. 10:24).
+ Teach one another (Col. 3:16).
+ Pray for one another (James 5:16; 1 John 5:16; see also Col. 4:3–4; 1 Thess. 5:25).
+ Accept one another as Christ accepted us (Rom. 15:7).
+ Forgive one another (Col. 3:13; Eph. 4:32).
+ Honor one another (Rom. 12:10; 1 Cor. 12:26).
+ Be humble toward one another (Rom. 12:16; Phil. 2:3; 1 Peter 5:5).
+ Be tolerant toward one another, making allowance for each other's faults (Eph. 4:2).
+ Above all—love one another (John 13:34–35; 15:12, 17; Rom. 13:8; 1 Thess. 3:12; 4:9; 2 Thess. 1:3; 1 Peter 1:22; 1 John 3:11, 23; 4:7, 11–12; 2 John 5).

On our walk with God along our spiritual journey, as with any long and difficult trek, we have certain needs. We need to know where we are going and how to get there. We need strength for the strenuous stretches and encouragement for the struggle against our spiritual foes. Finally, for our inevitable cuts and bruises, we need restoration and healing. A glance at the above list of "one anothers" reveals that all of these needs are provided for us through our fellow believers.

Guidance

The words of the psalmist—"Your word is a lamp to my feet and a light to my path" (Ps. 119:105)—imply that our path in this world is a way through darkness that holds the dangers of losing our way and falling into deep ravines. But God has given us the heavenly light of his Word to both shine a floodlight on the pathway ("a light to my path") and to focus a beam for our next steps ("a lamp to my feet").

Growing in our spiritual walk comes from growing in the knowledge and understanding of God and his ways revealed in his written Word. Immature children, according to the apostle, are easily confused and deceived by the lies that surround them in this world. They are "tossed back and forth by the waves, and blown here and there by every wind of teaching and by the cunning and craftiness of people in their deceitful scheming" (Eph. 4:14 NIV). God's desire is that "we all reach unity in the faith and in the knowledge of the Son of God and become mature" (v. 13 NIV).

As we saw in chapter 7, an important way through which we increase our knowledge of Christ is through personal study and meditation of God's written Word. But our growth in knowledge also takes place in the community of God's people.

God has placed teachers in the community to aid us in the understanding and application of his Word to our lives (Eph. 4:11).* In addition, Scripture encourages all believers to teach one another: "Let the message of Christ dwell among you richly as you teach and admonish one another with all wisdom through psalms, hymns, and songs from the Spirit, singing to God with gratitude in your hearts" (Col. 3:16 NIV).† Believers are to speak the truth in love (Eph. 4:15), addressing one another with the truth based on the gospel.[3] By so doing, they "console, strengthen and correct one another through the gospel and so build up their communities."[4] Richard Baxter rightly said, "Every good Christian is a teacher, and has a charge of his neighbour's soul."[5]

Mutual instruction also takes place through ministries such as admonition, encouragement, and comfort, all of which are done on the basis of truth from God's Word. Even singing—as the Colossian text above indicates—was an avenue of mutual teaching. This no doubt took place through congregational singing but also individually as in Tertullian's second-century description of a Christian love feast where "each is invited to sing to God in the presence of the others what he knows from Scripture or from his own heart" (*Apology*, 39.18).[6]

The value of the community for understanding and growth in God's Word is seen in Paul's prayer for the Ephesian believers that they "may be able to *comprehend with all the saints* what is the breadth and length and height and depth, and to know the love of Christ which surpasses knowledge, that you may be filled up to all the fullness of God" (Eph. 3:18–19). As John Stott explains,

> We shall have power to comprehend these dimensions of Christ's love . . . *only with all the saints*. The isolated Christian can indeed know something of the love of Jesus. But his grasp is bound to be limited by his limited experience. It needs the whole people of God to understand the whole love of God, *all the saints* together, Jews and Gentiles, men and women, young and old, black and white, with all their varied backgrounds and experiences.[7]

---

* See also Rom. 12:7; 1 Cor. 12:28.

† Whether this text is translated to understand the teaching as done through singing psalms, hymns, and spiritual songs as in the NASB, or as an activity in addition to singing as in the NIV, the concept of teaching one another is still present. In truth, the early church considered the practice of singing together as having a significant didactic purpose.

To one extent or another, our understanding of God's truth is always limited by our personality and life experience. The truth of Christ is more robust and rich than any one person can see. Listening to another person's explanation of Scripture can help us see dimensions of truth to which we were previously blind.

Hearing another believer testify to God's work in his or her life in the assembly of God's people—a reality frequently mentioned in the Psalms (e.g., 22:22, 25; 35:18; 40:9–10)—can also enrich our understanding. Even more, it can drive the truth deeper into our heart by touching our emotions and thus our actions as only concrete examples and stories can do. One of the reasons that the great apostle Paul desired to go to Rome was that he might "be encouraged together with you . . . each of us by the other's faith" (Rom. 1:12). Their "faith" no doubt included lived demonstration of truth as well as trust.

As we have noted before, growing in the Christian life is the activity of learning a skill. Like becoming a medical doctor, it requires cognitive knowledge *and* observation of those who have gone before and developed the skills. We gain cognitive knowledge and see vivid examples of those who walked with God in the past through the study of the Scriptures (e.g., Heb. 6:12—"be . . . imitators of those who through faith and patience inherit the promises"). But we are also called to observe the lives of followers of Christ in our own time and circumstances.

Learning how to walk with God by following the example of others is strong in Scripture. "Be imitators of me," the apostle says, "just as I also am of Christ" (1 Cor. 11:1). "The things you have learned and received and heard and *seen* in me, practice these things" (Phil. 4:9; cf. 1 Cor. 4:16; Phil.; 3:17; 1 Thess. 1:6; 2 Thess. 3:7, 9). Entire communities, such as the church at Thessalonica, could be examples for others (1 Thess. 1:7).

The leaders in particular were to be models of the faith for the instruction of others (1 Tim. 4:12; Titus 2:7; 1 Peter 5:3). The writer to the Hebrews exhorts his readers to "remember your leaders, who spoke the word of God to you. Consider the outcome of their way of life and imitate their faith" (Heb. 13:7 NIV). Such "consideration" or careful observation requires an intimate knowledge of the example that can come only through continual close relationship.

Focusing on Godly Models for Change

"The unique significance of the Bible rests in part on the fact that it contains a large selection of realistic models, from Adam to Paul. The Bible was able to become one of the most important textbooks of human behavior and experience precisely because in it 'dominating' models recede and models that first fail but then overcome are so numerous. For Paul himself, for example, Abraham and Christ had exemplary significance."[8]

In community we learn to live God's transforming truth together, gaining insight into its meaning from one another and being mentored in living it out in differing situations. We get to know Christ through others and learn to live out the Christian story with them.

In community, where our strengths and weaknesses are revealed, we also come to know ourselves. The measure of our love is tested only in relationship with others. Our spiritual giftedness, or where we fit in the body of Christ, becomes known only as we actually live as part of that body. Even the knowledge of God's leading for our individual lives is aided as we enlist others who know us well to help us listen for the Spirit's voice.

In sum, the knowledge of the way of our spiritual journey that enables us to walk well comes in and through relational living in a community of fellow travelers.

Empowerment

Growth in our walk with God also requires strength and courage. We know from experience what Scripture tells us that walking with God is not a casual jaunt. There are hills to climb (sometimes steep), rocky stretches, deserts, swamps, and rivers that have to be traversed. Powerful spiritual enemies bent on hindering our walk and even destroying us constantly assail us—our own fleshly desires, the world system around us, and personal evil spirits. At times, circumstances get the best of us. Spiritual dryness comes on us for no apparent reason. All told, the road is not easy. We need help.

Scripture tells us to look to God for such help: "God is our refuge and strength, a very present help in trouble" (Ps. 46:1). "Cast your burden upon the LORD and He will sustain you" (Ps. 55:22); "Cast all your anxiety on him because he cares for you" (1 Peter 5:7).

But Scripture also informs us that God channels his help through his people. We are to "care for one another" (1 Cor. 12:25), to "bear one another's burdens" (Gal. 6:2), and to "serve one another" (Gal. 5:21). We are called to edify or build up one another—that is, to mutually strengthen our hearts and our lives—in the reality of the gospel. Each believer is given a spiritual gift for the building up of others (1 Cor. 14:12, 16). All are to "pursue the things which make for . . . the building up of one another" (Rom. 14:19; cf. 1 Thess. 5:11).

In his farewell address, Paul commended the Ephesian elders "to God and to the word of His grace which is able to *build you up*" (Acts 20:32). This power to build up, that is in the word of God's grace, is communicated by believers as they speak that word to one another and live it out in loving relationships.

In our struggles with our spiritual enemies, we are not intended to fight alone. The apostle encourages the Philippian believers to stand firm in one spirit with one mind, *"striving together* for the faith of the gospel" (Phil. 1:27). Such united striving is illustrated in "the shield of faith" that believers are to take up against the evil forces (Eph. 6:16). The shield that is mentioned is the large door-shaped shield measuring 2½ by 4 feet—not the small round shield (approximately 2½ feet in diameter) that was sometimes used. Made of wood and trimmed with metal, this large shield was covered on the surface with canvas and leather. Often before battle it was soaked with water making it an anti-incendiary able to ward off the destructive power of burning arrows shot against it.

The real value of this shield was when it was used in conjunction with others. Alone, individual soldiers with such a large shield could easily be encircled. But when all of the members of the company placed their shields side-by-side and above themselves, they became a formidable force both for defense and attack. As Markus Barth explains, "Men advancing behind their huge shields . . . were as threatening in the ancient world as soldiers riding in an armored car are today; and closely formed units, advancing shield by shield and with a compact cover of shields above their heads, were as much instruments of attack as modern tanks."[9]

In the battles against our spiritual foes, we all need the shields of others alongside our own. To go it alone is not only dangerous, but disobedient to our Commander.

Whether in the midst of a battle or simply trudging along the way, we also need the bolstering of encouragement. The word "encouragement" in most instances in the New Testament is the translation of the Greek term *parakaleō*, with the basic meaning of "to call someone to oneself."[10] The purpose for the call or summons of another person may be to seek help from him or her. But more commonly the word is used for calling someone for the purpose of helping that person with words of encouragement, exhortation, or comfort, depending on the situation.[11]

Among the ancient Greeks it was used especially as a rallying cry for those going into battle. Describing ships about to go into naval battle, the ancient playwright Aeschylus said, "The long galleys cheered (*parakalein*) each other, line by line" (*Persians*, 380).[12]

As these sailors stirred up one another with courage and strength for battle, so we are called to bolster one another in our struggles. "Encourage one another day after day . . . so that none of you will be hardened by the deceitfulness of sin" (Heb. 3:13). "Let us hold fast the confession of our hope . . . Let us consider how to stimulate one another to love and good deeds, not forsaking our own assembling together, as is the habit of some, but encouraging one another; and all the more as you see the day drawing near" (10:23–25). "Therefore encourage one another and build up one another, just as you also are doing" (1 Thess. 5:11; cf. 4:18 NIV).

Most of the time this encouragement and empowering of one another was done by simply speaking a pertinent word based on the saving work of God—either about something God had already done or what he has promised for the future. The apostle writes of having hope through "the encouragement of the Scriptures" (Rom. 15:4).

But believers also encouraged and empowered others through the bestowal of honor on one another in obedience to the apostle's instructions to "love each other with genuine affection, and take delight in honoring each other"—commending the ministries of one another (Rom. 12:10 NLT; cf. 1 Cor. 12:23–31). Mutual strengthening also came through caring for each other's needs. Both the recipient and the giver of the care received encouragement and strength in accord with the Scripture: "He who sows bountifully will also reap bountifully" (2 Cor. 9:6).

Finally, believers infused one another with new enthusiasm and confidence for coping with life through communal worship where they unitedly praised God in song, heard testimonies of the great works of God, and simply witnessed the faithful walk of others. Derek Kidner beautifully describes the power of communal worship for spiritual growth in his comment on the psalmist's desire to offer his sacrifice of thanksgiving and pay his vows to the Lord "in the presence of all His people . . . in the courts of the LORD's house" (Ps. 116:18–19). Noting that the psalmist's words are marked by an "intensely personal faith and love," Kidner said, "This flame is not withdrawn, to burn alone. Placed in the *midst*, it will kindle others, and blaze all the longer and better for it."[13]

Healing

Finally, we inevitably suffer wounds on our spiritual walk, and the community is the place of healing. Some of our wounds are self-inflicted by willfully veering from God's path of life and ending up in a thistle patch or at the bottom of a ditch. By self-centered attitudes and actions we literally tear at the very fabric of what makes us truly human—our relationship with God and others. We even rend our self as our conscience rails against us bringing the pain of guilt, shame, and self-loathing.

Because all sin is ultimately against God, he alone can be the ultimate healer.

But his healing doesn't come only through our private confession and repentance. As with all of God's grace for our spiritual journey, the grace of healing also comes through other believers.

It should be noted in passing that our sin against God is also always sin against others. For all sin is against love. Thus our sin whether private or not cannot help but affect our ability to love others. The healing of forgiveness therefore works not only to restore our relationship to God, but all relationships through which we experience true life.

As a festering wound must first be opened and cleaned before a healing agent can be applied, so the wound of sin must be opened before the balm of forgiveness can be applied. But sin resists exposure (John 3:20–21). Dietrich Bonhoeffer wisely noted what we all know by experience: "Sin demands to have a man by himself. It withdraws him from community. . . . Sin wants to remain unknown. It shuns the light. In the darkness of the unexpressed it poisons the whole being of a person."[14]

Sin wants us away from community because in community our old self-centered ego cannot be hidden. We come to know who we really are. Strife, jealousy, and almost all of the other works of the flesh mentioned in Galatians 5:19–21 become obvious when living close to other people. We learn how much we really love—that we don't actually love everybody as we thought.

But it is also in community where others are called to help us in healing our exposed sin. Writing to the Galatian believers, the apostle says, "If anyone is caught in any trespass, you who are spiritual, restore such a one in a spirit of gentleness; each one looking to yourself, so that you too will not be tempted. Bear one another's burdens, and thereby fulfill the law of Christ" (Gal. 6:1–2). Whether we take "caught in any trespass" to mean that the individual is "overtaken" or "entrapped" by a sin,[15] or that others "caught" him sinning ("detected in a transgression," NRSV), the person's sin somehow becomes known in the community.

And when his sin is known, those who are "spiritual"—those who are walking by the Spirit and can approach the person in the gentleness of Christ—are to "restore" (*katartizō*) the person. The idea of the Greek word is to "put in order," "restore to a former condition"[16] The word was used in medicine for setting a fractured or dislocated bone, or for outfitting a ship, or as in Mark 1:19 for "cleaning, mending, and folding together" fishing nets in preparation for the next time out (Mark 1:19).[17] Restoring the sinner, therefore, meant doing whatever it took to bring the person back to his or her former good state, preparing him or her for renewed life and service. It was amendment, not punishment.

Several ministries functioned in the New Testament fellowship to help the members become aware of their sin and aid in the healing process. Exhortation, from the Greek word *parakaleō*, "to call someone to oneself," which as we saw earlier can also signify encouragement, refers to a friendly appeal on the basis of the Word of God for people to live according to the ethics of the gospel. Exhortation was primarily the responsibility of the mature leadership of the community (Acts 20:1–2; 1 Thess. 2:11; 4:1; 1 Tim. 4:3; 2 Tim. 4:2), but it could be practiced by other members as well (Rom. 12:8; 1 Cor. 14:31).

The ministry of admonishing, which sought to turn the person from wrong thinking and actions, through "appropriate instruction, exhortation, warning and correction,"[18] also took place within the community. Like exhortation, admonishing was a responsibility of the community leaders (e.g., Col. 1:28; 1 Thess. 5:12). But all members were also encouraged to admonish each other even as the apostle Paul told the Roman believers, "I . . . am convinced that you yourselves are full of goodness, filled with all knowledge and able also to admonish one another" (Rom. 15:14). Similarly, believers in Colosse were instructed to "let the message of Christ dwell among you richly as you teach and admonish one another with all wisdom" (Col. 3:16 niv; cf. 1 Thess. 5:14; 2 Thess. 3:15).

Being a part of a close-knit family of believers was itself a powerful influence in helping the individual stay on course. Paul's letters to various churches included many exhortations for believers to help one another in inculcating and carrying out the ethical demands of the faith. But, in the opinion of one interpreter of the Thessalonian letters, the most important factor in maintaining the norms of Christian behavior was the group influence exerted through *"the sense of community fostered* by the apostle among his converts."[19] Living in a community as brothers and sisters in the family of God is a strong field of spiritual power that we all need for growth against the power of sin.

These mutual ministries that encourage us in our walk and help us to see where we are stumbling and straying from the path of life are not yet fully

The Molding Power of Community

"Without a community to reinforce the new beliefs and values and to encourage proper Christian behavior and practice, it is unlikely that Paul's converts would have survived as Christians. . . .

"Evangelical Christianity needs to strive to create a social context or community in which converts may be resocialized into a new and distinctively Christian pattern of behavior and practice. Without this, conversion is not complete and has little chance of being genuinely transformative in the long term."[20]

healing. Our sin needs not only to be exposed but healed through the grace of God's forgiveness. Again, this healing grace is communicated through the mutual relationship of the members of the community. God tells believers to do the following:

+ "Bear with each other and forgive one another if any of you has a grievance against someone. Forgive as the Lord forgave you" (Col. 3:13 NIV).
+ "With all humility and gentleness, with patience, showing tolerance for [or bearing with] one another in love" (Eph. 4:2).
+ "Be kind to one another, tender-hearted, forgiving each other, just as God in Christ also has forgiven you" (Eph. 4:32).
+ "Therefore, accept one another, just as Christ also accepted us to the glory of God" (Rom. 15:7).
+ "Bear one another's burdens [which in the context of the restoration of the person caught in sin surely includes the bearing of the other's sins], and thereby fulfill the law of Christ" (Gal. 6:2).

The law of Christ is the law of *bearing*—the bearing of the cross in which he bore the burden of our sins. We are called to follow Christ in living out that same cross with one another. We, of course, are not the source of forgiveness as he was. But we can be the expression of his forgiveness to others. As Luther said, because Christ dwells in us, we "are Christs one to another and do to our neighbors as Christ does to us."[21] Through our visible concrete acts of forgiveness we help another experience the reality of the grace of Christ's own invisible forgiveness.

In sum, we encounter God's grace for the healing of our wounds of sin not only through coming to him privately in confession and repentance, but also in the community—in the face of our brothers and sisters in whom Christ lives. Spiritual transformation apart from the fellowship of Christ's body is therefore not only to shun healing grace; it is to place ourselves in spiritual danger.

Along with the wounds from our own sin, we are destined to suffer wounds from persecution and various hurts that come to all people simply from living in a fallen world—fear, grief, loneliness, insecurity, hopelessness, and sufferings of all kinds. Certainly, God can and does apply his healing balm for these wounds directly to the individual. But he also deigns to communicate it through the community of believers in whom he lives by his Spirit. Even as there is a fellowship of suffering—"if one member suffers, all the members suffer with it" (1 Cor. 12:26)—so there is a fellowship of God's comfort.

Writing to the church at Corinth, Paul said,

> Praise be to the God and Father of our Lord Jesus Christ, the Father
> of compassion and the God of all comfort, who comforts us in all our
> troubles, so that we can comfort those in any trouble with the comfort
> we ourselves receive from God. For just as we share abundantly in the
> sufferings of Christ, so also our comfort abounds through Christ. If we
> are distressed, it is for your comfort and salvation; if we are comforted,
> it is for your comfort, which produces in you patient endurance of the
> same sufferings we suffer. And our hope for you is firm, because we
> know that just as you share in our sufferings, so also you share in our
> comfort. (2 Cor. 1:3–7 NIV).

Such mutual comforting is woven throughout the New Testament. The
Corinthians who were comforted through Paul, in turn give comfort to the vis-
iting Titus who then goes on to bring comfort to Paul (2 Cor. 7:6–7). Paul sent
Tychicus to the Ephesian believers to let them know about his circumstances
and so comfort their hearts (Eph. 6:22; Col. 4:7–8). All believers are encouraged
to comfort one another with the truth of the resurrection in the grief of the loss
of a loved one (1 Thess. 4:18).

No matter what our hurt may be, our great Comforter has provided a refuge
of encouragement and comfort in the community of his people where we meet
him in the face of our fellow believers. The pain of loneliness is eased by the
sense of belonging that comes through being a part of an accepting community.
Fears and insecurities are diminished by the strength and courage of others who
in reality are part of us. The truth of Ecclesiastes 4:10 is profoundly applicable

How Others Change Our Heart

The benefits derived through the interchange in close relationships are also commonly
described in terms of three general functions explained by Stephen Greggo: "*Informa-
tional support* is communication offering guidance, direction, perspective and/or useful
resources. *Emotional support* is any behavior that communicates care and love for
another. *Instrumental support* refers to any behavior that offers assistance in task completion or increases coping skill and/or resources."

Greggo ties these support areas to what we have seen of the heart and its
transformation when he notes that these areas "can be linked to the common depiction
for one's internal personality, namely, how one thinks, feels, and acts. External social
support nurtures the cognitive, affective, and behavioral domains central to the
individual's external world."[22]

to the healing of the wounds that we all suffer along the way in our spiritual walk: "Woe to one who is alone and falls and does not have another to help" (4:10 NRSV).

The Supreme Effect: Growth in Love

Finally, the supreme effect of community, and in a very real sense the summation of all of the effects noted above, is the growth of love. More than any other "one another" command, God tells us to "love one another" (at least sixteen times). For example,

+ "A new command I give to you, that you love one another, even as I have loved you, that you also love one another. By this all men will know that you are My disciples, if you have love for one another" (John 13:34–35).
+ "Owe nothing to anyone except to love one another" (Rom. 13:8)
+ "Now as to the love of the brethren, you have no need for anyone to write to you, for you yourselves are taught by God to love one another" (1 Thess. 4:9).
+ "Since you have in obedience to the truth purified your souls for a sincere love of the brethren, fervently love one another from the heart" (1 Peter 1:22)
+ "Beloved, let us love one another, for love is from God and everyone who loves is born of God and knows God" (1 John 4:7).*

Believers were also to greet one another with "a kiss of love" (1 Peter 5:14) or "a holy kiss" (Rom. 16:16; 1 Cor. 16:20; 1 Thess. 5:26). This word "kiss" (*philēma*) is related to the Greek word for "love" (*phileō*) that has the basic idea of loving what *belongs* to you. To kiss one another with "a holy kiss" was therefore to actualize the love that bound believers together in the community as a family, as those who *belonged* to each other.[23]

Because it is our nature as the image of God to love, the more we give and receive love, the more we become the human persons that we were created to be. We began our spiritual life by receiving God's love in Christ and we grow through that same love which is communicated in the fellowship of believers. "If we love one another," the apostle John wrote, "God abides in us, and His love is perfected in us" (1 John 4:12).

It has been rightly said that only heart communicates to heart. Thus as God's

---

* See also John 15:12, 17; 1 Thess. 3:12; 2 Thess. 1:3; 1 John 3:11, 23; 1 John 4:11, 12; 2 John 5.

love and grace for our spiritual growth comes from his heart to our heart, so our mutual ministries of his grace must be expressions of fervent "love . . . from the heart" to one another (1 Peter 1:22). The biblical proverb, "As iron sharpens iron, so one man sharpens another," can only function with swords when they are removed from their scabbards. So the more our hearts are open to give our self in love to another and to receive the other into our heart, the more the love of God is present for our growth.

The reciprocal process of our spiritual growth through loving relationships is well described in the following comment on the dynamic of human growth: "The more I relate the more I become myself; the more I become myself, the more I relate."[24] To run from others is therefore actually to run from my own heart, which longs for communion with others.

To love one another is not just the command of God. Like the first great commandment, to "love God with all your heart," and, in fact, all of God's commands (Ps. 19:7), to love one another is to experience life. The more we love, the more we live.

Love: The Passion of Life

"To give up one's life means to go outside oneself, to love, to expose oneself, and to spend oneself. In this passionate renunciation one's whole life becomes alive because it makes other life alive. . . . Only the passion of love makes a person alive right down to the very fingertips. At the same time it makes a person able and ready to die.

"That which abides in the passion of life, in the midst of living and dying, is *love*, the mysterious center of life and death, the passionate yes to life, and the passionate no to the negation of life."[25]

Conclusion

Since we were created to live in relationship with God and our fellow human beings, our spiritual transformation is ultimately nothing more than the restoration and spiritual maturing of true human life through fellowship with God and his people. God, the source of all love and life, communicates himself to us both directly and through other believers in whom he lives so that we might become knit together in community like his own divine fellowship—Father, Son, and Spirit.

When we open our heart to another believer, we not only receive that person into our heart. We receive God himself and his grace of transformation. As members of the body of Christ, believers minister to one another as the hands and feet of Christ. The word of another believer can be the voice of God's guidance. The touch of the everlasting arms that sometimes seem so far off can be felt in the touch of a Christian friend.

The goal of all spiritual transformation is Christlikeness and this is found preeminently in loving community. "All men will know that you are my disciples," Jesus said, "if you have love for one another" (John 13:35). He prayed that his disciples "may all be one . . . so that the world may believe that You sent me" (John 17:21).

The community of God's people united in love is the greatest manifestation of Christ's presence to the world around us. Church historian Henry Chadwick testifies to this truth when he writes concerning the success of the church in the first centuries: "The practical application of charity was probably the most potent single cause of Christian success. The pagan comment 'See how these Christians love one another' (reported by Tertullian) was not irony."[26]

God and his transforming grace are most evident in the sphere of a loving community, even as the apostle John wrote: "No one has seen God at any time; if we love one another, God abides in us" (1 John 4:12). The results of genuine fellowship are well expressed in the following:

> I sought my soul, and my soul eluded me.
> I sought my God, and my God I could not see.
> I sought my brother, and I found all three.[27]

Questions for Thought

1. In the picture of our transformation as a journey with God, have any of your fellow travelers provided help for you—guidance, empowerment, healing? Think about it in terms of general help such a teaching, but also specific instances and the effect of the help.

2. In the same picture of the journey, think about any instances where you helped others with their needs for their journey? In loving them and doing something to help them grow, what was the effect on your own growth?

3. In our journey with God and pursuit of spiritual transformation, we can expect strong resistance from the enemy of our souls. Have you ever found it difficult to fight those battles against his temptations (including fear and worry) alone? Have you ever been helped in these battles by another believer? Think of the time when others walked with you, helping you through a dark time.

4. Meditate on the thought that "to run from others is therefore actually to run from my own heart, which longs for communion with others." Do you need to do anything to grow in this area?

▪▪ 13 ▪▪

All Together Now

Spiritual Transformation as Holistic Salvation

> For by grace you are saved through faith, and this is not from your-
> selves, it is the gift of God; it is not from works, so that no one can
> boast. For we are his workmanship, having been created in Christ
> Jesus for good works that God prepared beforehand so we may do
> them.
>
> EPHESIANS 2:8–10 NET

> My entire hope is exclusively in your very great mercy. Grant what
> you command, and command what you will.
>
> AUGUSTINE

We have now looked at the basic nature of our heart and functions of mind, emotion, and volition and how they mutually interact together. We have also seen how God works through these dynamics of our heart to bring about change and growth in that new abundant life, which he designed for us and desires to give us. To summarize what we have seen: we are transformed by receiving God and his truth into the depth of our heart whereby the living power of God's presence through the Spirit works to transform our heart—our thoughts, our emotions, and our actions—into the likeness of his own heart and thereby conforming us to Christ our Savior.

In this chapter and the next, we want to gather together the various dynamics of change that we have seen into a more holistic picture of biblical spiritual transformation. This will provide further insight into the nature and characteristics of genuine spiritual transformation and also aid in evaluating our progress in our spiritual journey. Hopefully, it will also provide a deeper theological understanding of the process and answer some questions such as how the necessity of our activity or work in our own transformation relates to salvation by grace through faith and not works.

In this chapter we will see three primary traits of genuine biblical transformation. It is (1) a personal and holistic transformation, (2) fundamentally a transformation of love, and (3) a transformation that is totally by grace through faith. In the final chapter we will focus on the vital truth that spiritual life and growth is realized ultimately only by living in a personal relationship with God through Christ by the Holy Spirit.

Spiritual Transformation Is Personal and Holistic

We have seen throughout our discussion that we are changed by renewing our thoughts, our feelings, and our actions in an integrated unity. Our transformation has thus rightly been described as "one single, comprehensive experience in which all the three are united in such a manner that each contributes its share, and all cooperate unto man's salvation and God's glory. This experience is personal in character."[1]

Spiritual Transformation Is Re-creation to Personal Wholeness

Jesus concisely summed up this integrated process of our transformation in the following words to his heavenly Father: "I have made Your name known to them, and will make it known, so that the love with which You loved Me *may be in them*" (John 17:26). Coming to know God means being transformed into a loving person.

Such transformation is what the Scripture means when it speaks of "being saved" as in the apostle's statement, "the word of the cross is foolishness to those who are perishing, but to us who are *being saved* it is the power of God" (1 Cor. 1:18; cf. 2 Cor. 2:15). Salvation is more than deliverance from God's wrath and punishment and thus the gift of eternal life. It includes our restoration to wholeness as human persons. Thus when Paul says we are presently "being saved" he is declaring that as believers we are presently in the process of being restored to the wholeness of true human life.

In the Old Testament, salvation is frequently pictured as rescuing someone from an oppressive constricting situation in which life is cramped and choked off and placing him in a spacious roomy environment where he has freedom to develop and enjoy fullness of life without hindrance.[2] A number of the psalmists testify to this salvation: "You gave me room when I was in distress" (Ps. 4:1 NRSV). "He brought me forth also into a broad place; He rescued me, because He delighted in me" (18:19; cf. v. 36). "From my distress I called upon the LORD;

the LORD answered me and set me in a large place" (118:5).[3] This liberating salvation enables the heart to grow in the ways of God as the writer of Psalm 119 testified, "I shall run the way of Your commandments, for You will enlarge my heart (v. 32).

The New Testament Greek word for "salvation" (*sōtēria*, "salvation"; *sōzō*, "save, rescue") is similarly used for healing and restoration to wholeness as well as for salvation from sin and judgment. To the woman who was healed of her hemorrhaging, Jesus declared, "Daughter, your faith has made you well [or saved you]" (Mark 5:34). Those freed from the oppression of demons are described as "made well," or "saved" (Luke 8:36).[4]

God's salvation is thus a comprehensive work. It rescues us not only from the penalty of our sin, but from all the destructive effects of sin and its disorder in our life, and restores us to wholeness. Although this restoration in terms of our physical body will occur only in the future through a new resurrected body, salvation is already at work in our "inner person" since the day we received a new heart. We are in the process of "being transformed" from death and ruin[*] "into . . . [Christ's] image with ever-increasing glory" (2 Cor. 3:18 NIV), growing toward our destiny of conformity to the perfect humanness of Jesus (Rom. 8:29). It is this "salvation" that we are challenged to continually "work out" in the process of "being saved," or in spiritual transformation (Phil. 2:12).

Such holistic transformation requires that we learn to live as a *new person* in a *new realm of life*—as people who are part of a "new creation." As Scripture declares, "If anyone is in Christ, he is a new creature; the old things passed away; behold, new things have come" (2 Cor. 5:17). Transformation, or learning to live as a new creation, thus entails "a total restructuring of life that alters its whole fabric—thinking, feeling, willing, and acting."[5]

Before we came to Christ, we lived as players in the story of this old fallen world order that is passing away (1 John 2:17)—this "present evil age" (Gal. 1:4). We lived according to the values of this world, which the apostle John describes as doing "what the sinful self desires, what people see and want, and everything in this world that people are so proud of" (1 John 2:16 GNT).

The apostle Paul provided a rather comprehensive description of our former life when he said, "And you were dead in your trespasses and sins, in which you formerly walked according to the course of this world, according to the prince of

---

* Antonyms of "salvation" are "death" (2 Cor. 7:10) and "destruction," "ruin," and "perishing" (1 Cor. 1: 18; 2 Cor. 2:15). The restoration of the disorder in our physical being awaits the future salvation of the transformation of the body in glorification. But it is part of the same salvation in Christ.

the power of the air, of the spirit that is now working in the sons of disobedience. Among them we too all formerly lived in the lusts of our flesh, indulging the desires of the flesh and of the mind" (Eph. 2:1–3). To put it plainly, "we did what everybody else did . . . we did what the devil wanted . . . we enjoyed it because we did what pleased our flesh and our thoughts."[6]

This is no longer our life. As new persons, we live in a new story—the great biblical drama of God's historical saving activity. We still reside in this old world and are involved in its affairs, but we are no longer "of this world" (John 15:19; 17:14). We don't belong to this old world's system—it's no longer the matrix of our life. The perspectives of life and values of this present world are no longer ours. God has "rescued us from the domain of darkness, and transferred us to the kingdom of His beloved Son" (Col. 1:13). We are "aliens and strangers" in this present evil age (1 Peter 2:11; cf. Heb. 11:13). The kingdom of God with heavenly values and principles of life is our real "homeland," which in the age to come will be new heavens and new earth where righteousness dwells (Phil. 3:20; 2 Peter 3:12).

Living in this new realm, we already experience something of its newness. In the depth of our heart, we are new persons. Our identity is new—we are sons and daughters in the family of God. We pray to a Father in heaven. Our life has a new perspective with new meaning (or more properly, real meaning for the first time). We have new values that now include God and eternity. But with all the reality of our newness, our daily life still has many of the characteristics of our old life of this world.

We are like vagabond children who have been adopted by a loving king to live in his palace. Brought up in a dysfunctional family and accustomed to an unruly life, these children must learn to take on the characteristics of their new home. So we, who formerly lived a life shaped by a sinful, twisted, ego-centered hateful heart (Titus 3:3), must learn to live life according to the new realities of the kingdom of our heavenly Father.

Like an actor seeks to inhabit or live in the story of the script in which he or she has a role, so we learn to live our life in accord with our new kingdom citizenship.* We do this by indwelling the Scriptures, the new story of God's historical redemption, until the realities of our new home—*as it really is "in*

---

* Although the church is not the kingdom and we yet await Christ's kingdom to be established on earth at his coming, the Word (e.g. Matt. 13:19) and power of the kingdom through the Holy Spirit (1 Cor. 4:20) are present today in and through the church to enable members of the church as citizens of that kingdom to fulfill God's will for their lives and to live according to kingdom characteristics (e.g. "righteousness, peace and joy," Rom. 14:17).

Christ"—become real in us. This means incorporating the truth of Scripture in all its various forms—whether historical stories, propositional teaching, or emotional prayers—into our hearts so that our total person is transformed and we learn to think, feel, and act in accord with Jesus.[7]

Spiritual Transformation Is Change of Person, Not Simply Change of Behavior

Scripture provides the pattern of our new life in the form of instructions, commands, and examples that cover our attitudes and behavior for all of life.[*] As we have seen in the previous chapter, attending to our actions in obedience to God's Word is vital to our transformation. But it is possible for us to attend so much to obeying the commandments—especially those that deal with our external behavior that can be seen—that we overlook the truth that biblical transformation is the change of the *person* and not simply the *external behavior* of the person. It is the creation of a new self, not behavior modification of the old self.

We tend to focus on the commands dealing with our external life—our words, emotional displays, and actions. Being more obvious, our external behavior can impact our life more immediately with pangs of guilt and shame in the case of wrongful displays, and positive feelings when they are good. It also more directly impacts our relationships with others. Finally, we may desire to control our behavior in order to please our Lord.

Beyond these explanations, however, something more sinister and often unperceived lurks in much of our commandment-keeping. We desire to be well thought of by others and even by ourselves. In the words of Jesus, we "accept glory from one another" (John 5:44).

Whatever the motive or mixture of motives, we try hard to be people of integrity that tell the truth, that don't lie or steal. We try to exercise patience and control our temper. We seek to be faithful in our obligations to our family and especially to God, attending church, giving our tithes and offerings and being involved in some form of service. In general, we try to be a good person and a good neighbor to those around us.

Keeping our Lord's behavioral commandments should be the desire of every

---

* This is not to say that God did not address his word to humankind before our fall into sin. According to the Genesis creation account, God communicated with human beings from the beginning as Person to person through words (language). We also know something of the basic principles of the pattern of our new life by nature through God's law written on our heart (Rom 2:14–15). But this knowledge was dimmed and even perverted by our rebellious heart in accommodation to our self-centered desires.

believer and is vital to our transformation. But we must never lose sight of the truth that genuine transformation is transformation of the heart and thus of the whole person.

According to the psalmist, the believer is "like a tree firmly planted by streams of water, which yields its fruit in season and its leaf does not wither; and in whatever he does, he prospers" (Ps. 1:3; cf. Ps. 92:12–14; Jer. 17:7–8). Leaves and fruit give evidence of the tree's life, but they do not determine it. Rather the tree's life stems from roots hidden deep in the soil that are nourished by streams of water, which in this context is the Word of God (v. 2; cf. Isa. 44:6; Rev. 22:1–2).

Picking off withered leaves and bad fruit may make the tree look better, but it makes no real change in the nature or condition of the tree. In the same way, dealing with our outward behavior brings little genuine transformation of us as persons. It is like taking medication that alleviates the painful symptoms of a disease without dealing with the systemic root cause.

In a word, striving to conform our attitudes and actions to the commands of our Lord is truly transformative only if it is part of an obedience of the whole person from the heart. Any real change in our life through obedience to biblical commands ultimately flows from a change of our person. Historian Will Durant put it this way: "Caesar hoped to reform men by changing institutions, and laws; Christ wished to remake institutions, and lessen laws by changing men."[8]

Spiritual Transformation Is Gaining a New Self through the Dying of the Old Self

Jesus taught the one ultimate change necessary in all genuine heart transformation when he declared, "If anyone wishes to come after Me, he must deny himself, and take up his cross daily and follow Me. For whoever wishes to save his life will lose it, but whoever loses his life for My sake, he is the one who will save it" (Luke 9:23–24).

All true biblical transformation flows from this radical denial of self, which was demonstrated by Jesus himself who, when faced with his own desire to avoid the awful "cup" of the suffering of the cross, said to his heavenly Father, "Not my will, but Yours be done" (Luke 22:42).

At its core, spiritual transformation is the change of lords over our lives— from the lordship of self to the lordship of Christ. We began our walk with Christ by repenting of our old selfish life and in faith surrendering ourselves to him. The process of continued transformation of heart and life is simply growing

Christ's Self-Denial and Ours

The self-denial of Jesus is not exactly like our denial of ourselves in that, although faced with his own desire, he never actually chose his own will in opposition to that of his heavenly Father, which as sinners we often do. In these instances our self-denial must include repentance from sin—from living according to our own "godhood"—which Christ did not need as he always accepted the will of God as his own. Our renunciation of self obviously will not and cannot be done by the self; only the power of God can enable the self to surrender itself to God. Thus Jesus begins and ends his call for renunciation of self with a call to himself: "If any wishes to come after Me, he must deny himself, and . . . follow Me (Luke 9:23). Only by coming to him (placing our faith in him) and continually following him, hearing and obeying his Word, are we able to deny self and take up our cross, and live daily as those whose old self is dead.

in the actualization of this exchange in our daily experience until all of life is fully centered in God.

This renunciation of self, at the root of all transformation, is more than *renouncing various sins* of failure to keep God's commandments—a kind of sin management. It is the *renunciation of myself* as the "god" of my life. It is more than forsaking the activities of the autonomous self-centered self. It is giving up that self. It is not incorporating Christ into *my* life, but endeavoring "to transpose our life into Christ and entrust it to Him: indeed, to be possessed by Him."[9] It is ceasing to be my old independent self, running my life as my own lord, and instead, seeing myself as a new person living in union with my new Lord.

Spiritual transformation requires seeing our old self as dead—daily taking up our cross (Luke 9:23), which according to the Roman custom was the action of one already condemned to death and made to bear his cross to the place of crucifixion.[10] Thus Scripture challenges us to "consider yourselves dead to sin" (Rom. 6:11) which, in fact, we are. Through faith in Christ, we have been joined to him so that we participate in his redeeming work. The apostle Paul puts it this way: "Our old self was crucified with Him . . . so that we would no longer be slaves to sin: for he who has died is freed from sin" (Rom. 6:6–7). What the apostle says is that when we came to Christ, our old person—who we really were at the core of our heart—died with Christ and was raised a new person who now shares in Christ's resurrection life never to die again.

Although there is no evidence that Paul's words or concepts were borrowed from the religious practices of the Jews or Greeks of that time, these surrounding practices, no doubt, suggest something of how Paul's words of becoming a new person would have been understood by his hearers. One of the requirements for a pagan to come into the Jewish religion was the ritual of baptism. According to William Barclay, this baptism

> was held to be complete regeneration; the man was a new man; he was born anew. He was called a little child just born, the child of one day. . . . The completeness of the change is seen in the fact that certain Rabbis held that a man's child born after baptism was his first-born, even if he had had children before baptism. Theoretically, it was held—although the belief was never put into practice—that a man was so much a completely new man that he might marry his own sister or his own mother. He was not only a changed man, he was a new man, a different man. Any Jew would fully understand Paul's words about the necessity of a baptized man being a completely new man.[11]

Entrance into a Greek mystery religion similarly involved an initiation that made the person new.

> [It] was always regarded as a death followed by a new birth, by which the man was *renatus in aeternum*, reborn for eternity. . . . In one of the mysteries the man to be initiated was called *moriturus*, the one who is to die, and . . . he was buried up to his head in a trench. When he had been initiated he was addressed as a little child and fed with milk. In another of the mysteries the person to be initiated prayed [to a god]: "Enter though into my spirit, my thought, my whole life; for thou art I and I am thou."[12]

In a much more profound and real way than in these religious practices the believer in union with the Christ, the One who died to sin and was raised in newness of life, is a radically new person who in the depth of his heart—the core of his person—has likewise died and been resurrected a new person.

This is more than theology; it is reality. As Christians *we are no longer slaves of sin*. Through faith we are joined to Christ and have his new life even as a newborn baby has new life. But an infant does not immediately experience the fullness of human life—it unfolds and blossoms only through growth. So the experience of our new life in Christ requires growth in actually living "in Christ" through continually affirming, "not my will, but yours be done." Our spiritual growth requires that we continually ask our hearts: "Is this God's thought or my own? Is my attitude toward this situation or person the attitude of my Lord or it is the feeling of my old self-centered, god-playing self who wants his way? Is what I desire to do at this moment what God wants me to do or simply what I want? Is my motive in doing this love for God and others—genuinely seeking their good—or selfish love for myself? What is my ambition in life, God's goals or my own? Who (or what) is the practical god of my life—is it pleasure, importance, success, security, or anything else that serves and enhances me as the ultimate ruler of my life, or is it the one true God?"

Without growth in recognizing and learning to say "no" to self when we recognize it as usurping the place of God in our lives, spiritual transformation cannot take place.

Because sin brings spiritual death—alienation from the living God—the sinful impure person in the Old Testament could find access into God's presence only through the blood (representing the giving up of life in death) of an animal substitute. The same is true for our spiritual life and growth—fellowship with God comes only through death of the sinner.

Christ's death as our substitute gives us access into God's presence. But even as the Old Testament worshipper was required to personally identify with the death of the sacrificial animal by placing his hands on the head of the animal, so our fellowship with God requires that we personally identify with Christ's death for us by dying to self, considering our old self as dead.

In order to experience the fellowship of God and his life-changing power in our daily life, dying to self through participation in Christ's death must be continually affirmed. Thus frequently, if not each time that we come to our Lord in prayer and worship, it can be helpful to affirm afresh our original denial of self that brought us into fellowship with our divine heart changer.

Such saying "no" to the old self is far from making our spiritual growth a negative experience. For it is only through a continual denial of the old self that we grow in the new self and the experience of its new life. It is the person "who loses his life for My sake," Jesus said, "who will save it" (Luke 9:24, or "find it," Matt. 10:39).*

As he approached his own death, Jesus told his disciples, "Truly, truly, I say to you unless a grain of wheat falls into the earth and dies, it remains alone; but if it dies, it bears much fruit." He goes on to apply this same principle to all people: "Anyone who loves their life will lose [destroy][13] it, while anyone who hates their life in this world will keep it for eternal life" (John 12:25 NIV).

---

* This thought is central to Paul's teaching that knowing or experiencing Christ and the power of his resurrection in our life involves participation in his sufferings (as a believer exposed to the evil powers of this present age) and being conformed to his death (i.e., dying to self in all circumstances).

Defining the love of one's self as wanting one's own will, Augustine said, "Prefer to [do] God's will; learn to love thyself by not loving thyself."[14] Far from throwing self away, we are simply giving up life centered in self—the old life of this world that is passing away—for life centered in Christ who is truly life. We are exchanging the old self that depended on its own resources and was consequently burdened with guilt, fears, and inadequacies of every kind for a new self that participates in the richly adequate and abundant life of God.

Spiritual Transformation Is Ethical Transformation in Love

Holistic personal transformation means changes in all areas of life. If our heart is changing, there will be changes in our morals and ethics, in our relationship with God and others, and in our attitudes and actions toward everything. All of these various changes, however, are the fruit of the one change that underlies all genuine spiritual growth—the change of love, the supreme mark of the Christian believer's life.

The great desire of Jesus, as someone has vividly expressed it, was "to tear

Love Is the Crucial Barometer of Spiritual Life

Scripture teaches many important characteristics of the believer's life that might be mentioned along with love, such as holiness, fear of God, glorifying God. But several truths point to love as the crucial mark of the believer's life:

(1) All of the commandments, the keeping of which would render one holy, are summed up in love (Mark 12:28–33; cf. Deut. 6:5). As church historian Everett Ferguson says, "God's covenants are not so much legal relationships as love relationships, a fact shown by the marriage analogies employed by the prophets (Jer. 2:2; Ezek. 16:8–14; Hos. 2:1–3:1)."[15]

(2) Love, modeled after Jesus' own sacrificial love for his people, is the great commandment of Jesus to his disciples under the new covenant and the mark by which his people give evidence to the world that they are his disciples (John 13:34–35; 15:12, 17).

(3) Love is the basis or root of commandment keeping (John 14:21, 23–24); it goes beyond the outward action involved in commandment keeping to the inner attitude, which is probably the harder to obey and therefore most revealing of our sinful self-centeredness.

(4) Love is the greatest of theological virtues (1 Cor. 13:13; cf. Col. 3:14). This is no doubt so because as God's people we are destined to reflect the love of Trinitarian relationships (John 17:11–26). Thomas à Kempis rightly said, "Nothing is sweeter than love, nothing stronger, nothing higher, nothing wider, nothing more pleasant, nothing fuller or better in heaven or earth; for love is born of God, and can rest only in God, above all created things."[16] In sum, our spiritual life is fundamentally based on a relationship with God, and of all of the marks of the believer, love is the greatest relational term.[17]

the heart of man from the rancid swamp of his ego, and plant him in the sweet soil of love."[18] Spiritual transformation that is not growth in love is not biblical transformation.

Love Is Our Nature as Children of the God Who Is Love

Because we are sons and daughters of a God whose very nature is love, it is logical as Scripture teaches that the crucial evidence of our new life is also love. "Love is from God; and everyone who loves is born of God and knows God. The one who does not love does not know God, for God is love. . . . God is love, and the one who abides in love abides in God, and God abides in him" (1 John 4:7–8, 16). "Follow God's example, therefore, as dearly loved children and walk in the way of love" (Eph. 5:1–2 NIV). "By this all men will know that you are My disciples, if you have love for one another" (John 13:35). To "know the love of Christ" is to become "filled with all the fullness of God"—that is, the fullness of the life of God that is in Christ (Col. 1:19; 2:9).

The story of God's redemption in which we live is a love story: "For God so loved the world, that He gave His only begotten Son, that whoever believes in Him shall not perish but have eternal life" (John 3: 16). It is, in fact, this story that gives the true meaning of love as the apostle John explained, "This is love: not that we loved God, but that he loved us and sent his Son as an atoning sacrifice* for our sins" (1 John 4:10 NIV). To put it succinctly, Jesus is the paradigm of love—God in human flesh living and dying for the welfare of others, even for those who did not love him (Eph. 5:2; Rom. 5:8).

Love Is the Fruit of Our New Life

In Jesus' metaphor of the vine and the branches there are only two commandments given to believers as the fruit-bearing branches, and these are inseparable—"abide in Me" and "abide in My love" (John 15:5, 9). Abiding in Christ, to be alive with his life, is to abide in his love—to live in the experience of Christ's love both *for* us and *through* us to others.

To abide in his love, as Jesus explained, is to obey his commandments (v. 10), the chief of which is "love one another, just as I have loved you" (vv. 12, 17; 13:43; cf. 1 John 3:23; 2 John 5). This primacy of love in the life of the believer is echoed by the apostle Paul when he described the growth of the church as growth "in love" (Eph. 4:15–16).

---

* "Atoning sacrifice" is literally "propitiation," which here means the *satisfaction* and thus the turning away of God's wrath against us because of our sins by the sacrifice of God himself in the person of Christ on the cross.

Love also stands at the head of the list of virtues that describe the "fruit" produced by the Spirit in our new life—"love, joy, peace, patience, kindness, goodness, faithfulness, gentleness, self-control" (Gal. 5:22–23). As Richard Longenecker explains, all of the other qualities in the list of the Spirit's fruit are in reality only various displays of love:

> It appears that Paul is not so concerned with precisely how each of these matters works out in practice, but with the underlying orienta-tion of selfless and outgoing concern for others. For in commitment to God through Jesus Christ one discovers a new orientation for life that reflects the selfless and outgoing love of God himself. It is not, as in Eastern philosophy, the denial of the ego or the created self. Rather, it is freedom from the contaminating effects of egoism and self-centeredness, with the result that now such virtues as 'love, joy, peace, patience, kindness, goodness, faithfulness, gentleness, and self-control' can be expressed in the Christian life in ways that are beneficial to oth-ers and that reflect God at work in the Christian's life, apart from one's own sinful egocentricity.[19]

Love Is the Supreme Command That Encompasses All Commands

When questioned concerning the greatest commandment of the Law, Jesus replied that all of the commandments of the Israel's Old Testament covenant (Jewish tradition counted 613),[20] and all of the exhortations for godly living by the prophets depend on two great commandments of love—"You shall love the Lord your God with all your heart, and with all your soul, and with all your mind," and, "You shall love your neighbor as yourself" (Matt. 22:37–40).

If our spiritual transformation is essentially learning to walk according to the many commands and instructions of our Lord that direct us in the way of life, then it is clear that our transformation centers on learning to love.

The apostles echo the truth of Jesus, declaring that "one who loves another has fulfilled the law" (Rom. 13:8 ESV; cf. Gal. 5:17; James 2:8). Since it is the nature of love to seek the good of others, love inevitably produces the righteous relationships toward God and others commanded by the Law. "Love does no wrong to a neighbor; therefore love is the fulfilling of the law" (Rom. 13:10).*

---

* Love as the obedience to God's commands is also seen in the comparison of 1 John 2:3–4 with 4:7–8. In the first reference our knowledge of God is evidenced by keeping his commandments while in the second, love is the evidence.

After listing a number virtues that we are to put on like clothes, Paul added, "Beyond all these things put on love, which is the perfect bond of unity" (Col. 3:14). As Peter O'Brien explains, love is the crowning grace because it is "the bond that leads to perfection," that is, the power that enables people to live for the good of others and the whole in perfect unity and harmony.[21]

There can be no obedience to our Lord's commands without love, for love and obedience are mutually related. Love leads to obedience and obedience leads to love. "If you love me," Jesus said, "you will keep my commandments" (John 14:15, cf. 21, 23). "If you keep My commandments, you will abide in My love" (John 15:10).

We love because God first loved us (1 John 4:19), and our love manifests itself in obedience to his commands. But our obedience also draws us ever deeper into God's love. Thus there is an endless spiral of God's love at work in us. The dynamic of the believer's life is simply "faith working through love" (Gal. 5:6). In short, the faith that first united us to God and his love continues as the channel to work that love in our life.

All of this is to say that without love, all of our obedience to the biblical commands and instructions for godly living is of no value and brings no change in our life. We may obediently spend time in the Bible and grow in knowledge, but without love, knowledge leads to arrogance (1 Cor. 9:1). We may energetically get involved in ministry utilizing our spiritual gifts and do works of great sacrifice for the benefit of others, but without love there is no spiritual growth—in the words of Paul, "I am nothing. . . . It profits me nothing" (1 Cor. 13:1–3). We may discipline our lives to put away sinful practices and take on certain virtuous behaviors. But without love these activities do not change the heart, they only change the outward appearance like the practices of many pharisaical religious leaders in Jesus' day.

Because the change of our love—dying to self in order to live for others—is the essence of our spiritual transformation—it is here where we most directly confront the power of sin in our lives. As a result much of our obedience in the process of our growth is a mixture of love and other motives. We are like children who obey their parents partly through love, but also partly from fear of punishment or to gain favors. But only the aspect of our obedience that is motivated by love produces genuine spiritual transformation.

The Way of the Spiritual Transformation of Love

Understanding our spiritual transformation as a transformation of love enables us to see the basic outline of the process of transformation. Since love is deeply personal and involves the total person, spiritual transformation requires change in our thoughts and beliefs, in our attitudes and emotions, and in our actions. Only when all of our personal functions are active are we really loving, and thus bringing about a change of love. A car can only be steered in a different direction when it is moving. So also the direction of our love can only be changed when we are in the process of loving—not simply when we think about love, or feel loving, but when we actually love with our whole person.

Because the only source of genuine love is our Creator, our transformation must begin from outside of our self. We change from a self-centered love to a love for God and other people only by opening our heart to the God who loves us and longs to communicate his life of love to us through his Son. Coming into our heart God creates it new, making it alive with his life—a life whose very essence is love.

The schematic of this transforming process is thus: from outside (God's love toward us) → inside (a created human love in the likeness of God) → outside (love flowing out for the welfare of others). God's love is transmitted to us like the force of a powerful magnet that in turn magnetizes us, causing us to reach out in love to others until all are united by the magnetic power coursing through every piece. Our love thus exists only as we have a constant input from God and an outflow to others.

To be sure, people living apart from a relationship with God do still love. But that love, which is a remnant of the image of God in them, is now a deformed love oriented inward on self—a love that in reality is the ultimate cause of the rancorous enmity among people as each person apart from God, in the depth of his heart, seeks his own good rather than that of the other.*

It was through this pattern, responding to God's love, that our relationship with God began and it is by the same pattern that we grow in that relationship. At the establishment of a covenant relationship with his Old Testament people at Mount Sinai, God said, "You yourselves have seen what I did to the Egyptians and how I bore you on eagles' wings, and brought you to Myself. Now then, if your will indeed obey My voice and keep My covenant, then you shall be My own possession among all the peoples" (Exod. 19:4–5).

The people came into relationship with their God by responding to his prior love. And that relationship was maintained and deepened by constantly remembering this initial act of their redemption and the blessings that their loving God continued to work among them.

---

* See chapter 3, "Two Fundamental Defects" subsection "Pride" and "The Christian's Heart"; and chapter 5, "The Character of the Heart Determined by Its Content."

We began our relationship with God in the same way—responding to his love revealed in his Son—and so it continues. This is why God commonly tells us of his love for us and what he has done for us in Christ before he gives us instructions on how to live in response to that love. For example, in both the letters to the Ephesians and the Colossians the first half explain what God's love has done for us in providing salvation whereas the last half instruct us how to live now that we have received that love.

This pattern of spiritual life and growth depending on first receiving God's love is also evident in Romans 12:1: "Therefore, I urge you, brethren, *by the mercies of God*, to present your bodies a living sacrifice, acceptable to God, which is your spiritual service of worship." The exhortation for us to give ourselves as a living sacrifice, which involves obedience to God's call on our lives, is grounded on God's "mercies" manifested in his saving work—mercies that we have already received and that continue to exercise their power in us through the Spirit.[22] As John Murray says, "It is the mercy of God that melts the heart and it is as we are moved by these mercies of God that we shall know the constraint of consecration."[23]

If this is the case that transformation begins with the input of God's love, then if we would be transformed our first task is not to intensify our efforts to gain virtues or try to be good, but rather to increasingly "comprehend with all the saints what is the breadth and length and height and depth, and to know the love of Christ which surpasses knowledge, that you may be filled up to all the fullness of God" (Eph. 3:18–19).

In other words, our spiritual change begins with meditating with hearts full of praise and gratitude on the biblical story of God's acts of redemption, and on his loving grace in our own experience. We are able to love (i.e., obey God's commands) only because God first loved us (1 John 4:19). And the measure of our love is directly related to the extent of our realization of his love in our lives, even as Jesus said, "He who is forgiven little, loves little" (Luke 7:47).

Above all, it is knowledge of God's infinite love manifested in the sacrifice of his Son for the forgiveness of our sins that enables us to love others with similar love. But every good thing in our life is an expression of God's love. The more we are aware of that love and gratefully welcome it into our hearts, the more that love transforms us into lovers. For when we welcome God's love, we are welcoming the God of love, who is the ultimate heart changer.

The transformation of the love of our heart not only requires that we grasp God's love in the depth of our heart, but also that we let its power move us to actively love others. The amount of water that can flow through a pipe depends both on the amount coming in *and* flowing out. If the input is constricted the outflow is reduced. But also if the outward flow is restricted, the inward flow is diminished. Similarly, the growth of the love in our heart depends both on growing in the reception of God's love toward us and growing in our active loving of others.

Spiritual Transformation Is by Grace through Faith

Throughout this study we have emphasized that all of our personal functions—our mind, emotion, and will—must be active in order for us to grow spiritually. We must hear God's Word, receive it, and obey it. This necessity of active obedience may raise questions of how faith and works are related in our spiritual growth.

We readily acknowledge that our initial salvation was totally by God's grace through faith, completely apart from any work on our part. All we did was receive what Christ did for us—he did it all. But now, we may reason, since we have new life and the Spirit living in us and empowering us to do good works, we need to add works to our faith. Aren't we given many commands to obey in our Christian life and told to "work out" our "salvation"? Doesn't this call for our activity mean that our spiritual growth and the attainment of our final salvation and glorification come by faith plus works? The answer to these questions is a resounding "no."

Spiritual Transformation Is All Grace

Scripture teaches that our salvation in its totality—past, present, and future, from start to finish—is solely by God's grace received through faith.

When some in the church in Galatia were tempted to add their human effort to God's grace in order to grow spiritually, the apostle Paul challenged them with these words: "Did you receive the Spirit by the works of the Law, or by hearing with faith? Are you so foolish? Having begun by the Spirit, are you now being perfected by the flesh?" (Gal. 3:2–3).

Paul's argument is simple: You know that you began your Christian life totally by God's grace through faith. You received the Spirit, who is God himself working the powerful grace of his salvation in your life simply by believing the good news of Christ and what he has done for you—nothing more.

If God's gracious work was sufficient to bring Christ and his saving work into your life—making you a new person with a new heart and giving you spiritual life when you were formerly spiritual dead (Eph. 2:5)—then surely that same grace is sufficient to complete the task of working out that saving work in your

Grace Is More Than an Attitude

Grace is more than a gracious attitude or disposition for Paul. It is "an effective divine power in the experience of men and women" that overlaps in meaning with "Spirit" as illustrated in the parallel concepts of being "under grace" (Rom. 6:13) and being "led by the Spirit" (Gal. 5:18).[24] That the apostle sees grace as the working of the Spirit is also evident in his own testimony: "By the grace of God I am what I am . . . I labored even more than all of them [the other apostles], yet not I, but the grace of God with me" (1 Cor. 15:10). The writer to the Hebrews also speaks of being "strengthened by grace" (Heb. 13:9).

daily experience. After all the presence of the Spirit is God's guarantee of our final salvation (1 Cor. 1:22; Eph. 1:14). What possible work of your own could you add to his work?

Trying to grow by adding our own effort to grace is not only foolish, but harmful. In doing so we are actually denying God's gracious work and cutting ourselves off from it. To those who were tempted to add to God's grace by keeping the rules and regulations of the Old Testament Jewish Law in order to attain final salvation,* Paul warned that in doing that "Christ will be of no value to you at all. . . . You . . . have been alienated from Christ; you have fallen away from grace" (Gal. 5:2–4 NIV).†

According to Paul, salvation is not a combination of the grace of God in the gift of his Son plus something that we add to that. But rather as John Stott explains the apostle's caution:

You have got to choose between a religion of law and a religion of grace, between Christ and circumcision. You cannot add circumcision (or anything else, for that matter) to Christ as necessary to salvation,

---

* The focal issue in the church of Galatia was whether Christians need to practice circumcision, which was a theological symbol for placing oneself under obligation to the rules and regulations of the Old Testament Jewish Law (cf. Gal. 5:3, "And I testify again to every man who receives circumcision, that he is under obligation to keep the whole Law"; cf. also 6:13). This teaching that Paul opposed in Galatia was apparently similar to those at the Jerusalem council in Acts 15 who insisted that in order to be saved, even as a believer in Christ it was necessary to keep the Mosaic Law (cf. Acts 15:1, "unless you are circumcised . . . you cannot be saved"). The apostle saw this as "a different gospel" (Gal. 1:6) contrary to the gospel of salvation that is attained only through faith in Christ and his saving work (cf. Gal. 2:20–21; 6:14–15).

† In saying that they "have been alienated from God; . . . fallen away from grace," Paul is not saying that they have lost their salvation. Rather he is simply pointing out the incompatibility of salvation that comes by grace through faith alone and salvation gained by our works. As Longenecker says, "It was the attempt to combine a legal attitude toward life with faith in Christ that Paul denounces as being incompatible." Richard N. Longenecker, *Galatians*, WBC 41 (Dallas: Word Books, 1990), 228.

because Christ is sufficient for salvation in Himself. If you add anything to Christ, you lose Christ. Salvation is in Christ alone by grace
alone through faith alone.[25]

The apostle knew this truth in his own life. Recognizing that his old god-
playing self had been crucified and raised with Christ, he declared, "It is no
longer I who live, but Christ lives in me; and the life which I now live in the flesh
[i.e., this present body] I live by faith in the Son of God who loved me and gave
himself up for me" (Gal. 2:20).

Faith unites us with Christ so that our spiritual life is nothing less than the
resurrection life of Christ living in us through the Spirit, which is the equivalent
of "living by the Spirit" (see Gal. 5:25). We cannot possibly add anything to
Christ's life at work in us; we can only receive it by faith. Thus the apostle prays
for the Ephesians that the Spirit would strengthen them in their "inner man"
(or heart) so "that Christ will live in you as you open the door and invite him in"
(Eph. 3:16–17 MSG).

The words of Ephesians 2:8–10, recognized by many scholars as "the best
brief summary . . . of Paul's understanding the Gospel,"[26] concisely summarize
the biblical teaching of salvation as totally by God's grace through faith alone:
"For by grace you have been saved through faith and that not of yourselves, it is
the gift of God; not as a result of works, so that no one may boast. For we are
his workmanship, created in Christ Jesus for good works, which God prepared
beforehand so that we would walk in them" (cf. v. 5).

In saying, "you have been saved," the apostle used a form of the Greek word
for "save" that indicates an action that took place in the past with its effects continuing into the present.[*] He is therefore talking not only of our initial salvation
when we first believed, but also of continuing comprehensive salvation with all
of its blessings including our present spiritual transformation. This salvation, he
says, is totally "by grace . . . through faith . . . the gift of God; not as a result of
works." It is God's work from beginning to end—"He who began a good work in
you will perfect it until the day of Christ Jesus" (Phil. 1:6).[†]

---

[*] "Have been saved" is a Greek perfect periphrastic construction which "draws attention to
the resulting state of salvation." Peter T. O'Brien, *The Letter to the Ephesians*, PNTC (Grand
Rapids: Eerdmans, 1999), 169.

[†] That salvation is totally by grace is also seen when "the grace of God" is used as the equivalent of the gospel (Col. 1:6; Acts 20:24) and the gospel is "the power of God for salvation to
everyone who believes" (Rom. 1:16). "Grace" is also used as the equivalent of "salvation" in the
apostle's warning "not to receive the grace of God in vain" and so miss out on the "day of salvation" (2 Cor. 6:1–2). Harris comments on this text as follows: "In the Pauline corpus [*he charis*

Spiritual Transformation Involves Our Work through God's Grace at Work in Us

But doesn't Scripture command us to "work out your salvation with fear and trembling" (Phil. 2:12)? How can salvation be totally the work of God's grace when we are commanded to "work out" our salvation?

These questions are answered in the words that immediately follow the command. We are to work out our salvation, the apostle says, "for [or because] it is God who is at work in you, both to will and to work for His good pleasure" (Phil. 2:13). In other words, the *working out* of our salvation is totally the result of God's continual *working in* us to supply "both *the determination to obey* his own gracious purpose and *the power to carry it out*."[27]

Yes, our working is a necessary part of our transformation, but it is not in addition to God's grace. It is totally the effect of that grace at work in us.

The true place of our works in salvation is explained by the apostle Paul when, after declaring that salvation is by grace through faith apart from works, he added, "For we are His workmanship, created in Christ Jesus for good works, which God prepared beforehand so that we may walk in them" (Eph. 2:10).

Salvation is the *creative* work of God from beginning to end. We are "His workmanship,"* and this includes our "good works," which have already been prepared by him. All of our activity, so necessary for our transformation, is thus the fruit of God's grace. As Andrew Lincoln aptly explains, "To say that God has prepared the good works in advance in his sovereign purpose is also to stress in the strongest possible way that believers' good deeds cannot be chalked up to their own resolve, but are due solely to divine grace. It is grace all the way. Even the living out of salvation in good works is completely by grace."[28]

Again Paul testifies to this truth in his own life. "We have conducted ourselves in the world in godly holiness and sincerity . . . *relying on God's grace*" (2 Cor. 1:12).[29] It is "the grace of God . . . that offers salvation," that "teaches [or trains] us to say 'No' to ungodliness and worldly passions, and to live self-controlled, upright and godly lives in this present age" (Titus 2:11–12 NIV). It is God's grace

---

tou theou, the grace of God] is often simply the apostle's shorthand for all the benefits of the gospel that are secured by Christ and mediated by the Spirit. . . . All of this is included in what Paul calls *sōtēria* [salvation] in 6:2." Murray J. Harris, *The Second Epistle to the Corinthians: A Commentary on the Greek Text*, NIGTC (Grand Rapids: Eerdmans / Milton Keynes, UK: Paternoster, 2005), 457–58.

* In addition to its use in Eph. 2:10, the Greek word for "workmanship" (*poiēma*) is used for all of God's creative works in the Septuagint (the early Greek translation of the Old Testament, abbr. LXX) in Pss. 92:4 (91:5 LXX) and 143:5 (142:5 LXX) and also in Romans 1:20.

that trains the believer in the virtuous life—not the man-centered and habit-forming disciplines of the philosophical world of New Testament times.

Biblical disciplines, such as the regular nourishing of our heart through feeding on the Word of God and communing with our heavenly Father in times of prayer as well as times of worship and fellowship with other believers are absolutely necessary for spiritual growth. But these are productive for spiritual growth only as channels of God's grace.

Rigorous disciplines may bring certain outward changes of life, but only God's grace has the power to transform the heart. Only grace—not rules and regulations—can free us from the lordship of sin and make us servants of God and his righteousness (Rom. 6:14–22). Only grace is the mighty power that "reign[s] *through righteousness* to bring eternal life through Jesus Christ our Lord" (Rom. 5:21).* In the words of John Stott,

> Nothing could sum up better the blessings of being in Christ than the expression "the reign of grace." For grace forgives sins through the cross, and bestows on the sinner both righteousness and eternal life. Grace satisfies the thirsty soul and fills the hungry with good things. Grace sanctifies sinners, shaping them into the image of Christ. Grace perseveres even with the recalcitrant, determining to complete what it has begun. And one day grace will destroy death and consummate the kingdom. So when we are convinced that "grace reigns," we will remember that God's throne is a "throne of grace," and will come to it boldly to receive mercy and to find grace for every need.[30]

Spiritual Transformation Is the Obedience of Faith through Grace

The truth that our good works are produced by God's grace must not lead us to the conclusion that our activity is thereby eliminated. God has prepared our good works beforehand "so that we would walk [or live] in them" (Eph. 2:10). Only as we actively live out the good works that God in grace has prepared for us does the life of our new creation actually become part of us in the process of our transformation.

---

* The righteousness through which grace reigns in this context (Rom. 5:17–19) is first and foremost the gift of Christ's righteousness reckoned to us and through which we are justified or declared righteous and given eternal life. But it also includes the righteousness of Christ that is formed in our life through the ministry of the Spirit in our transformation or our sanctification. For our ultimate eternal life is the outcome of both our justification and sanctification (see Rom. 6:22, "But now having been freed from sin and enslaved to God, you derive your benefit, resulting in sanctification, and the outcome, eternal life").

Our Will and Our Works Are All of God's Grace

Pointing out that the Spirit creates in the believer a "new will," T. J. Deidun explained how the gift of salvation and our working it out (our task) are both the result of God's grace: "The Christian is under obligation to comply with this 'new will,' which has now become the deepest instinct of his being. Here indicative [i.e., what God has given us in our salvation] and imperative [i.e., what the believer is commanded to do in salvation] are conjoined: the Christian's 'new will', constantly flowing from the activity of the Spirit, is the divinely wrought indicative which *carries within itself* the Christian imperative. There can be nothing more 'indicative', and, at the same time more 'imperative' than the activity of the Spirit creating and sustaining my own most personal instinct."[31] Along with a new heart with a new will oriented toward God's pattern for your life, Scripture tells us that the Spirit guides and directs us (Rom. 8:14; Gal. 5:18), motivates and empowers us (Rom. 8:2–4, 13; Gal. 5:16, 25), and even prays for us (Rom. 8:26–27). All of this is in order that God's creative purpose may be perfected in us—a life "for good works."

Our salvation is thus both a *gift* and a *task*. It is the gift of the crucified and resurrected Christ living in us through the indwelling Spirit, and the task of living out this new life in obedience to our Lord. But this does not mean that this salvation is both by grace and works. For both of these dimensions of salvation—gift and task—are the product of God's grace.

We can see this most clearly in the gift of Christ's saving work *for* us—he accomplished salvation and all we can do is receive his finished work. But his saving work *in* us for our transformation is also his gracious gift through the work of the Spirit in us.

Consider for a moment the matter of love. Scripture frequently commands us to love (e.g., Gal. 5:13–14). But it also informs us that love is the "fruit" of the Spirit. So our activity of loving is not the product of our laboring but the activity of the Spirit in and through us (Gal. 5:22). In truth, obedience to all of God's commands comes only as we walk or conduct our life by the Spirit, the gift of God's grace (Gal. 5:16, 25).

Our task in *working out* our salvation is therefore to receive this saving grace and allow it to reign freely in our lives through faith. In the words of the great Reformation theologian John Calvin, faith is "a kind of vessel" with which "we come empty and with the mouth of our soul open to seek Christ's grace."[32]

Because it is God's will that we come to him and find life, he not only invited us to have faith, he commanded it (1 John 3:23; Acts 17:30). Our initial saving faith can therefore be described as an "obedience of faith" (Rom. 1:5; 16:26; cf. Acts 6:7) in which we surrendered ourselves to God and received him into our lives with the power of his saving grace.

The Root of Obedience in the "Obedience" of Faith

The phrase "obedience of faith" either identifies faith as an act of obedience, making faith appositional to obedience ("obedience which is faith"), or understands obedience as a quality or characteristic of faith ("faith's obedience").[33] Either way, faith involves obedience. As Douglas Moo explained, "We understand the words 'obedience' and 'faith' to be mutually interpreting: obedience always involves faith, and faith always involves obedience. They should not be equated, compartmentalized, or made into separate stages of Christian experience."[34] This interpretation is supported by the places where faith and obedience are found in parallel statements (Rom. 1:5 and 15:18; 1:8 and 16:19; 10:16a and 10:16b; 11:23 and 11:30, 31) and instances where Paul speaks of "obeying" the gospel or truth (Rom. 2:8; 10:16; 2 Thess. 1:8; cf. 1 Peter 2:8; 3:1). Moreover, to believe is expressed as a command to which the correct response could only be obedience (1 John 3:23—"This is His commandment, that we believe in the name of His Son Jesus Christ"; cf. Acts 17:30—"In the past God overlooked such ignorance, but now he commands all people everywhere to repent" (NIV).

This obedient faith of submission to the lordship of Christ and openness to receiving his gracious salvation apart from our works continues as the basis of our spiritual life. The root of obedient submissive receiving faith issues forth in active works or the outworking of genuine faith (James 2:14–16). There is thus a root of obedience already in saving faith, in having submitted to Christ and humbly received his gracious salvation, which issues now in active works of faith, "good works" (Eph. 2:10). To put it another way, the initial obedience in saving faith is the obedience of receiving God's saving grace through no "good works" on our part, but totally by God's grace. On the other hand, the obedience that flows from that grace received now works out from our new life in the active obedience of "good works." In sum, we can give in "good works" only what we have first received. Both the receiving and giving involve obedience to God's Word.

It is through this same "obedience of faith"—a humble openness to God and his saving power—that we receive the grace that transforms.

When the Scripture says that the gospel of Christ "is the power of God for salvation to everyone who believes" (Rom. 1:16), it is not saying that the gospel is God's power only to bring initial salvation to the one who believed. Rather it declares that the gospel is the power of God for complete salvation—from beginning to end—to the person who *believes* (present tense), or continues to believe. Faith is "both the initial and the continuing access point for the saving power of God into human life."*[35] Faith is the "'yes' by which the Christian, at the time of his conversion and *throughout* his life of faith, receives God's [power] as the source of his own dynamism."[36]

---

* The Greek grammatical construction of "believes" (*pisteuonti*) is the present tense participle of the verb "believe" (*pisteuō*), presumably indicating (as Dunn remarks) that Paul "wishes to focus not solely on the initial act of faith but on faith as a continuing orientation and motivation for life."

Our salvation is thus through faith alone from beginning to perfection. God simply invites us to let him come into our lives and save us. Our initial obedience of faith welcomed Christ and his saving power into our lives. We grow through the continuance of that same faith in the Lord who now lives in us, to empower and direct us in living the new life. All the way faith is simply letting God come in, getting ourselves out of the way (renouncing self-works) and letting him work his grace to transform our heart in all of its activities.

When God asks us to change our thoughts or emotions or actions, he supplies the grace (direction and power) to obey. When we don't exercise the obedience of faith but instead function autonomously in our own strength, we resist his transforming grace in our lives. In healing the man with the withered hand, Jesus commanded him to stretch out his hand (Mark 3:5). When the man obeyed and stretched forth his incapacitated hand, it was instantly and completely made whole.

In this particular incident the man's affliction may have actually made it impossible for him in his own ability even to extend his hand (see 1 Kings 13:4). If such was the case, the man in faith obeyed by internally willing to stretch out his hand believing that somehow even the power to do so would be given by the Lord. If on the other hand he was able at least to extend his incapacitated hand, he obediently did so in faith believing that it would be healed. Either way it was through faith that the powerful grace of God worked instant healing—something that the man in his own strength was totally powerless to do.

The same is true with the healing of the disabled man at the pool of Bethesda and the paralytic who was let down through the roof. Jesus commanded both of them *to do something that they were incapable of doing apart from his grace:* "Get up, pick up your pallet and walk" (John 5:8; Mark 2:11, cf. v. 9).*

In the same way, our obedience of faith to the commands and leading of God opens our lives to the operation of his healing and transforming grace so that we can do what in our own strength we are powerless to do—overcome the power of sin in our lives.

Transformation in Spiritual Life Like Physical Life

The relation of our activity to the transforming grace of God in our spiritual life may be seen by considering the place of our activity in our physical life and growth. Our physical life was bestowed on us through the process of natural

---

* While nothing is said explicitly of their faith, especially that of the man at the pool, they must have had some faith to move themselves in obedience to Jesus' command.

generation and birth, so also our spiritual life was given to us through a new birth by the Spirit. As our physical life is not of our work, so our spiritual life is totally the gracious gift from God. He is the one who opens our heart to receive new life "in Christ" through the obedience of faith. At this point we are simply the receptors of life.* Where formerly we were spiritually dead, we are now alive with the eternal life of God.

Our new spiritual life, as in our physical life, begins in the state of infancy and is designed to unfold its reality through growth and the maturing process. Planted in the depth of our heart the new life initiates the process of transforming or re-creating our whole heart and total life. As it does so, it begins to manifest itself in the activities of our life—our thoughts, emotions, and actions. At the beginning, our obedience of faith simply received the new life. Now through continued and growing faith we receive spiritual nourishment causing our new life to grow stronger and increasingly manifest itself in us as good works. By the animating power of new life we are active in these works, but they are still totally the effect of God's grace through faith.

If we take the analogy one step further, we see that our activity is not only the product of the gift of our new life; it is also involved in the very sustenance and growth of that life. Once given physical life, we begin to *breathe, drink* liquid, and finally *eat* solid food. The various functions of our body are active in taking in this nourishment and digesting it for the maintenance and growth of our life.

But again, all of this activity necessary for growth is itself completely dependent on the nourishment that is received. The very activities of eating, drinking, and breathing that enable us to receive outside nourishment—activities performed by us—are dependent for their operation on the life-giving air, food, and water that they bring into the body. Any activity or work (i.e., any good work) that flows from this nourishment of a healthy person is likewise completely dependent on what is given to us from outside of ourselves—provisions that we do not in any way generate or provide.

In sum, the gift of physical life once received enlivens the body to become actively involved in its own sustenance and growth of that life. But this activity

---

* This is not an attempt to explain or solve the debate concerning divine and human activity in coming to salvation. It is only to say that apart from some initial divine gracious activity no human would be saved, just as Scripture clearly states that no person naturally seeks God apart from his gracious seeking of us (Rom. 3:11) and that "those who are in the flesh [a description of the person apart from God] cannot please God." This surely includes the idea that a person apart from God and thus unaided by divine grace cannot choose to believe as an act of faith, an act that is surely pleasing to God (Rom. 8:7).

that is essential for continued life and growth—without it we would die—is itself completely dependent on sources of life outside of ourselves that are in no way the product of our activity or work.

So with our spiritual life, as new living persons we become active in the reception and assimilation of nourishment for our spiritual growth. Like "newborn babies" we "long for the pure milk of the word" so that we may grow "in respect to salvation" (1 Peter 2:2). Jesus said, "He who eats My flesh and drinks My blood has eternal life . . . . He who eats My flesh and drinks My blood abides in Me, and I in him" (John 6:54–56).*

Eating and drinking Christ's body and blood are vivid metaphors for our need to ingest through faith the spiritual food and drink of the One who surrendered his body to death and shed his blood as a sacrifice for our sin that we might share in his resurrection life. Every time we celebrate the Lord's Supper, it should remind us of the truth that our spiritual life and growth is dependent on our continual feeding on the living Christ even as our physical life depends on the ingesting of physical nourishment.

The nourishing food of Christ comes through consuming and digesting God's Word even as we consume and digest food and drink. After speaking of eternal life coming through eating his flesh and drinking his blood, Jesus went on to tell his disciples, "The words that I have spoken to you are spirit and are life" (John 6:63).† God's Word as our food and drink for our eternal life and its nourishing is frequently taught in Scripture:

> Man shall not live on bread alone, but on every word that proceeds out of the mouth of God (Matt. 4:4; cf. Deut. 8:3).

> Ho! Everyone who thirsts, come to the waters; and you who have not money come, buy and eat. . . . Why do you spend money for what is not bread, . . . Listen carefully to Me [i.e., to My word], and eat what is good, . . . Incline your ear and come to Me. Listen, that you may live . . . (Isa. 55:1–3).

---

* "My flesh" refers to the appropriation of Christ who surrendered his body in death and "My blood" to the shedding of his blood as a sacrifice for our sin. That Jesus is not suggesting that we can physically eat his flesh and blood is clear as just prior to these words he said that the same eternal life that belongs to the person who eats his body and blood belongs to the person who "comes to Me" and "believes in Me" (vv. 35, 40).

† Compare also the statement that "he who eats My flesh and drinks My blood abides in Me, and I in him" (John 6:56) with "If you abide in Me and My words abide in you . . ." (John 15:7; see also John 8:31–32 where Christ's word sets us free and v. 36 where Christ himself sets us free).

Your words were found and I ate them, and Your words became for me
a joy and the delight of my heart (Jer. 15:16; cf. Ps. 119:103).

The adage regarding our bodily life—"We are what we eat"—is equally true
of our spiritual life. Like the food we eat and digest is absorbed and assimilated
into our very being to become who we are, so Christ and his life communicated
to us through his Word is incorporated by faith into our heart to make us who
we are spiritually.

But taking in more nourishment alone is not sufficient for good health, it
must be utilized in bodily activity. When for some reason we become bedridden
and are unable do any physical activity, we lose our appetite and strength. We
actually lose muscle mass if we are inactive for more than a week. The same is
true in our spiritual life; when we don't utilize spiritual nourishment in activity
or works, we begin to lose our appetite and restrict our intake of spiritual food.
As a result our spiritual vitality wanes and our strength for loving service and
resistance of evil is weakened.

Thus we must acknowledge that the activity of our new personhood is vital to
our spiritual health and growth. God works through me—through my personal
activities of thought, emotion, and will—to make me a new person. How could
it be otherwise? How could God change my thoughts without me actively thinking? If he could somehow put thoughts in my mind apart from my own thinking,
how would these thoughts be mine? The same applies to my will and emotions.
For my transformed thoughts, emotions, and will to actually be *mine* and not
only *God's* (they can, of course, be both), it is necessary for my personal activity
to be involved in the interactive process in which such change occurs.

We must, however, never let this activity cause us to lose sight of the "by
grace through faith" dynamic. As Jesus taught in his illustration of the vine and
the branches, we have no ability as branches to bear fruit. In fact, we "can do
nothing"—we cannot even live, let alone grow—apart from Christ, the life of the
vine, living in us (John 15:4–5).* The dynamic of our growth and transformation is thus the effect of God's life in Christ at work in us.

To summarize, when we open ourselves in faith to receive God's life, that life
begins to work to make us alive. As new persons alive with the life of God, we
cannot help but become active, for activity is the inevitable manifestation of life.
Planted in the depth of our heart—the core of our person—this new life now

* Compare Jesus' words in Matt. 6:27, which some versions take to refer to physical stature:
"Which of you by taking thought can add one cubit unto his stature?" (KJV, cf. HCSB).

begins the process of transforming us as persons, increasingly manifesting its nature in all of our personal activities—our thoughts, our emotions, and our will and actions.

Recognizing that our transformation is all by grace through faith does not mean that we therefore need not be concerned with the activities of our life or obedience to God's Word. For his instructions and commands are part of the means through which he works to activate his life in us by calling us to think, feel, and will in accord with his own thoughts, feeling, and actions and thus come to realize his kind of life in our experience.

Conclusion

The important question is, How do I see my activity? Is it something added to my faith in the sense that faith makes me a Christian, and now as a believer I need to work on obeying my Lord's commands? If this is my perspective, the focus in my pursuit of spiritual growth will tend to be on the activities of my life. My stress will be on working hard to transform my behavior.

If on the other hand, I believe that all of my genuinely spiritual activities are produced by the life of God in me, my concern for transformation will drive me to attend more to my openness to God and his life, in other words, to my faith. I must attend to my activities and even discipline my behavior. But my ultimate goal in all of these activities will be to grow in faith or openness to God and his grace.

A helpful way to pose the questions may be to ask: Is the basic issue in my success or failure in spiritual growth a matter of my behavior or of my faith? When I wrongfully respond with anger to someone, is the problem one of behavior or of faith? If I fudge the truth in a difficult situation, is it a failure in good works or faith? Was the first sin of Adam and Eve in eating the forbidden fruit wrong behavior or unbelief?

The answer in all of these situations is, of course, both—sin is a failure both of works and of faith. But it is only through faith that we really obey the commands of our Lord in our behavior. Our works as believers are all the product of the life of Christ lived in us by the Spirit. And it is only our faith that unites us to Christ so that his life becomes "our life" (Col. 3:4; cf. Gal. 2:21).

Thus we can work the good works that God commands only as we open ourselves in faith to Christ, living and working in us through the Spirit. I must attend to the commands of Scripture, for they are the pattern of my new life. But I cannot actualize that pattern except through the power of Christ living in me in every situation of my life. If the Christian life is as the apostle states, the reality that "Christ lives in me," then growing in the experience of that life is simply growing in the appropriation of Christ into my life through "faith expressing itself through love" (Gal. 5:6 NIV).

Questions for Thought

1. What are your thoughts about the truth that biblical transformation is the change of the whole person and not simply a change of behavior? Does it have any effect on the way you view spiritual growth?

2. What does it mean that renunciation of self is more than renunciation of various sins? Do you think that it is helpful in our spiritual transformation to recognize that transformation is fundamentally gaining a new self through dying to old self rather than simply attempting to overcome sins? Why? Or why not?

3. Do you think that most people think of spiritual growth or transformation as growing in keeping the various commandments or growing in love? Is this truth that transformation is growing in love encouraging or discouraging to you as you think of your own spiritual growth state? Why?

4. How does our active obedience contribute to our heart transformation? Is it necessary or optional?

5. Do you think that the analogy in the chapter between our activity in our physical growth and health (eating, drinking, exercising, etc.) and our activity (obeying, praying, fellowshipping, etc.) in our spiritual growth and health is valid? How does this affect your motivation to do good works?

6. How have you looked at your obedience in relation to attaining final salvation? What difference does it make in one's pursuit of heart transformation if we believe that our works of obedience are totally the effect of God's grace rather than that they are necessary to gain God's grace of final salvation? What will be the difference in our focus if we believe that all of our activities or works are produced by the life of God in us through the Spirit of Christ?

■■ 14 ■■

The Ultimate Issue

Spiritual Transformation through Relationship with God

You make known to me the path of life; you will fill me with joy in your presence, with eternal pleasures at your right hand.

PSALM 16:11 NIV

As for me, the nearness of God is my good.

PSALM 73:28

True religion is a union of the soul with God, a real participation of the divine nature, the very image of God drawn upon the soul, or, in the apostle's phrase, "it is Christ formed within us."

HENRY SCOUGAL

The complexity of our human nature and personhood that we have seen thus far may lead us to conclude that our spiritual growth is a complicated matter. But such is not the case. If it were, only the brightest among us could succeed. Like driving an automobile, it can be helpful to know something about the inner workings of the drivetrain of an automobile, but we can successfully drive simply by knowing the operating procedure and of course the rules of the road. So it is with our spiritual formation: it is not knowledge of the complexities of life that lead to successful living; it is living life according to the pattern designed for us by our Creator. The activities of God and of our self that are involved in our spiritual transformation may be complex and sometimes difficult to fully understand. But the realization of our transformation is clear and easily understood—we are transformed through living life in a personal relationship with God.

A Heart-to-Heart Relationship with God

The God of the Bible is a relational God, not only within himself between Father, Son, and Spirit, but also toward his personal creatures. Scripture describes his relationship with his people in the intimate metaphors of Father and children, husband and wife, and friend. The original relationship of humans with God is suggested in the story of Adam and Eve hiding because of their disobedience as God came walking in the garden where they lived (Gen. 3:8). Commenting on this picture, Old Testament scholar Gordon Wenham said, "The description of Eden with trees, rivers, gold, and so on emphasized God's presence there. Therefore it seems likely that it was not unusual for him to be heard walking in the garden . . . . Maybe a daily chat between the Almighty and his creatures was customary. . . . It is not God's walking in the garden that was unusual, but the reaction of man and his wife."*

The essence of spiritual transformation is simply the restoration of this original personal relationship. Scripture tells us that it was for this purpose that God sent his Son into the world. Standing in our place as "the second man" and "the last Adam" (1 Cor. 15:45, 47) Jesus suffered the consequences of our sin in his death on the cross and was resurrected to newness of life so we might be brought back into a relationship with God, the "fountain of life" (Ps. 36:9; cf. Jer. 2:13; 17:13). As the writer of Hebrews exclaims, "He is able to save forever those who *draw near to God through Him*" (7:25).

This transforming relationship with God is intimately personal, much more than we often think of living with him and sometimes do. It is more than living with God as we might live in a field of magnetic energy where we go about the affairs of our life with little consciousness of him except for the times we attend church or a funeral, and even then he seems distant, like someone we don't know very well. It is more than living with God as the all-powerful and ever-present one who created and sustains us, or as the Cretan poet quoted by the apostle Paul expressed it, the one in whom "we live and move and exist" (Acts 17:28).

The transforming relationship is also more than living with God in what might be called a judicial or legal relationship—somewhat like our relationship with our government—in which because of Christ we know our sins are forgiven and

---

* Wenham also notes that "the term 'walking' [*halakh*] . . . is subsequently used of God's presence in the Israelite tent sanctuary (Lev 26:12; Deut 23:15; 2 Sam 7:6–7) again emphasizing the relationship between the garden and the later shrines," places such as the tabernacle and later temple where God's presence was among his people. Gordon J. Wenham, *Genesis 1–15*, WBC 1 (Waco: Word Books, 1987), 76. Victor Hamilton also notes that the form of the verb translated "walking" "suggests iterative [repetitive or frequentative] and habitual aspects." *The Book of Genesis: Chapters 1–17*, NICOT (Grand Rapids: Eerdmans, 1990), 192.

as a consequence we won't be condemned at the judgment. It is even something beyond mentally believing the truth that Christ lives in us through the indwelling Spirit and thus we have some kind of a spiritual relationship with God.

The relationship that transforms our heart is a deep personal relationship in which we relate to God from all of our heart—our mind, emotions, and actions, a heart open to share ourselves with him and let him share himself with us. This is the relationship that Jesus taught when he said, "Abide in me, and I in you. As the branch cannot bear fruit of itself unless it abides in the vine, so neither can you unless you abide in Me. I am the vine, you are the branches; he who abides in Me and I in him, he bears much fruit, for apart from Me you can do nothing" (John 15:4–5).

To "abide" in Christ and have him abide in us is to live with Christ in an enduring relationship of life similar to the description of his own relationship with his heavenly Father in John 14:10: "Do you believe that I am in the Father and the Father is in Me? The words that I say to you I do not speak on My own initiative, but the Father abiding in Me does His works." Because Christ and his Father were abiding in each other, Christ's speech and actions were those of the Father through him (John 10:37–38). When we abide in Christ and he in us, our speech and actions likewise become the speech and actions of Christ through us.

This mutual indwelling with Christ—a real spiritual union with God—already exists in the depth of the heart of Christians. But this invisible union in the heart is designed to grow and transform the "issues" of our daily life. As it does, we come to experience the reality of a relationship with God in our life like that described by the psalmist: "I am continually with You; You have taken hold of my right hand. With Your counsel You will guide me, and afterward receive me to glory. . . . God is the strength [lit. the rock] of my heart and my portion [i.e., my life's sustenance] forever. . . . As for me, the nearness of God is my good" (Ps. 73:23–24, 28). The great "good" in the psalmist's life was not prosperity, not even prosperity from the hand of God. It was *God's presence with him in the reality of life*—being able to say, "Even though I walk through the valley of the shadow of death [or 'the darkest valley,' NRSV], I fear no evil, for You are with me" (Ps. 23:4).

Just before returning to his heavenly Father Jesus told his disciples as well as each of us as believers, "Remember, I am with you always, to the end of the age" (Matt. 28:20 NRSV). As the one who is "God with us" ("Immanuel," Matt. 1:23), Jesus is the reality of the promises that God gives to his people to be present with them in the experiences of life, promises such as:

+ "Do not fear, for I am with you; do not anxiously look about you, for I am your God. I will strengthen you, surely I will help you, surely I will uphold you with My righteous right hand." (Isa. 41:10).

+ "Be strong and courageous, do not be afraid or tremble at them, for the LORD your God is the one who goes with you. He will not fail you or forsake you." (Deut. 31:6).

+ "He will call upon Me, and I will answer him; I will be with him in trouble; I will rescue him and honor him" (Ps. 91:15).

+ "Do not fear, for I have redeemed you; I have called you by name; you are Mine! When you pass through the waters, I will be with you; And through the rivers, they will not overflow you. When you walk through the fire, you will not be scorched, Nor will the flame burn you. For I am the LORD your God, the Holy One of Israel, your Savior" (Isa. 43:1–3).

Jesus also spoke of giving us "abundant life" (John 10:10), and giving us his joy and his peace even in the midst of our trouble-filled lives (John 15:11; 16:33). He answered the suffering apostle's prayer by saying, "My grace is sufficient for you, for power is perfected in weakness" (2 Cor. 12:9).

The apostle experienced the reality of that grace through the presence of Christ in his life. Imprisoned and abandoned by everyone else, he testified, "The Lord stood with me and strengthened me" (2 Tim. 4:17). The reality of Christ's presence enabled him to say from his own experience—not simply from the teaching of Scripture, "I can do all things through Him who strengthens me"* (Phil. 4:13; cf. 1 Tim. 1:12).

Only in a relationship with Christ, in which we actually experience his presence and power in the circumstances of our own lives, are we being transformed into his likeness. We sometimes speak of a person with whom we have a close relationship as having that person in our heart. This is more than sentimental talk, it is reality. Most of us who had a close relationship with our parents have something of their person deposited in our heart. This may diminish when we are no longer physically close to them and they are less in our consciousness, but it is never totally absent. Going through life, we continue to incorporate other

---

* Although most versions translate the Greek construction in this verse in an instrumental sense, "through Him," it may also, and perhaps preferably, be translated in "an incorporative sense," that is, "in vital union with Him who strengthens me." Peter T. O'Brien, *The Epistle to the Philippians: A Commentary on the Greek Text*, NIGTC (Grand Rapids: Eerdmans, 1991), 527.

persons into our hearts through relationships—the closer the relationship, the greater their presence and impact on the shape of our life.

Through a similar close relationship with Christ, although much more powerful because of the ministry of the indwelling Spirit, the risen Jesus is assimilated into our heart to live out his life in our experience, or as the apostle puts it, "Christ is formed in you" (Gal. 4:19). And while other people may be in our lives and have great influence on us, only the presence of Christ—perhaps through other people—is able to transform our hearts to actually experience the God-centered life of the new creation.

Living in such a heart-to-heart relationship with the almighty God who created and sustains the vast universe may seem a bit preposterous. Is such a majestic Supreme Being really interested in relating to us who are but tiny insignificant specks in his immense domain? Is it even possible for me as a finite human being to relate to the incomparable God? Moreover, can he really be in intimate personal relationship with each individual believer at the same time? How can he listen to everybody's prayers and answer each one with a personal response?

How God is able to relate to every believer simultaneously is surely part of his incomprehensible *greatness* lauded by the psalmist when he exclaimed, "Great is the LORD, and greatly to be praised, and his greatness is unsearchable" (145:3). We cannot know all of the *how* of God's relating, but that he does relate, and does so personally and intimately, is the testimony of his Word and of his people throughout the ages.

Through the prophet God declared, "I dwell on a high and holy place, but also with the contrite and lowly of spirit" (Isa. 57:15). He calls Abraham "My friend" (Isa. 41:8), and Jesus extends this to all of his disciples, calling them "my friends" (John 15:14; in both instances "friend" is more literally, "beloved"). God often speaks of us as his children calling us his "sons and daughters" (2 Cor. 6:18; cf. Rom. 8:14–15). Like a loving compassionate father, he knows us individually and is ready to respond to our personal requests with good (Ps. 103:13; Matt. 7:11).

In contemplating our relationship with the God of the universe, we must remember that he created us in his own image and likeness. As the persons of the triune God (Father, Son, and Spirit) relate to each other, so we as finite created "replicas" of God are persons designed for relationship with God and other persons. Because Jesus was God manifest in the flesh, the relationship that the disciples had with him was in reality a relationship with God. In answer to Philip's request, "Show us the Father," Jesus said, "He who has seen me has seen the Father" (John 14:8–9).

The Likeness of Divine and Human Personhood Revealed in the God-Man

The likeness of divine and human personhood is seen most clearly in the truth that the Son of God, the second person of the Trinity, could take on the nature of a human being that when united with the personhood of the Son of God also became personal with the result that the one person, Jesus Christ, was truly personal God and truly personal man. This union of divine and human natures in one person is possible only if the personhood of God and man bear a similarity.

The risen Jesus is no longer among us in bodily form so we can see him with our eyes and touch with our hands, but he is still present with us. Before departing to go back to heaven, he told his disciples that he would send the Spirit to "be with you forever." He then added, "I will not leave you as orphans; *I will come to you.*"* He further said, "If anyone loves me, he will obey my teaching. My Father will love him, and *we will come to him and make our home with him*" (John 14:18, 23). Despite the fact that he would leave them physically, Jesus assures his disciples that he would be present with them through the Spirit. The Spirit will "glorify me because it is from me that he will receive what he will make known to you" (John 16:14 NIV).

The ministry of the Spirit is to bring Christ—his life, his words, and saving work—to us. As expressed in the apostle Paul's prayer for the Ephesians, the Spirit strengthens us in our inner being so that "Christ may dwell in your hearts through faith" (Eph. 3:16–17). In sum, through the ministry of the Spirit we have a relationship with Christ and through him with the Father that needs to be reality in our daily lives.

Developing a Heart-to-Heart Relationship

Since transformation comes through a relationship with our Creator, the all-important question is, How can we develop such a personal relationship with God? How does the relationship with God, which began when we received his Son into our lives, grow and mature so that we come to experience his presence and life more and more in our daily life? In reality developing a relationship with

---

* Some interpreters see this coming of Jesus only in his temporary resurrection appearance to his disciples. But the reference to not leaving them orphans and the near statements that on that day they would know that he is in them (v. 20) and that he and the Father would abide with them (v. 23) suggest that this coming is permanent. See Raymond E. Brown, *The Gospel according to John, XIII–XXI*, AB 29A (Garden City, NY: Doubleday, 1970), 644–48.

God may be compared in many ways to the way we come to know any person as a friend.

Frequent Contact

Relationships develop and grow only through frequent contact. Noting that Jesus' command to "abide in Me" came to all of his disciples, Adrian van Kaam rightly concluded:

> There must be a way of keeping in touch with him that is open to each of us, even the most simple among us. How do we keep in touch with our family, our best friends, our beloved? We do it in many ways: visits, postcards, letters, telephone calls, conversations, a prayer, a memory. It is necessary that we do it often enough to keep the relationship alive. Remaining in Jesus happens somewhat in the same way.[1]

The depth of a relationship depends on how well we know one another; and this is closely related to how much time we spend together. As we noted earlier, it is possible to be impacted by a close friend even when we are not with him or even conscious of him. For something of him—perhaps his thoughts or the example of his life—has been deposited in our hearts as a result of fellowship. Normally, however, the more time we are away from a friend, the less he is in our conscious thought, and consequently the less impact he has on our life. The same is true in our spiritual life. The transforming effect of Christ on our hearts comes only with frequent fellowship with him.

Scripture compares the need for spiritual nourishment to the need of food in our physical life. Jesus said, "Man does not live on bread alone, but on every word that proceeds out of the mouth of God" (Matt. 4:4; cf. Deut. 8:3). He also said, "The one who feeds [continuously] on me will live because of me" (John 6:57 NIV). Most of us eat daily (usually more than once) in order to sustain our bodily health and strength, and the prayer—"Give us this day our daily bread"—suggests that this is normal human behavior.

The picture of feeding our inner spiritual life as we do our body therefore suggests that spiritual health and transformation come through daily (if not more frequent) fellowship with God through prayer, listening to his words, and fellowshipping with his people. The relationship between any lovers cannot grow or even be sustained without frequent contact. So our relationship with God—the supreme love of the believer's life—cannot develop and be transforming without frequent fellowship with him.

Abiding in God's Word

A personal relationship of "abiding" in Christ also requires that we abide in his Word and his Word abides in us. Jesus said, "If you abide in Me, and My words abide in you, ask whatever you wish, and it will be done for you" (John 15:7). Abiding in me and so having your prayers answered, Jesus says, means letting my words abide in you. He expressed the same truth when he said, "If you continue [or abide]* in My word, then you are truly disciples of Mine" (John 8:31).

Words are the primary way that we express ourselves as persons and therefore the primary way through which we have personal relationships. When we hear and receive the words of Jesus, which encompass all of Scripture (John 5:39; Luke 24:47), we are receiving the presence of Jesus himself—the powerful living Word of God—into our lives, even as he explained, "the words that I have spoken to you are spirit and are life" (John 6:63).

Abiding in the Word is therefore hearing the speech of the living God. It is reading and meditating on Scripture *relationally*, hearing the words of a person as we would a personal letter from a dear friend, hearing our friend's voice and his heart speaking to our own heart.

This kind of hearing or abiding requires an open heart, for God speaks to those who listen with their heart. If the ears of our heart are dull to our Lord's voice because we already have our assured opinion on the matter, or perhaps we don't like the challenge that his words bring to our own willful desires, the transforming operation of his Word on our hearts will be choked.

To be changed, we must be open to the truth of all of God's Word—its instruction in the way of life and its conviction and rebuke of our deviations from that way. We must let the Word of the vinedresser—our heavenly Father—come into our hearts to prune away the fruitless branches in our lives (John 15:2). Any hindrance to the entrance of God's Word into our hearts is an impediment to a full heart-to-heart relationship with him and thus the transformation of our heart.

---

* The Greek verb rendered "abide" in John 15:7 is *menō*. The similarity between the "abide" in John 15 and that in John 8:31 is seen in D. A. Carson's comment on the latter verse: "The verb rendered 'hold' [NIV] is *menō*, to abide, to remain—a theme of critical importance that returns in a concentrated way in ch. 15. . . . A genuine believer remains in Jesus' 'word' (*logos*), his teaching . . . : *i.e.* such a person obeys it, seeks to understand it better, and finds it more precious, more controlling, precisely when other forces flatly oppose it." D. A. Carson, *The Gospel according to John*, PNTC (Grand Rapids: Eerdmans, 1991), 348.

Abiding in God's Love

The relationship of abiding in Christ is further explained by his command: "Abide in my love." Abiding in his love is, of course, related to abiding in his Word. For we who were not witnesses of his life and death for us come to know Christ's love today primarily through the witness of the Scriptures.* Furthermore, as Jesus added, abiding in his love means living in obedience to his commands: "If you keep my commandments, you will abide in my love" (John 15:9).

It is not that we earn more of God's love by being obedient to his commands. Rather when we are obedient we are able to receive more of his love and experience its power in our lives. When the prodigal son left his father to go off to live a profligate lifestyle in a distant country, his father's love for him did not for one moment diminish. But his son far away could not experience that love in the same way that he could if he were living at home in a close relationship with his father. So with us, the closer we live to God in obedience to his commands, the more we abide in his love and experience that love in daily life.

Abiding in Christ's love is immediately hindered in many believers because of the difficulty of grasping and receiving the immensity of that love—a love that is willing to serve others, even enemies, to the point of sacrificing self (John 15:13; Rom. 5:8). When Jesus was here on earth some people found his love repulsive and became his adversaries. Even his disciples found his love baffling. When Jesus approached Peter to wash his feet, Peter's first response was, "Never shall You wash my feet" (John 13:8). He simply could not grasp the radical humility of a love that would cause his Lord to stoop to such lowly service. According to the scriptural record, none of the disciples really understand the love that motivated their Lord to sacrifice himself on the cross until after his resurrection (Matt. 16:21–23; Luke 18:31–34). It is still difficult to receive Christ's love because it is so different from any of the natural love we see about us. It is indeed a love that "surpasses knowledge" (Eph. 3:19).

But perhaps more than its radical difference, we fail to receive Christ's love because we are not fully aware of its magnitude and what it has done for us. We don't see the desperate plight of our sinful condition from which his love in mercy and grace rescued us. This can be true especially in the case of those who became Christians at an early age and have never experienced the destructive

---

* We, of course, know the love of Christ as it flows to us through the words and actions of other believers in whom he lives. But it seems impossible to know the full magnitude of God's love in Christ without knowing of the demonstration of that love in the reality of his historical words and actions.

consequences of sin that many do before coming to Christ later in life. On the opposite end, some who have lived a life of sin may fail to receive the fullness of Christ's love because we are overwhelmed by our sinfulness and simply can't believe the greatness of his love even for such a person.

Finally, we often draw away from God's love when we misinterpret it. When the sun in our life is eclipsed by dark rain clouds and suffering engulfs us, we feel that God has abandoned us. As one member of our Bible study who had not been reading his Bible or praying explained, "My life has been rough this week. I feel that God has abandoned me, so I abandoned him." We forget that our heavenly Father never promised that life in his love would be painless in this present world—in fact just the opposite. In reality, as every Christian can testify, times of suffering have often brought about the greatest spiritual growth.

Like a loving father disciplines his children, our heavenly Father sometimes moves us along our spiritual journey by allowing us to experience suffering, but he is always there in his love. An African friend shared the true story of a group of ladies who were studying Malachi 3:3, "He will sit as a smelter and purifier of silver." Puzzled about what this really meant about the character of God, one of the women volunteered to go and try to find out by watching a silversmith at work.

As she watched, the silversmith took a piece of silver and held it in the middle of the fire, explaining that it needed to be where the flames were the hottest to

The Deep, Transforming Effect of Suffering

The dynamic of suffering in our life as Christians is well stated in the testimony of a friend who recently died in her mid fifties after a four-year battle with cancer. The following words read at her funeral were found written in the margin of her Bible:

"A person who has a heart after God will be prepared to face anything the world throws at him. At times God doesn't rescue us from hard situations because He is providing something better. We may feel that He is abandoning us, but in reality He is protecting us—not by deliverance, but through strengthening. Changing something within my heart is a greater demonstration of the Lord's power than changing something around me. Experiencing God's presence and strengthening in the midst of trials is a greater faith builder than being delivered from the trial. A tested and refined faith is a greater reward, greater than immediate relief from discomfort. This will result in praise and glory at Christ's return. The greater answer to prayer is His leaving me in a trial and having an internal peace that nothing can steal—not even my circumstances. If God removes the situation, you may never learn that He is sufficient for everything I need. Let God change me and discover His joy in whatever circumstances comes your way."

burn away all the impurities. Relating this to God holding us in such a hot spot, the woman thought again of God sitting as a refiner and asked the silversmith if it was necessary for him to sit in front of the fire the whole time. "Yes," he responded, adding that he not only had to hold the silver, but he had to keep his eye on it the whole time. If it was in the flames a moment too long, the silver would be destroyed. "But how do you know when the silver is fully refined," she asked. The silversmith smiled and said, "Oh, that's easy—when I see my image in it."[2]

No matter what our experience might be, in good times or bad, whether we see it or not, we need to lay hold of the truth that God's love is always there. Referring to all kinds of suffering, the apostle wrote, "In all these things we overwhelming conquer through Him who loved us." Nothing "will be able to separate us from the love of God, which is in Christ Jesus our Lord" (Rom. 8:37, 39). His prayer was that God would enable us to comprehend and to know Christ's love (Eph. 3:14–19), suggesting that we are all in need of grasping this love more fully if we desire to grow spiritually. Peter O'Brien is surely correct when he said, "No matter how much we know of the love of Christ, how fully we enter into his love for us, there is always more to know and experience. . . . We cannot be spiritually mature as we should be unless we are empowered by God to 'grasp the limitless dimensions of the love of Christ.'"[3] Our growth in the knowledge of Christ's love comes through continually opening our heart to God's Word—the story of his love in reaching down to rescue us from our lost state.

By gazing by faith at the life of our Lord, listening to his teachings, and especially seeing him on the cross suffering and dying for our sins, we increasingly come to see the reality and deadly power of the sin in our lives and the corresponding greatness of his amazing love. Through receiving and experiencing more of that love, we not only grow in our love relationship with our Lord, but we also increasingly become loving people who through love keep his commandments and *abide in his love*—the transforming relationship.

Living in Harmony with God

The relationship of abiding in Christ through abiding in his Word and love clearly implies living a life in harmony with him. However, this aspect is so vital to a heart-to-heart relationship that it deserves explicit note. It is impossible to experience a close personal relationship with another person without sharing deep convictions and values. As Scripture says, "What partnership has righteousness with lawlessness? Or what fellowship has light with darkness?"

(2 Cor. 6:14 ESV). For us to experience the transforming presence of God in the depth of our heart, we must see things the way he does. We must love the things he loves and hate the things he hates. We must walk the way he is going. In short, we must live life close to him as the psalmist testified: "the nearness of God is my good" (Ps. 73:28).

Through the work of Christ, God has brought all who are "in Christ" near to him: "But now in Christ Jesus you who formerly were far off have been brought near by the blood of Christ" (Eph. 2:13).* But as sons and daughters in earthly families can lose the experience of their relationship with their parents by turning away from them, so we as sons and daughters of God can draw away from our heavenly Father and lose the experience of our relationship with him.

To experience our relationship with him we must respond to his loving initiative. We must, as Scripture says, "Draw near to God and He will draw near to you" (James 4:8).† Such nearness requires the whole heart of each partner. God has demonstrated his wholehearted love for us in the gift of his beloved Son. Now he calls us to a wholehearted response: "You will seek Me and find Me when you search for Me *with all your heart*" (Jer. 29:13).

Since we always love something, our failure to love God with "all of our heart" means that something has drawn our love away from God—something in our life is functioning as a competitor with God for our love. The psalmist's description of those who are far from God as "those who are unfaithful to You" (Ps. 73:27) is literally, and more vividly, "those who go a whoring from You" ("those who desert You for harlotry," NKJV). When our relationship with God seems distant, it is not simply that our love has grown cold. We have allowed something else in our life—maybe career, wealth, prestige, pleasure, or even other people—to intrude and steal our wholehearted love away.

Loving God with *all* of our heart, of course, does not mean that we cannot love any other than God. A husband and wife can have an undivided loyal love for each other and still love their children. A deep love between parents actually engenders a richer overflow of love for the children. Our love for others,

---

* "Those who formerly were far off" in Eph. 2:13 refers to the Gentiles who formerly were "without God in the world." Jewish believers in God had already been brought near through God's covenant blessings on them in previous history. But even the Old Testament Jewish believers gained new "access in one Spirit to the Father" through the finished redemptive work of Christ (Eph. 2:17–18).

† The same thought is repeated in a variety of ways: "The LORD is with you when you are with Him. And if you seek Him, He will let you find Him; but if you forsake Him, He will forsake you" (2 Chron. 15:2). "'Return to Me,' declares the LORD of hosts, 'that I may return to you'" (Zech. 1:3; cf. Mal. 3:7).

however, must be in harmony with our wholehearted love for God. The things that we love must be things that he loves, for we can only truly love with his love flowing through us. Jesus said that we demonstrate our love for him by keeping his commands (John 14:15)—which includes loving others even as he does.

Our love relationship with our God therefore includes loving all of the good things that God gives to us—but all in accord with God's design for our lives and our relationship with him. Even as a mother or father can love their children in ways that harm their love for each other as husband and wife, so an improper love, even for the good things that God gives us, can degrade our love for him. And, to be sure, to love things that the other person hates is sure to seriously damage the depth of any relationship.

For a personal relationship with God in which we experience the nearness of his transforming presence, we must therefore draw near to Him—not simply on Sunday during worship service, or during a special spiritual discipline, or on spiritual retreat, but continually throughout every day of our life. We can live in such a relationship of nearness to God only by entering into the holiness of God's world. Thus to the exhortation for us to draw near to God, James added, "Cleanse your hands . . . and purify your hearts" (James 4:8).

These requirements for living in the presence of God echo the words of the psalmist: "Who may ascend into the hill of the LORD? And who may stand in His holy place? He who has clean hands and a pure heart" (Ps. 24:3–4). For a transforming relationship with God we must walk with our Lord, continually

We Are All Responsible Creators of Our Own World

Theologian John Frame's comments about the reality that we as creatures made in the image of God are all secondary creators in fashioning the world in which we live are pertinent to our spiritual formation. Our thoughts are not like God's in that what he thinks comes to pass when he spoke the original creation into reality. Nevertheless, Frame says, "our thoughts are also creative in a sense. We are secondary creators. On the one hand, when we refuse to think according to God's norms, we are at the same time refusing to live in His world and devising a world of our own to replace it. On the other hand, when we think obediently, we are re-creating for ourselves what God has created for us. As Romans 1 teaches, fallen man exchanges the truth for a lie. Adopting a lie affects not only the contents of our heads but every area of our lives. Fallen man lives as if this were not God's world; he lives as if the world were his own ultimate creation. . . . Thus in an important sense, the sinner is a 'secondary creator,' one who chooses to live in a world—a dream world—that he has invented. The believer, too is a secondary creator, one who adopts God's world as his own."[4]

taking stock of our actions (clean hands) and our attitudes (pure heart). Is what I am doing or thinking right now pleasing to our Lord? Is it in harmony with God's purposes in the world? His purposes in my life? Am I loving in act and attitude the things that he loves and thus showing love for him? Or am I grieving my Beloved by giving my love to things that are far from his world?

When we think, feel, or act contrary to God's norms, we are in reality rejecting life in his world and devising a world of our own. He, of course, is still with us in the world of our creation and continually working for our return. But like the father in Jesus' story of the prodigal son, he cannot really go with us in a relationship of *nearness* into a world that is alien and antagonistic to his world.

When we reject the norms of his world, we are in essence telling him that we do not want him near us. So, in love, he lets us go into the world of our creation to suffer its disorder and spiritual starvation so we might come to our senses and return to him. And when we do, again like the father of the prodigal, he runs to meet us and again bestow on us that good which comes from nearness to him in his world.

We can experience the nearness of our God only in a mutual relationship of love. Jesus said, "He who has My commandments and keeps them is the one who loves Me; and he who loves Me will be loved by My Father, and I will love him and will disclose Myself to him" (John 14:21). As God's love was and still is active in transforming us, so our love must be active in working out our salvation through obedience to his Word.

In sum, we cannot experience the transforming relationship of nearness to God without a sincere concern for holiness in our life. "Make every effort . . . to be holy," the writer to the Hebrews declared, for "without holiness no one will see the Lord" (12:24). Even as our final face-to-face relationship with God in glory requires our striving for the things of God in our lives, so our present yet imperfect relationship grows deeper as we refuse to tolerate sin in our lives and seek to grow in the likeness of our Lord.

It is futile to seek the experience of God in our lives through various spiritual exercises without turning from the things of this world system and our own fleshly desires—desires that are independent of God. We cannot enjoy physical health without consuming food that is suited to the nature of our body. So we cannot be spiritually transformed without seeking to live according to the order and loves of God's world for which we were made.

Speaking of God meeting the righteous person, the prophet Isaiah said, "You meet him who rejoices in righteousness, who remembers You in Your ways" (Isa. 64:5). John Oswalt helpfully applies these words to our relationship with God:

"Let a person begin to live according to *(remember)* God's ways, joyfully doing righteousness, expectantly waiting for him, and sooner than we might think, we are going to meet him coming to meet us. . . . If we wonder where God is in our lives, the key is to begin doing what we know, allowing him to manifest himself when and where he chooses."[5]

Our pursuit of holiness, however, must always be out of a love relationship. Without love we are not keeping God's commandments and pursing biblical holiness. To obey someone with whom we share a love relationship—they love us and we love them—is much easier than obeying simply because we recognize their authority over us. Our striving to live in harmony with God in his world thus flows out of our relationship with God and leads to an ever deepening of that relationship—and our transformation.

Unceasing Prayer

A personal relationship with God is above all marked by a life of prayer.* As the very breath of our newborn heart, prayer is the natural response to God's Word first spoken to us. "Because you are sons," the apostle wrote, "God has sent forth the Spirit of His Son into our hearts, crying, 'Abba Father!'" (Gal. 4:5–6). The Spirit who re-creates our heart immediately turns our heart toward God and cries out on our behalf, "Father." By the Spirit we also utter the same cry—"Abba! Father!" in the similar passage in Romans 8:15.

Because we are adopted sons of God "in Christ," we share in the relationship that Christ in his humanity had with his heavenly Father.† Thus it is natural for us to discourse with our Father even as Jesus constantly prayed to his heavenly Father. Prayer, as Jean Daniélou explains, is "the expression of an ontological bond that exists between God and us. It is the outward manifestation of a fundamental reality; we continuously receive ourselves from God and we continuously refer back to him."[6]

Prayer was vital to Jesus' personal life and his ministry. The gospel writers

---

* For an excellent biblical-theological study of prayer, see Graeme Goldsworthy, *Prayer and the Knowledge of God: What the Whole Bible Teaches* (Leicester: Inter-Varsity Press, 2003). See also W. Bingham Hunter, *The God Who Hears* (Downers Grove, IL: InterVarsity Press, 1986) for an overall biblical and practical study of prayer.

† In addition to his human sonship, Christ was also a divine Son as a member of the triune God—Father, Son, and Spirit. We, of course, do not share in his divine nature. But we share in all that he is as man—the "last Adam" and the "second man," the head of a new humanity. This includes his relation to the Father as a human religious son who prayed and trusted his heavenly Father even as we must. Jesus did so not as God but as a human being through the power of the Holy Spirit, and likewise this is what God intends for everyone who believes, namely, to live the Christian life by the power of his Spirit.

tell us that he "would often slip away" to pray" (Luke 5:16).* He discussed prayer with his disciples and instructed them in their prayers (Matt. 6:5–13; par. Luke 11:1–13; 18:1). We also find God's people at prayer throughout Scripture. Frequently their prayers are recorded in order to help us in our own prayers. The book of Psalms, whose Hebrew title is "Songs of Praise," has been called "the Prayer-book both of Jews and Christians."[7]

Finally, we are repeatedly exhorted to pray: "Devote yourselves to [or persist in] prayer keeping alert in it with an attitude of thanksgiving" (Col. 4:2). Be "devoted to prayer" (Rom. 12:12). "With all prayer and petition pray at all times in the Spirit" (Eph. 6:18). "Be anxious for nothing, but in everything by prayer and supplication with thanksgiving let your requests to made known God" (Phil. 4:6). "Pray without ceasing" (1 Thess. 5:17).

The last command—"pray without ceasing"—tells us that prayer should be the constant experience of our spiritual life. Not that we should be verbally praying all the time, but that we should be living in continual fellowship with our God with an attitude of dependence—living, as has been said, in the light of God, as a sunflower lives in the light of the sun and follows it throughout the day basking in its life-giving rays. As Leon Morris explains:

> Prayer is not to be thought of only as offering petitions in set words. Prayer is fellowship with God. Prayer is the realization of the presence of our Father. Though it is quite impossible for us always to be uttering the words of prayer, it is possible and necessary that we should always be living in the spirit of prayer.
>
> But believers who live in this way, conscious continually of their dependence on God, conscious of his presence with them always, find that their general spirit of prayerfulness in the most natural way overflows into uttered prayer.[8]

Living in the "spirit of prayer" means that we live with God as an intimate friend with whom we converse about all that is going on in our life. In addition to specific times of prayer, without uttering words we talk to him throughout the day about the tasks that we face, our relationships, our problems, our blessings and joys. In our thoughts we worship him for his awesome greatness and wonderful works of grace and love.

The importance of prayer for our spiritual life and growth is the reality that

---

* See also Matt. 14:23; Mark 1:35; 6:46; Luke 6:12; 9:18, 28.

The Indispensable Place of Praise in Transformation

Scripture abounds with calls for the worship of God by all people—great and small, old and young. The psalmist wrote, "Kings of the earth and all peoples; princes and all judges of the earth; both young men and virgins; old men and children. Let them praise the name of the LORD" (148:11–13).

Similarly, the apostle John hears a voice coming from the throne of God in heaven: "Give praise to our God, all you His bond-servants, you who fear Him, the small and the great" (Rev. 19:5).

The absolute indispensability of praise for our spiritual growth in our new humanity is evident in the words of Hans Walter Wolff: "Where the praise of God is absent, man has misunderstood the discord between his neediness and his capabilities. Here too inhuman man is not far away. . . . In praise . . . the destiny of man—his destiny to live in the world, his destiny to love his fellow men, and his destiny to rule over all non-human creation— finds its truly human fulfillment. Otherwise man becoming his own idol, turns into a tyrant; either that or, falling dumb, he loses his freedom."[9]

it is in prayer where we most consciously live out our relationship with God— whether praise, thanksgiving, petition, or even lament.

In *praise* of our Lord we come to the real essence of human life. "Let my soul live that it may praise You," the psalmist exclaimed (Ps. 119:175). "The dead do not praise the LORD" (Ps. 115:17).[*] Such statements are not denying a life after death in which believers will worship God with praise.[†] They simply express the attitude of God's Old Testament people living within the covenant community that had received many divine promises of blessing related to earthly life.[‡] For these saints, true life on earth consisted in living for the glory of God and declaring his praise in the worshipping community and before all nations. They believed, as Old Testament scholar Claus Westermann explained, that "praise of God is essential to existence; it is itself a manner of existence. If it has ceased, authentic life has also ceased."[10]

In our prayer of *praise*, we continually recognize and affirm our God for who he really is. We declare that he is "the LORD our Maker . . . And we are the people of his pasture and the sheep of his hand" (Ps. 95:6–7). We proclaim the Lord's great historical acts of salvation for his people and as well as what he has

---

[*] Cf. Pss. 6:5; 30:10; 88:10; Isa. 38:18.

[†] See Pss. 49:15; 73:23–24; Isa. 26:19; Dan. 12:2; Heb. 12:22–23; Rev. 5:11–14.

[‡] The situation of God's Old Testament community people, although marred by sin, can be compared to that of original humankind who were called to serve God as his vice-regents over creation (Gen. 1:28) and to live in a conscious fellowship with God and thus praise would be their mode of existence.

done for us personally. With the psalmist we command our own soul: "Bless the LORD, O my soul . . . and forget none of His benefits" (Ps. 103:2). In extolling the virtues of our Lord we are reminded of the greatness of his power and the immensity of his love for us. Praise is thus a rich form of meditation on God and our relationship with him—a great faith builder.

Prayers of *petition* likewise express consciously the truth of our dependent relationship on our Creator. Coming to our heavenly Father with requests is simply putting into practice our belief that all of our life—"every good and perfect gift" including our daily bread—comes from God (James 1:17). God has provided all things necessary for true life in Christ, and he invites us to come to him in prayer and receive them. "Nothing is promised to be expected from the Lord, which we are not also bidden to ask of him in prayers. So true is it that we dig up by prayer the treasures that were pointed out by the Lord's gospel, and which our faith has gazed upon."[11]

Even our brokenhearted cries of lament and complaint—when God seems distant—give expression to a vital relationship with God. As Hans Walter Wolff says, in laments "the man who cannot himself remedy his situation of need, clings to the God of the testimonies. The laments document resistance to the temptation to renounce God (Job. 2:9) no less than the songs of praise."[12]

Since our transformation takes place through a personal relationship with God, we cannot be transformed without prayer. In prayer we take God as real and personal. We become aware of his presence. To pray is to rise above the earthly realities of our life and connect with the ultimate level of our existence.

As the Lord was "enthroned upon the praises of Israel" (Ps. 22:3), so he is present in our prayers of praise. The prophet Isaiah told us that the name of the gates of the new Jerusalem will be "Praise" (Isa. 60:18). For those who enter into God's presence will do so with praise even as the psalmist encouraged ancient Israel to "enter His gates with thanksgiving and His courts with praise" (Ps. 100:4). The more we praise the Lord, the more we contemplate his manifold glory. And the more we gaze at his glory, the more we are transformed into his true image to reflect his glory in our lives.

Our petitions likewise are requests for the manifestation of God's presence in our lives. In the words the great Reformer John Calvin, when we call on the name of our heavenly Father,

> we invoke the presence both of his providence, through which he
> watches over and guards our affairs, and of his power, through which

he sustains us, weak as we are and well-nigh overcome, and of his good-ness, through which he receives us, miserably burdened with sins, unto grace; and, in short, *it is by prayer that we call him to reveal himself as wholly present to us.*[13]

Simply put, in calling on God we open our heart to his gracious work. As Daniélou notes, "One begins to open oneself to God when, aware of one's impo-tence to deal with things on one's own, one turns to God for help; from this moment on, one is open to the work of grace."[14]

This explains why, even though God longs to bestow his blessings on us as his children, he commands us to come to him in prayer in order obtain them. The prophet Isaiah declares, "Therefore the LORD longs to be gracious to you. . . . How blessed are all those who long for Him" (30:18). God's gifts are obtained only through his presence—through a personal relationship with him. He can-not give us himself and his blessing when our heart is closed to him in prayer-lessness and we are seeking life some other place.

Finally, prayer is vital in our transformation because through prayer we are called to participate in the work of fulfilling God's purposes, including those for our personal transformation. If our prayers are biblical, they are all simply elab-orations of the opening petitions of our Lord's model prayer: "Our Father who is in heaven, hallowed be Your name ['may your name be honored as holy,' HCSB], *Your kingdom come, Your will be done on earth as it is in heaven*" (Matt. 6:9–10).

In his valuable work on the theology of prayer, Graeme Goldsworthy said, "It comes down to this: having revealed his purpose, God graciously allows us, as his

Why Pray for Things That God Has Already Planned?

On the issue of praying for things that God has already purposed to do, Graeme Goldsworthy said, "God loves us to ask for the things he has revealed that he wants to give us. This is part of the process he has chosen to use in order to carry out his plan for the whole universe (Jer. 29:1–17; Ezek. 36:37; 1 John 5:14). . . . God is pleased to involve us in the outworking of his will as responsible, praying people. Generally, he does not carry out his will without bringing his saved people into the process through their prayer."[15] To be sure, God does not always reveal his specific will for the details of our life. But even in these instances our prayer must be in accord with what we do know of God's will from the Scriptures with the added acknowledgement that our request is ultimately for his will to be done in every instance knowing that his will is for our best.

dear children, to be involved in the carrying out of his will. . . . Prayer is *not* try-ing to persuade God to do something he otherwise would not do. It is our being caught up in the purposes of God and the expression of this privilege as his dear children who know him as Father. We do not know God if we ignore his revealed will and it's outworking through the Son."[16] Even "the details of our lives can never be conceived of as merely the means of maintaining a stable life-situation. If we pray for health, safety or our daily bread, it is in order to be able to live another day to serve God and to share in the outworking of his purposes."[17]

Prayer, as noted above, makes conscious our relationship with God as active participants with him in his plans and work to finally bring the kingdom on earth as it is in heaven.* Like a parent who in his love for his children and desire for them to mature, calls them into responsible participation in the family affairs, God calls us to participate with him through the communion of prayer and, of course, also in the activity of carrying out those affairs. He could certainly carry out his purpose by himself. But he loves to draw us close to him in the fellowship of his work through prayer. He wants us—who even as believers are tempted to live life independently from him—to learn that apart from him we cannot do anything to accomplish his purpose or truly live an abundant life. We were cre-ated to live with faith in God recognizing that all of our life flows from him, and prayer is "the chief exercise of faith"† and the avenue through which faith grows in our life.

In sum, prayer is at the center of a personal relationship with God that trans-forms. For, as we have said, it is in prayer that we consciously open our hearts and lives to receive his transforming grace. It is in prayer, when our heart beats with God's heart in participating in the outworking of his saving activity, that God's transforming grace reaches its goal of making us loving persons. As we partici-pate in God's saving activity in the world through prayer, so it is through prayer that we participate in the "working out" of our own spiritual transformation.

---

* In a very real sense, our participation with God in the personal relationship of prayer and work is the fulfillment of God's original command for us to rule over his creation as his representa-tives (Gen. 1:26, 28; Ps. 8:4–8; Heb. 2:6–8).

† John Calvin, *Institutes of the Christian Religion*, vol. 2, ed. John T. McNeill, trans. Ford Lewis Battles, Library of Christian Classics 21 (Philadelphia: Westminster, 1960), 3.20. In addition, Calvin wrote: "But after we have been instructed by faith to recognize that whatever we need and whatever we lack is in God, and in our Lord Jesus Christ, in whom the Father willed all the fullness of bounty to abide [cf. Col. 1:19; John 1:6] so that we may all draw from it as from an overflowing spring, it remains for us to seek in him, and prayers to ask of him, what we have learned to be in him. . . . Just as faith is born from the gospel, so through it our hearts are trained to call upon God's name [Rom. 10:14–17]." Ibid., 3.20.1.

Questions for Thought

1. What does it mean that transformation involves a heart-to-heart relationship with God? Do you like the thought of living in a personal relationship with an awesome God better than seeing transformation as obeying God's commands? Why or why not? Which seems easier to you?

2. What should our focus be in our pursuit of spiritual growth, bearing fruit in our lives or abiding in Christ? What has been your focus?

3. How do the things mentioned that enable us to have a heart-to-heart relationship with God relate to your own experience (e.g., frequent contact, abiding in God's Word and love, harmony, prayer)? Do you feel strong in some of those things and weak in others? Is it possible to be strong in some of those things and weak in others, or do they all fit together so closely that strength in one is strength in all?

4. Do you think that our prayer life is indicative of our faith in God and his transforming power? What part does unceasing prayer play in spiritual transformation? What part does it play in your pursuit of transformation?

Conclusion

God so loved the world that he gave his only Son that we might have life, abundant life. This truth from Scripture tells us at least two profound realities. First, the life we have without Christ is not life, but death. To live we must be reborn, re-created with true life. Second, that true life is available for all who will accept God's gift of salvation in his Son, the One who took our death upon himself and rose to newness of life that in him we might also live a new kind of life.

In his Word, God sets before us the way to the experience of that new life. Not yet the perfect life when he wipes every tear from our eyes and there is no pain or sorrow or death. We await that fullness of life in our final transformation and the ultimate making new of all creation (Rev. 21:3–4). But today, God offers us the beginning of that life in the midst of a world increasingly filled with pain, sorrow, and death to which we are not immune. Through the ministry of the Spirit whom he sent, Jesus promised to give us his joy and peace, and produce the fruit of the Spirit beginning with love in our experience now. The apostles in the New Testament along with many believers throughout all history testify to this reality.

For most, if not all of us, the way of this life is far from natural. In fact, it is strange. Growing in life through death. Gaining through losing. If we would be transformed in heart to know more of this new life in our experience it will come only through coming to understanding and choosing to submit to God's strange, but true, wisdom and not the wisdom of this world, which still often seems so natural to us as believers. These two ways of wisdom are clearly set before us in the following poem attributed to a young Civil War veteran whose battlefield injuries left him crippled.

> I asked for strength that I might achieve;
>> I was made weak that I might obey.
> I asked for health that I might do greater things;
>> I was given infirmity that I might do better things.

> I asked for riches that I might be happy;
>   I was given poverty that I might be wise.
> I asked for power that I might have the praise of men;
>   I was given weakness that I might feel the need of God.
> I asked for all things that I might enjoy life;
>   I was given life that I might enjoy all things.
> I have received nothing I asked for, all that I hoped for.
>   My prayer is answered.[1]

The transformation that took place in this war veteran's heart is possible only through the supernatural power of the indwelling Spirit of God who forms in us the life of Christ who is God's wisdom in person and is made God's wisdom for us (1 Cor. 1:24, 30). There is no avenue, no regimen, no religious practices that can bring real transformation of our heart except those that enable us to live constantly in the presence of our Savior in heart-to-heart fellowship. This process of transformation is captured in chorus of the old hymn:

> Moment by moment I'm kept in His love;
> Moment by moment I've life from above;
> Looking to Jesus till glory doth shine:
> Moment by moment, O Lord, I am Thine.[2]

Continually looking to Jesus, aware of being kept in his love and receiving his life, transforms us radiating his glory in our life (2 Cor. 3:18), and through us to the world about us.

Such transformation of our heart and the change of life that issues from it does not come overnight. Although we might desire it, God never promises nor provides a means for instant transformation. We are instantly born to new life as we are united to Christ through faith. But Scripture teaches no instant growth in strength and maturity in our new life. It is a long walk, or perhaps an endurance race (Heb. 12:1), but certainly not a broad jump.

Interestingly, throughout the Bible the Christian life is pictured like the growth of a tree. The psalmist said,

> The wicked sprouted up like grass, . . .
> The righteous man will flourish like the palm tree,
> He will grow like a cedar of Lebanon
> Planted in the house of the LORD,

They will flourish in the courts of our God.
They will still yield fruit in old age [we are never too old to grow]
They shall be full of sap and very green." (Ps. 92:7, 12–14)

Grass sprouts up quickly but soon dies in the scorching sun. A tree stands solid with deep roots watering and nourishing it. But a tree takes time to grow. It doesn't spring up to full height instantly. So like trees, we should not be discouraged if our transformation sometimes seem slow. There will be times when it almost seems to stop as the root of our new heart reaches down deeper into the recesses of the remnants of the old heart that still remain and comes to the rocky soil or "hardpan"—old patterns that have been there for a long time. But there is nothing that can stop the transforming power of God's presence in our life if we live life with a humble heart wide open to his heart, which in his love is wide open to us to work in us "everything pertaining to life and godliness through the true knowledge of Him who called us by His own glory and excellence" (2 Peter 1:3).

Finally, biblical spiritual transformation is "hard," but finally "easy." The one who is seeking spiritual transformation will not "be carried to the skies on flow'ry beds of ease" as the old hymn puts it.[3] As "good soldiers of Christ Jesus" we will "suffer hardship" (2 Tim. 2:3). There will be battles with the enemy within—the remnants of our old god-playing self—and battles with the forces of evil in a hostile world around us. Thus Jesus himself said that "the way is hard* that leads to life, and those who find it are few" (Matt. 7:14 ESV).

But Jesus also still extends to us today the same offer that he did to his hearers some two thousand years ago: "Come to Me, all who are weary and heavy-laden, and I will give you rest. Take My yoke upon you and learn from Me, for I am gentle and humble in heart, and you will find rest for your souls. For my yoke is easy and My burden is light" (Matt. 11:28–30). The hard way of following Jesus is the easy way that leads to rest.

The yoke was a wooden frame that was fit over the necks of draft animals (usually two oxen) so that the pull was against their shoulders, much like the

---

* The Greek word *tethlimmenē* (from *thlibō*) translated "hard" is in some versions translated "narrow" in this verse (e.g., NASB, NIV). But it is a different word than the one used for "narrow" (*stenos*) in v. 13. The word for "hard," which describes the "way" in v. 14, is related to the Greek word *thlipsis*, which has the basic meaning of "press, crush," and thus is used figuratively for "oppression, affliction, and tribulation," which is how it is almost always used in the New Testament. D. A. Carson thus describes the "hard" way as "the way of persecution and opposition." "Matthew," in *Matthew, Mark, Luke*, vol. 8, *EBC*, ed. Frank E. Gaebelein (Grand Rapids: Zondervan, 1984), 189.

softer leather horse collars used with work horses in more recent times. It became a symbol of submission and servitude (e.g., Gen. 27:40; 1 Tim. 6:1). Rabbinic tradition spoke of submission to God's will as taking on "the yoke of the Law."[4] In inviting us to take his yoke, Jesus is calling us to submit to him and his way of life, to listen to his words and obey them—to the way of spiritual transformation.

When we submit to his yoke, we will find it "easy"—a word often used for God's kindness and benevolence. Our yoke which is fitted just for us personally will be kindly, pleasant, suitable, and easy to bear. It is so because it is finally the yoke of love that perfectly fits the design of our human life and the impulse of our new heart. Thus the more we submit to his yoke, the more we realize that it is not alien to us, but rather the means to God's shalom (the sense of well-being) that come from living the life for which we were created.

But even more than being perfectly suited to us, his yoke is "easy" and his burden "light" because he is there with us. Unlike the religious leaders of his day, Jesus does not simply lay heavy burdens on us and do nothing to lighten them. He bears them with us, He comes with his Word to give us himself, to give us his own life and all that it entails—his love, joy, peace, strength, comfort, encouragement, direction—so that his life might become our life. To those who are new creatures and can say, "It is no longer I who live, but Christ who lives in me" (Gal. 2:20), his yoke is not burdensome.

The way of spiritual transformation is the way of taking on our Lord's yoke. To the extent that we truly receive his yoke and incorporate it into our heart, to that extent we will find it easy and its burden light—and find rest for our souls even when the way is hard.

Notes

Introduction

1. Reprinted by permission.
2. Dallas Willard, *Renovation of the Heart: Putting on the Character of Christ* (Colorado Spring: NavPress, 2002), 22.
3. Ibid., 23.

Chapter 1: Born to Grow

Epigraphs. John 10:10; William Barclay, *The Gospel of John*, vol. 2, Daily Study Bible (Philadelphia: Westminster, 1956), 6.

1. C. K. Barrett, *The Second Epistle to the Corinthians*, Black's New Testament commentaries 8 (1973; repr., Peabody, MA: Hendrickson, 1993), 146.
2. K. Kock, *"derekh," TDOT*, 2:281–82.
3. Derek Kidner, *Psalms, 1–72: An Introduction and Commentary on Books I and II of the Psalms*, TOTC (London: Inter-Varsity Press, 1973), 86
4. Claus Westermann, *Genesis 12–36: A Commentary*, trans. John J. Scullion (Minneapolis: Augsburg, 1985), 2:259.
5. Erwin Schrödinger, *What Is Life? And Other Scientific Essays* (Garden City, NY: Doubleday, 1956), 69–70.
6. Bruce K. Waltke, *"nefesh," TWOT*, 2:587–91; cf. also Hans Walter Wolff, *Anthropology of the Old Testament*, trans. Margaret Kohl (Philadelphia: Fortress, 1974), 10–25.
7. William Barclay, *Flesh and Spirit: An Examination of Galatians 5.19–23* (London: SCM Press, 1962), 77.
8. John Eadie, *Commentary on the Epistle to the Galatians* (Edinburgh: T&T Clark, 1869; 1894 ed.; repr., Grand Rapids: Zondervan, 1964), 422.
9. G. G. Findlay, "Joy," *Dictionary of the Bible*, ed. James Hastings (New York: Charles Scribner's Sons, 1952), 500.
10. Fenton John Anthony Hort, *The Way, the Truth, the Life*, 2nd ed. Hulsean Lectures, 1871 (Cambridge: Macmillan, 1894), 98.
11. Ibid., 99.
12. G. Lloyd Carr, *"shalom,"* TWOT, 2:931.

13. Richard N. Longenecker, *Galatians*, WBC 41 (Dallas: Word Books, 1990), 261.

14. Gordon J. Wenham, *Numbers: An Introduction and Commentary* (Downers Grove, IL: InterVarsity Press, 1981), 90.

15. Cornelius Plantinga Jr., *Not the Way It's Supposed to Be: A Breviary of Sin* (Grand Rapids: Eerdmans / Leicester: Inter-Varsity Press, 1995), 10.

16. Leon Morris, *The Gospel according to John*, rev. ed., NICNT (Grand Rapids: Eerdmans, 1995), 233, 376.

17. Hort, *The Way, The Truth, The Life*, 99, 101.

Chapter 2: The Real Person

Epigraph. F. H. von Meyenfeldt, "The Old Testament Meaning of Heart and Soul," in *Toward a Biblical View of Man: Some Readings*, ed. Arnold H. De Graaff and James H. Olthuis (Toronto: Association for the Advancement of Christian Scholarship, 1978), 70.

1. Stewart Kampel, "Profile: Milton Glaser," *Haddash Magazine* 91, no. 3 (December 2009/January 2010), http://www.hadassahmagazine.org/site/apps/nlnet/content2.aspx?c=twI6LmN7IzF&b=5724115&ct=7782493.

2. Hans Walter Wolff, *The Anthropology of the Old Testament*, trans. Margaret Kohl (Philadelphia: Fortress, 1974), 40.

3. Ibid. The 858 occurrences include 850 in Hebrew (two forms) and 8 in Aramaic (a language closely related to Hebrew in which portions or the book of Daniel were written). Fabry gives the total number of occurrences of the words for heart in the Old Testament as 853 (845 Hebrew, 8 Aramaic) (H. J. Fabry, "*lev, levav,*" *TDOT*, 7:407).

4. Bruce Waltke, "*nefesh,*" *TWOT*, 2:587–91.

5. Gustave F. Oehler, *Theology of the Old Testament* (1883; repr., Grand Rapids: Zondervan, 1950), 153. Analogously Edmund Jacob stated, "the heart is the soul in its inner worth." Edmund Jacob, "*psuchē,*" *TDNT*, 9:626.

6. I. Cohen, "The Heart in Biblical Psychology," in *Essays Presented to Chief Rabbi Israel Brodie on the Occasion of His Seventieth Birthday*, ed. Hirsch Jacob Zimmels, Joseph Rabbinowitz, and Israel Finestein, Jews' College Publications, n.s., no. 3 (London: Soncino Press, 1967), 41.

7. D. Martyn Lloyd-Jones, *Studies in the Sermon on the Mount* (London: Inter-Varsity Press, 1959), 1:108.

8. William McKane, *Proverbs: A New Approach*, OTL (Philadelphia: Westminster, 1970), 616.

9. Robert J. Bouffier, "The 'Heart' in the Proverbs of Solomon," *Bible Today* 52 (1971), 249.

10. Ibid.

11. J. Ramsey Michaels, *1 Peter*, WBC 49 (Waco, TX: Word Books, 1988), 161.

12. This translation of Ps. 64:6 is from Marvin E. Tate, *Psalms 51–100* WBC 20 (Dallas: Word Books, 1990), 130.

13. Bruce K. Waltke, *The Book of Proverbs: Chapters 1–15*, NICOT (Grand Rapids: Eerdmans, 2004), 1:590.

14. Paul S. Minear, "A Theology of the Heart," *Worship* 63 no. 3 (May 1989): 253.

15. Von Meyenfeldt, "Old Testament Meaning of Heart and Soul," 70.

16. John Calvin, *Institutes of the Christian Religion*, vol. 1, ed. John T. McNeill, trans. Ford Lewis Battles, Library of Christian Classics 20 (Philadelphia: Westminster, 1960), 1.1.1–2.

17. Martin Luther, in his preface to Melanchthon's *Commentary on Colossians*, cited by Philip Schaff, *History of the Christian Church*, 2nd ed., rev., vol. 7, *Modern Christianity: The German Reformation* (1910; repr., Grand Rapids: Eerdmans, 1953), 7.193.

18. Martin Luther, "From Depths of Woe I Raise to Thee," *Trinity Hymnal* (Philadelphia: Committee on Christian Education, Orthodox Presbyterian Church, 1961), no. 461.

19. Franz Delitzsch, *Biblical Commentary on the Proverbs of Solomon*, trans. M. G. Easton, BCOT (1874; repr., Grand Rapids: Eerdmans, 1950), 1:115.

20. William R. Newell, *Romans: Verse by Verse* (Chicago: Moody Press, 1950), 83.

21. Frederick Dale Bruner, *The Christbook: Matthew 1–12*, Matthew: A Commentary, vol. 1 (Dallas: Word, 1987), 465.

22. C. S. Lewis, *Mere Christianity*, rev. ed. (New York: Macmillan, 1960), 149–50.

23. Bernard Ramm, *Offense to Reason: A Theology of Sin* (San Francisco: Harper & Row, 1985), 41.

24. Herman Ridderbos, *Paul: An Outline of His Theology*, trans. John Richard de Witt (Grand Rapids: Eerdmans, 1975), 120.

25. D. A. Carson, "Matthew," in *Matthew, Mark, Luke*, vol. 8, *EBC*, ed. Frank E. Gaebelein (Grand Rapids: Zondervan, 1984), 177.

Chapter 3: The Real Problem in Life

Epigraph. Augustine, *The Confessions of St. Augustine: Modern English Version* (Grand Rapids: Baker Book House, 2005), 90. This version of the *Confessions* employs paraphrase to better capture the meaning of the original text for the contemporary reader. Thus "it was wholly me and my wicked heart that divided me from myself" in the statement above is more literally "the whole was myself and what divided me against myself was my impiety" (Augustine, *Confessions*,

5.10.18, trans. Henry Chadwick, World's Classics [Oxford: Oxford University Press, 1992], 84.) However, since as we have seen in the previous chapter, "myself" is really my "heart," "my impiety" seems well expressed in "my wicked heart."

1. "Ra'," *The Hebrew and Aramaic Lexicon of the Old Testament,* CD-ROM ed., ed. Ludwig Koehler and Walter Baumgartner, rev. Walter Baumgartner and Johann Jakob Stamm, trans. and ed. by M. E. J. Richardson (Leiden: Brill Koninklijk, 2000).

2. See David W. Baker, "ra'a," *New International Dictionary of Old Testament Theology and Exegesis,* ed. Willem A. VanGemeren (Grand Rapids: Zondervan, 1997), 3:1154–58.

3. M. Scott Peck, *People of the Lie: The Hope for Healing Human Evil* (New York: Simon & Shuster, 1983), 42.

4. Ronald B. Allen, "'aqash," *TWOT,* 2:693. See also, G. Warmuth, "'aqash," *TDOT,* 11:323–26.

5. Hans-Joachim Kraus. *Psalms 60–150,* Continental Commentary, trans. Hilton C. Oswald (Minneapolis: Fortress, 1993), 279.

6. Cornelius Plantinga Jr., *Not the Way It's Supposed to Be: A Breviary of Sin* (Grand Rapids: Eerdmans / Leicester: Inter-Varsity Press, 1995), 40.

7. Bruce K. Waltke, *The Book of Proverbs: Chapters 15–31,* NICOT (Grand Rapids: Eerdmans, 2005), 2:422.

8. Lucius Annaeus Seneca, *Letters from a Stoic: Epistulae Morales Ad Lucilium,* trans. Robin Campbell (New York: Penguin, 1969), 225.

9. *The Jerusalem Bible,* ed. Alexander Jones (Garden City, NY: Doubleday, 1966).

10. Augustine, *The City of God,* trans. Marcus Dods (New York: Random House, 1950), 14.13.

11. Robert W. Kellemen, *Soul Physicians: A Theology of Soul Care and Spiritual Direction,* rev. ed. (Taneytown, MD: RPM Books, 2005), 389.

12. C. S. Lewis, *Mere Christianity,* rev. ed. (New York: Macmillan, 1960), 94.

13. Blaise Pascal, *Pensées,* 34.494, in *Pensées and Other Writings,* trans. Honor Levi (Oxford: Oxford University Press, 1995), 118–19.

14. Gordon Allport, *The Individual and His Religion: A Psychological Interpretation* (New York: Macmillan, 1950), 94–95.

15. Plantinga, *Not the Way It's Supposed to Be,* 125–26.

16. Augustine, *City of God,* 14.13.

17. Reinhold Niebuhr, *The Nature and Destiny of Man,* vol. 1, Gifford Lectures (New York: Charles Scribner's Sons, 1964), 207.

18. Stephen K. Moroney, "Thinking of Ourselves More Highly Than We Ought: A Psychological and Theological Analysis," in *Care for the Soul: Exploring the*

Intersection of Psychology and Theology, ed. Mark R. McMinn and Timothy R. Phillips (Downers Grove, IL: InterVarsity Press, 2001), 309–31.

19. "*khlv* II," *A Hebrew and English Lexicon of the Old Testament* by F. Brown, S. R. Driver, and C. A. Briggs (Oxford, 1907), 316.

20. John N. Oswalt, *The Book of Isaiah: Chapters 40–66*, NICOT (Grand Rapids: Eerdmans, 1998), 237–38.

21. Aleksandr I. Solzhenitsyn, *The Gulag Archipelago 1918–1956: An Experiment in Literary Investigation*, vol. 2, trans. Thomas P. Whitney (New York: Harper & Row, 1975), 602–3.

22. John Chrysostom, *Homilies on the Gospel of Matthew*, 73:2:442; cited by Frederick Dale Bruner, *The Churchbook: Matthew 13–28*, Matthew: A Commentary vol. 2 (Dallas: Word, 1990), 827.

23. Quoted in Iian H. Murray, ed., *David Martyn Lloyd-Jones: The First Forty Years, 1899–1939*, vol. 1 (Edinburgh; Carlisle, PA: Banner of Truth Trust, 1982), 100–101.

24. Albert Einstein, "The Real Problem Is in the Hearts of Men," in an interview with Michael Amrine, *New York Times*, June 23, 1946.

25. V. H. Kooy, "Integrity," *IDB*, 2:718.

26. G. Lloyd Carr, "*shalem*," *TWOT*, 2:930.

27. Derek Kidner, *Psalms 73–150: An Introduction and Commentary on Books III–V of the Psalms*, TOTC (London: Inter-Varsity Press, 1975), 313.

28. D. A. Carson, "Matthew," in *Matthew, Mark, Luke*, vol. 8, *EBC*, ed. Frank E. Gaebelein (Grand Rapids: Zondervan, 1984), 135.

29. L. Alonso-Schökel, "*yashar*," *TDOT*, 6:465–66.

30. Cynthia Crossen, "From Talk Shows to Offices, America Lacks Good Listeners," *The Wall Street Journal*, July 10, 1997.

31. Walter Grundmann, "*tapeinos* [humble], etc.," *Theological Dictionary of the New Testament*, ed. Gerhard Kittel and Gerhard Friedrich, trans. and abr. in one vol. Geoffrey W. Bromiley (Grand Rapids: Eerdmans, 1985), 1152.

32. J. R. R. Tolkien, *The Silmarillion*, 2nd ed., ed. Christopher Tolkien (New York: Ballantine Books, 1999), 3–4.

33. Ibid., 4–5.

34. Paul S. Minear, "A Theology of the Heart," *Worship* 63 no. 3 (May 1989): 249.

35. Robert Jewett, *Paul's Anthropological Terms: A Study of Their Use in Conflict Settings* (Leiden: E. J. Brill, 1971), 313.

36. Peter Kreeft, *Heaven: The Heart's Deepest Longing*, expanded ed. (San Francisco: Ignatius Press, 1989), 45.

37. Augustine, *Confessions*, trans. Henry Chadwick, World's Classics (Oxford: Oxford University Press, 1992), 278.

38. Jewett, *Paul's Anthropological Terms*, 322–23.

39. Edward Sanford Martin, "My Name Is Legion," in *Masterpieces of Religious Verse*, ed. James Dalton Morrison (New York: Harper & Row, 1948), 274, no. 846.

Chapter 4: Living with Heart

Epigraphs. William Cowper, *The Task: A Poem, in Six Books* (London: J. Johnson, 1785), 6.85; Paul L. Peeters, "*Dominum et Vivificantem*: The Conscience and the Heart," *International Catholic Review: Communio* 15 (Spring 1988): 150.

1. *Science of the Heart: Exploring the Role of the Heart in Human Performance*, comp. Rollin McCraty, Mike Atkinson, and Dana Tomasino (Boulder Creek, CA: HeartMath Research Center, Institute of HeartMath, 2001), 8.

2. Franz Delitzsch, *A System of Biblical Psychology*, 2nd ed., trans. Robert Ernest Wallis (1899; repr., Grand Rapids: Baker, 1966), 310.

3. Andrew Bowling, "*lev, levav*," *TWOT*, 1:466.

4. Hans Walter Wolff, *The Anthropology of the Old Testament*, trans. Margaret Kohl (Philadelphia: Fortress, 1974), 46.

5. Robert Jewett, *Paul's Anthropological Terms: A Study of Their Use in Conflict Settings* (Leiden: E. J. Brill, 1971), 327.

6. John Laidlaw, *The Bible Doctrine of Man; or The Anthropology and Psychology of Scripture*, rev. ed., Cunningham Lectures, Seventh Series (1879; Edinburgh: T&T Clark, 1895), 124–25.

7. Marianne Szegedy-Maszak, "Hearts and Minds," *U.S. News & World Report* 135, no. 19 (2003): 70, http://health.usnews.com/usnews/health/articles/031201/1minds.htm.

8. Johannes Pedersen, *Israel: Its Life and Culture*, vol. 1, trans. Mrs. Aslaug Møller. (1926–40; repr., London: Oxford University Press, 1973], 108 (emphasis added).

9. Otto A. Piper, "Knowledge," *IDB*, 3:43.

10. Pedersen, *Israel*, 1:125.

11. Gerhard Kittel, "*akouō*," *TDNT*, 1:218.

12. Ibid.

13. Wolfhart Pannenberg, *Anthropology in Theological Perspective* trans. Matthew J. O'Connell (Philadelphia: Westminster, 1985), 244.

14. Ibid., 250. The quote is Pannenberg's explanation of Schleiermacher's understanding of feeling.

15. Antonio R. Damasio, *Descartes' Error: Emotion, Reason, and the Human Brain* (New York: Putnam, 1994), xv.

16. Paul Lauritzen, *Religious Belief and Emotional Transformation: A Light in the Heart* (Lewisburg: Bucknell University Press / London and Cranbury, NJ: Associated University Presses, 1992), 44.

17. Robert C. Roberts, *Spirituality and Human Emotion* (Grand Rapids: Eerdmans, 1982), 15.

18. Martha C. Nussbaum, *Upheavals of Thought: The Intelligence of Emotions* (Cambridge: Cambridge University Press, 2001), 49.

19. Roberts, *Spirituality and Human Emotion*, 21.

20. Charles Bridges, *An Exposition of Proverbs* (1846; repr., Grand Rapids: Christian Classics, n.d.), 60.

21. John Henry Newman, "Secret Faults," Psalm 19:12 (sermon, St. Mary the Virgin, Oxford, England, 1825–1843, published in vol. 1 of Parochial and Plain Sermons, 1868), in *Selected Sermons*, ed. Ian Ker, Classics of Western Spirituality (Mahwah, NJ: Paulist Press, 1994), 78.

22. John Flavel, *Keeping the Heart* (1668; repr., Grand Rapids: Sovereign Grace Publishers, 1971), 102.

23. Franz Delitzsch, *Biblical Commentary on the Psalms*, vol. 1, 2nd ed., trans. Francis Bolton, BCOT (1867; repr., Grand Rapids: Eerdmans, 1959), 350.

24. William Cowper, *The Task: A Poem, in Six Books* (London: J. Johnson, 1785), 6.88.

25. Bernard J. F. Lonergan, *Method in Theology* (New York: Herder and Herder, 1972), 33–34.

26. Plutarch, *Of Curiosity, or An Over-Busy Inquisitiveness into Things Impertinent*, sec. 3, vol. 2, trans. William W. Goodwin [Boston: Little, Brown, and Co., 1878], 428

27. Richard Sibbes, *The Soul's Conflict, and Victory Over Itself by Faith*, 15:7:6, in *The Complete Works of Richard Sibbes*, vol. 1 (Edinburgh: James Nichol, 1862), 200, quoted in David A. Powlison, "To Take the Soul to Task." *Journal of Biblical Counseling* 12, no. 3 (1994): 2.

28. This discussion of the forms that our life takes in relation to the reality of the heart is adopted from the helpful discussion of Adrian van Kaam, *The Art of Existential Counseling* (Wilkes-Barre, PA: Dimension Books, 1966), 61–104.

29. Cornelius Plantinga Jr., *Not the Way It's Supposed to Be: A Breviary of Sin* (Grand Rapids: Eerdmans / Leicester: Inter-Varsity Press, 1995), 107, referencing

Martin Buber, *Between Man and Man*, trans. Ronald Gregor Smith (New York: Macmillan, 1965), 18.

30. Oscar Wilde to Lord Alfred Douglas, January–March 1897, Reading Gaol (prison), Reading, Berkshire, England, originally published posthumously in heavily expurgated form by Robert Ross under the title *De Profundis* in 1905, first fully correct version published in 1962, reprinted in *Selected Letters of Oscar Wilde*, ed. Rupert Hart-Davis (Oxford: Oxford University Press, 1979), 194.

31. Timothy Keller, *The Reason for God: Belief in an Age of Skepticism* (New York: Dutton, 2008), 177.

32. Van Kaam, *Art of Existential Counseling*, 68–69.

33. Paul Tournier, *The Person Reborn* (New York: Harper & Row, 1966), 65.

Chapter 5: Radical Surgery

Epigraphs. Robert Jewett, *Paul's Anthropological Terms: A Study of Their Use in Conflict Settings* (Leiden: E. J. Brill, 1971), 313; *The Bible: James Moffatt Translation* by James A. R. Moffatt (Grand Rapids: Kregel, 1994).

1. "Surgery: The Ultimate Operation," *TIME*, December 15, 1967, http://www.time.com/time/magazine/article/0,9171,837606,00.html.

2. John Laidlaw, *The Bible Doctrine of Man; or The Anthropology and Psychology of Scripture*, rev. ed., Cunningham Lectures, Seventh Series (1879; Edinburgh: T&T Clark, 1895), 122.

3. Max Lucado, *Come Thirsty* (Nashville: W Publishing Group, 2004), 11.

4. John E. Hartley, *The Book of Job*, NICOT (Grand Rapids: Eerdmans, 1988), 409.

5. Ibid., 247.

6. F. J. Stendebach, "'ayin," *TDOT*, 11:32–33.

7. Jewett, *Paul's Anthropological Terms*, 313.

8. Hendrik Hart, "Conceptual Understanding and Knowing Other-wise: Reflections on Rationality and Spirituality" in *Knowing Other-Wise: Philosophy at the Threshold of Spirituality*, ed. James H. Olthuis, Perspectives in Continental Philosophy 4 (New York: Fordham University Press, 1997), 24.

9. U.S. Geological Survey "The Water Cycle: Transpiration," accessed on April 15, 2011, http://ga.water.usgs.gov/edu/watercycletranspiration.html.

10. Bengel, ad loc.; cited by G. Bertram, "stenos," *TDNT*, 7:608. Trans. of Bengel, Murray J. Harris, *The Second Epistle to the Corinthians: A Commentary on the Greek Text*, NIGTC (Grand Rapids: Eerdmans / Milton Keynes, UK: Paternoster, 2005), 488.

11. Bruce K. Waltke, *The Book of Proverbs: Chapters 1–15*, NICOT (Grand Rapids: Eerdmans, 2004), 1:351.

12. William McKane, *Proverbs: A New Approach*, OTL (Philadelphia: Westminster, 1970), 327.

13. Paul Minear, "A Theology of the Heart," *Worship* 63, no 3 (May 1989): 249.

Chapter 6: God and Us

Epigraph. William Arnot, *Studies in Proverbs: Laws from Heaven for Life on Earth* (1884; repr., Grand Rapids: Kregel, 1978), 127. William McKane, *Proverbs: A New Approach*, OTL (Philadelphia: Westminster, 1970), 559.

 1. William McKane, *Proverbs: A New Approach*, OTL (Philadelphia: Westminster, 1970), 559.

 2. Hans-Joachim Kraus, *Theology of the Psalms*, trans. Keith Crim (Minneapolis: Fortress, 1992), 157.

 3. Peter Kreeft, *The God Who Loves You: Knowing the Height, Depth, and Breadth of God's Love for You* (Ann Arbor, MI: Servant Books, 1992), 140–41.

 4. Douglas J. Moo, *The Epistle to the Romans*, NICNT (Grand Rapids: Eerdmans, 1996), 375.

 5. John R. W. Stott, *Romans: God's Good News for the World*, Bible Speaks Today (Downers Grove, IL: InterVarsity Press, 1994), 184.

 6. Henry Scougal, *The Life of God in the Soul of Man, or Nature and Excellency of the Christian Religion.* (1677; Philadelphia: Westminster, 1948), 49.

 7. John Calvin, *Institutes of the Christian Religion*, vol. 1, ed. John T. McNeill, trans. Ford Lewis Battles, Library of Christian Classics 20 (Philadelphia: Westminster, 1960), 2.3.6.

 8. Johannes Pedersen, *Israel: Its Life and Culture*, vol. 1, trans. Mrs. Aslaug Møller. (1926; repr., London: Oxford University Press, 1973), 166.

 9. Franz Delitzsch, *A System of Biblical Psychology*, 2nd ed., trans. Robert Ernest Wallis (1899; repr., Grand Rapids: Baker, 1966), 438.

10. Robert Jewett, *Paul's Anthropological Terms: A Study of Their Use in Conflict Settings* (Leiden: E. J. Brill, 1971), 323.

11. John Flavel, *Keeping the Heart* (1668; repr., Grand Rapids: Sovereign Grace Publishers, 1971), 5.

12. "*katergazomai*," BDAG, 531.

13. William Hendriksen, *Philippians*, New Testament Commentary (Grand Rapids: Baker, 1962), 120.

14. Richard N. Longenecker, *Galatians*, WBC 41 (Dallas: Word Books, 1990), 180.

15. Paul L. Peeters, "*Dominum et vivificantem*: The Conscience and the Heart," *International Catholic Review: Communio* (Spring 1988): 150.

16. John Murray, *Redemption: Accomplished and Applied* (1955; repr., London: Banner of Truth, 1961), 148–49.

17. Peter T. O'Brien, *Commentary on Philippians: A Commentary on the Greek Text*, NIGTC (Grand Rapids: Eerdmans, 1991), 285.

18. Ethelbert Stauffer, "*agapaō*," *TDNT*, 1:50.

19. For a discussion of the meaning of this clause in Colossians 2:23 favoring the alternate translation, see Peter T. O'Brien, *Colossians, Philemon*, WBC 44 (Waco: Word Books, 1982), 154–55.

20. John Witherspoon, "The Dominion of Providence Over the Passions of Men," Psalm 86:10 (sermon, Princeton, New Jersey, May 17, 1776).

Chapter 7: Minding the Mind

Epigraph. Quoted from the "The Translators to the Reader" prefixed to the Authorized [King James] Version of the Bible of 1611, in *The Bible: Authorized King James Version*, ed. Robert Carroll and Stephen Prickett, Oxford World's Classics (Oxford: Oxford University Press, 1997), lvi. The spelling and the use of italics has been modernized.

1. Harold W. Hoehner, *Ephesians: An Exegetical Commentary* (Grand Rapids: Baker, 2002), 608–9.

2. Leonhard Goppelt, "*typos,*" *TDNT*, 8:246.

3. Cf. Douglas J. Moo, *The Epistle to the Romans* NICNT (Grand Rapids: Eerdmans, 1996), 402; Robert A. J. Gagnon, "Heart of Wax and a Teaching That Stamps: *TYPOS DIDACHES* (Rom 6:17b) Once More," *Journal of Biblical Literature* 112, no. 4 (1993): 667–87.

4. Bruce K. Waltke, *The Book of Proverbs: Chapters 1–15*, NICOT (Grand Rapids: Eerdmans, 2004), 1:295.

5. Derek Kidner, *Psalms 73–150: An Introduction and Commentary on Books III–V of the Psalms*, TOTC (London: Inter-Varsity Press, 1975), 424.

6. Philip E. Hughes, *Commentary on the Second Epistle to the Corinthians*, NICNT (Grand Rapids: Eerdmans, 1962), 353.

7. Andrew T. Lincoln, *Ephesians*, WBC 42 (Dallas: Word Books, 1990), 286.

8. "*nous,*" *BDAG*, 680.

9. Paul S. Minear, "Theology of the Heart," *Worship* 63, no 3 (May 1989): 250.

10. D. A. Carson, *The Gospel according to John*, PNTC (Grand Rapids: Eerdmans, 1991), 566.

11. Quoted in Frederick Dale Bruner, *The Christbook: Matthew 1–12*, Matthew: A Commentary, vol. 1 (Dallas: Word, 1987), 261.

12. *Commentariorum in Isaiam libri XVIII*, prologue: PL 24, 17b; quoted in Erich

Sauer, *From Eternity to Eternity: An Outline of the Divine Purposes*, trans. G. H. Lang (Grand Rapids: Eerdmans, 1954), 65.

13. Alexander MacLaren, *Expositions of Holy Scripture: John 1–14*, vol. 10, (1894; repr., Grand Rapids: Baker, 1974), 140.

14. J. I. Packer, interview by Sue Nowicki, "Theologian J. I. Packer Reflects on Sharing His Faith," *The Washington Post*, December 26, 2009: http://www.washingtonpost.com/wp-dyn/content/article/2009/12/25/AR2009122501711.html.

15. Douglas Derryberry and Mary Klevjord Rothbart, "Emotion, Attention, and Temperament," in *Emotions, Cognition, and Behavior*, ed. Carroll E. Izard, Jerome Kagan, and Robert B. Zajonc (Cambridge: Cambridge University Press, 1984), 138–39.

16. Daniel J. Siegel, *The Developing Mind: How Relationships and the Brain Interact to Shape Who We Are* (New York: Guilford Press, 1999), 124–28.

17. Richard Bondi, "The Elements of Character," *Journal of Religious Ethics* 12, no. 2 (Fall 1984): 206.

18. David D. Burns, *Feeling Good: The New Mood Therapy* (New York: Penguin, 1981), 29.

19. Richard S. Lazarus, "Thoughts on the Relations between Emotion and Cognition," *American Psychologist* 37, no. 9 (1982): 1022.

20. Richard S. Lazarus, "On the Primacy of Cognition," *American Psychologist* 39, no. 2 (1984): 124.

21. Matthew A. Elliott, *Faithful Feelings: Rethinking Emotion in the New Testament* (Grand Rapids: Kregel, 2006), 133.

22. Charles Bridges, *An Exposition of Proverbs* (1846; repr., Grand Rapids: Christian Classics, n.d.), 20.

Chapter 8: Meditation (Part 1)

Epigraph. Eugene H. Peterson, *Eat This Book: A Conversation in the Art of Spiritual Reading* (Grand Rapids: Eerdmans, 2006), 4.

1. Dietrich Bonhoeffer, *Meditating on the Word*, ed. and trans. David McI. Gracie (Cambridge, MA: Cowley Publications, 1986), 127–28.

2. John E. Hartley, "*tsaleakh*," *TWOT*, 2:766.

3. Johannes Pedersen, *Israel Its Life and Culture*, vol. 1, trans. Mrs. Aslaug Møller (1926; repr., London: Oxford University Press, 1973), 196.

4. Louis Goldberg, "*sakal*," *TWOT*, 2:877.

5. Trent C. Butler, *Joshua*, WBC 7 (Waco: Word Books, 1983), 3, 5.

6. Derek Kidner, *Psalms 73–150: An Introduction and Commentary on Books III–V of the Psalms*, TOTC (London: Inter-Varsity Press, 1975), 416.

7. Derek Kidner, *Psalms 1–72: An Introduction and Commentary on Books I and II of the Psalms*, TOTC (London: Inter-Varsity Press, 1973), 48.

8. H. Ringgren, "*haghah*," *TDOT*, 3:323.

9. A. Negoita, "*haghah*," *TDOT*, 3:323.

10. "*logizomai*," *BDAG*, 598.

11. Johannes P. Louw and Eugene Albert Nida, *Greek-English Lexicon of the New Testament: Based on Semantic Domains*, electronic ed. of the 2nd ed. (New York: United Bible Societies, 1989), 1:352.

12. William D. Mounce, *Pastoral Epistles*, WBC 46 (Nashville: Thomas Nelson, 2000), 263.

13. Jeffrey M. Schwartz and Sharon Begley, *The Mind and the Brain: Neuroplasticity and the Power of Mental Force* (New York: HarperCollins, 2002), 332, 330, 339.

14. M. M. Merzenich and R. C. deCharms, "Neural Representations, Experience, and Change," in *The Mind-Brain Continuum: Sensory Processes*, ed. Rodolfo R. Llinás and Patricia S. Churchland (Cambridge, MA: MIT Press, 1996), 76.

15. Kidner, *Psalms 1–72*, 131.

16. Henry Scougal, *The Life of God in the Soul of Man, or Nature and Excellency of the Christian Religion* (1677; repr., Philadelphia: Westminster, 1948), 49, citing 2 Cor. 3:18.

17. Brevard S. Childs, *Memory and Tradition in Israel*, Studies in Biblical Theology 37 (Naperville, IL: Alec R. Allenson, 1962), 56.

18. Quoted in Anthony C. Thiselton, *The First Epistle to the Corinthians*, NIGTC (Grand Rapids: Eerdmans, 2000), 876–77.

19. "An African American spiritual that probably predates the Civil War, 'Were You There' was first published in William Barton's *Old Plantation Hymns* (1899)." *Psalter Hymnal Handbook* (Grand Rapids: CRC Publications, 1998), quoted under "Notes" section for "Were You There," Hymnary.org, http://www.hymnary .org/text/were_you_there_when_they_crucified_my_lo.

20. W. Schottroff, "*zkr* to remember," *TLOT*, 1:384.

21. Jeremiah Burroughs, *The Saints' Treasury: Being Sundry Sermons Preached in London* (London: T. C. for John Wright, 1654), 46, quoted in Earnest F. Kevan, *The Grace of Law: A Study of Puritan Theology* (1964; repr., Grand Rapids: Baker, 1976), 236.

22. Quoted by Chuck Colson, "Astronauts Who Found God: A Spiritual View of Space," *BreakPoint*, November 5, 1998, http://www.breakpoint.org/commen taries/4557-astronauts-who-found-god.

23. G. Liedke and C. Petersen, "*torah* instruction," *TLOT*, 3:1415–22.

24. Peter C. Craigie, *Psalms 1–50*, WBC 19 (Waco: Word Books, 1983), 60.

25. George J. Zemek, *The Word of God in the Child of God: Exegetical, Theological and Homiletical Reflections from the 119th Psalm* (Brandon, FL: self-published, 1998), 43.

26. Craigie, *Psalms 1–50*, 62.

27. Charles Wesley, "Thou Hidden Source of Calm Repose," (1749), vv. 3–4, Hymnary.org, http://www.hymnary.org/text/thou_hidden_source_of_calm_repose.

28. Timothy Keller, *The Prodigal God: Recovering the Heart of the Christian Faith* (New York: Dutton, 2008), 115.

29. Martin Luther, *A Commentary on St. Paul's Epistle to the Galatian*, ed. and trans. Philip S. Watson (1535; repr., London: James Clarke, 1953), 101.

30. Katherine Hankey, "Tell Me the Old, Old Story" (1866), v. 2, hymnal.net, http://www.hymnal.net/hymn.php/h/1075.

Chapter 9: Meditation (Part 2)

Epigraphs. Ephesians 1:18; George Müller, *Autobiography of George Müller, or A Million and a Half in Answer to Prayer*, 3rd ed., comp. G. Fred Bergin, preface and concluding chap. Arthur T. Pierson (1905; repr. London: J. Nisbet and Co., 1914), 152–53.

1. Henri J. M. Nouwen, *The Return of the Prodigal Son: A Meditation on Fathers, Brothers, and Sons* (New York: Doubleday, 1992), 10–11.

2. Ibid., 10–11.

3. Ibid., 11.

4. Otto A. Piper, "Knowledge," *IDB*, 3:43.

5. Martin Luther, *Luther's Works*, vol. 14, *Selected Psalms: III*, ed. Jaroslov Pelikan (St. Louis: Concordia, 1958), 297–98.

6. R. Bultmann, "*lypē, lypeō*," *TDNT*, 4:313.

7. Richard Baxter, *The Saints Everlasting Rest* (London: printed by Rob. White for Thomas Underhill and Francis Tyton, 1650) in *The Practical Works of Richard Baxter: Select Treatises* (1863; repr., Grand Rapids; Baker, 1981), 96–97.

8. Gerhard von Rad, *Old Testament Theology*, vol. 1 of *The Theology of Israel's Historical Traditions*, trans. D. M. G. Stalker (New York: Harper & Brothers, 1962), 200.

9. Jonathan Edwards, *Religious Affections* (1746), ed. John E. Smith, vol. 2 of *The Works of Jonathan Edwards*, ed. Perry Miller (New Haven: Yale University Press, 1959), 100–101.

10. Ibid., 102.

11. Richard Baxter, *The Saints Everlasting Rest* (1650) in *The Practical Works of Richard Baxter: Select Treatises* (1863; repr., Grand Rapids; Baker, 1981), 297.

12. Martha C. Nussbaum, *Upheavals of Thought: The Intelligence of Emotions* (Cambridge: Cambridge University Press, 2001), 33, 55.

13. Augustine, *Expositions of the Psalms 73–98* (ca. 392–422), trans. Maria Boulding, pt. 3, vol. 18, *The Works of Saint Augustine*, ed. John E. Rotelle (Hyde Park, NY: New City Press, 2002), 410. Augustine's words are: "Now the feet that carry us on our journey are our intentions [Latin, *affectus*—disposition, emotions]. Each of us draws nearer to God or moves further from him in accordance with the intention we have, the love that is in us."

14. Franz Delitzsch, *Biblical Commentary on the Psalms*, vol. 1, 2nd ed., trans. Francis Bolton, BCOT (1867; repr., Grand Rapids: Eerdmans, 1959), 1:312.

15. John N. Oswalt, *The Book of Isaiah: Chapters 40–66*, NICOT (Grand Rapids: Eerdmans, 1998), 235.

16. John N. Oswalt, *The Book of Isaiah: Chapters 1–39*, NICOT (Grand Rapids: Eerdmans, 1986), 193n6.

17. Joseph Ratzinger (Benedict XVI), *Introduction to Christianity*, trans. J. R. Foster (1969; repr., San Francisco, CA: Ignatius Press, 1990), 39.

18. William Bridge, *The Works of the Rev. William Bridge* (1649; repr., Beaver Falls, PA: Soli Deo Gloria Publications, 1989), 3:125.

19. Donald S. Whitney, *Spiritual Disciplines for the Christian Life* (Colorado Springs: NavPress, 1991), 44.

20. Peter Toon, *Meditating as a Christian: Waiting upon God* (London: Collins, 1991), 182.

21. Ibid.

22. Dietrich Bonhoeffer, *Meditating on the Word*, ed. and trans. David McI. Gracie (Cambridge, MA: Cowley Publications, 1986), 32–33 (emphasis added).

23. Martin Luther, *What Luther Says: An Anthology*, comp. Ewald M. Plass (St. Louis: Concordia, 1959), 3:1485, par. 4798.

24. George Müller, "Soul Nourishment First," (booklet, 1841) in Müller, *Autobiography of George Müller*, 152–53.

25. Paul Meier, "Spiritual and Mental Health in the Balance," in *Renewing Your Mind in a Secular World*, ed. John D. Woodbridge (Chicago: Moody Press, 1985), 26–28.

26. Ibid., 27–28.

27. Horatius Bonar, *God's Way of Holiness* (New York: Robert Carter & Brothers, 1865), 197–98.

28. Richard J. Foster, with Kathryn A. Helmers, *Life with God: Reading the Bible for Spiritual Transformation* (New York: HarperCollins, 2008), 63.

29. John Calvin, *Commentary on the Book of Psalms*, trans. James Anderson (Calvin Translation Society, 1845–1849; repr. Grand Rapids: Baker, 1979), 5:63.

Chapter 10: Habits of the Heart

Epigraphs. Karol Wojtyla (John Paul II), *The Acting Person*, trans. Andrzej Potocki, Analecta Husserliana 10, ed. Anna-Teresa Tymieniecka (Dordrecht, Holland: D. Reidel, 1979), 97; Eugene H. Peterson, *Eat This Book: A Conversation in Spiritual Reading* (Grand Rapids: Eerdmans, 2006), 71.

1. Martin Bolt and David G. Myers, *The Human Connection: How People Change People* (Downers Grove, IL: InterVarsity Press, 1984), 13.

2. See chapter 4.

3. David G. Myers, *The Human Puzzle: Psychological Research and Christian Belief* (San Francisco: Harper & Row, 1978), 97, referring to Seymour Lieberman, "The Effects of Changes in Roles on the Attitudes of Role Occupants," *Human Relations* 9 (1956): 385–402, doi: 10.1177/001872675600900401.

4. Myers, *Human Puzzle*, 101.

5. Gary A. Anderson, *A Time to Mourn, a Time to Dance: The Expression of Grief and Joy in Israelite Religion* (University Park, PA: Pennsylvania State University Press, 1991), 9–14.

6. Gerhard Wallis, "'āhabh," *TDOT*, 1:102, 105.

7. Gottfried Quell, "*agapaō*," *TDNT*, 1:26.

8. C. S. Lewis, *Mere Christianity*, rev. ed. (New York: Macmillan, 1960), 101.

9. Anderson, *A Time to Mourn, a Time to Dance*, 48.

10. Ibid., 49, 82–87.

11. Charles Taylor, *Human Agency and Language: Philosophical Papers*, vol. 1 (Cambridge: Cambridge University Press, 1985), 67.

12. Ibid., 95–97.

13. The following evidence comes from Myers, *Human Puzzle*, 94–104.

14. Robert C. Roberts, "What an Emotion Is: A Sketch," *Philosophical Review* 97, no. 2 (1988): 204.

15. Roger Brown, *Social Psychology* (New York: Free Press, 1965), 153–54, quoted by Myers, *Human Puzzle*, 97.

16. Ibid., 97.

17. John Paul II (Karol Wojtyla), *Veritatis Splendor*, Encyclical letter regarding certain fundamental questions of the church's moral teaching, Vatican Web site, August 6, 1993, par. 71, http://www.vatican.va/holy_father/john_paul_ii /encyclicals/documents/hf_jp-ii_enc_06081993_veritatis-splendor_en.html.

18. James Burtchaell, *Philemon's Problem: A Theology of Grace* (Grand Rapids: Eerdmans, 1998), 309.

19. Bruce K. Waltke, *The Book of Proverbs: Chapters 1–15*, NICOT (Grand Rapids: Eerdmans, 2004), 1:223.

20. Otto A. Piper, "Knowledge," *IDB*, 3:44.

21. Brevard S. Childs, *Old Testament Theology in a Canonical Context* (Philadelphia: Fortress, 1985), 51.

22. Waltke, *Book of Proverbs: Chapters 1–15*, 1:77.

23. A. S. Kapelrud, "*lamad*," *TDOT*, 8:5; cf. Ernst Jenni, "*lmd* to learn," *TLOT*, 2:646.

24. J. Goetzmann, "Mind, *phronēsis*," *NIDNTT*, 2:617.

25. Peter T. O'Brien, *The Epistle to the Philippians: A Commentary on the Greek Text*, NIGTC (Grand Rapids: Eerdmans, 1991), 507, citing Victor Paul Furnish, *Theology and Ethics in Paul* (Nashville: Abingdon, 1968), 89.

26. Wallis, "*'āhabh*," *TDOT*, 1:102–103, 105.

27. John Calvin, *Institutes of the Christian Religion*, vol. 1, ed. John T. McNeill, trans. Ford Lewis Battles, Library of Christian Classics 20 (Philadelphia: Westminster, 1960), 1.6.2.

28. Waltke, *Book of Proverbs: Chapters 1–15*, 1:244.

29. Ibid., 181.

30. Ibid.

31. Georg Fohrer, "*sophia*," *TDNT*, 7:487.

32. Leslie C. Allen, *Psalms 101–150*, WBC 21 (Waco: Word Books, 1983), 143.

33. David Alan Williams, "Knowing as Participation: Toward an Intersection between Psychology and Postcritical Epistemology," in *Care for the Soul: Exploring the Intersection of Psychology and Theology*, ed. Mark R. McMinn and Timothy R. Phillips (Downers Grove, IL: InterVarsity Press, 2001), 343.

34. Robert C. Roberts, "Outline of Pauline Psychotherapy," in *Care for the Soul: Exploring the Intersection of Psychology and Theology*, ed. Mark R. McMinn and Timothy R. Phillips (Downers Grove, IL: InterVarsity Press, 2001), 141–42.

35. James B. Adamson, *The Epistle of James*, NICNT (Grand Rapids: Eerdmans, 1976), 130.

36. I. Howard Marshall, *The Epistles of John*, NICNT (Grand Rapids: Eerdmans, 1978), 221; so also Stephen S. Smalley, *1, 2, 3 John*, WBC 51 (Waco: Word Books, 1984), 255.

37. Derek Kidner, *The Proverbs: An Introduction and Commentary*, TOTC (Downers Grove, IL: InterVarsity Press, 1964), 68 (emphasis added).

38. John Calvin, *Institutes of the Christian Religion*, ed. John T. McNeill, trans. Ford

Lewis Battles, Library of Christian Classics, vol. 20 (Philadelphia: Westminster, 1960), 3.6.4.

39. M. Sæbø, "ysr to chastise," TLOT, 2:549.

40. A frequent saying of an unnamed pastor, quoted in Edward M. Curtis and John J. Brugaletta, *Discovering the Way of Wisdom: Spirituality in the Wisdom Literature* (Grand Rapids: Kregel, 2004), 24.

41. Henry Drummond, *The Greatest Thing in the World and Other Addresses*, rev. ed. (1880; London: Hodder and Stoughton, 1920), 38–39, http://www.ccel.org/ccel/drummond/greatest.ii.ii.html.

42. J. A. Thompson, *Deuteronomy: An Introduction and Commentary*, TOTC (Downers Grove, IL: InterVarsity Press, 1974), 122; C. F. Keil and F. Delitzsch, *The Pentateuch*, vol. 3, trans. James Martin, BCOT (1870; repr., Grand Rapids: Eerdmans, 1959), 323; Gustave Friedrich Oehler, *Theology of the Old Testament*, ed. George E. Day (1883; repr., Grand Rapids: Zondervan, n.d.), 153–54.

43. Quoted by Bruce Larson, *A Call to Holy Living: Walking with God in Joy, Praise, and Gratitude*, Christian Growth Books (Minneapolis: Augsburg, 1988), 70.

44. Frederick Dale Bruner, *The Christbook: Matthew 1–12*, Matthew: A Commentary, vol. 1 (Dallas: Word, 1987), 439.

45. C. S. Lewis, *Mere Christianity*, rev. ed. (New York, Macmillan, 1960), 147–48.

Chapter 11: No Man Is an Island

Epigraphs. John Donne, "For Whom the Bell Tolls" Meditation 17, *Devotions upon Emergent Occasions* (1624), in *The Works of John Donne: With a Memoir of His Life*, vol. 3, ed. Henry Alford (London: John W. Parker, 1839), 574–75; Romans 12:5; Aristotle, *Politics* (350 B.C.?), trans. Benjamin Jowett, Great Books of the Western World, ed. Robert Maynard Hutchins (Chicago: Encyclopedia Britannica, 1952), 9:446.

1. Kallistos Ware, "The Hesychasts: Gregory of Sinai, Gregory Palamas, Nicolas Cabasilas," in *The Study of Spirituality*, ed. Cheslyn Jones, Geoffrey Wainwright, and Edward Yarnold (New York: Oxford University Press, 1986), 242–58.

2. Olivier Clément, *On Human Being: A Spiritual Anthropology*, trans. Jeremy Hummerstone (New York: New York City Press, 2000), 43–44.

3. M. Scott Peck, *The Different Drum: Community Making and Peace* (New York: Simon & Schuster, 1987), 55.

4. Walther Eichrodt, *Theology of the Old Testament*, trans. John A. Baker, OTL (London: SCM Press, 1967), 2:126.

5. Karl Barth, *Church Dogmatics*, ed. G. W. Bromiley, trans. G. T. Thomson, vol. 3, pt. 4, *The Doctrine of Creation* (Edinburgh: T&T Clark, 1961), 12.163.

6. Claus Westermann, *Genesis 1–11: A Commentary*, trans. John J. Scullion (Minneapolis: Augsburg, 1984), 1:227.

7. Derek Kidner, *Genesis: An Introduction and Commentary*, TOTC (Downers Grove, IL: InterVarsity Press, 1967), 65.

8. Thomas F. Torrance, *Reality and Scientific Theology*, Theology and Science at the Frontiers of Knowledge 1 (Edinburgh: Scottish Academic Press, 1985), 171–72; Joseph Ratzinger (Benedict XVI), "Retrieving the Tradition: Concerning the Notion of Person in Theology," *Communio* 17 (Fall 1990): 439–54.

9. Torrance, *Reality and Scientific Theology*, 172.

10. John Bowlby, *Loss: Sadness and Depression*, vol. 3. of *Attachment and Loss* (New York: Basic Books, 1980), 442.

11. Jean Vanier, *Community and Growth*, rev. ed. (Mahwah, NJ: Paulist Press, 1989), 13.

12. Daniel J. Siegel, *The Developing Mind: How Relationships and the Brain Interact to Shape Who We Are* (New York: Guilford Press, 1999), 67.

13. Ibid., 85.

14. W. Norris Clarke, *Person and Being*, Aquinas Lecture 57 (Milwaukee: Marquette University Press, 1993), 66.

15. Eric L. Johnson, "Human Agency and Its Social Formation," in *Limning the Psyche: Explorations in Christian Psychology*, ed. Robert C. Roberts and Mark R. Talbot (Grand Rapids: Eerdmans, 1997), 161.

16. Siegel, *Developing Mind*, 86. On the capacity of the brain and mind to change throughout life, see Jeffrey M. Schwartz and Sharon Begley, *The Mind and the Brain: Neuroplasticity and the Power of Mental Force* (New York: HarperCollins, 2002).

17. The following evidence from social psychology is from C. Stephen Evans, "The Relational Self: Psychological and Theological Perspectives," in *Judeo-Christian Perspectives on Psychology: Human Nature, Motivation, and Change*, ed. William R. Miller and Harold D. Delaney (Washington, DC: American Psychological Association, 2005), 77–80.

18. Ibid., 80.

19. Karl Barth, *Church Dogmatics*, ed. G. W. Bromiley, trans. G. T. Thomson, vol. 3, pt. 4, *The Doctrine of Creation*, (Edinburgh: T&T Clark, 1961) 12.163.

20. Karl Rahner, *Christian Commitment: Essays in Pastoral Theology*, trans. Cecily Hastings, vol. 1 of *Mission and Grace* (New York: Sheed and Ward, 1963), 77–78.

21. Clarke, *Person and Being*, 80.

22. James R. Beck and Bruce Demarest, *The Human Person in Theology and Psychology: A Biblical Anthropology for the Twenty-First Century* (Grand Rapids: Kregel, 2005), 319.

23. G. Ernest Wright, *The Challenge of Israel's Faith* (London: SCM Press, 1946), 92.

24. Dean Ornish, "Changing Life Habits" (interview by Bill Moyers), in Bill Moyers, *Healing and the Mind*, ed. Betty Sue Flowers and David Grubin (New York: Doubleday, 1995), 107, 105.

25. Erich Fromm, *The Art of Loving* (New York: Bantam Books, 1963), 6–7.

26. Ibid., 7–8.

27. Ludwig Köhler, *Old Testament Theology* (Philadelphia: Westminster Press), 130.

28. Johannes Pedersen, *Israel: Its Life and Culture*, vol. 1, trans. Mrs. Aslaug Møller. (1926; repr., London: Oxford University Press, 1973), 308, quoted in Wright, *Challenge of Israel's Faith*, 94.

29. Thomas Smail, *Like Father, Like Son: The Trinity Imaged in Our Humanity* (Grand Rapids: Eerdmans, 2006), 124.

30. G. Ernest Wright and an ecumenical committee in Chicago, *The Biblical Doctrinal of Man in Society* Ecumenical Biblical Studies 2 (London: SCM Press, 1954), 18.

31. Paul D. Hanson, *The People Called: The Growth of Community in the Bible* (San Francisco: Harper & Row, 1986), 447.

32. Wright et al., *Biblical Doctrinal of Man in Society*, 48.

33. A.W. Towzer, *The Pursuit of God* (no place: W.L.C., 2009), 53.

34. Alister I. McFadyen, *The Call to Personhood: A Christian Theory of the Individual in Social Relationships* (Cambridge: Cambridge University Press, 1990), 54.

35. Torrance, *Reality and Scientific Theology*, 179–80.

36. The following material is drawn from Jean-Marc Laporte, "Kenosis as a Key to Maturity of Personality," in *Limning the Psyche: Explorations in Christian Psychology*, ed. Robert C. Roberts and Mark R. Talbot (Grand Rapids: Eerdmans, 1997), 229–44.

37. Willem VanGemeren, "Psalms," in *Psalms, Proverbs, Ecclesiastes, Song of Songs*, vol. 5, *EBC*, ed. Frank E. Gaebelein (Grand Rapids: Zondervan, 1991), 817.

38. T. S. Eliot, "Choruses from 'The Rock'" (1934) in T. S. Eliot, *The Complete Poems and Plays, 1909–1950* (New York: Harcourt, Brace & World, 1952), 101.

39. Emil Brunner, *The Misunderstanding of the Church*, trans. Harold Knight (Philadelphia: Westminster, 1953), 12.

40. "Organism," *Wikipedia, The Free Encyclopedia*, http://en.wikipedia.org/w/index.php?title=Organism&oldid=117289696 (accessed March 23, 2007).

41. John Murray, *The Epistle to the Romans: Chapters 9–16*, NICNT (Grand Rapids: Eerdmans, 1965), 2:120.

42. John Chrysostom, *Commentary on the Epistle to the Galatians, and Homilies on the Epistle to the Ephesians*, new rev. ed., Library of Fathers of the Holy Catholic Church 6, trans. and ed. members of the English Church, including E. B. Pusey, J. H. Newman, J. Keble and C. Marriott. (London: Walter Smith, 1884), 256–57.

43. Robert Banks, *Paul's Idea of Community: The Early House Churches in Their Cultural Setting*, rev. ed. (Peabody, MA: Hendrickson, 1994), 60.

44. Siegel, *Developing Mind*, 66, 71.

45. Miroslav Volf, *After Our Likeness: The Church as the Image of the Trinity*, Sacra Doctrina (Grand Rapids: Eerdmans, 1998), 211–12.

46. George T. Montague, *Growth in Christ: A Study of Saint Paul's Theology of Progress* (Kirkwoord, MO: Maryhurst Press, 1961), 161.

47. Quoted in ibid., 160.

48. Dietrich Bonhoeffer, *Life Together*, trans. John W. Doberstein (New York: Harper & Row, 1954).

Chapter 12: Love One Another

Epigraph. George T. Montague, *Growth in Christ: A Study of Saint Paul's Theology of Progress* (Kirkwoord, MO: Maryhurst Press, 1961), 161.

1. Stephen P. Greggo, "Biblical Metaphors for Corrective Emotional Relationships in Group Work," *Journal of Psychology and Theology* 38, no. 2 (2007): 159.

2. Ibid., 157–61.

3. Andrew T. Lincoln, *Ephesians*, WBC 42 (Dallas: Word Books, 1990), 259–60.

4. Ernest Best, *A Critical and Exegetical Commentary on Ephesians*, International Critical Commentary (Edinburgh: T&T Clark, 1998), 407.

5. Richard Baxter, *The Saints Everlasting Rest* (1650) in *The Practical Works of Richard Baxter: Select Treatises* (1863; repr., Grand Rapids: Baker, 1981), 60.

6. Quoted by F. F. Bruce, *The Epistles to the Colossians, to Philemon, and to the Ephesians*, NICNT (Grand Rapids: Eerdmans, 1984), 158.

7. John R. W. Stott, *God's New Society: The Message of Ephesians*, Bible Speaks Today (Downers Grove, IL: InterVarsity Press, 1979), 137.

8. Gerd Theissen, *Psychological Aspects of Pauline Theology* trans. John P. Galvin (Philadelphia: Fortress, 1987), 9.

9. Markus Barth, *Ephesians: Translation and Commentary on Chapters 4–6*, AB 34A (Garden City, NY: Doubleday, 1974), 772.

10. Otto Schmitz and Gustav Stählin, "*parakaleō*," *TDNT*, 5:774.

11. J. Thomas, "*parakaleō*," *Exegetical Dictionary of the New Testament*, ed. Horst

Balz and Gerhard Schneider (Grand Rapids: Eerdmans, 1993), 3:24. Cf. the translation of the cognate term *paraklētos* as "Helper" in relation to the Holy Spirit (John 14:16; 15:26).

12. Quoted by William Barclay, "*Paraklētos*: The Word of the Holy Spirit," in *More New Testament Words* (London: SCM Press, 1958), 134.

13. Derek Kidner, *Psalms 73–150: An Introduction and Commentary on Books III–V of the Psalms*, TOTC (London: Inter-Varsity Press, 1975), 411.

14. Dietrich Bonhoeffer, *Life Together*, trans. John W. Doberstein (New York: Harper & Row, 1954), 118.

15. Richard N. Longenecker, *Galatians*, WBC 41 (Dallas: Word Books, 1990), 272.

16. "*katartizō*," BDAG, 526.

17. Ibid.

18. J. Behm, "*noutheteō*," *TDNT*, 4:1019.

19. Charles A. Wanamaker, *The Epistles to the Thessalonians: A Commentary on the Greek Text*, NIGTC (Grand Rapids: Eerdmans, 1990), 190 (emphasis added).

20. Charles A. Wanamaker, *The Epistles to the Thessalonians: A Commentary on the Greek Text*, NIGTC (Grand Rapids: Eerdmans, 1990), 15, 139.

21. Martin Luther, "Treatise on Christian Liberty," in *Works of Martin Luther*, Philadelphia Edition (Philadelphia: Muhlenberg Press, 1943), 2:339.

22. Greggo, "Biblical Metaphors for Corrective Emotional Relationships," 155.

23. Gustav Stählin, "*phileō*," *TDNT*, 9:115, 120, 129, 138–40; in general the kiss expressed "close relationship and the corresponding love" (120).

24. Robert A. Connor, "The Person as Resonating Existential," *American Catholic Philosophical Quarterly* 66, no. 1 (1992): 48.

25. Jürgen Moltmann, *The Open Church: Invitation to a Messianic LifeStyle*, trans. M. Douglas Meeks (London: SCM Press, 1978), 26.

26. Henry Chadwick, *The Early Church*, rev. ed., Penguin History of the Church 1 (1967; London: Penguin Books, 1993), 56.

27. Popularly attributed to the English poet William Blake.

Chapter 13: All Together Now

Epigraph. Augustine, *Confessions*, 10.29, trans. Henry Chadwick, World's Classics (Oxford: Oxford University Press, 1992), 202.

1. William Hendriksen, *A Commentary on the Gospel of John*, 2 vols. in 1 (London: Banner of Truth Trust, 1959), 2:11.

2. J. F. Sawyer, "*yesha*," *TDOT*, 6:442.

3. See also Pss. 31:8; 66:12.

4. Georg Fohrer, "sōzō," *TDNT*, 7:990.

5. Murray J. Harris, *The Second Epistle to the Corinthians: A Commentary on the Greek Text*, NIGTC (Grand Rapids: Eerdmans / Milton Keynes, UK: Paternoster, 2005), 434.

6. Harold W. Hoehner, *Ephesians: An Exegetical Commentary* (Grand Rapids: Baker, 2002), 324.

7. Kevin J. Vanhoozer, "Lost in Interpretation? Truth, Scripture, and Hermeneutics," *Journal of the Evangelical Theological Society* 48, no. 1 (2005): 109–10.

8. Will Durant, *Caesar and Christ: A History of Roman Civilization and of Christianity from Their Beginnings to A.D. 325*, Story of Civilization (New York: Simon & Schuster, 1972), 3:562.

9. Dietrich von Hildebrand, *Transformation in Christ: On the Christian Attitude of Mind* (1948; repr., San Francisco: Ignatius, 2001), 493–94.

10. I. Howard Marshall, *The Gospel of Luke: A Commentary on the Greek Text*, NIGTC (Grand Rapids: Eerdmans, 1978), 373.

11. William Barclay, *The Letter to the Romans*, Daily Bible Study (Philadelphia: Westminster, 1957), 84–85.

12. Ibid., 85.

13. The Greek word *apollymi* translated here "lose" also means to "ruin" or "destroy" ("*apollymi*," BDAG, 116).

14. Augustine, *St. Augustin: Sermons on Selected Lessons of the New Testament*, trans. R. G. MacMullen, in *A Select Library of the Nicene and Post-Nicene Fathers of the Christian Church*, ed. Philip Schaff, vol. 6 (New York: The Christian Literature Co., 1888), 408.

15. Everett Ferguson, *The Church of Christ: A Biblical Ecclesiology for Today* (Grand Rapids: Eerdmans, 1996), 18.

16. *The Imitation of Christ* (ca. 1418–27), 3.5 (Grand Rapids: Zondervan, 1967), 83–84.

17. See Francis A. Schaeffer, *The Mark of a Christian* (Downers Grove, IL: InterVarsity Press, 1970).

18. James Tunstead Burtchaell, *Philemon's Problem: The Daily Dilemma of the Christian* (Chicago: Foundation for Adult Catechetical Teaching Aids, 1973), 168.

19. Richard N. Longenecker, *Galatians*, WBC 41 (Dallas: Word Books, 1990), 267.

20. The 613 consisted of 248 positive commands and 365 prohibitions. W. Grundmann, "*megas*," *TDNT*, 4:535.

21. Peter T. O'Brien, *Colossians, Philemon*, WBC 44 (Waco: Word Books, 1982), 204.

22. Douglas J. Moo, *The Epistle to the Romans*, NICNT (Grand Rapids: Eerdmans, 1996), 749–50.

23. John Murray, *The Epistle to the Romans: Chapters 9–16*, NICNT (Grand Rapids: Eerdmans, 1965), 2:113.

24. James D. G. Dunn. *Romans 1–8*, WBC (Dallas: Word Books, 1988), 17.

25. John R. W. Stott, *The Message of Galatians*, Bible Speaks Today (London: InterVarsity Press, 1968), 133–34.

26. C. Crowther, "Works, Work and Good Works," *Expository Times* 81, no. 6 (1969–70): 170: cf. C. Leslie Mitton, *The Epistle to the Ephesians: Its Authorship, Origin, and Purpose* (Oxford: Clarendon Press, 1951), 268–69.

27. Peter T. O'Brien, *The Epistle to the Philippians: A Commentary on the Greek Text*, NIGTC (Grand Rapids: Eerdmans, 1991), 287 (emphasis added).

28. Andrew T. Lincoln, *Ephesians*, WBC 42 (Dallas: Word Books, 1990), 116.

29. This is the translation provided by Harris, *Second Epistle to the Corinthians*, 183.

30. John R. W. Stott, *Romans: God's Good News for the World*, Bible Speaks Today (Downers Grove, IL: InterVarsity Press, 1994), 157–58.

31. T. J. Deidun, *New Covenant Morality in Paul*. Analecta Biblica 89 (Rome: Pontifical Biblical Institute, 1981), 79–80.

32. John Calvin, *Institutes of the Christian Religion*, vol. 2, ed. John T. McNeill, trans. Ford Lewis Battles, Library of Christian Classics 21 (Philadelphia: Westminster, 1960), 3.11.7.

33. Herman Ridderbos, *Paul: An Outline of His Theology*, trans. John Richard de Witt (Grand Rapids: Eerdmans, 1975), 237.

34. Douglas J. Moo, *The Epistle to the Romans*, NICNT (Grand Rapids: Eerdmans, 1996), 52.

35. James D. G. Dunn, *Romans 1–8*, WBC 38A (Dallas: Word Books, 1988), 40.

36. T. J. Deidun, *New Covenant Morality in Paul*, Analecta Biblica 89 (Rome: Pontifical Biblical Institute, 1981), 82.

Chapter 14: *The* Ultimate Issue

Epigraph. Henry Scougal, *The Life of God in the Soul of Man, or Nature and Excellency of the Christian Religion*. (1677; Philadelphia: Westminster, 1948), 30.

1. Adrian van Kaam, *The Mystery of Transforming Love* (Denville, NJ: Dimension Books, 1982), 22.

2. Faustin Ntamushobora, *From Trials to Triumphs: The Voice of Habakkuk to the Suffering African Christian* (Eugene, OR: Wipf and Stock, 2009), 58.

3. Peter T. O'Brien, *The Letter to the Ephesians*, PNTC (Grand Rapids: Eerdmans,

1999), 264, 264n185 citing D. A. Carson, *A Call to Spiritual Reformation: Priorities from Paul and His Prayers* (Grand Rapids: Baker, 1992), 195.

4. John M. Frame, *The Doctrine of the Knowledge of God*, Theology of Lordship (Phillipsburg, NJ: P&R, 1987), 27–28.

5. John N. Oswalt, *The Book of Isaiah: Chapters 40–66*, NICOT (Grand Rapids: Eerdmans, 1998), 624.

6. Jean Daniélou, *Prayer: The Mission of the Church*, trans. David Louis Schindler Jr., Ressourcement (1977; Grand Rapids: Eerdmans, 1996), 15.

7. J. J. Stewart Perowne, *The Book of Psalms: A New Translation, with Introductions and Notes Explanatory and Critical* (1868; 1879; repr., Grand Rapids: Zondervan, 1966.), 1:22.

8. Leon Morris, *The First and Second Epistles to the Thessalonians*, rev. ed. NICNT (1959; Grand Rapids: Eerdmans, 1991), 173.

9. Hans Walter Wolff, *Anthropology of the Old Testament*, trans. Margaret Kohl (Philadelphia: Fortress, 1974), 228–29.

10. Claus Westermann, "ḥll to praise," *TLOT*, 1:374.

11. John Calvin, *Institutes of the Christian Religion*, vol. 2, ed. John T. McNeill, trans. Ford Lewis Battles, Library of Christian Classics 21 (Philadelphia: Westminster, 1960), 3.10.2.

12. Wolff, *Anthropology of the Old Testament*, 255n18.

13. Calvin, *Institutes of the Christian Religion*, vol. 2, 3.20.2 (emphasis added).

14. Daniélou, *Prayer*, 24.

15. Graeme Goldsworthy, *Prayer and the Knowledge of God: What the Whole Bible Teaches* (Leicester, England: Inter-Varsity Press, 2003), 61, 62.

16. Ibid., 61, 65.

17. Ibid., 192.

Conclusion

1. Quoted by Ben Patterson, *Waiting: Finding Hope When God Seems Silent* (Downers Grove, IL: InterVarsity Press, 1989), 148.

2. Daniel Webster Whittle, "Moment by Moment" (1893), Hymnary.org, http://www.hymnary.org/text/dying_with_jesus_by_death_reckoned_mine.

3. Isaac Watts, "Am I a Soldier of the Cross" (1724), v. 2, Hymnary.org, http://www.hymnary.org/text/am_i_a_soldier_of_the_cross.

4. Pirke Aboth 3:5; *Sanhedrin* 94b; *Genesis Rabbah* 67:7.

Scripture Index

Subject Index

Name Index

Sidebars